CAPTURING IMAGINATION

Hau
BOOKS

Editors
Giovanni da Col
Niloofar Haeri
Julie Archambault

Editorial Office
Faun Rice
Sheehan Moore
Michael Chladek
Michelle Beckett
Justin Dyer
Ian Tuttle

www.haubooks.com

CAPTURING IMAGINATION
A PROPOSAL FOR AN ANTHROPOLOGY OF THOUGHT

By Carlo Severi

Translated by Catherine V. Howard, Matthew Carey,
Eric Bye, Ramon Fonkoue, and Joyce Suechun Cheng

Hau Books
Chicago

© 2018 Hau Books
Cover: Nail figure, Congo, Musée du Quai Branly, Paris

Cover and layout design: Sheehan Moore

Typesetting: Prepress Plus (www.prepressplus.in)

ISBN: 978-0-9991570-0-8
LCCN: 2018952264

Hau Books
Chicago Distribution Center
11030 S. Langley
Chicago, IL 60628
www.haubooks.com

Hau Books is printed, marketed, and distributed by The University of Chicago Press.
www.press.uchicago.edu

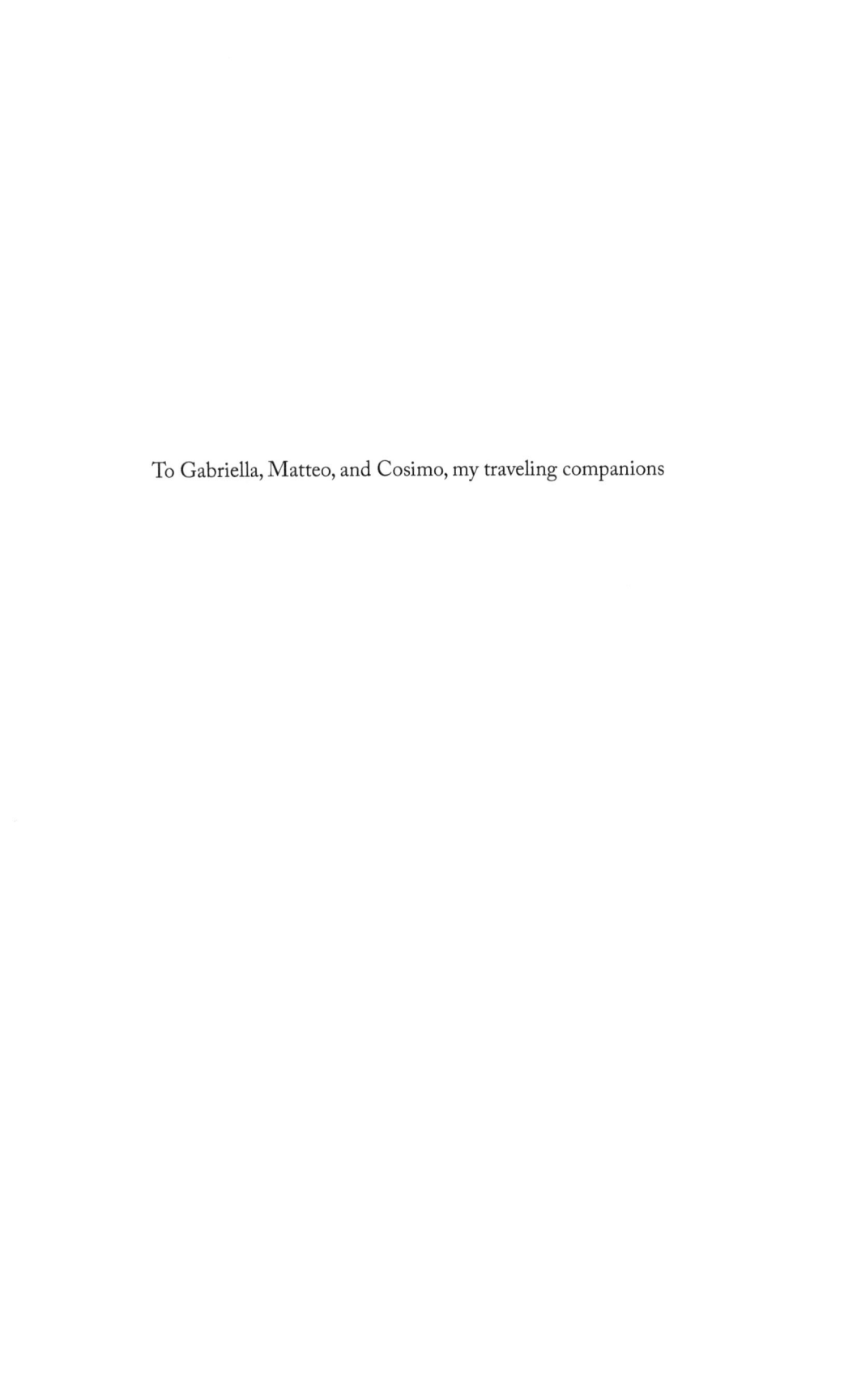

To Gabriella, Matteo, and Cosimo, my traveling companions

I' vo come colui ch'è fuor di vita,
che pare, a chi lo sguarda, ch'omo sia
fatto di rame o di pietra o di legno,
che si conduca sol per maestria
e porti ne lo core una ferita
che sia, com' egli è morto, aperto segno.

I wander like a lifeless being,
who looks, they say, as though he's made
of copper, stone, or wood,
and moves by strings another wields.
Upon his breast, an open wound
reveals the tale of how he died.
—Guido Cavalcanti, Rima VIII

Table of Contents

List of Figures   xiii
Translator's Note   xix
Acknowledgments   xxi

Chapter One. On Living Objects and the Anthropology of Thought   1
    Kūkai's Vision   7
    Levels of Cognition   16
    Anthropology and Pragmatics   19
    Ethnography and Thought   22

Chapter Two. Primitivist Empathy: Intensifying the Image and Deciphering Space   25
    The Stakes of Formal Borrowings   34
    Carl Einstein, or Immobile Ecstasy   41
    Primitivism without Borrowing: Imaginary Filiation   46
    Iconography and Gaze-Games   56

Chapter Three. The Universe of the Arts of Memory   61
    An Exercise in Methodology   61
    Amerindian Arts of Memory: A Case Study   70
    Pictography and Memory: A Model   77
    Eponymous Animals: Northwest Coast Visual Culture   83

Pictograms and Andean *Khipus* 90
Principles of Mnemonic Encoding 96

Chapter Four. Authorless Authority: Forms of Authority in Oral Traditions 99
Evidentials, Pragmatics, and Artifacts 101
The Fang *Mvet*: Singer, Song, and Harp 103
Rethinking the West African Nail Figure 111
The Complex Artifact 120

Chapter Five. Giving Voice: When Images Speak 123
Speech and Ritual Images 124
Here-Now-I: Demonstrative Images and Speech Acts 132
Kolossoi and *Kouroi*; or The Pragmatics of Images 138
Conclusion 149

Chapter Six. Becoming Patroclus: Funerary Rituals and Games in the *Iliad* 153
The Image Through the Text: Identification, Hierarchy, and Prefiguration 162
Funerary Games as Quasi-Rituals 169
Reflections on Funeral Rituals among the Wari' 173
The Universe of Object-Persons 179

Chapter Seven. The Anthropology of Abstract Art 183
Claude Lévi-Strauss and the Anthropology of Art 184
Principles of Analysis: An Example from Kandinsky 191
Visual Strategies in Abstract Art 197

Chapter Eight. Chimeric Space: Perception and Projection 207
The Visible and Invisible in Works of Art 210
Perception and Projection in the Gaze 213
Symbolism and Transitional Space 221
Chimeras and Ambiguous Images 227
Wayana and Yekuana Iconography: Chimeras in the Amazon 237
Conclusion 251

**Chapter Nine. The Semblance of Life: The Epistemology
of Western Perspective**   253
    A Science of Description: *Imitare* and *Ritrarre*   258
    Models of Truth   270
    Poetry Without Words or Blind Painting?   272
    The Counterfactual Image   286
    New Meditations on a Hobby Horse   293
    Perspective and the Anthropology of Images   298
    From Presence to the Active Gaze   299
    The Witness-Figure and *Capriccio*   313

Chapter Ten. On Irrefutable Hypotheses   321

References Cited   333

List of Figures

Cover. Nail figure (*nkisi*), Congo, Musée du Quai Branly, Paris.
Figure 1. Emil Nolde, *Dancer* (1913), Museum of Modern Art, New York (© Nolde Stiftung Seebüll).
Figure 2. Henri Matisse, *Blue Nude (Memory of Biskra)* (1907), Baltimore Museum of Art, Baltimore (© Estate of Henri Matisse).
Figure 3. Wassily Kandinsky, *The Lyrical* (1911), Museum Boyjmans van Beuningen, Rotterdam.
Figure 4. Henri Matisse, *Portrait of Madame Matisse* (1913), State Hermitage Museum, St. Petersburg (© Estate of Henri Matisse).
Figure 5. Shira Punu mask, Gabon, former collection of Ernst Winizki, Zurich.
Figure 6. Giuseppe Castiglione, *The Qianlong Emperor in Ceremonial Armor on Horseback* (1739 or 1758), Palace Museum, Beijing.
Figure 7. Pahouin carved head, Gabon, former collection of Paul Guillaume, Paris.
Figure 8. Baule wooden mask, Ivory Coast, Museum Folkwang, Essen.
Figure 9. Barnett Newman, *Genetic Moment* (1946–47), Beyeler Foundation, Riehen/Basel (©The Barnett Newman Foundation, Adagp, Paris).
Figure 10. *Saint Nicolas* (twelfth–fourteenth centuries), Tretjakov Gallery, Moscow.
Figure 11. Andrea Pozzo, *Apotheosis of Saint Ignatius* (1691), nave vault, Church of Saint Ignatius of Loyola, Rome.

Figure 12. Kranz Kline, *Accent Grave* (1955), Cleveland Museum of Art, Cleveland (© Adagp, Paris).
Figure 13. Hayashi Jikko, *Dragonfly* (1777–1813), private collection.
Figure 14. Yekuana "pictograms" illustrating the myths collected by Marc de Civrieux (from Civrieux 1970).
Figure 15. "Toad" and "bat" in traditional Yekuana iconography (from Guss 1989).
Figure 16. Alternate figure–ground relationships in images of Awidi, the serpent (left), and Odosha, master of evil (right), derived from the same graphic theme (from Guss 1989).
Figure 17. Logical nesting of lists of proper names in the Kuna "Song of the Demon."
Figure 18. Picture from the Dakota Bible (1870s) from a Sioux village, Great Lakes region, Museum of Ethnology, Berlin.
Figure 19. Ordering and salience in Yekuana pictography.
Figure 20. Haida totem pole from the village of Skedans (from Smyly and Smyly 1975).
Figure 21. Some examples of the Northwest Coast "form alphabet" (from Holm 1965).
Figure 22. Representation of the sea monster Sisiutl on a Kwakwaka'wakw drum, made by Willie Seaweed, Royal British Columbia Museum, Victoria.
Figure 23. Representative space and distributive space (from Holm 1965).
Figure 24. A Hopi chimera in a polychrome ceramic pot (© President and Fellows of Harvard College, Peabody Museum of Archaeology and Ethnology).
Figure 25. Development of salience in Northwest Coast iconography.
Figure 26. Development of order in Andean *khipus*.
Figure 27. Fang harp used for play the mvet: (a) chord rings; (b) secondary resonators; (c) main resonator; (d) bridge; (e) strings. Image from Boyer (1988). Reproduced with the permission of Société d'ethnologie, Paris.
Figure 28. Two rhythmic and melodic sequences in *mvet* music from Boyer (1988, 121). Reproduced with the permission of Société d'ethnologie, Paris.
Figure 29. A Haida mask, American Museum of Natural History, New York.

LIST OF FIGURES

Figure 30. A Congolese nail figure (*nkisi*), from Gell (1998). Reproduced with the permission of the Musée du Quai Branly and the Réunion des Musées Nationaux, Paris.

Figure 31. The skein of spatiotemporal relations mobilized by the use of the *nkisi* (adapted from Gell 1998).

Figure 32. Chain of ritual identifications attributed to the *nkisi*.

Figure 33. Relationships and behavior in the *Naven* ritual.

Figure 34. Two examples of Greek funerary statues: left, a female *kore*, Acropolis Museum, Athens (© Tarker/Bridgeman Images); right, a male *kouros*, National Archaeological Museum, Athens (© De Agostini Picture Library/G. Nimatallah/Bridgeman Images).

Figure 35. François Clouet, *Portrait of Elizabeth of Austria* (1571), Louvre Museum, Paris.

Figure 36. Wassily Kandinsky, *Picture with an Archer* (1909), Museum of Modern Art, New York.

Figure 37. William Turner, *Shade and Darkness (The Evening of the Deluge)* (1843), Tate Britain, London.

Figure 38. William Turner, *Light and Colour (Goethe's Theory): The Morning after the Deluge* (1843), Tate Britain, London.

Figure 39. Gottfried Wals, *A Roman Landscape with Figures* (c. 1616), Metropolitan Museum of Art, New York.

Figure 40. Gottfried Wals, *A Country Road by a House* (1620), Fitzwilliam Museum, Cambridge.

Figure 41. Piet Mondrian, *Pier and Ocean* (1915), Kröller-Müller Museum, Otterlo.

Figure 42. Robert Delaunay, *Simultaneous Disk* (1913), private collection.

Figure 43. Siberian ivory buckle with the double image of a wolf's head/sea lion. Pitt Rivers Museum, Oxford.

Figure 44. Plan of the Church of the Holy Sepulcher, Jerusalem (from Santo Brasco 1481, 58 v°).

Figure 45. Enguerrand Quarton, *Coronation of the Virgin* (1454), Musée Pierre-de-Luxembourg, Villeneuve-lès-Avignon.

Figure 46. Bartolomeo Suardi, *Virgin with Child* (c. 1515–20), Ambrosian Library, Milan.

Figure 47. Hieronymus Bosch, *The Martyrdom of St. Liberata* (c. 1500–1504), Doges Palace, Venice.

Figure 48. Anonymous German painter, *The Trinity* (eighteenth century), Carolino Museum, Salzburg.
Figure 49. Albrecht Dürer, hieroglyphs for the *Triumphal Arch of Emperor Maximilian* (c. 1515), woodcut print (from Dürer 1970).
Figure 50. Juan de Flandres, *Salome* (c. 1496), Museum of Art and History, Geneva.
Figure 51. Andrea Mantegna, *Saint Sebastian* (c. 1459), and detail of clouds from upper left corner, Kunsthistorisches Museum, Vienna.
Figure 52. Andrea del Sarto, *Madonna of the Harpies* (1517), Uffizi Gallery, Florence.
Figure 53. Paolo Veronese, fresco detail (1560–61), Villa Barbaro, Maser (Treviso).
Figure 54. Juan de Flandres, *Saint Michael Altarpiece* (c. 1506), Diocesan Museum, Salamanca.
Figure 55. Barnett Newman, *Onement VI* (1953), private collection (© The Barnett Newman Foundation / Adagp, Paris).
Figure 56. Edgar Degas, *Steep Coast* (1892), private collection.
Figure 57. Baga *A-tshol* anthrozoomorphic mask, contemporary era, Guinea, Musée du Quai Branly, Paris.
Figure 58. Mughal School, *The Shah Bahram-Gour Fairy Harpist on a Composite Camel* (seventeenth century), Museum of Islamic Art, Berlin.
Figure 59. Ritual helmet, called the "Helmet of Philip V of Macedonia," Getty Museum, Malibu.
Figure 60. Hopi polychrome ceramic pot (see also Figure 24).
Figure 61. Duplicated image of "maguari stork's bill" design used in Wayana basketry, drawn on paper by Dola (from Velthem 2003).
Figure 62. Complex iconography: "Crab/tapir eye" design in Wayana basketry (from Velthem 2003).
Figure 63. Drawing by Anakari depicting decorations inside a supernatural being, utilizing the "jaguar/periwinkle" design also used in Wayana basketry (from Velthem 2003).
Figure 64. Waura representation of anaconda (from Barcelos Neto 2002).
Figure 65. Wayana *maruana*, the painted ceiling wheel in the ceremonial house, described as a "stingray-*qua*-anaconda," Museum of Ethnography, Geneva.

Figure 66. Amazon red squirrel and "squirrel" design in Wayana basketry (from Velthem 2003).
Figure 67. "Jaguar" design in Wayana basketry (from Velthem 2003).
Figure 68. Michelangelo, detail of *Night* on tomb of Lorenzo de' Medici (1524–34), New Sacristy of the Basilica of San Lorenzo, Florence.
Figure 69. Donatello, *Del Bosco Christ* (c. 1460), Convent of Bosco ai Frati, San Piero a Sieve.
Figure 70. Brunelleschi, *Crucifix* (1410–15), Santa Maria Novella, Florence.
Figure 71. Hans Holbein the Younger, *The Body of the Dead Christ in the Tomb* (1521), Kunstmuseum, Basel.
Figure 72. Rhetorical model of composition in painting (from Baxandall 1986, 135).
Figure 73. Giotto di Bondone, *La Navicella* (1305–13), Saint Peter's Basilica, Rome.
Figure 74. Baldassarre d'Este, *Death of the Virgin* (c. 1450), Pinacoteca Ambrosiana, Milan.
Figure 75. Leonardo da Vinci, *Deluge* (c. 1515), Royal Library, Windsor.
Figure 76. Leonardo da Vinci, *Deluge* (c. 1515), Royal Library, Windsor.
Figure 77. Leonardo da Vinci, *Matilda* (c. 1515), Royal Library, Windsor.
Figure 78. Andrea Mantegna, *The Flagellation of Christ* (c. 1475), Kupferstichkabinett, Berlin.
Figure 79. *Vase with Black Figures*, second half of the sixth century BCE, Museum für Kunst und Gewerbe, Hamburg.
Figure 80. Cosmè Tura, *Pietà* (1460), Correr Museum, Venice.
Figure 81. Giovanni Bellini, *Triptych* (1488), Basilica Santa Maria Glorosia dei Frari, Venice.
Figure 82. Piero della Francesca, *The Resurrection* (c. 1463), Municipal Museum, San Sepolcro.
Figure 83. Andrea Mantegna, *Death of the Virgin* (c. 1461), Museum of the Prado, Madrid.
Figure 84. A hobby horse.
Figure 85. Giotto, *Adoration of the Magi* (1303–6) (detail), Arena Chapel, Padua.
Figure 86. Federico Barocci, *The Pardon of Assisi* (c. 1575), Church of Saint Francis, Urbino.

Figure 87. Giorgione, *Madonna and Child Enthroned between Saint Francis and Saint George* (c. 1502), Cathedral of Castelfranco Veneto, Castelfranco.
Figure 88. Lorenzo Lotto, *Portrait of a Young Man* (c. 1530), Picture Gallery of the Castello Sforzesco, Milan.
Figure 89. Jacopo da Pontormo, *Portrait of Two Friends* (1523–24) (detail), Giorgio Cini Foundation, Venice.
Figure 90. Andrea Mantegna, *The Martyrdom of Saint Sebastian* (1490), Ca' d'Oro, Venice.
Figure 91. Giambattista Tiepolo, *Scherzi e Capricci* (c. 1744), private collection, Venice.
Figure 92. Giandomenico Tiepolo, *The New World* (1791), Ca' Rezzonico, Venice.

Translator's Note

CATHERINE V. HOWARD

The project of bringing Carlo Severi's magnificent book to life in this English edition has drawn on the efforts of many people, including the translators who contributed to giving it voice. Although their translations were produced at different times for different occasions, all of them were edited and harmonized to ensure that the text's new incarnation as *Capturing Imagination: A Proposal for an Anthropology of Thought* would reflect the unity of the French original and enable readers to follow the author's process of constructing his interpretive model through the entire book. Each of the translators deserves credit for their contributions. Ramon Fonkoue and Joyce Suechun Cheng were responsible for translating the article (Severi [2008] 2012) that was incorporated as Chapter Two in this book. Matthew Carey translated two articles (Severi [2009] 2012, [2008] 2016) that became Chapters Three and Four, respectively, as well as drafts that were revised for Chapters Five and Eight. Eric Bye translated the lengthy Chapter Nine, while I translated Chapters Six, Seven, Ten, part of the new Chapter One, and the front matter, and edited the text as a whole.

The text has also gone through some notable changes in the transition from the French edition to the English. The major difference is the addition of an entirely new chapter to open the book and frame its approach. Furthermore, the author amplified many passages throughout the book expressly for this publication.

One of the invaluable features of Severi's work is that he draws on an astonishing breadth of sources, published in various languages and in various countries, enabling readers to encounter numerous works and authors for the first time. To assist scholars in tracking down references, the citations and bibliographic data for foreign works have been converted to English publications if they exist. Since Severi's analyses are sensitive to the historical context in which the sources first appeared, the original publication date, if known, has been added to each citation. Similarly, direct quotations are drawn from published English versions that exist; otherwise, they have been translated by one of the translators who contributed to this book.

It is our hope that this translation will open up new perspectives on anthropological questions to a wider audience and thus enrich the debates that surround them.

Acknowledgments

This book was written over several years, composed of revisions of previous articles and unpublished texts. It was first published in French as *L'Objet-personne: Une anthropologie de la croyance visuelle* (Severi 2017) and has gone through further revisions for this English edition. It could not have come into being without the seminar, "Anthropology of Memory," held at the École des Hautes Études en Sciences Sociales (EHESS, School of Advanced Studies in the Social Sciences), which provided me a vibrant space for research. I would like to thank, first of all, the young researchers and many colleagues who participated in the seminar. This book also benefited from other enriching exchanges in France, Brazil, United States, and Great Britain, which took place thanks to three research projects: the Agence Nacional de la Recherche (ANR, National Research Agency) project, "Anthropology of Art," which I codirected along with Julien Bonhomme (École Normale Supérieure), between 2008 and 2012 at the Laboratoire d'Anthropologie Sociale (Social Anthropology Laboratory) of the Collège de France and the Département de la Recherche et de l'Enseignement (Department of Research and Teaching) of the Musée du Quai Branly; the project, "Art, Image, Memory," funded by the Coordenação de Aperfeiçoamento de Pessoal de Nível Superior (Capes, Coordinating Agency for Advanced Training in Graduate Education) and the Comité Français d'Évaluation de la Coopération Universitaire et Scientifique avec le Brésil (Cofecub, French Committee of Evaluation of University and Scientific Cooperation with Brazil), and the Saint-Hilaire Franco-Brazilian Program, for which I was jointly responsible, along with Carlos Fausto of the Museu Nacional-Universidade do Rio de

Janeiro, between 2007 and 2012; and the project, "Translating Words/Traduire les Mondes," which I codirect with William Hanks of the University of California, Berkeley, and which is now supported by Le Laboratoire d'Excellence TransferS (Paris Sciences et Lettres).

I presented chapters of this book at the invitation of several universities: Aarhus Universitet, University of Michigan, University of Texas at Austin, Universitetet i Bergen, University of California, Berkeley, Wissenschaftskolleg zu Berlin, Università di Bologna, Brown University, Cambridge University, Columbia University, Københavns Universitet, Université de Genève, Harvard University, Johns Hopkins University, Ritsumeikan University in Kyoto, Universidad Nacional Autónoma de México, University of Oregon, Oxford University, Scuola Normale Superiore di Pisa, Museu Nacional-Universidade Federal do Rio de Janeiro, Universidad Nacional de San Cristóbal de Huamanga, Universidade de São Paulo, Università degli Studi di Siena, University of Tokyo, Tufts University, and Vassar College. I thank all the participants in the seminars at these universities, who often helped me greatly with their comments and critiques. In France, I presented my work at the École des Hautes Études en Sciences Sociales (EHESS) in Paris and Toulouse; the Department of Anthropology of Paris-Ouest-Nanterre; the École Normale Supérieure (ENS Ulm); the Collège de France; the Musée du Quai Branly (specifically as part of the seminar, "Iconographic Traditions," which, in different years, Claude Imbert, Giovanni Careri, or Denis Vidal helped me to organize); and, thanks to Jean-Hubert Martin, the Centre Pompidou. The discussion with the group of philosophers organized by Danièle Cohn at the Université Paris I also afforded me a precious opportunity for work and reflection.

In 2012–13, when I was a visiting fellow at King's College, Cambridge, I was able to test and enrich many of the hypotheses that were as yet unresolved in my manuscript. The seminar I have given every year since 2004 as a visiting professor at the Istituto Universitario di Architettura in Venice has also contributed a great deal to the progress of my research. I would also like to thank the Research and Education Department of the Musée du Quai Branly for its generous hospitality and friendly help. My deep gratitude goes to Sara Shroukh, who helped me with equal parts kindness and rigor in locating bibliographic sources, and to Lucie Marignac and Marie-Hélène Ravenel at Éditions Rue d'Ulm, who did a great deal of work on the original French version of this book in both form and substance.

For the translations of the various chapters into English, I want to thank Catherine V. Howard, Matthew Carey, Eric Bye, Ramon Fonkoue, and Joyce Suechun Cheng. In particular, Catherine has done splendid work both in translating certain chapters and in editing the entire manuscript for this English publication.

The staff in the editorial office of Hau Books provided exceptional assistance in producing this book, notably Michelle Beckett, who copyedited the manuscript; Faun Rice, who guided it through the production stages; and Sheehan Moore, whose graphic design expertise enhanced the book's visual dimension.

Last but not least, I wish to thank Giovanni da Col. The dialogue with him and the seminar on the "Anthropology of Imagination" that we co-organized at the Musée du Quai Branly in Paris between 2014 and 2018 have been a source of constant inspiration for this book.

CHAPTER ONE

On Living Objects and the Anthropology of Thought

> When we were living in Berlin, Kafka often went for a walk in Stieglitz Park. I sometimes accompanied him. One day, we came upon a little girl who was crying and seemed to have lost all hope. As we spoke with her, Franz asked the reason for her grief. We learned that she had lost her doll. On the spot, he invented an entirely plausible story to explain the disappearance. "Your doll is just taking a little trip. I know because she sent me a letter." The little girl looked at him suspiciously. "Do you have it with you?" she asked him. "No, I left it at home, but I'll bring it tomorrow." Suddenly curious, the little girl almost forgot her grief. Franz went home immediately to write the letter.
>
> He set to work with as much seriousness as if it were a matter of writing an actual literary work. He entered the same state of nervous tension that would overcome him whenever he sat down at his desk, even if only to write a letter or postcard. . . .
>
> This make-believe lasted at least three weeks. Franz dreaded the moment when he would have to bring it all to a conclusion.
>
> Such a conclusion would have to be an authentic one, creating a new order to take the place of the disorder triggered by the loss of the toy. He pondered long and hard before finally deciding to have the doll get married. He first described the young man, the engagement party, the wedding preparations, and then, in great detail, the newlyweds' house. The doll concluded her letter by telling the little girl, "I have traveled a great deal. I now have a house and a husband. You, too, will realize that we have to give up ever seeing each other again." (Diamant 1998: 228–29)

This story, related by Kafka's partner, Dora Diamant, exemplifies a certain type of presence an object can have, one that is perhaps universal, when an artifact is transformed into a person. Once lost, the doll ceases to be inanimate and becomes a girl. She comes to life. She speaks. She cries. She consoles. She writes letters. The fascination with what Diamant calls Kafka's "instinctive impulse" to attribute life to the doll is immediate. In this series of letters (unfortunately, probably lost), he undoubtedly used literature—or, rather, the act of writing in itself—as a sort of magic. According to Diamant, Kafka's intention was to enter the inner universe of the little girl to help her move forward and thus create an order to replace the disorder caused by the doll's disappearance. Beyond this, however, we need more to understand the magical effect of Kafka's letters. What reality, what exercise of thought is involved in claiming that this doll met a young prince in Stieglitz Park, took a long trip with him, became engaged, and had a happy marriage? Under what conditions is an object, clearly inanimate in the eyes of all the protagonists of this story (the storyteller, the witness, and even the little girl), capable of thinking, imagining, or speaking?

To understand the nature of this remarkable form of thought, the first step should be to reflect on the effects of narration on space and time. Thanks to the story that Kafka's letters gradually reveal, a shared space of thought emerges. Within this space, a complex relationship is established between the writer, the little girl, the doll, and the witness, Diamant. The first effect is clear: because of this new relationship, the lost doll *does not disappear*. More precisely, her disappearance from sight no longer means she vanished for no reason. Through the letters Kafka reads to the little girl every day, the doll remains present. She stays with the child for as long as the story lasts. Through Kafka's voice, the doll gives advice to the little girl, recounts her travels, expresses desires, shares thoughts, and promises to write more letters. Through such means, the little girl is able to reach an agreement with the doll and gradually separate from her with less pain. Over a certain period of time and within a certain space, the object has thus become a person. How should this space and this time be described? How shall we conceive of the self of the one who narrates, the self of the child (so bound up with the object), and the self of the absent doll that returns to narrate its own story through Kafka?

In innumerable social contexts of different cultures, people attribute the status of living beings to inanimate objects. In situations like play or ritual, objects may be endowed with a range of human characteristics, such as perception, thought, action, or speech. Puppets, dolls, and ritual statuettes cease to be merely *addressees* and begin to *address us*. We see life in them. What type of thought animates the object in these situations, making it both alive and memorable? The aim of this book is to formulate some answers, albeit partial and provisional, to this question, through the study of a number of ethnographical cases, from non-Western masks and ritual statuettes to paintings and sculptures in the Western tradition. This task, however, needs to be founded, as any anthropological enterprise, on more than empirical analyses; it also requires a new approach to the question of the anthropological study of thought. My exploration of the kind of life that might be mentally attributed to inanimate beings is intended to be an initial experiment in this domain. In this chapter, then, I will outline the argument of the book and, in more general terms, the theoretical strategy I have adopted to construct it. But let me first pay a well-deserved tribute to the work of Alfred Gell.

In *Art and Agency* (1998), Gell made the point that the museum artifacts that we label "art" are not merely instances of a universal instinct underlying artistic creativity. Besides being the products of the particular aesthetic of the societies in which they were conceived, many of these objects were also originally treated as living beings, notably within sequences of ritual actions. Through the process that Gell calls an "abduction of subjectivity," these artifacts are endowed with their own "agency." As such, they become the means of expressing specific networks of relationships among members of society. Whether it is a question of performing a sacrifice, marking out a symbolic space, or correctly accomplishing a rite of passage, "living" artifacts play a crucial role.

Gell's approach has been highly influential, and his work is still invaluable for the anthropology of art. However, twenty years after the publication of his book, we can look at his argument with fresh eyes and pose some new questions. Here, I will raise two points in particular. The first concerns the relationship between agency and aesthetics. On this topic, Gell famously wrote that "the anthropology of art cannot be the study of aesthetic principles of this or that culture, but of the mobilization of aesthetic principles (or something like them) in the course of social interaction" (1998, 5). According to him, "a purely cultural, aesthetic, 'appreciative' approach to art objects is an anthropological dead end" (1998, 5). If the anthropology of art can be pursued, it has to develop an "imitative strategy" of the other branches of social anthropology by becoming a "theory about social relationships, and not anything else" (1998, 5).

Gell's proposal has proven successful and productive. Yet we can argue that the question of aesthetics is not entirely resolved by the proposal of simply neglecting it. Even if we admit that a merely aesthetic appreciation would be unhelpful to understand the life of ritual objects in Melanesian or Amerindian cultures, the influence that Western conceptions of art, and of modern primitivism in particular, still holds on our way of looking at them is left unexplored in Gell's book. In the ensuing chapters, I will try to show that a critical examination of modern primitivism is necessary in order to free our gaze from Western conceptions and to approach the analysis of artifacts in a new light, looking at *both* their social effectiveness *and* the kind of aesthetics they mobilize.

My second point concerns the context and the network of social relationships in which agency may be attributed to an artifact. Gell refers to a kind of "spontaneous anthropomorphism" that we constantly experience in everyday life. His favorite example is his old Toyota, a "reliable and considerate" object that "does not just reflect the owner's personhood; it has a personhood as a car" (1998, 18). He notes how common it is for us to speak to objects as if they were human, at some level almost expecting them to respond, even though logically we know better. This kind of everyday experience led Gell to elaborate a theory of how agency and subjectivity are attributed to things. His claim is that artifacts become part of our social existence precisely because we so easily treat them as human. "Because anthropomorphism is a form of 'animism' which I actually and habitually practice," writes Gell, "there is every reason to make mention of it as a template for imagining forms of animism that I do not happen to share, such as the worship of idols" (1998, 19). As a consequence, his theory tends to conceptualize the presence of an "animated being" as the result of a direct replacement: a certain object corresponds to a certain person and vice versa. Through this perspective, for instance, the celebrant of a ritual and the object that takes on the celebrant's functions maintain a relationship of absolute equivalence. One has exactly the same value and meaning as the other. In ritual action (and in the universe of truth that it generates), the object seems to act like a shadow or a mirror image of the human being who replaces it.

Admittedly, this kind of anthropomorphism is very common in everyday life. But it is also highly unstable. It is a *fragile* state of mind, as it is constantly subjected to critical examination. Moreover, anthropomorphism does not invariably take the diffuse, everyday, and relatively superficial form discussed by

Gell. In other situations, our relationship to artifacts assumes more stable forms. This is notably the case in ritual action: the progressive construction of a truth regime different from the one we follow in our day-to-day existence creates a context in which our anthropomorphic thinking crystallizes and gives rise to enduring beliefs. Does the concept of anthropomorphism used by Gell enable us to account for the complex, stable, and counterintuitive identities embodied by inanimate objects in contexts such as ritual action or play? To understand these cases—and the kind of "suspension of disbelief" they imply—we need to look closer at the mental operations underlying this kind of elaborated anthropomorphism. My hypothesis is that in such situations, the object ceases to entertain a dual relationship with the person or "supernatural being" it represents. Within a ritual context, it becomes more complex than a mirror image or a "double." It resembles more a crystal, where a plural identity, constituted by fragments of different identities, is gradually constructed. The investigations presented in this book will show that this complex relational structure may account for the attachment of a stable belief to the living artifact. I will try to show that if we decipher the complexity of the bond of belief created between objects and persons, the very idea of a "living object" appears in a completely different light.

The story of Kafka and the doll offers a luminous example of this complexity. What does the doll represent? Whose image is it? By following Kafka's game, we gradually realize that it assumes a changing identity, at once plural and provisional. In one letter after another, the doll is a girl, a close friend, then a fiancée and the future wife of a young prince. But there is more involved in the make-believe: the doll's presence is imagined in the universe described by the narration: long journeys to wondrous, far-off countries, fabulous palaces, and so on. Moreover, the narration is not just a story; it is also an act. It translates the presence of a narrator, not simply the characters Kafka talks about. Beyond appearances, the doll is thus equally close to the image and the voice of this thin, inspired young man who reads his letters aloud—or even to the silent presence of Diamant, who captured the memory of this curious episode.

Through the tools of comparative anthropology, I will offer an analysis of this type of complexity, which concerns the presence as well as the image of an object, while seeking to identify the space of thought that engenders it. Although this will involve constructing an anthropological theory of anthropomorphism, I wish to do more in the pages that follow. In fact, the existence of anthropomorphic thought is not at all surprising. The traces of the exercise of this mode of thought are evident throughout our daily experience, even if we may not notice them because of their very banality.

In other places, times, or situations, anthropomorphic thought undergoes a profound change. On certain occasions, it intensifies, becoming more serious, sometimes solemn and indisputable. The attitude that attributes life to an artifact in such cases is no longer revocable or provisional. Anthropomorphism thus appears to be a "serious game" with rules that people may follow or transgress. Such occasions call to mind the domain of religion, yet they can also occur without any religious belief being involved, such as when the picture of a recently deceased husband comes "alive" for a while and becomes a conversation partner with a widow.

These situations, which I will discuss mainly in ritual contexts, are also illustrated in Ernst Gombrich's memorable example in his *Meditations on a Hobby Horse* (1971). The broomstick that a child can "ride" (an action that, as we will see later, Gombrich rightly links to the artistic act) is a horse—in fact, it is the horse that makes the child a knight, just as it makes his friend a princess of the Middle Ages—precisely because anthropomorphic thought makes this rudimentary object the final term in a chain of associations. Like Kafka's doll, the broomstick points to a complex exercise of thought, which the image can only partially translate.

Here, I will focus my analyses on situations in which the establishment of a belief links an object and a person in a persistent, complex, and to a certain extent, orderly manner. These situations are not always "rituals" in the strict sense of the term. Other situations exist where games of substitution and partial identification may be established between humans and objects, or even between humans and humans. I thus propose to describe such situations as *quasi-rituals*. Without corresponding to the usual conditions prevailing when ritual action is exercised, these situations can nonetheless be described through the relational theory that Michael Houseman and I formulated for ritual action twenty years ago (Houseman and Severi 1998). In this work, we argued that a rite is determined more by its relational form than by its meaning or function. By "form," we meant a particular relational configuration that confers a distinctive ontological dimension on ritual interaction. This dimension, which we viewed as a "serious fiction," to borrow Gregory Bateson's phrase ([1972] 1999, 35–40), implies more than the traditional anthropological principle that the world evoked within a ritual must be interpreted according to a symbolic register. It implies further that the identity of the subjects of ritual action is defined through the condensation of what would be seen in ordinary life as contradictory modes of relationship.

As an example of this kind of *quasi-ritual* situation, which likewise involves the condensation of different modes of relationships, I will propose an analysis in an ensuing chapter of the Homeric funerary games based on a reading of the *Iliad*. Later in the book, I will go a step further by considering instances of Western art as generating specific relational situations in which artifacts may reveal agency and even a certain kind of life. This approach to what we call "art" experimentally reverses the perspective of modern primitivism. Instead of seeing "works of art" in artifacts endowed with agency outside the West, I will analyze certain Western works of art according to their own logic as object-persons. My final claim will be that studying situations where an object is thought to come alive enables us to deepen and extend the scope of our understanding not only of ritual action and the act of play but also of art, both Western and non-Western.

Let me now briefly define the strategy I have chosen to develop my argument. To do so, I will first examine in what ways my approach differs from the two main currents in contemporary anthropology that aim to deal with thought and mental operations: the ontological and cognitive approaches. I will next outline the approach I develop in the analyses presented in this book. Let us start with an experiment in ontological thought.

KŪKAI'S VISION

At the turn of the ninth century, a young Japanese scholar named Kūkai (Kōbō Daishi, 774–835) met an ascetic Buddhist monk, who introduced him to an esoteric text of the tantric tradition. This text stated that by reciting the mantra it contained one million times in the proper way, "the meanings of everything that had been heard will be thoroughly understood, retained in the mind, and never lost or forgotten" (Kūkai 2010, 4). Kūkai believed that any word attributed to the Buddha was (or had to be) literally true. From that day forward, he devoted himself without rest to the practice of reciting the mantra. "Wandering in deep mountains and secluded valleys" (Kūkai 2010, 5), he never stopped chanting the mantra. One day, he had a vision. In the valley where he was reciting, he suddenly realized that trees, rocks, and birds loudly resounded with the sound of his whispered mantra. Everything he perceived was speaking his own words.

This experience was not due simply to the attainment of heightened powers of memory and vision (also promised by the mantra). What Kūkai understood from the message conveyed to him by his "sudden awakening" was that

> nature itself is vibration, sound, and language. Every phenomenon, in all nature, is . . . a manifestation of a primordial language carved into the fabric of space. . . . Long before human language ever evolved, the entire universe was . . . a text written in this primordial language. (Takagi, in Kūkai 2010, 5)

Later, in his treatise devoted to *The Meaning of Sound, Letter, and Reality*, Kūkai commented on the meaning of his vision in more speculative terms:

> The moment that the inner breath and the outer air began to move, vibration inevitably arises. This is called *sound*. . . . Sound arises and is never meaningless; it is always the name of a thing. This is called *letter*. Names evoke the essence. This is called *reality*. Distinguishing the three—sound, letter, and reality—is called *meaning*. (Kūkai 2010, 84)

According to Kūkai, then, language and reality coincide. In order to understand a meaningful statement, one has to understand that words actually work as an acoustic image of the world. They do not represent it; they *are* the world.

How are we to understand this statement? One possibility is to reconstruct its historical context. Buddhism often presents the practice of experiencing visions as an "undetermined, spontaneous, absolute" (Faure, 1993, 158). Many scholars have shown that this kind of vision was linked to a specific discursive practice, an "art of speaking" that required a long initiation. Moreover, we know that Kūkai had studied Daoism in China, and it has been noted that his vision of the "speaking valley" reflects a passage of one of the great books of Daoism, the Zhuangzi:

> A colorless and soundless wind blows through the infinite reaches of the cosmos. . . . When this wind blows in the deep forests of the Earth, the trees immediately begin to rustle, and sounds arise everywhere. In that ancient forest, there are huge trees measuring a hundred arms lengths around. In their trunks and branches are infinite holes of different shapes. When the wind strikes those holes they each produce different sounds: some roar like torrents dashing against the rocks, some murmur like the shallows, some rumble like thunder in the sky, some

hiss like flying arrows, and others sound of wailing, anger, sadness, or happiness. (Kūkai 2010, 85)

Kūkai is thus not alone in assimilating language with reality. What appears at first sight to be a spontaneous vision of an enchanted valley is actually an image deeply rooted in a particular conception of the world, one that originated in the Chinese philosophy of the fifth century. From this point of view (sometimes called a "lateral" comparison, in this case, between China and Japan), we can say that Kūkai's vision reflects a scholarly tradition and a specific school of thought.

Another way to evaluate a cosmology of this kind is to "frontally" (Candea 2016) compare it to Western cosmology. European or American authors of all sorts have traditionally stated that, in the Western perspective, signs are opposed to objects, not confused with them. Signs are arbitrary, conventional, and in some measure abstract. They do not "resemble" objects nor do they convey their acoustic image. Furthermore, in contrast to what Kūkai writes, Western cultures hold that sounds can be perfectly meaningless. The distinction between inanimate matter and language is paralleled by another crucial one, that between subject and object. Western thought is, we are often told, "dualistic." Eastern doctrines, on the contrary, tend to posit a kind of synthesis of the subject and the object, incarnated, in Kūkai's case, by the idea of a "speaking landscape." Such a vision is associated with a "religious" or metaphysical vision of the world, whereby language (and the mind behind it) are not opposed to each other but, rather, are part of a single being.

Recently, it has become usual to oppose Eastern Monistic spiritualism to Western Cartesian dualism. Is this opposition really well founded? We will have to look more closely to Kūkai's vision and its connections with Buddhism to fully answer this question. Before doing so, however, we may also wonder whether the *image of ourselves* that this kind of comparison implies is correct, whether from a theoretical or a historical point of view. Among the philosophers of Western antiquity, we find a number of nondualist thinkers. Epicurus, for instance, taught that both reality and the human mind are materially composed of the same atoms. His theories do not fit comfortably into the pattern in Western society that Philippe Descola ([2005] 2013, 172–200) describes as "naturalism," which implies the existence of, on the one hand, a continuity between human and nonhumans in terms of the physical matter they are composed of, and on the other, a discontinuity between physical matter and the mental faculties that are exclusively human. Epicurus saw continuity and a common nature in the structures of both matter and human mental activities. In Lucretius's *De Rerum Natura*, one of the richest sources for understanding Epicurism, all phenomena belonging to nature are said to be composed of an infinite but fixed and immortal set of "atoms." Thought processes, including inference and imagination, are not fundamentally different from other "natural" phenomena; they are simply generated by different combinations of atoms. Furthermore, human bodies and minds are not different from animal bodies and minds. Death is not the end of a "soul" or its travel to another world; it is just a transformation of atoms guided by the laws of a Mind, which is common to all creatures. Lucretius describes, for instance, how horses feel, think, and dream like human beings. And, for him, since atoms combine in the same way the letters of an alphabet combine to generate words, the organization of human language is the best model for understanding the material structure of the universe.

This vision of a fundamental continuity between the "object" (matter) and the "subject" (mind) was far from being confined to Greek materialism. Since Lucretius's *De Rerum Natura* and other ancient texts were rediscovered, the materialism of antiquity has indeed permeated an entire tradition of Western materialistic thought, from Giordano Bruno (who remarkably wrote that "if God is not the same as nature, it is to be conceived of as the nature of nature"), to Baruch Spinoza, to Denis Diderot, and down to contemporary debates in the cognitive sciences. Although the competing paradigm of naturalism has always had advocates such as René Descartes, who distinguished the *res extensa* (the Matter) from the *res cogitans* (the Subject), the long tradition of materialism, which considers these two domains to be coinciding, has had equally vigorous proponents.

Where is the supposedly monolithic "Western dualism" that is so often opposed to an equally monolithic "Eastern monism"? This kind of comparison, no matter how it is framed, whether sophisticated or simplistic, inevitably leads down the wrong path, for both theoretical and ethnographical reasons. As for theory, I have argued elsewhere (Severi 2013, 2014) that anthropologists usually do not adequately understand the concept of ontology. Many of our colleagues (e.g., Viveiros de Castro 1998; Descola [2005] 2013) tend to call any discourse about the origins and nature of the world an "ontology." However, ever since Parmenides, the term *ontology* has not referred to the various material constituents of the universe (fire, water, air, etc.) and their different ways to combine. Parmenides's ontological argument is about "being itself." It aims to construct an ontology as a science of abstract principles—founded on the analysis of predicates of being (such as necessity versus contingence, possibility versus impossibility, subsistence versus potentially, and the like)—not as a discourse about the origins of what physically exists. Nor does Parmenides seek to classify the different beings inhabiting the universe. He intends, on the contrary, to identify an abstract relationship between *nous* and *physis* and to discover the conditions under which the world is thinkable. This is why a classification of different beings into categories based on, for example, the distinctions of animate/inanimate, human/animal, male/female (which are often considered "ontological" by anthropologists) technically does not make for an "ontology." It is better defined instead as a "natural philosophy *without* ontology."

From a technical point of view, the negative (or indeterminate) results of this kind of comparison appear as an effect of the way "ontology" is usually constructed as an ethnographic object. The first problem is the exclusive focus on the content of "cosmology" as a notion, accompanied by a lack of analysis about the ways it comes to be shared and by whom. If the "stuff a cosmology is made of" is shared knowledge, how is this knowledge shared or transmitted? We may hope to understand this process only if we adopt a perspective in which the analysis of the forms of knowledge transmission is given priority over the analysis of content. In this respect, Kūkai's vision no longer appears as the inverted *analogon* of an abstract notion of "Western naturalism." Rather, it is the result of ritual action implying a certain form of thought-enactment ("contemplation"), a certain form of language use, typically nonpropositional ("the repetition thousands of times of a certain sequence of words"), and an exercise in techniques of memory aimed at defining an exceptional form of subjectivity. From this perspective, the relationship of these practices to the other ritual tradition Kūkai also followed (the meditation technique aimed at transforming him in a way to "become the Bodhisattva immediately in his body") is clearly relevant to understanding his vision. Notably, the only other treatise that we have by Kūkai is precisely about meditation. In other words, the kind of variation in the realm of thought that I am attempting to define here is not only characterized by a symbolic content; it also implies forms of enacting thought, which emerge through specific forms of language use and ritual action. It is only through the study of these conditions that we may comprehend the many ways in which "cosmological knowledge" is shared, transmitted, and transformed.

My third objection to the ontological approach concerns the use of the verb *to be*. From a philosophical point of view, since at least Alfred Ayer (1936, 52), the ambiguity of this verb has been criticized. As Ayer writes,

> If we were guided merely by the form of the sign, we should assume that the "is," which occurs in the sentence "He is the author of that book," was the same symbol as the symbol "is," which appears in the statement, "The cat is a mammal." But when we come to translate[1] the sentences, we find that the first is equivalent to "He, and no one else, wrote that book," and the second to "The class of the mammals contains the class of cats." And this shows that each "is" is an ambiguous symbol, which must not be confused with the other, nor with the ambiguous symbols of existence, a class membership, and identity, and entailments, which are also constituted by signs of the form "is." (Ayer 1936, 52)

This way of generating ambiguity has heavy consequences in the analysis of ethnography. If we want to avoid them, we should recognize that things do not "exist" in human societies in an undifferentiated way. To understand how an "ontology" applies to a specific society, we have to reconstruct the grammar of the verb "to be" on a case-by-case basis.

In the anthropological literature, an eloquent illustration of this point can be found in the discussion E. E. Evans-Pritchard devotes to the grammar of the verb "to be" among the Nuer. He starts by arguing that a specific form of the use of the verb "to be" is crucial for understanding sacrifice:

> When a cucumber is used as a sacrificial victim, Nuer speak of it as an ox. In doing so, they are asserting something rather more than that it takes the place of an ox. They do not say, of course, that cucumbers are oxen, and in speaking of a particular cucumber as an ox in a sacrificial situation, they are only indicating that it may thought of as an ox in that particular situation; and they act accordingly by performing the sacrificial rite as closely as possible to what happens when the victim is an ox. The resemblance is conceptual, not perceptual. (Evans-Pritchard 1956, 128)

Once he establishes this point concerning the existence of conceptual analogies, Evans-Pritchard takes a more general approach to this question by distinguishing among several forms of existence revealed by the use of the verb

---

1. When Ayer uses the concept of "translation" here, he is referring to Bertrand Russell's "theory of definite descriptions" (Russell and Whitehead 1910), according to which "We define a symbol in use, not by saying that it is synonymous with some other symbols, but by showing how the sentences in which it significantly occurs can be translated into equivalent sentences" (Ayer 1936, 49).

"to be." First, he remarks that the Nuer use the verb in one sense, such as "the crocodile is an animal, not a spirit," which only means that such a reptile exists as a beast. The Nuer are not immersed in the mystical, nonlogical, "primitive mentality" described by Lucien Lévy-Bruhl ([1922] 1978), nor do they see spirits or essences everywhere. The proof given here by Evans-Pritchard is simple: even when the Nuer say that "a crocodile is Spirit," they would constantly and firmly deny that "a spirit is a crocodile." Evans-Pritchard next introduces a subtle distinction between "being Spirit" and "being a spirit." "Being Spirit" can sometimes function just as the name of a natural phenomenon, such as lightning or any natural sprite, which involves a sort of "refraction of Spirit" (Evans-Pritchard 1956, 138). The "is" appearing in this statement, however, "is not one of identity" (1956, 138), since Spirit is, for the Nuer, quite independent of any natural phenomenon. However, the use of "is" designating a stable and general identity is not found in the statement "X is a spirit" either: this expression simply refers to an individual being that, in certain cases, might assume the "symbolic" role of representing a specific spirit. In other cases, this statement refers to a different kind of situation, the totemic relationship between an "animal spirit" with the members of the clan it designates. In this specific relationship, where a single animal might assume the role of "spirit" only for members of a particular clan, the indication "to be a snake or a crocodile" comes closer to the description of a personality. In none of these cases, however, is the verb "to be" a tool for indicating stable or unconditional identities. From the point of view we might call "ontological," this means that these variations in the grammar of the verb "to be" reflect the fact that the Nuer do not consider Spirit as something that exists in a general and undifferentiated way. Evans-Pritchard explains this in the following way:

> There are gradations of the conceptions of Spirit from pure unattached Spirit to Spirit associated with human; animal and lifeless objects are more and more closely bound to what it is associated with the farther down the scale one goes. So when Nuer say of something that it is Spirit, we have to consider not only what "is" means, but also what "Spirit" means. (Evans-Pritchard 1956, 139)

We could add that this "graduated" character is also typical of what we might call "matter" or "reality." Spirit and matter do not constitute the terms of an opposition; both of them exist only in degrees. One obvious consequence of this point is that "patterns of existence" are not the same for all beings in the Nuer universe. Nonhumans do not "exist" in the same way humans do; the same goes for cucumbers, oxen, and other sacrificial victims.

These analyses of Evans-Pritchard, relevant to Nuer ontology, are followed by his famous discussion of the relationships between twins and birds. The focus of the argument is on the logic of relationships underlying the use of the verb "to be." Here, as we have already seen, the form subject X "is" predicate Y (e.g., twins are birds, or twins are the same person) hides the fact that the relationship is not dual; it presupposes a third term, "God," to whom both are related. In this case, writes Evans-Pritchard, "The formula does not express a dyadic relationship between twins and birds, but a triadic relationship of twins, birds, and God. In respect to God, twins and birds have a similar character" (Evans-Pritchard 1956, 132).

For the Nuer, constructing a progressive series of predicates in these forms of existence is a way of establishing an ordered set of relationships among graduated instances of beings, be they "material" or "spiritual." It is clear that adopting this relational approach (in which, as in sacrificial actions, relations take priority over the description of the empirical appearance of beings) is a way to identify a rich, detailed sequence of intermediary steps between "true" (material) and "untrue" (spiritual) things. In other words, the concepts of truth and falsity do not disappear in this context, since both of them are present: a crocodile is a beast, not Spirit; a vulture is not Spirit is the sense that rain or an earthquake is; a twin is not a bird in terms of their appearance; and a cucumber is not an ox, unless it becomes an ox by convention. But they play different roles according to the different linguistic forms in the grammar of the verb "to be" and the different contexts of enunciation in which they are expressed. This is the reason why, instead of trying to establish whether they obey some sort of general rationality, we must use the utmost exactitude to grasp the limits and scope of the conceptual universe they express.

This carefully graduated and contextual interpretation of reality need not be deciphered as a proposition or an ensemble of propositions forming a "conception" of the world. Nor does Evans-Pritchard's proposal to consider this way of thinking as the product of the Nuer's poetic sense or verbal art seem much more useful. Elsewhere (Hanks and Severi 2014), Hanks and I have argued that, instead of looking for a category where this kind of discourse would belong, it is far more valuable to follow the process of translation to which this "experience on an imaginative level of thought" (Evans-Pritchard 1956, 142) is constantly subjected in the culture where it is used. In Claude Lévi-Strauss's language, we could say that this kind of conceptualization constantly mobilizes sensory data in terms of other sensory data, without invoking the question of rationality (in the sense this term has in linguistics). Furthermore, in this case, instead of seeing the possibility of translation as a theoretical difficulty for defining thought (as it has traditionally been viewed), we could, on the contrary, consider the ethnography of translation as an opportunity to observe the dynamics of thought processes and to study how they operate by adapting to constraints and by exploiting possibilities of the means of expression they use in different contexts.

Finally, let us consider the case of negation from this point of view. As noted earlier, when anthropologists use the concept of ontology, they often describe various "forms of existence." However, the concept of "existence," which is the foundation of the idea of "ontology," cannot be formulated without referring to its contrary, the concept of "nonexistence." It is unimaginable that a culture, while mentioning the "existence" of something, could spare itself the distinction between "existent" and "nonexistent" instances of reality. For Aristotle, the properties pertaining to all existent beings are only four: the existence of a being can be necessary or contingent, possible or impossible. However, it should be noted that these four "ontological properties" represent four possible mediations between being and nonbeing. In fact, it is quite possible to reformulate the terms used to qualify the existence of a being in terms of nonbeing. If something exists necessarily, it cannot be nonexistent; if something exists in a contingent way, it can become nonexistent by accident. If an object has only a possible existence, it can equally (to the same extent) become nonexistent. To say that the existence of an object is impossible is to state that it could never exist. What is crucial for social anthropology is that these classic relationships between being and nonbeing do not rule out a further possibility: situations in which the relationship between being and nonbeing assume a paradoxical form where "Being" implies "Nonbeing." Anthropologists know these paradoxical definitions well, since they often characterize the relationship societies establish with the dead, the spirits, or entities like the "speaking trees" or the "rocks expressing fear or sadness" that appear in Kūkai's vision. To designate these imaginary situations, in which the relationship with reality assumes the form of a paradoxical ontology ("existent only if nonexistent" or "existing by negating the feature of existent things"), human societies have invented an array of special forms of communication, verbal and nonverbal alike. The study of these forms of "serious fiction" (which bear relationships with other, more ordinary forms of reality) is essential for understanding the coexistence of different "forms of thought" in a single society.

In conclusion, let me point out that the "ontological" perspective generates two blind spots. On one side, there is a naïve (nonanalytical) conception of the concept of "existence" and on the other, a refusal to admit the existence of a specific logic governing serious fiction as a parallel form of reality. In both cases, there is a refusal to recognize that social life is composed of different layers of reality governed by different logics.

LEVELS OF COGNITION

The refusal to apprehend plural perspectives of analysis also characterizes the field of cognitive anthropology. In this case, however, the problem concerns the rigidity of the conceptual model, not a mistaken conception of the ontological background. Cognitive anthropologists explicitly aim to study, as do I, the ways that mental processes propagate in a society (e.g., Sperber 1985; Sperber and Wilson 1986; Boyer 1988, 1992, 1993, 2002; Whitehouse 2004; Bloch 2012; Morin 2011). It seems natural, therefore, to ask how their approach might be compared with the one I am defending here. I will therefore first define the kind of cognition I am focusing on and then formulate a number of critiques to the main line of research in cognitive anthropology.

We can start by acknowledging that, in social life, not all individual fantasies become shared knowledge. Dreams, for instance, which might be seen as extremely "counterintuitive" and thus memorable, usually last only a brief period of time in individual memory. Furthermore, their representational content is famously difficult to share with others. Anthropology has not much to say about individual experiences of this kind. Its primary scope is the exploration of the many ways knowledge is shared. Furthermore, we know that a large amount of human shared cognition is basic and indifferent to cultural variation, simply because it is independent of any process of communication. A good example is what psychologists call "naïve physics" (Hayes 1985). At a certain age (Baillargeon 1995), all human children acquire the right expectations concerning a ball thrown upward. They instinctively "think" that the ball will come down. Usually, their daily experience confirms this rule. It is remarkable, however, that, from a logical point of view, this does not mean that this kind of knowledge is independent of truth: it still has to be confirmed to become fully true. As far as we know, knowledge belonging to this kind of cognition does not vary from one culture to another. It is a mistake to think that this level is irrelevant for the study of social cognition, but it is also irrefutable that this kind of cognition only describes a form of competence that belongs to the individual. The performances of social interactions, as well as their propagation in a society, only indirectly depend on this kind of basic cognition, which might be part of a general endowment of the human species but is not technically definable as a social phenomenon. From the point of view of a general psychology of human beings, then, the exploration of this kind of cognition might be quite interesting, but from the point of view of the forms of propagation of knowledge in a given society, it simply never strikes deeply enough. I would therefore argue that it is a mistake to conflate this kind of cognition with other kinds of cultural representations, which are also basic and shared but heavily dependent on the modalities of cultural communication, thus varying from one culture to another.

In my view, cognitive anthropology constantly mistakes one level for the other. This is one of the reasons for the rigidity of the method and the poverty of results that characterize this field of anthropology today. It is obviously impossible in such a short introduction to examine this question in detail, but let me briefly examine analyses proposed by Dan Sperber (1985, 1986), since they are shared by many other cognitive anthropologists and still reflect the mainstream perspective in this field. Sperber has often claimed to be the author of two influential and controversial theories: one concerns the identification of relevance (that is, intentional meaning) within an expanded and revised Gricean model of conversation (Grice 1989); the second concerns the definition of culture as a process of an "epidemic" propagation of representations. The natural development of this approach to social cognition—which one might consider the task of his followers—would be to go one step further, leading to the identification of a logical link between the two theories. This link would enable the unified theory to predict where and when a certain way of producing relevance in communication would generate a specific sort of social propagation of representations. However, this seems to be an impossible task for contemporary cognitive anthropology. Two reasons may account for this theoretical failure. The first is that Paul Grice's work offers an abstract model for understanding the role of intentions and a speaker's implicit meanings in situations of idealized conversation. However (or therefore), it is, quite intuitively, a poor tool for understanding other contexts of cultural communication where, as in Kūkai's vision, language is used in a nonpropositional way, or where, as in ancient Greek funerary rituals, the faculty of speaking is attributed to an inanimate artifact (Chapter Five), or where, yet again, as in many rituals, knowledge is expressed through action. In many cases, the use of this model simply leads to inaccurate or inappropriate descriptions of ethnography. To understand the ever-changing and usually unexpected forms of propagating representations that we find in ethnography, we obviously need a far wider conception of language use and communication. The second reason for cognitive anthropology's failure lies in the rather outdated concept of epidemics that Sperber uses in his famous paper on "cultural epidemiology." In that essay (1985), he describes the propagation of representations in a society as a process analogous to the propagation of a viral illness, when an ill body "infects" a previously healthy one. Contemporary epidemiology, however, long ago ceased to define epidemics in these terms. Epidemics are no longer defined as the physical contact of viruses of an illness that pass from a body to another body. The field of epidemiology has increasingly become the study of the reproduction of *the conditions* generating illnesses rather than their propagation. Today, epidemiologists currently speak of the epidemiology of obesity, asthma, or lung cancer (Doll and Hill 1950; Bonita, Beaglehole, and Kjellström 2006)—all illnesses where no contact between viruses or other microorganisms generate any symptoms. The same conceptual revision should be applied for the epidemiology of ideas. The cultural study of cognition should be based, thus, not on a typology of representations (such as intuitive, counterintuitive, apparently irrational, etc.) but, rather, on the conditions influencing the generation of specific forms of communicative interactions. If so, this inquiry should no longer be based on the content of cultural representations, which supposedly makes them "successful or unsuccessful," but instead on the analysis of the pragmatic forms of their propagation. The research that I have conducted on the propagation of the Native American messianic movement known as the "Ghost Dance" (between approximately 1880 and 1920) in the United States shows, for instance, that the propagation of this new "religion" was not based on the content of the representations themselves (whether categorized as counterintuitive, intense, salient, etc.) but on the *form of communicative interaction* that characterized the new rituals, which combined, in a paradoxical way, Christian prayers with traditional dances celebrating the ancestors (Severi [2007] 2015, 265–90).[2]

---

2. In Chapter Three of the present book, I give another example of using this approach when analyzing the form of ritual enunciation in oral traditions among the Fang of West Africa.

In short, the knowledge of human social cognition need not avoid, as is unfortunately often the case, the intricacies of ethnography. It should, to the contrary, be rooted in a detailed study of the forms of the transmission of knowledge. A crucial point that I share with cognitive anthropology, however, is that the focus of analysis shifts from reconstructing "conceptions of the world" to the study of the conditions of enunciation of shared knowledge in different contexts. In this perspective, to "study culture" becomes a way to explore the pragmatic conditions of cultural communication, verbal or otherwise, ritualized or ordinary. It is certainly from this perspective that, in this book, I analyze the communicative agency and forms of interaction that we find attributed to artifacts.

ANTHROPOLOGY AND PRAGMATICS

On the links between anthropology and pragmatics, the contribution of linguistic anthropology has been crucial. Thanks to the work of authors such as Dell Hymes (1981), Michael Silverstein (1976), Denis Tedlock (1983), Keith Basso (1996), Alan Rumsey (2002, 2003), William Hanks (2005, 2006), Francesca Merlan and Alan Rumsey (2017), Alessandro Duranti (2015), and Webb Keane (1997, 2011, 2015), anthropology has firmly integrated the study of the pragmatic conditions of speech acts, through which the identities of speakers are constructed, into its conceptual toolkit. These authors have demonstrated that studying the conditions of interlocution can enrich our understanding of the meaning of traditional discourse and help us situate myths and other narrative forms in specific oral genres and, more generally, shed new light on the uses of traditional knowledge. This pragmatic approach enables anthropologists to move beyond the mere deciphering of indigenous speech acts and endeavor, instead, to distinguish various forms of social communication and the modalities through which tradition functions.

However, as mentioned earlier, research in the field of pragmatics has forked into two distinct branches. On the cognitive side, the analysis of extremely simple (or fictitious) communicative acts leads to sophisticated but hardly applicable theoretical models (Grice 1989; Sperber and Wilson 1986). On the linguistic side, the detailed identification of complex sociolinguistic phenomena, using contextually specific explanatory tools, has prevailed in more theoretical concerns (Labov 1972). To this day, specialists in pragmatics tend to focus either on the wider criteria of generalized pragmatics, applicable to all communicative acts, or on the localized, specific variations that affect particular instances of linguistic performance. The unfortunate effects of this bifurcation in research strategies are clear: the degree of abstraction that Grice and his followers opt for makes their models unsuitable for analyzing data from the field, while the study of specific cases raised by other authors has rarely led to wider, more generalizable conclusions from an anthropological perspective. In its relationship with social anthropology, linguistic pragmatics has seemed either too abstract and based on fictitious examples, or else empirically grounded but too circumstantial and heterogeneous. This divergence is particularly striking in the study of ritual communication, a context where the "agency" attributed to artifacts is very frequently involved. Whereas a series of solid anthropological works (Bateson [1936] 1958; Barth 1975, 1987; Rappaport 1979, 2000; Kapferer 1977, 1979, 1983; Staal 1979, 1983, 1989; Humphrey and Laidlaw 1994; Bloch 1986, 1991) has sought to identify the constitutive traits of ritual action and to distinguish it from everyday action, linguists (even though they have produced precise descriptions of many different situations of social communication) have thus far not attempted to explore the special pragmatics of ritual speech. Were this to become a topic of research, their studies could converge in an approach illuminating the range of phenomena involved in this type of communication.

Anthropologists, for their part, have been slow to grasp and incorporate descriptive categories from pragmatics, such as situation, setting, context, indexicality, and implicature, into their analyses. They have made little attempt to delve deeper into the study of the ritual use of language, limiting themselves to highlighting a few superficial aspects of ritual language (repetition, semantic poverty, use of fixed formulas, etc.) without linking them to other aspects of ritual behavior. Some of them have indeed applied John Austin's classic work on speech acts ([1962] 1975) to the disparate elements of ritual speech and action (Tambiah 1985; Bloch 1974), but as Donald Gardner (1983) points out, these approaches are either rigorous but empirically useless or else approximative and theoretically negligible.

For linguists, pragmatics is still defined as the study of everything that is explicitly formulated through linguistic means under the conditions of a given speech context. Although they recognize the existence and efficacy of other contextual indicators that are not expressed in linguistic terms, they almost invariably treat them as either residual or negligible. This linguistic definition of the field of analysis, which only takes into account the "grammaticalized" elements

(Levinson 1983, 89), ignores a whole range of other phenomena that we need to take into account for understanding communication in ritual contexts.

This point is analyzed in detail in several chapters of this book (see Chapters Four and Five). Here I wish to raise only two points. The first concerns the way in which a ritual identity is established in contrast with ordinary life. Many pragmatists have highlighted the fact that, in ordinary speech, the identity of the speaker is an important element of social indexicality and thus helps determine the meaning of utterances. By contrast, in a ritual context, many of the usual conditions of ordinary communication are suspended, such as the ones identified by Erving Goffman—"shared experience, the occupation of the same space at the same time, and a form of reciprocity through mutual perception" (1963, 22; 1972)—and those later added by Hanks, namely, "mutual understanding among parties, and a framework of relevance" (2006, 118). The meaning of the utterance can only be grasped if we understand how the speaker is defined in a preformatted, often counterintuitive communicational game. As in a game of chess, we must first know the rules governing the game and the uses of all the pieces in order to understand why one piece made a certain move. Likewise, in ritual communication, we must first know what the components of a speaker's complex identity are in order to understand the framework and thus the context of speech acts. In logical terms, this means that the rules governing a speaker's identity cease to be normative (as in everyday speech) and become constitutive when they are applied to an entirely new game of interaction.[3]

My second point concerns the role of images and actions in ritual communication. In many cases, the images and actions are no more to be seen as a heterogeneous or residual element in relation to the speech act. On the contrary, speech and image reciprocally entail one another in the definition of the speaker and thus of the indexical field. Speech acts that occur in ritual contexts possess a specific form of complexity that is defined less by their semantic content

---

3. This is how John Searle (1969) explains the distinction (originally from Kant [1781] 1999) between "constitutive" and "regulative" (normative) rules: "Constitutive rules . . . create or define new forms of behavior. The rules of football or chess, for example, do not merely regulate playing football or chess, but as it were they create the very possibility of playing such games. . . . Regulative rules regulate a pre-existing activity, an activity whose existence is logically independent of the rules. Constitutive rules constitute (and also regulate) an activity the existence of which is logically dependent on the rule" (1969, 33–34). Note that the special use of speech governed by constitutive rules contributes to the memorability of a set of representations within a ritual tradition (see Severi 2003, [2007] 2015).

than by the definition of the specific "conditions of utterance," including where and when the act occurs and the nature of the speaker. To be anthropologically relevant, this context must be defined not only in linguistic terms but also with regard to other forms of communication, notably visual or gestural. To bridge the two approaches of pragmatics and anthropology, a model is needed that can account for this complexity.

ETHNOGRAPHY AND THOUGHT

Let us turn to the issue of thought. From Lévy-Bruhl's considerations of "prelogical mentality" ([1922] 1978) up to Sperber's arguments on apparently irrational beliefs (1982), a large part of the anthropological literature devoted to thought does not really concern the study of thought as a general human activity but, rather, the opposition between rationality and irrationality (Severi 2014). In this perspective, anthropologists usually compare an abstract definition of "rationality" with an empirical counterpart, mostly founded on the analysis of some forms of categorization and theories of causality. It is obvious, however, that there is much more to human thought than categorization or propositional rationality. Ideas about perception and space, language, and communication, right or wrong moral values, for instance, are constantly present in ethnography. It would be hard to qualify them as "rational" or "nonrational" (or even "symbolic"); following at least Austin ([1962] 1975), concepts of this kind would be better qualified as "appropriate" or "inappropriate," or as "felicitous" or "infelicitous," within a certain context, rather than as rational or nonrational.

In sum, when approaching the idea of an anthropology of thought, there is a preliminary choice to make. Either one chooses what we may call a Piagetian model of thought-as-rationality, seen in its various manifestations but defined only through the opposition between rational or nonrational (e.g., Piaget [1923] 2001, [1926] 2007); or one refers to a more extensive, and more realistic, definition of thought. One of the classic authors who have worked in this direction (and whom we could, in this respect, oppose to Piaget) is Lev Vygotsky, the great Russian psychologist (Vygotsky 1978). Not unaware of the problems posed by cultural differences, Vygotsky elaborated a multifaceted conception of the exercise of thought, which includes not only rational inference but also metalinguistic, metacommunicational, aesthetic, and narrative thought. In this book, I have chosen this Vygotskian option, and I try to develop it in a new direction. From a methodological point of view, the approach to thought I am taking here is resolutely ethnographic. Instead of predefining a kind of thought and looking for it in social life, I consider specific interactions and forms of communication and then try to understand the kind of thought they mobilize. This perspective may allow us to take further steps toward the definition of a new approach in the anthropology of thought. Roman Jakobson (1959) remarked once that when we pass from one language (or, more precisely, one grammar) to another, the variation between the two concerns what speakers *must* say in order to express a meaning rather than what they *may* say. I have argued that this kind of variation might become useful in the study of linguistic variation, but also in the domain of thought. I would claim first that variation in a necessary but far from sufficient level is not merely an empirical fact (as Jakobson probably thought), with no meaning in itself. To illustrate this point, I referred to the distinction currently used in logic between the *power* of symbolic systems (the possibility of identifying a limited number of features that are valid for a large number of cases) and their *expressivity* (the possibility of identifying a large number of features belonging to a limited number of cases) (Mangione 1964, 52–53). Any case-centered inquiry (such as fieldwork-based ethnography) needs to be in some measure expressive, while any comparative or statistical analysis needs to be reasonably powerful. With this distinction in mind, I have noted that a consequence of Jakobson's perspective on linguistic variation is that all human natural languages potentially have the same logical power, but they always differ in degrees of expressivity. This means that the grammatical differences between languages can be considered as specific forms of a general logical property of all symbolic systems ("degrees of expressivity"), not simply as "episodic" or contingent phenomena. Second, I have proposed that if this form of variation is considered as the variation of an abstract property, we may then extend this observation from language to the domain of thought. In short, we might state that language-games generate thought-games. Accordingly, I formulated the hypothesis that different "forms of thought" *only* concern what people *must* conceptualize in a certain context. Through this perspective, variation in the realm of thought might not indicate "kinds of thought" typical of different kind of societies; rather, the representations and operations that a specific kind of context might *require* people to think, without limiting what it may *allow* them to think. I have argued that this kind of variation is not limited to grammar rules. It also concerns practices linked to many forms of translation, in particular, to intersemiotic translation, which involves the passage from verbal to nonverbal ways for expressing meaning. The main intent of the investigations gathered in this book is to make a further step in this direction and to show that not only language-games but also interactions with images generate thought-games.

In my recent research, I have been looking at the type of thought (and context of social action) that is related to the social use and interpretation of images in the process of transmitting knowledge. As a first step, I analyzed iconographies used in techniques of memorization (Severi [2007] 2015). In studying these techniques, I sought to identify their *universe*, a concept I defined as the family of mental operations (classifying, inferring, and imagining) involved in these techniques. In this book, I now look at the attribution of subjectivity and agency to artifacts with the same perspective. I wish to demonstrate that endowing an artifact or image with "life" is another way of establishing a universe of thought, one that mobilizes a multiplex form of shared imagination.

These thought-games define the universe where certain inanimate objects are given life. The task of this book, as an initial experiment in the anthropology of thought, is to explore some of their many ways of capturing our imagination.

CHAPTER TWO

Primitivist Empathy
Intensifying the Image and Deciphering Space

> *What fascinated us in this art was its absolute primitivism, its intense, often grotesque expression of power and of life in the simplest form.*
> —Emil Nolde, *Das eigene Leben*

Power, life, simple form: at the beginning of the twentieth century, the Die Brücke group in Germany and the Fauves in France discovered primitive art almost simultaneously (Goldwater [1938] 1986).[1] Both groups, each in its own artistic terms, were essentially searching for a path toward a new intensity in works of art. With the rupture initiated by these two avant-garde movements, artistic activity began to pursue a two-pronged aim: to create a new type of space and, through it, to trigger intense emotions. For all these artists, it was essential, as Henri Matisse (1991, 154, 266) put it, "to express the idea of immensity from within a limited space." In exploring a new space of representation and freeing themselves from academic principles of imitating nature, they sought, above all, to achieve a new intensity in the image. It was not enough for them

---

1. Robert Goldwater also draws attention to the very precocious (but for a long time isolated) interest Kokoschka had in the works exhibited in the Museum of Ethnology in Vienna as early as 1902.

to "create previously unknown sensations; to strip art of everything routine and accepted," as Giorgio de Chirico wrote ([1912] 2014); they set out to find new power in the work of art that would go beyond the emotional registers typical of the closed universe of academic art. Motivated by the discovery of a new space, artistic experimentation aimed to shock. It reached beyond the classical conception of the passions and widened the sphere of emotions depicted in the artwork. The objective was both to integrate affective dimensions excluded from art in the past and to cast new light on what was in the present. Art, the Fauves and Die Brücke Expressionists insisted, must surpass the appearance of the real to reach the pure manifestation of emotion.

Since the beginning of the twentieth century, one of the main strategies of modern artists in their search for emotional intensity was to take inspiration from the arts of "primitive" peoples— the chaotic mixture of African, Asian, or Oceanian objects that, in Paris and elsewhere, was referred to as *art nègre*. When Emil Nolde painted *Dancer* in 1913 (Figure 1), or when Matisse created *Blue Nude* in 1907 (Figure 2), they adapted qualities they perceived in such objects to portray the essential, to invest their images with power. In contrast to photography, "primitivist art" sought to make the work of art unique, irreplaceable, full of energy like an idol—to render it "primitive" in the sense of being originary, inimitable, immediate, and freed forever from appearances.

For Robert Goldwater, whose book *Primitivism in Modern Art* ([1938] 1986) was the first to analyze this movement in depth, primitivism is essentially a way of simplifying the purely optical aspects of the work of art that are linked to the techniques of imitation. The goal is to produce an absolute image free from any reference to the real, thereby giving free rein to the intensity of affect. Goldwater describes the model for primitivism in these terms:

> The arts valued by the twentieth century are exotic arts in which it is imagined that technique has been properly kept subordinate by the intensity of the emotion expressed, or indigenous arts (those of the folk, children, and madmen) where, ideally, the medium would be obliterated in favor of a direct conveying of emotion. (Goldwater [1938] 1986, 254)

Artists pursuing primitivist aims, he says, select dramatic themes centered on the "fundamental passions of existence" (1986, 255). However, it is not the choice of subject matter that generates the primitivist style in their work; to obtain such a result, they must first invent some way to simplify the image. The artist

Figure 1. Emil Nolde, *Dancer* (1913), Museum of Modern Art, New York (© Nolde Stiftung Seebüll).

Figure 2. Henri Matisse, *Blue Nude (Memory of Biskra)* (1907), Baltimore Museum of Art, Baltimore (© Estate of Henri Matisse).

must "reduce the picture to a single, simple dominating scene, which will not be analyzed as a variegated formal composition, but will absorb, or be absorbed by him in a direct and undifferentiated fashion" (1986, 255). For Goldwater, this is a means of reducing, as much as possible, the psychic distance between the observer and the work of art. When a single figure (such as Nolde's *Dancer* and Matisse's *Blue Nude*) dominates the work, the image suddenly comes closer and our gaze goes straight to what is essential. Several examples of this method can be found in the works of the Fauves as well as those of the Die Brücke artists and, later on, the Blaue Reiter group. In the work of the young Wassily Kandinsky (for example, *The Lyrical* from 1911, in Figure 3) immediately preceding his pure abstraction period, the viewer can almost follow, step by step, the process of simplifying the subject, accompanied by a gradual intensification of the visual effect.

Figure 3. Wassily Kandinsky, *The Lyrical* (1911), Museum Boyjmans van Beuningen, Rotterdam.

Simplifying and reducing the subject to the essential is, however, only a first step. The second strategy in primitivism to attain intensity is of a slightly different order. For the artists, this consists in schematizing both the space and the figures in a way that erases any incidental aspect, whether these aspects are linked to a particular state of mind or related to a precise place or time. The point is to banish the episodic—or what used to be called *le roman peint* in avant-garde circles—in order to focus on the symbolic image. It is in this regard that the model of *art nègre* seems to have played a crucial initiatory role. As Carl Einstein states in his treatise on African sculpture (Einstein [1921] 1922), the art of so-called primitive peoples deals with masks but not with portraits. Western primitivist artists believe that, for an image to be intense it is not necessary to emphasize the psychological characterization of the human figure. On the contrary, the image must be relatively impersonal, almost anonymous. Through such an approach, it becomes generalizable in the same way as a symbol:

> This kind of symbolism is attained by the omission of such detail, in both formal and iconographic senses, as would particularize the situation presented in terms of the characters involved, and so would make it external, peculiar, and not susceptible of emotional identification by the spectator. Neither Gauguin's Bretons nor his Tahitians are individuals, nor are his landscapes in the countryside. (Goldwater [1938] 1986, 256)

Goldwater argues that most of the artists in the modern primitivist movement utilize two means to intensify the image: the immediate presentation of a scene in a rarefied space and a "symbolic" quality (simplified, generalized, devoid of details) of figures. Primitivists share these strategies whether they use what he calls an "emotional" approach or an "intellectual" approach to primitivism ([1938] 1986, 257–62). "The scenes depicted by both the Fauves and the Die Brücke have that strange enveloping 'jungle' quality that results from the combination of close-up rendering with a formal and psychological generalization" ([1938] 1986, 256).

Goldwater's account, which had all the qualities of a pioneering work, remained the authoritative interpretation of primitivism for nearly fifty years. Before his book, references to primitive art were largely incidental, linking it to legends recollected by artists or to often contradictory anecdotes by various protagonists. With Goldwater, primitivism became a key in the analysis of the aesthetic ideas that oriented the work of the first avant-garde artists. However, his interpretation of primitivism poses two essential problems. The first is historical in nature: if *art nègre* suddenly became so important between 1903 and 1905 for Vlaminck and Nolde, for Kirchner and Derain, and then for the Cubists, the Surrealists, and the abstract painters, it is because it came into contact with a persistent undercurrent of European thinking. Interest in *art nègre*, as a subject of artistic thought, emerged as an echo of this undercurrent, in which the reflections of a number of philosophers, anthropologists, and psychologists in the nineteenth century played a crucial role.[2]

Among the many, let me mention the notable work of Godfried Semper, an architect and theoretician of art, who might be considered the founder of the primitivist thought. When, at the beginning of the nineteenth century, with a small group of fellow researchers (like Bastian and Klemm), Semper starts to work on the problem of the "origins of Art," he does not look for the "history" or the "evolution" of human cultures; rather, he wants to identify the elementary forms of expression of the human mind. Following the example of Humboldt (above all the great treatise entitled Kosmos), Semper wanted to combine the analysis of the techniques with the identification of the elementary forms (*Urformen*) that preside over all artistic creation. In this perspective, the invention of a style does not simply mark a step in a process of evolution but represents a more complex phenomenon: the synthesis between a number of techniques subjected to evolution and the forms of representing space, which characterizes the human mind. From this multilayered conception of cultural evolution, Semper also draws up the idea of a Museum of Man, where artifacts were not ordered according to the Darwinian concept of evolution. The exposition imagined by Semper followed rather a system of forms, one founded upon a universal psychology of the elementary ideas (*Elementargedänken*) of humanity, from which any specific object would be, so to speak, logically deducted. The best example of this kind of analysis is the Carib Hut that Semper presented at the Universal Exhibition in London in 1851. To him, the Caribbean hut is "perfect" because it presents a vivid image of one of the possible relationships that can be created among the four essential elements composing any architectural space: Roof, Enclosure, Mound, and Center. This "perfection" shows that, when we look back over time or observe the output of "primitive" peoples, we do not encounter an inchoate art but, rather, a certain type of perfection that will never be outmoded by subsequent ulterior evolution. In this sense, the hut is a masterpiece, never to be surpassed by any other work of art. Semper takes the model that Goethe applied to the morphology of plants and transfers it to the forms invented by human beings. Since the Carib Hut exhibits, like Goethe's *Urplanz*, a perfect relation between the four elements of any architecture, it does not illustrate a step in evolution from simple to complex. On the contrary, the hut illustrates

---

2. On this question, see, for example, Boas and Lovejoy (1935).

a very different principle, which Semper tries to apply in all his research: when one looks for the origin of the plastic expression of thought, he argues, one never finds anything resembling a *childhood of art*. The hut illustrates an example of formal perfection, which—in its own terms—will never be overcome by any cultural evolution. The model of this epistemology is not Darwin but Cuvier. In a paper written in 1852, Semper writes that the great discovery of Cuvier is that all the beings belonging to nature depend from a small number of *simple ideas*, or *forms*. From that discovery, he draws the conclusion that forms are the "ideas of Nature." Let us take the apparently simple example of a snowflake, Semper suggests (1989, 198). It has an autonomous form, where a number of elements are organized around a single point. This organization can take three forms: a radial disposition starting from the center, a circle around, or a combination of these two axes. Two principles, which are both implicit and abstract, are at work here: proportionality, which organizes the elements among themselves; and symmetry, which arranges them into the two possible orders, circular or radial, in relation to the center. Semper uses the term "authority" for the visual indications that enable the eye to perceive the variations of specific forms generated from a general principle, which determines the unity of the set of forms. Thus, following his vocabulary, we could say that the "authority" of a snowflake, the "visible representative of its unifying principle" (Semper 1989, 209), lies in the implicit relation of its elements to the central point, visible or implicit, that represents its unity in space. "These elements," writes Semper, "relate to the authorities as resonant, modulating, and accompanying tones to the keynote" (1989, 209). Actually, for him, every artistic creation works like the snowflake, since it always organizes pluralities following the principle of a formal authority. In a word, the "aesthetic instinct" confers to the inventions of humanity the "same necessity" that natural forms possess. This is why, for Semper, if we reduce the study of human creations to a small number of elementary forms, we can pass from the study of nature to the study of human imagination. Adopting the method of Cuvier, we could thus eventually identify "the principles and the elementary forms of which all of the million appearances in art are but as much different modifications" (Semper 1989, 32).

Semper's reading of Cuvier's ideas is very rich; exploring it could lead to many other aspects of his theory. But let us draw an initial conclusion. Following his perspective, we may compare the form of the Carib Hut to that "central nugget" of the rules of a language, which Humboldt called the "genius" of a grammar. However, the kind of thought materialized in the form of the hut is independent of evolution. It is comparable not to the historical progress of a certain technique but, rather, to the permanent truth of a mathematical theorem. It is only natural to recognize the constant metamorphosis of techniques over time. But it is just as clear that, at the level of the laws governing human thought, there are simply multiple variations of a single Mind. The ground for the primitivist perception of non-Western art was thus established.

Unfortunately, Goldwater ignores everything of this intellectual background and insulates primitivism from its historical context. Although his account produced the first systematic interpretation of non-Western art in the context of European modernism and its aesthetic reflection, it also generated a paradox. This paradox is at the very heart of his reading of primitivist works. From his perspective, modernist primitivism owed almost nothing to observation—in the sense of formal interpretation—of primitive arts. After the first shock of the discovery of *art nègre*, Goldwater argues, modern art found its own identity and evolved not through inspiration but through a gradual distancing from "tribal" arts. For him, the relation with *art nègre* was only an incidental episode, a temporary step in an investigation that did not involve any real knowledge of non-Western arts.

For Goldwater, the effect that primitive art had on a group of artists was temporary and did not seem to have left any enduring traces. The vogue for the exotic primitive lasted only a few years, he writes in 1938, before artists (in particular, French and German) took an interest in other forms of primitive expression, which soon took the place of primitive art:

> The primitive works of art which provided inspiration began to be less exotic and removed and to come closer to home: children's art and folk art were at first mixed with the African and the Oceanic, and similarities were found between them. With the addition of subconscious art considered under its primitive aspects, they entirely replaced the aboriginal productions. (Goldwater [1938] 1986, 265)

To understand this interpretation, we must remember that, for Goldwater, there was never a direct relation, in the sense of formal influence, between African, Oceanian, or Amerindian arts and Western primitivism. "True" primitive art was only a catalyst for certain aesthetic ideas specific to modernity, he argues; the link between indigenous and modern arts was only metaphorical and did not concern artistic works at all. This link should be analyzed more from a psychological than a formal aspect:

Far from being the cause of any "primitive" qualities that may be found in modern art, primitive art only served as a kind of stimulating focus, a catalyst which, though not itself used or borrowed from, still helped the artists to formulate their own aims because they could attribute to it the qualities they themselves sought to attain. For these reasons, the very limited direct formal influence of primitive art is not to be wondered at. (Goldwater [1938] 1986, 252–53)

In other words, formal influences through direct borrowings from primitive art by modern artists played a minor role. From a technical as well as conceptual point of view, modern primitivism saw in primitive art only a metaphor of its own identity, a pretext among others to find its own path to "art of an absolute character." As Goldwater ([1938] 1986, 271) puts it, "Primitivism as it is embodied in modern painting and sculpture has little similarity with the chronologically, culturally, or the esthetically primitive in the arts."

Seen through this lens, primitivism thus did not contribute to any new understanding of non-Western art traditions. Rather, it accounted for quite a different process, above and beyond appearances. By following its own logic to develop ways to reduce the psychological distance that separates the image from its observer, the works of primitivism constituted a stage toward the emergence of abstract art. The two ways of intensifying the image identified by Goldwater ([1938] 1986)—simplification and generalization—led to abstraction and the reflection on form it implied. This intuition, quickly forgotten by his successors, remains essential for understanding primitivism. I will return later to the affinity, much deeper than usually imagined, between what Charles Baudelaire called the "fantastic" style,[3] abstraction, and primitivism, a link that Goldwater was the first to reveal. For the time being, let me simply note that his book is nowadays seldom read or cited. In fact, the knowledge that we have about primitivism, nearly sixty years after its publication, has significantly changed.

At a celebrated (and controversial) exhibition on primitivism held at the Museum of Modern Art (MoMA) in New York in 1984, William Rubin and his team demonstrated that, contrary to what Goldwater believed, the direct formal influence of non-European works of art (mostly African, Oceanian, and Amerindian) on the art of the European historical avant-garde artists was substantial and frequent (Rubin 1984, 7). The intensification of the image sought by modern artists very often implied direct borrowings from other cultures by Matisse, Derain,

---

3. Regarding this point, see Severi (1991).

Kirchner, Picasso, and many others whom Goldwater had studied. Therefore, according to Rubin and his colleagues, primitive art has much more than a merely metaphorical presence in primitivism. Although often inserted in contexts where its appearance is concealed by visual strategies (which Rubin teaches us to decode), art considered "primitive" is very much present and perfectly recognizable.

However, Rubin's work in identifying sources of primitivist influences, which obliges us to reevaluate Goldwater's perspective, by no means justifies the neglect of his work. It does not go to the heart of the second problem that Goldwater raised, which is a purely aesthetic matter: what are the new mechanisms of the gaze that, under the pretext of bearing affinities to the primitive, function as new catalysts of intensity in certain primitivist styles?

We should first acknowledge that, after bringing up this intriguing problem, Goldwater has, so to speak, deprived himself of the means to solve it. The first consequence of his claims about the metaphorical nature of the relationship between the "primitive" and "primitivists" is indeed the fact that the concept of primitivism itself tends to become vague and dissolve. How can we identify an approach that is defined as inherent to the relationship to non-European arts and yet also as independent, from a formal perspective, of these same arts? How can we understand this catalyzing process if we describe only the effects and not the sources? To elucidate the question of the operations of the gaze (and that of their link to the representation of affect), we must rethink the meaning of the word "primitivist" by taking into account what Goldwater earlier failed to observe: namely, the theoretical stakes behind the question of formal influence.

THE STAKES OF FORMAL BORROWINGS

Maurice de Vlaminck, André Derain, Henri Matisse, Pablo Picasso, Emil Nolde, Wassily Kandinsky, Franz Marc, Carlo Carrà: the works of artists called "primitivist" are displayed in our museums and art history books, buttressed with evidence to back the claim. The story behind some specific artifact, information about the literal transfer of some particular detail, and images side by side to show something borrowed from an African mask or an Oceanian sculpture often serve as unexpected revelations. These transfers of image—for example, between *Portrait of Madame Matisse* (Figure 4) and the Shira Punu mask (Figure 5) that appears to be its direct source—surprise us and win our agreement. The borrowing seems undeniable.

Figure 4. Henri Matisse, *Portrait of Madame Matisse* (1913), State Hermitage Museum, St. Petersburg (© Estate of Henri Matisse).

Figure 5. Shira Punu mask, Gabon, former collection of Ernst Winizki, Zurich.

Such was the claim made emphatically by Rubin and his team at the 1984 MoMA exhibition and catalogue, offering a series of proofs for what he called the "affinity of the tribal and the modern" (Rubin 1984). Yet the nature of this affinity turns out to be difficult to grasp once we examine some of its aspects closely. For Goldwater, at least, primitivism was a relatively short-lived phenomenon, an episode in an artistic investigation that had more or less ended by the time he wrote his book in 1938. Fifty years later, however, the curators of the MoMA exhibition saw the already long list of primitivist artists as continually being enriched. The choice to take non-European arts as a direct source of inspiration for new works of art has obviously not flagged, obliging us to dismiss Goldwater's opinion if we wish to understand the artistic endeavors of contemporary artists. In short, primitivism refuses to abandon the stage and be discarded in the archives of art history. As it did a century ago, it continues to explore new paths and metamorphose in unforeseen ways, making it difficult to adequately characterize it or comprehend its nature. A degree of indeterminacy persists, leaving it open to future developments.

This uncertainty concerns not only the present and the future of primitivism but also its historical origins. Where did primitivism come from? When and how did it become one of the significant moments in modern art?

For many historians of modern art, primitivism originated in the work of Paul Gauguin, an artist who abandoned the West and devoted himself to an allegedly primitive lifestyle in Tahiti. In these accounts, we owe the "discovery" of primitive art to Gauguin's desire to go beyond the limits of our civilization. However, once we move from the artist's biography to an analysis of his work, it appears that nothing actually supports such an assertion. As Rubin argues, "The Polynesian works of art functioned for Gauguin more as symbols and decorative devices than as agents of influence on his style" (Rubin 1984, 7). What was "primitivist" in Gauguin was more a life project than a process taking place in the work of art: "It would not be farfetched to consider Gauguin's visual account of his 'island paradise' a somewhat desperate example of life imitating literature, in effect, a mimetic reenactment of the 'myth of the primitive'" (1984, 7).

Although Goldwater's assessment of primitivism is entirely different than Rubin's, he concurs on this point. He, too, feels that Gauguin's work tended toward primitivism but never actually attained it. Gauguin's primitivist impulse remained a mixture of Romanticism and Jugendstil, "which tries to, but never succeeds in dominating the emotional tone of his pictures. Grace still properly belonged to Gauguin's conception of the primitive, and to the pictures which were its result, but only in spite of himself" (Goldwater [1938] 1986, 256). If Gauguin was a primitivist, he was one almost involuntarily. The source of primitivism, whether it implies a conscious borrowing of forms or other kinds of connection with primitive arts that can influence an artist's style, is not to be found in Gauguin's work.

When and where, then, was primitivism born in modern art? The search for the historical and conceptual origins of primitivism needs to go beyond individual memories of artists and critics, beyond legendary stories and episodes so often told by certain art historians.[4] The question implies two different kinds of issues: one is chronological, the other conceptual. No matter what the circumstances under which something like a "primitivism" in art was born, it is impossible to understand it without recognizing the background, an episteme that slowly formed around objects arriving in European collections since the beginning of

---

4. The account of the "discovery" of primitive art relied for a long time on an autobiographical text full of imprecise and contradictory data: the *Memoires* of Maurice Vlaminck. He dated the discovery to 1906 and located it in Argenteuil, France (see Flam 1984). However, thanks to Goldwater's work, we know that this "discovery" also occurred almost simultaneously in Germany in 1904, when Kirchner and the Die Brücke group of artists recognized the significance of African and Oceanic objects on display in the museum in Dresden. They were soon followed by the artists of the Blaue Reiter group (Goldwater [1938] 1986, 105ff.).

the fifteenth century. In the first part of this chapter, I outlined Semper's ideas and their influence on his intellectual heirs; elsewhere I have addressed the general lines of this episteme (Severi 1991, 1994, 1998). Here, I want to explain the concept of primitivism through another path, one that goes beyond circumstances and episodes and leads toward a morphology of cultural exchange.

Let us look at the 1758 portrait of the young Emperor Qianlong (Figure 6) painted by Giuseppe Castiglione (who took on the Chinese name of Lang Shining). Castiglione was a Jesuit missionary and painter from Milan living at the Beijing court between 1714 and 1766.[5] At first sight, Castiglione seems to have adopted the method of simplifying space that was typical of the tradition of courtly Chinese art: reducing it to a strictly flat surface and representing it from a frontal view, without any nuances of shadow or variations of light. Castiglione's mastery of this style was such that he received numerous orders from the emperor. However, by looking more closely at the portrait, it becomes clear that Castiglione inserted a beautiful imitation of a European equestrian portrait into the flat space imposed on him by the Chinese style. It is an iconographic model for the representation of monarchs that had enjoyed tremendous success in Western art, dating back at least as early as Titian's portrait of Charles V and taken up by Rubens, Van Dyck, and many others. Castiglione's painting is ingenious, subtle, and technically adept.

Yet a more attentive examination of the scene as a whole dissolves the illusion of unity so skillfully calculated by Castiglione. We realize that, although the image of the young emperor sitting on a horse, painted with such astounding technical perfection, seems to be situated in a space similar to perspective, it is actually conceptually divided into two independent parts. The figure of Quianlong, in accordance with the principles of courtly art, is composed statically in a flat, symmetrical space. By contrast, the image of the horse (and some of the landscape) follows the Western iconographic schema and timidly introduces an implicit depth. The rider thus remains suspended in an artificial position, not touching the ground, ensconced in a space that is not his.[6] Two distinct

---

5. On Giuseppe Castiglione, the Milanese painter who (with Attiret and Damasceno) belonged to the Jesuit group of artists in residence at the Beijing court in the eighteenth century, see Sullivan (1973, 46–89), Rogers (1988), and Beurdeley and Beurdeley (1971). Regarding the series of portraits of Emperor Qianlong produced by Castiglione, see in particular Musée du Petit Palais (1996, 148–66).

6. See the perceptive commentary on this portrait in Pirazzoli-t'Serstevens (1996, 271).

Figure 6. Giuseppe Castiglione, *The Qianlong Emperor in Ceremonial Armor on Horseback* (1739 or 1758), Palace Museum, Beijing.

iconographic models—that of the Chinese monarch and that of the European monarch—are found juxtaposed here without fusing to create a new image. Although situated in the same painting, the two models follow different visual and conceptual conventions. For each one, the lines of perspective operate according to their own laws. No synthesis is at work here.

What we have here is a good example of what primitivism is not. In this portrait, like other works by Castiglione, the implementation of Western perspective alternates with the atmospheric, flat vision of Chinese tradition.[7] It does not show any trace of the process seen in the works by primitivists, involving the reciprocal reconstruction by two models of spatial representation, of which direct borrowing is only one visible effect. In Western primitivism, this process leads to two seemingly different but related results: on the one hand, the invention of new images, and, on the other, the attribution of new meanings to other images produced by non-Western cultures.

Some art historians have noted that the emergence of primitivism marked the moment when artists were no longer interested only in what exotic arts represent but also in the way they produced representations (Messina 1993). This is true but insufficient for our purpose here. For a work of art to be deemed primitivist, a reciprocal tension between two styles of representation must always appear. Through this tension, one of the two visual languages can be defined through the other. This is how Einstein could consider some African works of art to be "Cubist" or "abstract" and, at the same time, describe Picasso's *Les Demoiselles d'Avignon* as characterized by an "African style."[8] The encounter between two traditions actually produces a new style and engenders a fresh poetics of the gaze, an alternative way of interpreting artistic objects coming from other civilizations. In this regard, a relationship of reciprocal interpretation, on a purely visual level, is created between two traditions. In Western culture, from the moment when the "savages" move from the time-honored status of "absolute strangers" to that of "potential ancestors" (Severi 1998), this relation is expressed in the terms of an imaginary filiation.

In light of this initial definition of primitivist borrowing, I will now attempt to identify certain operations at work in the gaze that are implied by this reciprocal interpretation of two spaces, which is linked to an imaginary relationship with primitive ancestors.

---

7. About the long cycle of paintings dedicated to the Emperor's deer hunt at his residence in Mulan (of which several now belong to the Guimet Museum), see Jinlang and Pirazzoli-t'Serstevens (1979) and Berinstein (1999).

8. The sources of inspiration for *Les Demoiselles d'Avignon* are in no way limited to African sculpture but also include numerous references to Spanish art. See Rubin's article on Picasso (Rubin 1984, 241–333).

CARL EINSTEIN, OR IMMOBILE ECSTASY

No author has captured this process of reciprocal interpretation between two figurative traditions (and of the two perceptual horizons they imply) as well as Carl Einstein. His work *Negerplastik*, first published in 1915 (Einstein [1915] 1986) in a collection of writings by Expressionist poets and writers, followed by *Afrikanische Plastik* in 1921 (Einstein [1921] 1922), were written in order to "consider African art only in relation to the principles that inspire art of our time" (Einstein [1921] 1922, 3). The "art of our time" is, for Einstein, mainly Cubism. He does not hesitate to declare that he "has examined African art from a Cubist point of view," going so far as to claim that he has "identified in Africa perfect examples of Cubist art" (Einstein [1921] 1922, 7) (Figure 7).

Figure 7. Pahouin carved head, Gabon, former collection of Paul Guillaume, Paris.

The premises of Einstein's thinking were already formulated in one of the great texts of nineteenth-century German aesthetics: *The Problem of Form in the Fine Arts* by Adolf von Hildebrand ([1893] 1994). One of Hildebrand's principal arguments, similar to Semper's viewpoint, is that each modality of artistic creation ought to aim toward the attainment of an ideal of absolute coherence with the nature of its distinctive form (in the sense of the mode of perception and the mental operations it implies).⁹ A sculptor himself, Hildebrand shows how the influence of perspective, an optical model dogmatized by academic art as well as Romanticism, had betrayed sculpture and its plastic nature. To give prominence to the frontal vision and to foreshortening in the perception of a sculpted figure—as Rodin, for example, had done in his Balzac or the Burghers of Calais—meant imposing a strictly pictorial apprehension on volume. This introduced a contradiction between aesthetic conception and practice, which Hildebrand vigorously opposes. As a "cosmopolitan spectator" (to borrow Baudelaire's expression), Einstein picks up this argument, using the same terms and some of the same examples as Hildebrand, and transforms it into an instrument for interpreting African sculpture. "It can be said that continental sculpture is strongly woven with pictorial substitutes," writes Einstein ([1915] 1986, 21).

> Indeed, in Hildebrand's work on "The problem of form," we find a perfect equilibrium between the pictorial and the plastic. An art tradition as significant as French sculpture seems, up to Rodin, to be precisely striving to abolish its plastic nature. Frontality itself must be considered as pictorial apprehension of volume . . . for here, three-dimensionality is concentrated in a few planes that reduce volume. (Einstein [1915] 1986, 347)

The central theme of these analyses, as in all important works on primitivism, concerns the decoding of space. What is at stake here is the efficacy of the image from the point of view of its emotionality. It is therefore not surprising that Einstein describes the impression of depth implied by the frontal consideration of sculpture as a veritable trap, almost a dangerous illusion. When we adopt the frontal vision, he says,

> we accentuate the parts that are closest to the spectator and arrange them while considering that the posterior parts are modulations of the front surface. The aspects put up front are thus accentuated, and we conjure away, by virtue of a movement of drawn or modeled form, the immediate expression of the third dimension. (Einstein [1915] 1986, 347)

---

9. See Wind (1963), whose analysis of Hildebrand's thinking is masterful.

Einstein thus concludes that "The construction of space was sacrificed to a secondary process that is alien to the sculptural. . . . Three-dimensionality disappeared and was replaced by feelings and . . . sculptures were considered as circumlocutions of the effect they produced" ([1915] 1986, 347). What radically changed this situation was Cubism, along with the simultaneous discovery of African sculpture:

> Just a few years ago we witnessed in France a decisive crisis. Thanks to a prodigious effort of consciousness . . . a few painters had enough strength to depart from an art that had been produced mechanically. Once free from the usual methods, they examined the elements in the perception of space in order to find what could actually create it. . . . At the same time, African sculpture was discovered, and it was admitted that in its isolation, it had cultivated pure forms of the sculptural. (Einstein [1915] 1986, 348–49)

To step out of the frontal and pictorial illusion is to capture pure form at its roots; it is to mentally create the multidirectional space where form appears. The argument in *Negerplastik* is that this mental understanding, embodied most fully by African sculpture and Cubist painting, is, above all, a *means of intensifying* the image. Certainly, the Cubist image, in terms of its construction, is independent from the observer's perspective as a unique point located in a space. It no longer caters to the spectator. It despises the fiction of a false depth, one simply suggested by pictorial means. It no longer calculates the optical mechanism following "frontality and distance" (1986, 350). In fact, the Cubist image constructs a multiplicity of points of view, revealing the mechanism of perception itself and thus demonstrating what Einstein calls the "logical consequences of plasticity." In fact, for Einstein (as for Hildebrand), it is only when an image (a "particular expression") perfectly captures a law of perception that a true form appears: "Form is the complete identity between perception and specific realization (the artwork), which, by virtue of their structure, perfectly coincide" ([1915] 1986, 350).

In this process of deployment, the decoding of depth still occupies a crucial position, but it is freed from the illusory character of the frontal position. For the gaze, this means identifying the invisible part embodied by the image; indeed, it is in this invisible part that the efficacy of the image lies. On this point, Einstein's analysis is illuminating:

> Sculpture has nothing to do with naturalist mass, but is only concerned with the organization of form. It is a matter of representing on the visible parts the

invisible ones in their formal function . . . and of representing the volume, or the coefficient of depth as I would like to call it [in such a way that] . . . each part finds its autonomy, and is distorted in a way that makes it absorb depth. ([1915] 1986, 351)

However, in creating a space as a totality and as a perfect similitude between individual perception and perception in general, this decoding of the coefficient of depth reveals the true nature of the sculptural work. For Einstein, form thus transforms the observer's experience into "a particular case of perception of absolute intensity" ([1915] 1986, 350). And for him, the model for this intensity is the African mask. Inhuman, impersonal, rigidly fixed, the mask may seem indifferent (Figure 8). But Einstein considers this view of the African

Figure 8. Baule wooden mask, Ivory Coast, Museum Folkwang, Essen.

mask to stem from a failure to understand the nature of the work and its intensity: "The fixity of the African mask is nothing else than the highest degree of intensity of expression, freed from any psychological motivation" ([1915] 1986, 353). The mask thus does not convey indifference; on the contrary, we should consider it as a model of Cubist creation precisely because "the elaboration of a purified structure" produces in it "a state of immobile ecstasy" ([1915] 1986, 353).

This reading of Einstein's text leads to two conclusions. On the one hand, it shows how his reciprocal interpretation of African art and Cubism simultaneously produces an aesthetic of the image and a poetics of the perception of African art. On the other hand, his interpretation, posed as one rigorously based on the identification of pure formal relationships, reveals another modality, different than that identified by Goldwater, of the intensification of the affective impact of the image. The *means to achieve immobile ecstasy* described by Einstein, which is the genuine issue in the Cubists' primitivist borrowing, presupposes the utopia of an omnidirectional gaze freed from any perspective, an immobile eye in which all dimensions that define the very existence of space are united on a sort of sublime level of sensibility. African art, in this sense, becomes the fulfillment of Hildebrand's utopia and his theory of form. This art liberates sculpture, or rather, plasticity as pure spatial thinking, from all pictorial aspects—and thus from all visual appearances.

However, this way of thinking about space, which African art embodies, does not undermine the sensitivity of the gaze. To grasp this point, it is necessary to recall André Derain's remarks about light in the context of *art nègre*: "It is madly expressive. But there is a second pattern in this surplus effect: these are forms . . . born of full light, and destined to reveal themselves in full light. It is therefore understood that the differences in volume can express a light, or the coincidence of light with such and such form" (Derain 1955, 196–97).

The great strength and the originality of Carl Einstein's thought should not let us forget that his analysis of African art would have been impossible without the transformations that turned African artists, makers of the masks who had hitherto been considered as "absolute strangers," into the "New Ancients," as Einstein ([1915] 1986, 354) calls them. In his eyes, they are "potential ancestors" who have access to a memory of pure form that has disappeared from Western consciousness. This notion of the universality of aesthetic sensibility is so significant and its impact in modern art so strong that it reveals a link between the artists and the primitive beyond the stakes of direct borrowing.

PRIMITIVISM WITHOUT BORROWING: IMAGINARY FILIATION

> *States of order, organic intensity energy and motion made visible memories arrested in space.*
> —Jackson Pollock[10]

At the beginning of the 1940s, a new trend appears in primitivist circles: artists stop the practice of borrowing forms (which disregarded their context or meaning) from primitive art. The new attitude involves understanding the mind of the primitive artist and establishing a relationship of direct empathy. This position, hostile to direct borrowing, is expressed with great lucidity in Barnett Newman's writings (1990), whose works bear no trace of imitation yet claim to possess a profound affinity with the Oceanic or Amerindian artists whose works he admires (Figure 9).

In several texts from the 1940s and 1950s, Newman asserts that artists who give in to the temptation of imitation (he was thinking mostly of Surrealists) are only inscribing images borrowed from exotic arts in a space defined according to Western categories. Far from reflecting an attempt to understand primitive arts, borrowing is merely a superficial way to attain a certain pictorial effect. The artist who resorts to borrowing, Newman writes, "imitates the magic" of African, Amerindian, and Oceanian art without ever understanding its nature or attaining its efficacy. Commenting on an exhibition of *Arts of the South Seas*, Newman says, "It was almost as if the object lesson of this important exhibition was to demonstrate the failure of the Surrealist to interpret correctly the meaning of magic—that they comprehended only its superficial aspects" (Newman 1990, 101). While taking inspiration from this or that detail of an African or Oceanian mask, the Surrealist artist remains entirely foreign to the spirit of these arts. Newman states:

> By insisting on a materialistic presentation of [this art] rather than a plastic one, by attempting to present it . . . in terms of Renaissance space . . . they hoped to make acceptable (the Surrealists prefer the term *surreal*) what they consciously know to be unreal. . . . This attempt to make the unreal more real by an overemphasis on illusion, ultimately fails to penetrate beyond illusion. (Newman 1990, 156)

---

10. This handwritten note, found in the artist's archives after his death, was quoted in Rose (1969, 102).

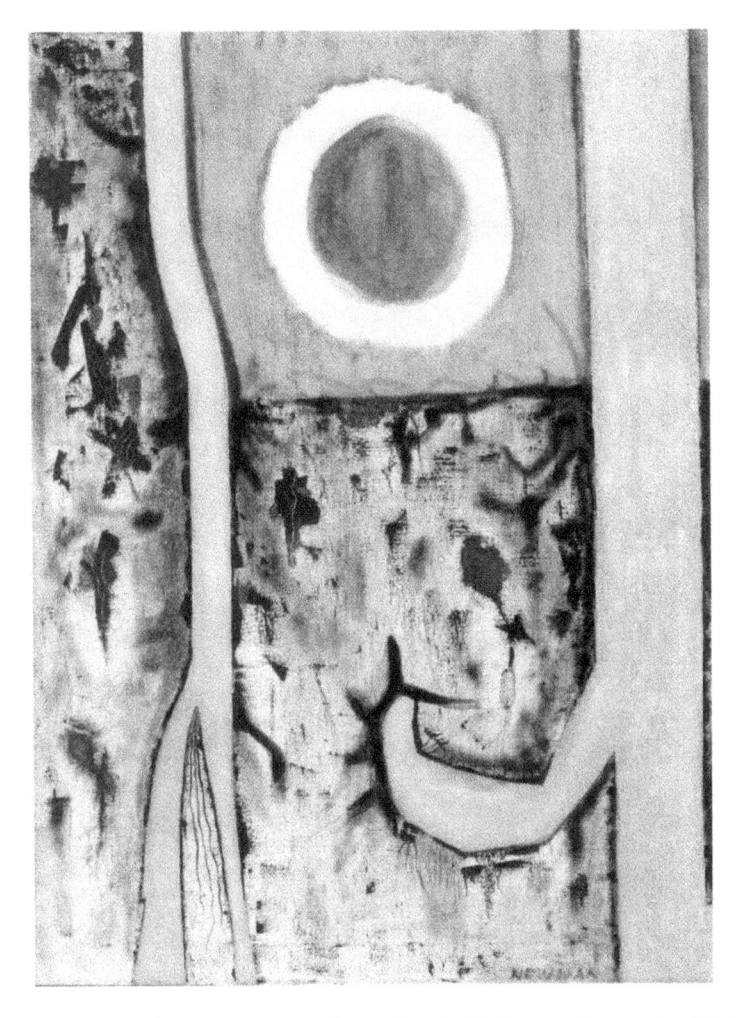

Figure 9. Barnett Newman, *Genetic Moment* (1946–47), Beyeler Foundation, Riehen/Basel (©The Barnett Newman Foundation, Adagp, Paris).

This failure is due to the Surrealists' indifference to the space implied by exotic objects, the space suggested by their own "coefficient of depth," in Einstein's terms. The primitivist artist's task should be to decode this space in his or her own language. The understanding of primitive art thus becomes more vital than imitation of these exotic objects. For Newman, as for Einstein, this understanding is entirely expressed in terms of space. However, while Einstein dreamed of an immobile eye, of a form entirely withdrawn into itself, capable of excluding any role for the spectator, Newman argues, on the contrary, for the necessity of intense activity by the eye.[11] Only this activity can make the space implied by exotic objects emerge around them. In terms of the operations of the gaze and the acts of perceptual interpretation that focus on primitive art, Newman's thinking approaches that of another prominent primitivist theoretician, Pavel Florensky, who was linked to the Russian avant-garde of the beginning of the twentieth century.

Florensky's critical work, published in his two most important books, *Reversed Perspective* ([1920] 2002) and *Time and Space in Art* ([1925] 1995), aims to identify the mechanisms of the construction of space in situations where classical perspective is not used. A single example of implicit space will suffice here: the way in which a flat object, such as a book, is represented in the Byzantine tradition (Figure 10).

Figure 10. *Saint Nicolas* (twelfth–fourteenth centuries), Tretjakov Gallery, Moscow.

---

11. On other aspects of Newman's viewpoint, see Severi (1989).

This image appears to give no indication about the actual optical space in which the vision of this object in reality took place. Depth seems to be totally ignored: only the contour of the object is carefully traced and emphasized with a gold line called a *razdelka*. Florensky focuses his analysis on this apparently minor detail. His first realization is that, from the point of view of the Byzantine iconographic tradition, nothing here suggests any abnormality or flaw in this technique for representing space. On the contrary, it is obvious that acute technical attention was devoted to making these contour lines.[12] For Florensky, these lines, considered in optical terms, may appear to distort the perception of depth, but they are actually meant to guide the perception of the image. By following these lines, the eye will find its way and thus make the image suggested by the icon emerge.

> The lines of the *razdelka* express a metaphysical schema of the given object, its dynamic, with greater force than its visible lines are capable of, although they are themselves quite invisible. Once outlined on the icon, they represent in the icon painter's conception the sum total of the tasks presented to the contemplating eye, the lines that direct the movements of the eye as it contemplates the icon. These lines are a schema for reconstructing the perceived object in the consciousness. (Florensky [1920] 2002, 206)

For Florensky, there are therefore two ways of representing space. One way, typical of Western European art, is essentially optical and seeks to imitate the mechanisms of everyday perception. The other, characteristic of the Byzantine icon as well as primitive art, has a symbolic nature, seeking instead to create a synthesis or mental equivalent of the image. The difference between the two methods is defined by Florensky in purely visual terms: the method suitable for perspective tends to immobilize the eye. The symbolic method, on the contrary, exploits its mobility. From its origins in the performing arts, the system of perspective has a double objective: to fix the gaze and to eliminate awareness of the act of perception. In this way, the eye is no longer conscious of its own activity and, at the same time, gains the illusion of having mastery over space. However, this apparent control is only the mask of a narrow limit imposed on perception. We need only look at any image created according to the rules of

---

12. This process is similar to that highlighted by Ernst Gombrich in his essay, "The Heritage of Apelles" (1976, 3–18).

perspective—even ones that may seem the most complex from a geometrical point of view, like the extraordinary Baroque constructions of Andrea Pozzo in the Church of St. Ignacius (Figure 11)—to realize that for the effect to be achieved requires an absolute immobility of the eye, which must be positioned at one single location in the space.

Such works are, for Florensky, "dead representations," meaning representations in which the image tends to communicate everything to the eye, leaving no room for mental synthesis. In these representations, he writes,

> all psycho-physiological processes in the act of vision are excluded. The eye looks motionlessly and dispassionately, the equivalent of an optical lens. It does not stir itself, it cannot, it has no right to stir, in spite of the fundamental condition of vision, its activeness, the active reconstructing of reality in vision as the activity of a living creature. Moreover, this looking is accompanied by neither memories, nor spiritual exertions, nor recognition. It is an external-mechanical process, at the most a physio-chemical one, but in no way is it that which is called vision. (Florensky [1920] 2002, 263)

The ideal of perspective is the strict equivalence of the physical image and the mental image, such that, from a single point of view, what reaches the retina and what is constructed by the artist tend to coincide. This is, for Florensky, the perfect example of a reproduction deprived of visual synthesis, memory, and analysis ([1920] 2002, 247).

Florensky's concept of visual synthesis is relevant to the perception of many examples of non-Western art. A representation that does not follow the rules of perspective seems less adequate to an immobile eye. But what the symbolic representation does is to make the eye actively explore a form and make it come alive—therein lies its power. During this exploration, based on *what the eye sees as well as what it notices is missing*, the gaze mentally produces a more complete internal mental representation, one that is more lively and incomparably more intense than the form that is materially imprinted on the surface of the icon. The art of Byzantine and Russian painters is about offering the gaze certain traces or clues that allow it to reconstruct the object, which is here evoked but not described in the image. And since the mind is far more powerful than the painter's brush, the icon produces a mental image much more intense than its representation in perspective.

Figure 11. Andrea Pozzo, *Apotheosis of Saint Ignatius* (1691), nave vault, Church of Saint Ignatius of Loyola, Rome.

This discovery of a mode of visual representation activated by the dialogue between the eye and the mind, an interaction taking place at the very heart of a mental synthesis induced by the perception of a clue to the form (such as the gold line highlighting the contours of an object in icons), is by no means limited to the interpretation of Byzantine art. Florensky himself clearly perceived the possibility of generalizing his analysis, suggesting that every image has an affinity with the methods used in painting icons. He described the process of creating images this way:

> Artistic vision is an extremely complex psychic process of merging psychic elements, accompanied by psychic resonances. In the image reconstructed in the spirit there accumulate memories, emotional echoes of inner movements, and around the dust motes of all the above the effective psychic content of the artist's personality is perceptibly crystallised. This clot grows and acquires its own rhythm, and it is this rhythm that expresses the artist's response to the reality he depicts. (Florensky [1920] 2002, 270)

In earlier works (Severi 1991, 1998, [2007] 2015), I have analyzed how the process of creating visual clues can help us understand various ethnographic statements about primitive works of art, notably those I have called "chimeric objects," where the visible surface of an object is conceived as a support for a series of invisible though precise developments of the image. I want to emphasize another point here: the work of mental reconstruction identified by Florensky helps to explain the exploration of implicit space that Newman considers essential for the attitude he claims for his own art: a primitivism without borrowing. Far from being the result of a technique for simplifying the image (as Goldwater would have it), or the result of a utopian liberation of any optical mechanism (as Einstein argued), the intensity of the image is the result of awakening the gaze.

The model for Florensky's reflection, the thinking with which he shares the deepest affinities, is surely that of Kandinsky. In his 1912 essay, "On the Question of Form," (Kandinsky 1994, 235–57), he said that the emotion we feel in the presence of the real is a crucial part of an artwork. On the canvas, the artist attempts to capture "the internal effect, which is produced by the inner sound, which is one of the most powerful and profound means of expression in every form of composition" (1994, 245). The instrument of this perception is precisely the form, which gradually frees itself from any connection to appearances, portraying "not the object itself, nor its external shell, but its inner sound, its life"

(1994, 244). It is through this gradual distancing from mere appearance that the form begins to convey empathy, which he called "resonance."

Einstein claims that the work of the eye is only an expedient, linked primarily to frontal vision, to perspective, and therefore to the pictorial aspect transferred onto sculpture. Florensky, Kandinsky, and Newman conceive of the work of the eye in an entirely different way. For the latter, the work of perception liberates visual perception from perspective and restores unsuspected life to the interpretation of nonimitative space on a flat surface. In fact, it is Goldwater's intuition that is at work here: the space that Florensky, from a primitivist perspective, attributes to the icon is also the space of abstract art and certain examples of non-European art. To understand this activity of the gaze (or the capturing of the resonance of a form, in Kandinsky's words), we can consider the example of some works by Franz Kline (Figure 12) and their hidden, never explicitly imitated source, namely, Japanese artworks (Figure 13). Here the eye is called upon to complement the image, even an abstract one, in accordance with the primitivist spirit that, without borrowing forms, strives nevertheless to adopt non-Western modalities of constructing and conceptualizing space. Instead of the Western illusion of depth, what emerges is the perception of a space that is implied rather than immediately made visible by the image. In this "art of an absolute character" (Goldwater), empathy no longer needs to borrow (see Figure 10, above).

Figure 12. Kranz Kline, *Accent Grave* (1955), Cleveland Museum of Art, Cleveland (© Adagp, Paris).

Figure 13. Hayashi Jikko, *Dragonfly* (1777–1813), private collection.

In a text dedicated to the Universal Exhibition of 1855, Charles Baudelaire ([1859] 1976) wrote that, to truly comprehend a work of art from a different culture, for example, "a Chinese piece of art, a strange and bizarre product, convoluted, with a deep color, or sometimes delicate to the point of making the spectator faint," the spectator must "undergo a transformation hanging on mystery, and through a phenomenon of the will acting on imagination, he must learn by himself to participate in the milieu that gave birth to this unusual flowering" (Baudelaire [1859] 1976, 574–97). Through this brief review from Matisse to Franz Kline, we might conclude that, for Baudelaire's observers to become "cosmopolitan spectators," for them to grasp, through "will and imagination," those forms for which "the gaze does not project according to the same magnetism" ([1859] 1976, 574–97), they must learn to implement the feeling of empathy through certain strategies.

In this chapter, I have explored a few aspects of this kind of empathy. This has led me to identify, beyond what artists and their interpreters say, three modalities specific to primitivist poetics: the gradual reduction of the psychological distance between the observer and the image; the achievement (through the freeing of the eye from the frontal perception of depth) of an "immobile ecstasy" linked to the utopia of absolute perception; and the work of projection involved in the elaboration of clues that, for Florensky, Kandinsky, and Newman, imbues the gaze with memory and allows the invisible aspects inherent in the image to emerge.

Each of these forms of empathy appears closely linked to a rethinking of the question of space. In each case, a reflection on the different forms of the gaze frequently grouped under the term *primitivist* has demonstrated that the reciprocal relationship between Western and non-Western art has little to do with iconographic imitation or borrowing. What is at issue in this relationship, even when all that remains from it is a metaphorical trace in the form of an imaginary filiation, is, instead, a certain dialectic between what is displayed in the image and what is marked as its invisible part. It is through these games of empathy, allied with the intensification of the image, that the primitive becomes, for the avant-garde, the imaginary ancestor of the modern artist.

These forms of primitivism, although different from each other, are nevertheless dependent on a paradox. Although primitivism made it possible, for the first time, a conversation (and even reciprocal interpretations) between so-called primitive art and the Western aesthetic tradition, it soon began defining itself in exclusively Western terms. Goldwater ([1938] 1986), like Rubin (1984), argues that avant-garde artists turn to primitive objects only to find a source of inspiration for their own style. For this reason, the interpretation of the object in itself becomes secondary, ignoring the reciprocal relationship. The dialogue between them, which in some works appears to be active, is actually only a figment of pure projection.

The primitivist aesthetic, which, as we will see in Chapter Seven, Claude Lévi-Strauss vigorously criticizes, claims to undermine ethnocentrism, but, in the end, it only perpetuates it in a new guise. Others who are more overtly ethnocentric reserve the term *art* for the Western tradition and deny that plastic or pictorial creations in so-called primitive societies can reflect attitudes comparable to that of the European artist. Conversely, the primitivist aesthetic postulates the absolute universality of artistic language: any art object whatsoever can be understood by anyone, independently of the meaning it embodies in the society in which it was created. If the ethnocentrism of a Ruskin rejects the universality of art, the primitivist aesthetic rejects the cultural and anthropological perspective on works of art. In either case, the anthropology of art has no place.

ICONOGRAPHY AND GAZE-GAMES

To find a way around this impasse, it is essential to recognize that a representational tradition is not only defined by a specific iconography, with its own *topoï*, style matters, authors, and periods; it also involves particular procedures, ideas, values, and interactions that, by forming a system, create the conditions for a game in which playing with the images is acceptable in its particular historical and cultural context. In his essay on marionettes, Heinrich von Kleist ([1810] 1972) provides an accurate idea of how this game works with images that form the background of an iconography. To "give life" to a marionette, Kleist says, the puppeteer's hand makes the simplest of movements, ones that seem to have no immediate relation to the movements made by the marionette itself. All the other elements responsible for the illusion of life—the attitudes, bounces, pursuits, attacks, and duels—that affect the behavior of the moving figure depend on two main conditions: first, a game of balancing weights and counterweights of the parts that form the marionette; and second, the innumerable acts of projection that these elements trigger in the spectators. There is indeed a mechanical dimension in manipulating marionettes that governs how it functions and how its identity is defined from an iconographic point of view. Nonetheless, all the thoughts it stimulates in the viewers (in a way that often escapes the puppeteer's intentions) are also an integral part of the universe of the illusion it sustains.

As in the marionette theater, iconography and gaze-games are always operating in iconographic traditions. The recognition of this double level is essential to the anthropologist for several reasons. First, it has significant consequences for the interpretation of cultural differences. Because of this distinction, it is possible to identify variations that concern one or the other level. In an exchange between different traditions, we may see iconographic variations and/or variations of the kind of gaze-game. Several art historians, notably Erwin Panofsky, have shown that an iconography presupposes not only specific images but, in addition, ways of organizing the figures that guide the viewer's gaze. Panofsky ([1927] 1991) proposed calling this level of organization of images "aesthetic space." The most familiar example is perspective, a set of criteria for organizing images in space, which implies the interpretation of indications arranged in an area in terms of depth, on the one hand, and, on the other, the understanding of the implicit movements attributed to immobile figures. These criteria can vary, of course, from one culture to another. A group of remarkable Sinologists, for example, have shown that, in Chinese painting in the Middle Ages, sepulchers were decorated by arranging figures from a point in space where the gaze of the deceased was conventionally located (Hay 2010). The gaze-game of this iconography was therefore to mark the implicit presence, indirectly suggested by the paintings, of the spirits of the dead in their grave. The deceased were thought to lead another life in the netherworld, from where they could see, "through the eyes of the deceased," the funeral palace built for them. According to Western traditional conventions these paintings were incomprehensible and apparently "full of visual contradictions." They revealed their coherence only after the discovery of the "ritual intention" that presided over their composition (2010, 52). Here, as in many other cases, studying the aesthetic space of an iconographic tradition is a good introduction to the analysis of the games played by the gaze implied by the image.

However, the liminal space in which the relationship between spectator and painted figure is played out can also be located, as we will see later, outside the image. Ethnography shows us cases where a simple gaze, without reference to the space where the image appears, can be enough to radically change the game. The case of Haitian vodou described by Alfred Métraux even testifies to the scandal it can provoke within a religious iconographic tradition by prompting a novel, illicit gaze-game. In Haiti, an iconography that was perfectly innocuous from the point of view of its traditional protagonists—the figures of the saints produced in chromolithography by the Catholic Church—was situated in a relational context that led the vodou practitioner to perform a ritual that was not directed toward the human saint who appeared in the image but rather the animal or the object associated with it. For example, the snake on which St. Patrick put his foot to symbolize his triumph over sin was, in Haiti, worshiped as the incarnation of the African god named Danbala-wedo, a supernatural serpent with many other meanings. Similarly, the Catholic image of the Virgin as *Mater dolorosa*, who wore numerous jewels, evoked the presence of the goddess Ezili-Freda-Dahomey, who was also magnificently adorned with jewels, although for very different reasons. Then again, the armor of St. James was interpreted by vodou practitioners as a reference to Ogun, the African god of iron. In all these examples, which drove the Catholic Church to organize a spectacular *auto-da-fé* in Port-au-Prince in the late 1950s, the iconography remained the same, while the game of worship rendered to the image made it the object of a subversive intervention (Métraux 1958, 325–26).

Thus, we can account for cultural variation in the field of iconography by understanding not only purely iconographic diversity but also the variations of the game. This distinction also makes it possible to grasp the nature of modern primitivism within the morphology of intercultural exchanges. This movement tries to portray itself as extremely "tolerant" of other iconographic traditions; from the primitivists' point of view, "everything can become art everywhere," from the Australian Aboriginal woman who traces a shape in the sand (Munn 1973) to the great masterpieces of the Western tradition. In the final analysis, however, this movement proves to be extremely rigid in the game it plays vis-à-vis the image. Primitivists may say that every image, in any society, is a "work of art," but for them, this means delving into the innermost being of the artist (and all the other ideas that flow from the concept of an "author," such as the notion of authenticity and the use of a biographical model as an organizing principle), even when dealing with societies in which the notion of an author is entirely different or nonexistent. To be convinced of this, it suffices to turn to certain Japanese traditions, where the challenge for the painter resides not in expressing the self but, as in the work of Hakuin and Enku, modifying and even annihilating the self (Seo and Addiss 2010; Bouchy 2003; Linhartová 1997). Any variation in a cultural game played with the image, and, indeed, in any other cultural register, such as ritual action, is excluded by the primitivist viewpoint, which recognizes only the language of the form and a reductionist psychological model of the relationship between the artist and the artwork.

In this book, I have chosen to invert this viewpoint. On the one hand, I will consider the production of images within their specific historical and cultural contexts, yet as inseparable from the exercise of thought, which is universal. On the other hand, I will define the Western "game of art" (or, more precisely, the game of the fine arts) as simply one of many possible games that can be played with images (and one that is highly variable in our own culture). Outside the West, we can identify at least two iconographic games involving aesthetics and the relationship between the artist and artwork. One of the issues I will explore is the game of memory, which mobilizes iconography as part of the conscious exercise of a technique for memorization, as I have discussed elsewhere (Severi [2007] 2015). Another focus here will be the game of attributing subjectivity and agency to an object, which engenders a link of belief between the image and the observer and leads to thinking of the image as a living, acting being.

Through the following chapters, I will attempt to progressively illuminate more facets of a particular type of game—one in which objects embody persons—and then return to considering the most prominent gaze-game in Western art, namely perspective. For now, what is incumbent upon me is to define the very notion of the "game" that will be used here. As stated earlier, this cannot be reduced to the idea of aesthetic space. How should we understand the relationship between a game and the space of representation? How should we proceed in order to uncover the set of operations that can be triggered by both the invention and the interpretation of specific iconographies? What is the most appropriate description of the process that leads to the creation of the universe of a particular iconographic tradition? How should we define the types of cognition, inference, imagination, and memory that iconographic traditions mobilize?

Because primitivists have so intently focused on form, they have resorted to familiar categories drawn directly from the language of the avant-garde: strength, life, energy, impulse, expression, and the like. Although this approach has provided one possible avenue for interpreting iconographic traditions, the language used has constantly betrayed the meanings of the original games. To succeed in interpreting these games and their iconographies, we need to take a different avenue and gradually formulate a new method for analyzing iconographic traditions and the forms of thinking associated with them. In a word, we must grapple with how the deployment of a game creates the universe of a particular iconographic tradition. We can arrive at an understanding of this universe only if, at each step in this journey, we rely on detailed ethnographic examples. Therefore, without proposing any a priori definitions, I will now consider the arts of memory in some Amerindian societies. Although the territory may be familiar, the questions I will pose will be new.

CHAPTER THREE

The Universe of the Arts of Memory

> *There must in the nature of human institutions be a mental language common to all nations. . . . This axiom is the principle of the hieroglyphs by which all nations spoke in the time of their first barbarism.*
> —Giambattista Vico, *The New Science*

AN EXERCISE IN METHODOLOGY

Social memory involves the remembrance of origins. Within the European tradition, ideas of the emergence of human society and its "early barbarism" were long associated with the myth of a universal language common to all humanity. This original language, posited by so many authors, raised an endless series of questions: What did its morphology, grammar, and logical structure look like? How did these first pioneers transmit it intact to future generations without a writing system? How did they communicate, both with one another and with their god?

In *The New Science*, Giambattista Vico ([1744] 1984) appealed to what we might call an *anthropological myth* to answer these questions. He suggested that initially social memory must have taken the form of emblems and symbolic figures, since images constitute the "mental language" that underpins the "principle of the hieroglyphs by which all nations spoke" (Vico [1744] 1984, 67, 77).

For Vico, this myth of a figurative language composed of icons was a logical necessity, a notion that would later have a significant impact on anthropological thought; indeed, its effects are still visible, albeit in implicit or fragmentary form, in contemporary social anthropology. Like so many of his contemporaries, Vico doubtless took Egyptian hieroglyphs as a historical model. When Horapollon's treatise on the Ancient Egyptian scripts was rediscovered during the Renaissance, provoking intense debate, hieroglyphs were still widely seen as *imagines symbolicae*, parts of a coded form of secret knowledge frequently attributed to Hermes Trismegistus or Moses. Some authors, such as Pico della Mirandola (following Plotinus), interpreted them as the last remaining traces of a divine language, which, by dint of careful riddling, could be made to give up the hidden order of the universe. Others, such as Alberti and Erasmus, more prosaically saw them as a possible model for a universal human language. Paolo Rossi's work ([1979] 1987) on seventeenth-century science, ably seconded by a number of more recent studies (e.g., Mauelshagen 2003), has raised a number of intriguing and still partially unexplored developments of this idea.

During the Baroque period, the notion of the hieroglyph was deployed in such unlikely fields as natural history, geology, and zoology. Medical experts and earth scientists considered rock crystals, fossils, geological strata, and anomalies (two-headed babies, hermaphrodites, or human–animal hybrids) as "hieroglyphs of nature"—prodigious signs by means of which the natural world revealed its secrets. Francis Bacon definitively characterized these monsters as "spontaneous" scientific experiments through which the laws of nature, unaffected by human intervention, are revealed. Later, Goethe theorized hieroglyphs to be prototypes of the originary forms (*Urform*) of living creatures, as immediate, abstract manifestations of the underlying unity connecting natural phenomena and the human spirit. Over the course of the eighteenth century, this naturalist interpretation of the hieroglyph was joined by the more abstract visions of Leibniz, D'Alembert, and Condorcet. At this point, an idea already implicitly present in Vico reached full expression: that of "mental hieroglyphs" or "universal characters," which could be expressed either linguistically or mathematically. One hundred years later, this same idea would drive Gottlob Frege ([1879] 1972) to elaborate his "mathematical ideography," a symbolic system independent of natural languages and capable of rigorously representing the laws of propositional logic.[1]

---

1. In his text, Frege ([1879] 1972) presents a "formulary language of pure thought" based primarily on arithmetical propositions.

The notion of mental hieroglyphs embodying a direct, linguistically unmediated relationship between concepts and images has been a widespread, persistent, and productive theme throughout modern thought (Assmann and Assmann 2003). For several centuries, however, its principal field of application was speculation on the origins of mankind. For linguists, anthropologists, and archaeologists up until the end of the nineteenth century, it was a given that the emblem always preceded the sign in "primitive society."

In *The New Science*, Vico had noted that hieroglyphs were an application of the same principles that regimented "mute" or sign languages, which made use of "gestures or objects that have natural relations with the ideas they wish to signify" (Vico [1744] 1984, 76). This, he suggested, explained why hieroglyphs the world over (from the West Indies of Mexico to the East Indies of China) seemed to derive from the same principles. For Vico, the hieroglyph was the model of the unitary principle of the human genus (*"senso comune del genere umano"*), which he placed at the heart of his theory. According to this principle, "uniform ideas originating among entire peoples unknown to each other must have a common ground of truth," and this, in turn, gave rise to the "mental dictionary" shared by all human cultures (Vico [1744] 1984, 63, 64).[2]

According to the myth of a universal language, human memory was initially preserved by means of images. This myth was particularly influential among historians of writing, who long distinguished between, on the one hand, a supposedly iconic, uncertain, and primitive "writing of things," and, on the other, a later, more evolved "writing of words." Such a view has also affected the wider study of the arts of memory. The two figureheads of this rich field of study, Paolo Rossi ([1983] 2000) and Frances Yates (1966), both emphasize the hieroglyphic character of these *artes memorandi*. The latter, influenced by the work of Aby Warburg, sets out to demonstrate the existence of a number of classical, astrological, magical, and more generally Neoplatonic ideas within the field of mnemonic techniques—and this as late as the middle of the Renaissance. In contrast, Rossi (followed by Jean-Philippe Antoine [1993]) adopts a philosophical approach that highlights the relationship between memorization and inferential techniques, showing how it played a central role in arts of memory from Raymond Lull to Linnaeus.

It would be an error, however, to overemphasize the opposition between Rossi's and Yates's approaches. In practice, the arts of memory reveal the same

---

2. On Vico and the origins of anthropological thought, see Berlin (1976, 1990).

double articulation as the myth of an original language. As mental languages, they are seen either as bearers of a sort of magic associated with the first language (by Camillo, Bruno, or Agrippa von Nettesheim, among others) or as precursors of a future universal tongue that must be forged from advances in science, particularly taxonomic and mathematical knowledge (by Erasmus, Leibniz, or D'Alembert). These ideas are still alive and well today, and not just in anthropology. In his contribution to a debate on the "universal language" promoted by the journal *Critique*, mathematician René Thom could happily exclaim, "Why speak of the myth of a universal language? Nowadays, there is at least one universal language—that of science" (Thom 1980, 291). This is close to the position of Rossi ([1983] 2000), for whom the historical outcome of the arts of memory can be seen in the work of Linnaeus. Yates (1966), for her part, identified "symptoms" of the quest for a scientific method in the classical arts. In short, both Rossi and Yates make references to a fundamental language and to the development of rational thought in their research on the arts of memory.

To study memory means studying thought at work. In his *Confessions*, St. Augustine revealed a clear awareness of this link: "Great is the force of memory, O Lord, I know not what, to be amazed at, profound, and of infinite multiplicity. And yet it is my mind: it is myself" (*Confessions* X.26.1–3, cited in Carruthers 1998, 31).[3] The arts of memory should not be framed as a survival (or possible development) of some magical or scientific paradigm but, instead, as historically and culturally situated practices of thought. This more anthropological approach to the subject is explored in the recent works of Mary Carruthers (1990, 1993, 1998) and Lina Bolzoni (2001, 2004). These two historians propose to address the *artes memorandi* as "crafts of thought" that bring together a whole range of memorization and mental imaging techniques. According to them, memorization techniques (along with the taxonomical organization of knowledge to which they give rise and the historical *longue durée* in which it is inscribed) should not be viewed as the conceptual foundation for a singular vision of the world. Rather, such practices are a type of historical artifact that can be used in a variety of contexts, ranging from the systematization of knowledge to pedagogics, from prayer to meditation, and even to the composition and reading of particular texts. The only aspect distinguishing this set of techniques from a material tool is that it is a *mental* artifact, a tool of thought. As Carruthers explains,

---

3. On this passage, see also the commentary in Brown (1967, 176ff).

We can no longer speak in the singular of the art of memory, except by analogy with the art of the carpenter or that of the painter—not as a set of established doctrines but as a set of tasks and methods that contribute to shaping a certain type of product. . . . Thus, the art of memory should not be restricted to an aspect of the philosophy of memory or treated as a simple entity in the history of ideas; it should also be seen as a skill used to generate creations that can be studied through the history of genres, influences, styles, forms, and techniques. (Carruthers 2002, 8)

Bolzoni adds that, in the arts of memory,

The schemas are primarily in the mind and take on form in various ways: through words, purely mental images, mixtures of words and images, illuminated manuscripts, images that are painted, sculpted, broken up, and recomposed in mosaic or made to gleam in stained-glass windows. They are schemas straddling the border between the visible and invisible, between reading and writing, memory and invention, exegesis and recycling. They constitute a basic *outillage*, wide-ranging and widespread, most of which no longer exists, having been removed physically . . . but, above all, removed from our critical perception, they become, paradoxically, invisible. (Bolzoni 2004, 6)

In this chapter, I will take the Carruthers's and Bolzoni's conclusions as the starting point for my analysis of the arts of memory utilized in several Amerindian traditions. My aim is twofold: first, to explain the nature of the universe of meaning constructed through the use of an iconography linked to the conscious exercise of memory; from this, I will extract implications for a general method to inform my subsequent analyses. Second is a wider goal of further developing an anthropology of memory, which I proposed in an earlier work (Severi [2007] 2015). The existence of several different arts of memory, each characterized by a precise constellation of what Rossi sees as key to the *artes memorandi*—the relationship between recollection, classification, and inference, on the one hand, and evocation, ideation, and imagination, on the other—is something that most anthropologists have overlooked. Diligent fieldwork has uncovered different memorization techniques in Oceania (Wassmann 1988, 1991; Harrison 1990; Silverman 1993), Africa (Nooter-Roberts and Roberts 1996; Kubick 1987), and the Americas (Hoffman 1897, 1898; Mallery [1893] 1972; Ewers [1939] 1979), but the idea that a logic of memorization might guide traditions in so-called oral societies has not gained much traction in the discipline, nor has the notion that an anthropology of the arts of memory could be elaborated as a complement to the work of historians.

This project necessitates several shifts in perspective. First, and most radically, we must tilt at the opposition between oral and written traditions—a dichotomy that has played a fundamental role in social anthropology. Elsewhere (Severi [2007] 2015), I have argued that this opposition underlies a number of anthropological misunderstandings: traditions that anthropologists have tended to describe as oral are often better thought of as *iconographic*. In many cultures where social memory may appear to rely only on the spoken word, closer scrutiny reveals that images play an indispensable role in the transmission of knowledge. To comprehend cultural facts that rely on such transmission, it is misleading to posit a symmetrical opposition between the domain of orality and that of writing. The counterpart of writing in many societies is not merely the spoken word but, more precisely, the hybridization of word and image in the form of a mnemonic device, most commonly in ritual contexts.

If the socialization of memory is to become a fully-fledged anthropological object, then a new definition of tradition is needed—one that is no longer defined in terms of semiotic means of expressing knowledge (traditions that are "oral," "written," and so on) but, rather, one that captures the precise nature of the multiple relationships that link words and images.

Historians of the *artes memorandi*, for their part, need to make room in their findings for new perspectives drawn from outside the Western world. This new approach implies a combined comparative and reflexive research strategy. If the idea of the arts of memory is to be applied beyond the Western framework, then it is not enough merely to show that some of the historians' concepts can be fruitfully applied to non-Western techniques of memorization. It is essential to also bring what Claude Lévi-Strauss called "the view from afar" to bear on the Western case. Seen from this perspective, both classical and medieval arts of memory can be classified as ideal types within a continuum of techniques for the exercise of thought—which inevitably raises the question of the relations between the arts of memory and the set of practices associated with writing.

The false opposition between orality and writing, the reluctance to compare the West with the Rest, and the complexity of the relationship between the arts of memory and writing techniques in our own tradition are epistemological dilemmas that have contrived to hamper our understanding of the memory techniques in non-Western traditions. This difficulty is, however, not merely theoretical. The study of these techniques often focuses on long-ignored graphic representations that are difficult to conceptualize. Our customary categories (drawing, symbols, ideograms, pictograms, semasiography,[4] writing, etc.) are ill adapted to such graphic representations, which are usually described in a vague fashion as "mnemonics." It is also frequently hard to grasp their underlying logic. One example of this is the Americanist debate surrounding *khipus*, the Incan cords containing different types of knots used to convey messages or memorize data. The work of a number of scholars (Ascher and Ascher 1981; Urton and Llanos 1997; Urton 1998, 2003; Quilter and Urton 2002; Salomon 2001, 2002, 2006; Pärssinen and Kiviharju 2004; Déléage 2007) has thrown new light on the technical uses and the social import of these mnemonic devices. This research builds on the finding that the primary purpose of *khipus* was to carry numerical information and that their use was tied up with the control of different elements (people, goods, ritual offerings, tributes, and even units of space and time) managed by the Incan bureaucracy. The use of *khipus* was thus, as Gary Urton pithily puts it, a particularly well-developed example of the "social life of numbers." Various historical sources confirm that the Quechua word *khipu* means both "knot" and "numerical calculation" and that the verb *khipuni* similarly means both "to tie a knot" and to "do a sum" (Gonzales Holguín [1608] 1989, 309; Vega [1609] 1991, I.6, chap. 7–9; Cummins 2002). Nevertheless, we know that the arithmetical interpretation only holds for certain *khipus*, those with sections or sets of chords organized into relationships that reveal regularity and can be assimilated to a numerical order. In these cases, a series (or even a series of series) of cords helped skilled users to rigorously record and memorize large sets of numbers (based on a decimal system). Urton notes that a significant number of *khipus* kept in museums (roughly one-third out of six hundred) lack this regularity and so should not be considered arithmetical aids. A small number of qualitative categories were signaled by color, the way the knot was folded, or the direction of the cords. Some historical sources (notably Guaman Poma de Ayala's *New Chronicle* [1615] 1980; see also the texts collected by Pärssinen and Kiviharju [2004]) suggest that these *khipus* were used to memorize texts containing names of people and places (Murra 1991), but the exact way the system of memorization might have worked is still largely inscrutable. How are

---

4. Ignace Gelb ([1952] 1963, 249) defines semasiography as the "forerunner of writing," composed of "various devices . . . to achieve intercommunication by means of visible marks, expressing meaning but not necessarily linguistic elements."

we to understand a mnemonic device that relies on the same mental operation (the creation of ordered series) to fulfill such diverse functions as numerical calculation and the memorization of a text? Contemporary debates on the issue are as lively as they are undecided, with partisans of the different camps frequently limiting themselves to fighting over whether *khipus* are "true" writing or "just" a mnemonic device. Most of these authors use the term *mnemonic device* to describe an "arbitrary and individual means of memorizing" that "follows no standard rules" (Cummins 2002, 195). Urton most clearly exemplifies this opposition, universally accepted by specialists, between "writing" and "mnemonic device." To show that *khipus* could not be reduced to mere mnemonic devices, he initially proposed (1998) to distinguish between different types of *khipus*: mnemonic ones for general use and more codified ones for bureaucratic use. He noted the capacity of certain *khipus* to record verbs or sentences and spoke of the *khipus* "high degree of syntactic and semantic information" (Urton 1998, 427). He specifically stated that "the *khipu* recording system more closely approximated a form of writing than is usually considered to have been the case" (1998, 427). Along these lines, he defended the argument that all *khipus* were derived from a pre-Hispanic form of actual writing. More recently (2003), he has proposed a third hypothesis: that *khipus were reduced to mere mnemonic devices* by the violent transformations undergone by Inca society during the early colonial period. The damage had been done as early as the 1590s, leading to "the elimination of fully grammatical constructions (of the type subject–object–verb), which were replaced by attenuated, non-narrative representations principally comprised of names and numbers" (2003).

Beyond the hypothetical powers of transcription (in forms and tenses of verbs, as well as certain epistemic classifiers)[5] attributed to *khipus* by Urton (1998, 428), it is hard to imagine how this precolonial knotted language might have functioned. It is worth remembering that "true writing," according to John de Francis's (1990) definition, uses a finite number of signs to give a complete representation of the spoken language. A system that can be called "writing" must therefore cover the entire range of words in a language—something that seems difficult for a notational system such as *khipus* to attain. As

---

5. An epistemic classifier (or "evidential") is a suffix indicating the nature of the information conveyed in a proposition. For instance, an evidential might indicate whether the information was generated by direct experience or derived from unverifiable rumor.

Thomas Cummins points out, *khipus* ordered the varied information they contained, whether words or numbers, by "producing an image of the memory, rather than by representing that which they are meant to preserve" (Cummins 2002, 209). In other words, the arrangement of *khipu* cords into a series of logical arborescent structures indicates a train or process of thought, but this tells us almost nothing about their actual content. Given these conditions, how can we conceptualize a coherent transition from the memorization of numerical series to historical narratives? The central question remains almost wholly unanswered by adversaries on both sides: what kind of conceptual unity underpins such different mnemonic usages? By extension, what is the logical status of the *khipus*? If they are not simply writing, mathematical symbols, or memory aids, what are they?

Further empirical research will doubtless shed light on this question. In the meantime, it is worthwhile considering a broader theoretical point: the opposition, inspired by the classic work of Ignace Gelb ([1952] 1963), between mnemonic devices and writing is, in fact, extremely fragile from a conceptual point of view. For Gelb, as for the other authors mentioned above, all these diverse techniques necessarily belong to one of two camps. Either a society relies on oral memory, giving rise to loose, fragile traditions, or it develops techniques for transcribing language, leading ultimately to writing. Many Amerindian cultures, however, fall outside this crude opposition: the practice of social memory and the use of organized iconographies go together in these traditions, which developed arts of memory that cannot be reduced to either writing or to individual mnemonic devices. I will return to these matters later; for the time being, let me note that *khipus* are not the only Amerindian graphic representations to call our categories into question by virtue of their hybridity and seemingly contradictory functions. Throughout the length of the Americas, we find pictographic traditions that, from the point of view of Western semiotics, seem to realize an "impossible combination" of picture and sign. Historians of writing have long hesitated over how to define these images. With the notable exception of Diego Valades, who, as early as the fifteenth century, spoke of them in no uncertain terms as memory images, most specialists have reduced pictograms to an opposition with alphabetic writing systems. This long list of authors might begin with Michele Mercati who, in 1598, referred to them as "Indian hieroglyphs," analogous to Egyptian ones, and end with Walter Hoffman and Garrick Mallery (Hoffman 1891, 1897, 1898; Mallery [1893] 1972), who defined Amerindian pictograms as crude means for recording elementary ideas. In between, we find countless European and American chroniclers and geographers dreaming up all kinds of mysterious *paleographic* interpretations, rarely accompanied by actual descriptions.

In some ways, the current debate surrounding *khipus* echoes these older controversies. I suggest that we can only understand the logical structure of Amerindian mnemonic devices by abandoning older, invariably ethnocentric approaches based on the opposition between *khipus* and writing in favor of a comparative anthropological perspective. The question, then, of whether pictographic systems or *khipus* are "true" writing or "just" mnemonic devices is of no interest here. Instead, I propose to explore whether *khipus* and pictograms, as organized mnemonic and graphic systems (however apparently distant they may be), share any common formal traits, thereby implying comparable mental operations. Can they, in other words, be fruitfully compared independently of any reference to writing systems? By focusing on the underlying mental operations, I wish to inquire into whether they belong to the same mental universe, and, therefore, whether Amerindian arts of memory share a common "mental language," to borrow Vico's term. In this way, it will become apparent that *khipus* and pictograms are not, in fact, unruly hybrids defying classification but, rather, mental artifacts with characteristics and functions that can be understood in their own terms. These analyses, based on the exploration of several case studies that are, of necessity, only coarse grained, will lead to a description of the logical elements that underpin the universe of Amerindian arts of memory. The word "universe" has both a geographical and a logical sense. I use it as a horizon for research, not as an attempt to reduce the immense diversity of Amerindian cultures to one common form. It is defined by the set of mental operations implied by the use of these memorization techniques as well as by a specific group of cultures.

AMERINDIAN ARTS OF MEMORY: A CASE STUDY

As I argued above, our traditional semiotic categories (drawings, pictograms, ideograms, etc.) fail to do justice to non-Western techniques of memorization. They do not provide the tools to produce coherent descriptions of how these graphic forms actually function. Instead of trying to classify these unfamiliar graphic systems a priori, we need to begin with empirical analyses of mnemonic iconographic systems and then delve into the mental operations on which they rely.

Let us begin with what superficially looks like a fairly straightforward case: Yekuana weaving. The Yekuana, hunters and agriculturalists who speak a Carib language, now live in the Upper Orinoco region between Venezuela and Brazil, although they may have originated in southern Amazonia. The work of a number of ethnographers, most notably Marc de Civrieux (1970, 1980), has given us detailed knowledge of their myths. They are part of a long cycle of narratives detailing the many episodes of a bloody conflict that the Yekuana believe orders the universe. On one side is Wanadi, a positive being associated with the sun and who presides over human culture (agricultural, fishing, hunting, and tool-making techniques), and, on the other, his twin brother, Odosha, who is the incarnation of evil, misfortune, illness, and death. For the Yekuana, this cosmic conflict is not simply a schematic representation of the origins of the universe. Although it dates back to the dawn of time, the brothers' struggle is unending: it continues to affect people's everyday lives, often with tragic consequences. This lack of harmony can be traced back to an original dissymmetry between good and evil, and between humans and their potential enemies, be they animal or vegetable in nature. For the Yekuana, evil always wins out over good. This is why their ally, Wanadi, lives in a far-off region of the heavens and has little contact with the human world. His twin brother, Odosha, however, is an ever-present danger; he lives in close proximity to humans, surrounded by his demons that are often represented as the invisible "masters" of animals and plants. This also explains why Odosha is represented by a whole series of malefic creatures: howler monkeys, serpents, jaguars, or cannibal strangers, whereas Wanadi, alone in his sky realm, singlehandedly protects his people. The Yekuana claim that each act of hunting, fishing, or gardening is performed in opposition to "invisible masters," who are seen as owners of animals and plants. This world, inhabited by potential threatening enemies, is that of Odosha and his demons. Each time humans pursue some act necessary to their survival, they risk retaliation, which they try, not always successfully, to ward off with specific chants. Besides being dissymmetric, good and evil are also constantly transforming into one another: the Yekuana believe that each of their cultural artifacts or techniques (weaponry, weaving, body ornamentation, or painting) is the result of a transformation of evil or of the beings who depend on evil. It follows that all living creatures are inherently ambiguous: everything that might be seen as useful or beneficent (including the woven baskets that men decorate in preparation for marriage) contains a transformed share of evil.

Although there is not space here to explore this mythical tradition at length, it is worth raising a telling point about the pictures that accompany Civrieux's original Spanish publication (1970). When he collected the myths from the Yekuana, he asked several of his informants to illustrate the stories of Wanadi and Odosha (Figure 14). Drawn in an uncertain hand, these crude representations of people and houses seem to illustrate Hoffman's (1897) notion of indigenous pictograms as being "rudimentary means to represent basic ideas."

Figure 14. Yekuana "pictograms" illustrating the myths collected by Marc de Civrieux (from Civrieux 1970).

We have David Guss (who carried out two major field studies among the Yekuana in 1976 and 1984) to thank for a double discovery concerning these myths. First, he was astonished to find that the Yekuana never actually recited their myths as autonomous narratives. Contrary to what he expected from Civrieux's myth collection, "there were no neatly framed 'story-telling' events into which the foreign observer could easily slip, no circles of attentive youths breathing in the words of an elder as he regaled them with the deeds of their ancestors" (Guss 1989, 1). Although mythology was omnipresent in everyday conversation, its enunciation was always fragmentary, allusive, and episodic. His initial goal of recording and transcribing their creation epic, *Watunna,* in the Yekuana language, would have taken years. Yekuana society, he noted, had only two contexts in which these myths received a fuller expression: in the images woven into baskets and in the chants sung during ritual festivals (which sometimes consisted only of lists of spirit names [1989, 36]). The handing down or transmission of myths, which mainly took place during weaving sessions, did not take the narrative form that Civrieux unwittingly led the reader to expect but involved, instead, an iconography and the enunciation, in a specific context, of events and proper names. In other words, the fact that Civrieux's collection of myths was presented as a sequence of narratives was the result not of Yekuana practices but of two processes quite alien to their tradition: an a posteriori organization of the myths into a corpus of chronologically organized episodes stretching from the beginning of time until the present, and the elicitation of supposedly "indigenous" pictograms for purposes of illustration. Guss realized that these twin processes had completely distorted the practical form taken by this mythical knowledge. Although Civrieux faithfully reproduced some of the myths' content, he fundamentally traduced them by misrepresenting the way they were performed and transmitted.

This ethnographic revelation has implications for our understanding of Yekuana iconography. Having spent much time learning local weaving techniques, Guss was in a position to confirm that the Yekuana did indeed have a form of graphic representation associated with their mythology. But this was not the pictographic representation of Civrieux's collection. Individual imagination played no part in this graphic tradition. Instead, the designs, based on weaving techniques, were regular, abstract, and geometric, and they followed a limited number of recognized themes. Guss managed to identify roughly thirty different, clearly identified themes. The crude human and animal figures, the tottering huts and crooked horizons found in Civrieux's book had no place in Yekuana tradition. Such differences were not restricted to mere form. The iconography identified by Guss was strictly limited in scope: none of the images represented mythical actions or particular episodes; only the names of certain key characters were translated into images. These woven patterns incorporated geometric, and vaguely iconic representations of only a few central figures, such as the toad, serpent, bat, monkey, and so on (see Figure 15).

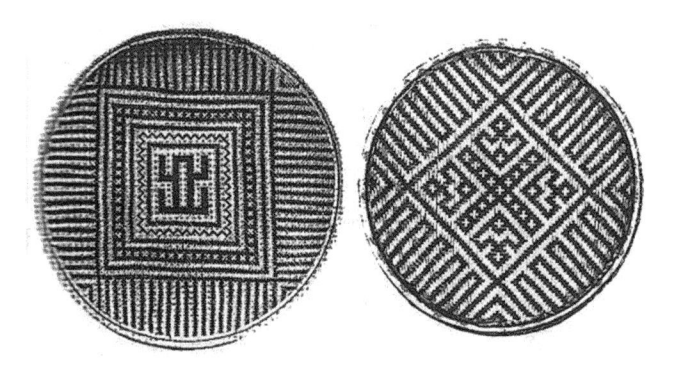

Figure 15. "Toad" and "bat" in traditional Yekuana iconography (from Guss 1989).

One of the most surprising aspects of Guss's observations is that these woven pictograms (like the ritual chants sung to crops and the "masters" or "owners" of prey) only record names. Guss convincingly argues that these lists of names, specifically toponyms and anthroponyms, serve as veritable *mnemonic foci* of Yekuana mythic narratives. The successive mythical eras are indicated by the use of particular toponyms, while stories are remembered around their central characters. The visual memory of myth thus amounts to a finite and well-identified catalogue of proper names.

What is the best way to describe the mode of operation of such visual memory? Analyzing the graphic schemata typical of the iconography reveals that, rather than presenting particular mythical sequences in more or less "realistic" fashion (as Civrieux's illustrations seem to have done), Yekuana pictograms reveal a deeper level at which mythical knowledge is organized. The two central principles of these myths, as we saw, are the constitutive opposition between two sets of characters and the constant process of transformation that affects them. These metamorphoses, in turn, take two distinct forms. On the one hand is the idea of a manifold creature (such as Odosha), who "adopts the form" of a whole series of other beings; on the other is the ceaseless process of metamorphosis (where good is necessarily the result of a domestication of evil), potentially endowing a creature with a constitutive ambiguity that is simultaneously positive and negative. Yekuana iconography allows for the precise, economical transformation of these two organizing principles of the mythic world into visual terms. In fact, the visual themes that translate the names of spirits are all derivations of a single graphic pattern, a sort of inverted

"T" representing Odosha (Figure 16). A few simple geometrical transformations allow the rest of the mythical characters to be generated from this single graphic pattern. These graphic representations underline the simultaneous multiplicity of these creatures (monkey, toad, serpent, bat, and so forth) and their deeper unity as forms derived from the same originary being. The various characters are thus constructed from one fundamental form and are part of a wider system that identifies particular characters as well as their possible relationships. These relationships of analogy, inclusion, and transformation bespeak an organizational structure within this system of representation, based on a criterion of unity.

Crucially, the visual technique in question also implies a slippage between figure and ground—understood in the sense used in Gestalt psychology, especially as elaborated by Roy Wagner (1986, 2012). This slippage allows for the representation of both a specific being and one of its possible metamorphoses. Such a possibility of a double representation—or, better yet, of representation in the form of a potentially dual being—applies to several mythical characters: monkeys, bats, and toads. The most striking example is, without doubt, the *Woroto sakedi*, an image that, depending on whether one focuses on the figure or the ground, shows either Odosha or one of his serpent avatars, Awidi (Figure 16). Ultimately, as Guss argues, the true subject of Yekuana iconography is not such or such a character but, more precisely, the ongoing transformation of one into the other (Guss 1989, 106, 121–24).

Working up from one elementary form of the pictogram (which is always both retained and transformed), this apparently simple iconographic series manages to organize the visual space of representation in increasingly complex ways. Within this visual space, all beings—even Wanadi—are the result of a transformation of Odosha. These forms are created by dint of additions, variations, and relationships of inclusion, repetition, and inversion, which conjointly testify to their fundamental unity. This technique translates the mythological universe into visual terms while simultaneously compiling an iconic memory of the names of key characters.

Yekuana weaving shows how crucial iconography can be in so-called oral societies. Between the two opposing poles of exclusively oral and written traditions, there is, in fact, a wide range of hybrid situations in which neither the use of spoken words nor that of written signs dominates. When the ethnographer makes the effort to identify the paths through which such knowledge

Figure 16. Alternate figure–ground relationships in images of Awidi, the serpent (above), and Odosha, master of evil (below), derived from the same graphic theme (from Guss 1989).

is transmitted, we find, as in the Yekuana case, a specific articulation for mnemonic purposes between a certain type of image (structured according to one dominant visual schema and belonging to a finite, often quite limited set) and certain categories of words, such as an organized series of proper names. In Western societies, we are inclined to assume that, since words and images are everywhere present in society, any form of visual representation or proposition can serve as an *aide memoire*. Field studies, however, suggest that the emergence of an iconographic tradition implies, above all, the formation of a specific *universe of discourse* specific to visual representation. In so-called oral cultures like that of the Yekuana, not everything can be visually represented; instead, their iconography tends to be applicable exclusively to one particular sphere, such as mythology. Within this universe, several levels of increasingly specific relations are created between the linguistic domain (in particular, special toponymic and anthroponymic lexicons) and that of iconic representation.

In analyzing several ethnographic cases, I have argued (Severi 1997, [2007] 2015) that three distinct operations underlie the emergence of such mnemonic "domains of representability" in the Amerindian context: the choice of which words to represent; the creation of a cognitively salient visual medium of representation; and the ordering of a particular space (which, for the Yekuana, involves a series of transformations of a basic geometric shape, giving rise to a range of visual terms). These three operations are further linked to particular linguistic forms used in traditional knowledge, such as the Yekuana chants. Unlike pictures in Western cultures, Yekuana pictograms do not simply illustrate stories nor do they resemble purportedly realistic images. Their graphic elements designate relations (of inversion, extension, inclusion, analogy, and so on) between various mythical beings in iconographic terms. Pictograms, as graphic images, presuppose the existence of a coherent iconography and a particular form of traditional knowledge. They should not be thought of as graphic elements invented by individuals but, rather, as *relationship markers* that signal connections between a set of known entities (and the mental operations implied by the set) and a graphic form determined by a particular iconographic tradition.

PICTOGRAPHY AND MEMORY: A MODEL

These initial reflections on an apparently simple case study suggest that the evolution of Amerindian pictography depends on the development of two parallel axes: on the one hand, the emergence of increasingly refined iconographies (with their particular themes and graphic styles), and, on the other, the development of ever more precise forms of taxonomically organized knowledge that can be pictographically represented. I have discussed this in detail elsewhere (Severi 1997, [2007] 2015), but here it will suffice to consider the pictographic representation of proper names. The knowledge set that, among the Yekuana, takes the elementary form of a simple list of mythical characters (jaguar, toad, serpent, monkey, etc.) can, in other cases, be organized along increasingly complex relational axes. This occurs in the pictography of the Kuna of the San Blas islands of Panama, among whom I conducted fieldwork from 1977 to 1982. Their iconography, one of the most highly developed Amerindian systems, makes use of lists of proper names represented by pictograms and associated with fixed narrative phrases that are only pronounced orally. In "Song of the Demon" (Severi [2007] 2015, 168–69), for instance, the spirit villages that the shaman must visit are depicted in fixed graphic form, accompanied by this formula: "Far away, there where the sun's canoe rises, the village [name] appeared." In "Song of the Rock Crystal," ([2007] 2015, 181–82), the names of the spirits are inserted into another formula: "At the river's mouth, spirit of [name], the first God placed your dwelling." In other passages of the latter text, we find even more complicated lists of names created by incorporating the names of spirits into village names. The third section of "Song of the Demon," which is called "The path that leads to spirit villages," contains the names of villages, such as the Village of Dances or the Village of Transformations, each of which is inhabited by a distinctive group of animal spirits: deer, birds, and butterflies in the former, monkeys, peccaries, and wild boars in the latter, and so on, while the Village of Homecoming is occupied by humans. Thus, the text consists of a series of logically nested groups of names, each associated with a particular pictogram and fixed oral expression (see Figure 17).

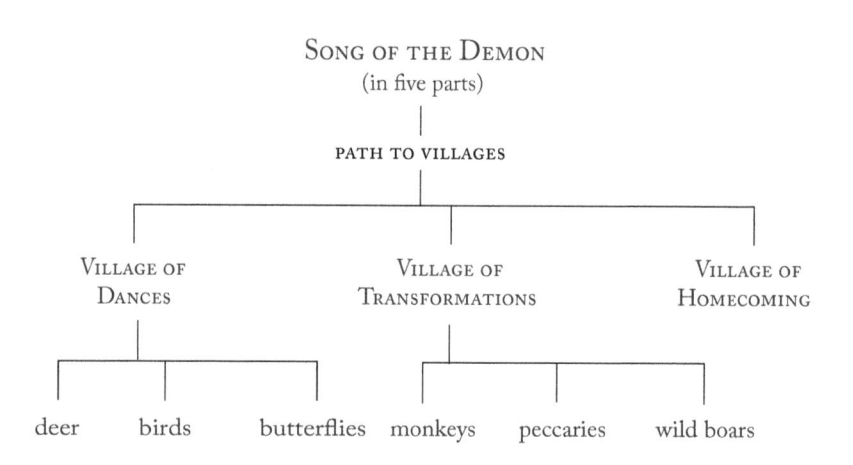

Figure 17. Logical nesting of lists of proper names in the Kuna "Song of the Demon."

In yet other cases, these types of nested series are replaced by alternating series or small clusters of proper names. Although the Kuna pictograms painted on boards may look like a straightforward series of images, they are, in fact, subject to relatively complex decoding processes (Severi [2007] 2015, 169–82).

In pictographic traditions elsewhere in the Americas (for example, those of the Nahuatl, Maya, and certain Great Plains groups), pictograms designating proper names and their accompanying formulas are inserted into other forms of stable graphic schemata. One good example is the "pictorial autobiographies" of from the Great Plains, in which pictograms detailing proper names are linked to images of a horseman heading off to hunt or do battle. In such cases, the proper name pictogram, such as "Bow Decorated with Feathers" (Figure 18), is slotted into a predetermined verbal formula, which, in this case, could be transcribed as "The bare-faced horseman, whose name is 'Bow Decorated with Feathers,' launches an attack."[6]

Figure 18. Picture from the Dakota Bible (1870s) from a Sioux village, Great Lakes region; Museum of Ethnology, Berlin.

In short, underpinning the wide range of local variation between different Amerindian cultures, we find a series of logical principles determining the use of pictograms. Different narrative themes (a journey, a spirit dialogue, or a war or hunting party) are played out in an oral genre (song, chant, or story) by means of parallelistic formulas with a fixed word order. This order transforms the narrative sequence into an alternation between fixed repetitive formulas and suites of variations, often in the form of lists of proper names. In the context of this

---

6. See Severi ([2007] 2015, 190–95) for an analysis of the pictograms of the Plains Ojibwa.

mnemonically organized ensemble of words, the role of the pictogram is to give mnemonic salience to the variations. In this way, via the iconographic transcription of variation, the pictogram makes it possible to efficiently memorize long, elaborate texts.

In other words, social memory in many Amerindian societies is based neither on a process analogous to alphabetic writing nor on some vaguely defined oral tradition. Rather, it depends on graphic mnemonic devices with the primary role of defining the relationship between a relatively stable iconographic set and a rigorously structured use of ritual language. Amerindian pictography is not some abortive forerunner of alphabetic writing but a supple and sophisticated mnemonic device in its own right, with a coherent graphic style shared by members of the society and a regular relationship to memorized texts. It is worth stressing that, from a graphic point of view, all pictographic iconography in Native America is

1. *conventional*: each "author" draws on an established, recognizable repertoire of graphic themes;
2. *closed*: within the discursive space described by the pictograms, it is only possible to refer to certain predefined situations and symbols;
3. *selective*: people drawing pictograms use conventional shorthand to evoke complex images; the use of these graphic schemata indicates that the drawings "select" a limited number of the real images' manifold traits;
4. *redundant*: the pictograms always add more information to what is conveyed in linguistic descriptions of the particular scene or episode; and
5. *sequential*: these pictographic systems range in complexity from straightforward examples, where the images follow only one form of geometric transformation, to cases where they obey a specific, rigorous linear order (for example, as boustrophedon among the Kuna or spirals among the Ojibwa).

Drawing on the examples discussed above, we can outline a preliminary set of mental operations involved in the use of pictograms. It is clear that none of these memorization techniques can be described as arbitrary or based simply on individual memory (Urton 1993). In America, the arts of memory are based on the ordering of shared knowledge (that is, a "tradition") and on the effect of salience, which makes it possible to distinguish among individual terms within a sequence. Together, these two operations produce *mnemonic relations*.

Unlike semiotic relations used in writing, mnemonic relations do not establish a connection between a sign and its real-world referent. Instead, they rely on a set of visual inferences, based on the decoding of complex images, which establish a relationship between the memory of images and the memory of words. The effectiveness of memorization techniques in iconographic traditions is not the result of an attempt to imitate the referential path taken by writing; it arises from the relationship the techniques establish between different levels of mnemonic elaboration. From this, we can conclude that all graphic memorization techniques depend on the *modular organization* of the types of knowledge they represent. This was illustrated above in the Kuna song in which graphic representations of proper names are inserted into increasingly complex linguistic structures (proper name + narrative sequence, based on inclusion or alternation).

This analysis can be pushed further. These first two mental operations—ordering and salience—involved in the iconographic process imply two more principles, of a more abstract nature, which throw new light on the relationship between pictograms and written signs. It is useful to draw a logical contrast between those traits that define a writing system and those that define mnemonics, whatever their degree of complexity. Let us take two logical properties characteristic of all symbolic sets: power and expressivity. The logical power of a system can be defined as its capacity to attribute predicates, however simple they may be, to a wide range of objects, whereas expressivity allows a system to describe a limited range of objects using a wide range of predicates. Thus, the highly detailed description of a person given by a single image (such as a portrait) is extremely expressive but lacking in power. In contrast, the utterance "all men are mortal" is extremely powerful but not very expressive. Working our way up from these premises, we can see that, in any writing system, such as a phonetic alphabet transcribing the sounds of a language, the power and expressivity of the language are equal to those of writing. In this perspective, writing disappears in language, since it is only its representation. The arts of memory, on the other hand, are systems of symbols having a power and expressivity that is never equal to those of language, even though they leave scarcely any room for individual choice and variation. As a mental artifact, the structure of an art of memory is made up of a relationship between operations that attribute salience (which give the system its expressivity) and forms of ordering (which give the system its logical power). The primary function of these two principles is a mental one:

the sequential ordering of images and their relations has an obvious function in encoding information. Salience, meanwhile, plays a crucial role in evoking and bringing things to mind. In short, the arts of memory can be defined in terms of three distinct relational orders: mnemonic (encoding/evocation), iconographic (ordering/salience), and logical (power/expressivity).

It follows that if we wish to analyze an iconographic tradition linked to the use of memory, we must begin by looking at the relationships it establishes between these three orders. Seen from this angle, Yekuana basket weaving, for instance, can be described as a mnemonic iconography with a relatively limited graphic range, a weakly organized set of themes (monkey, toad, anaconda, and so forth), which are all derived from one basic theme (Odosha). This makes the system relatively unexpressive and gives it a limited capacity for ordering (Figure 19).

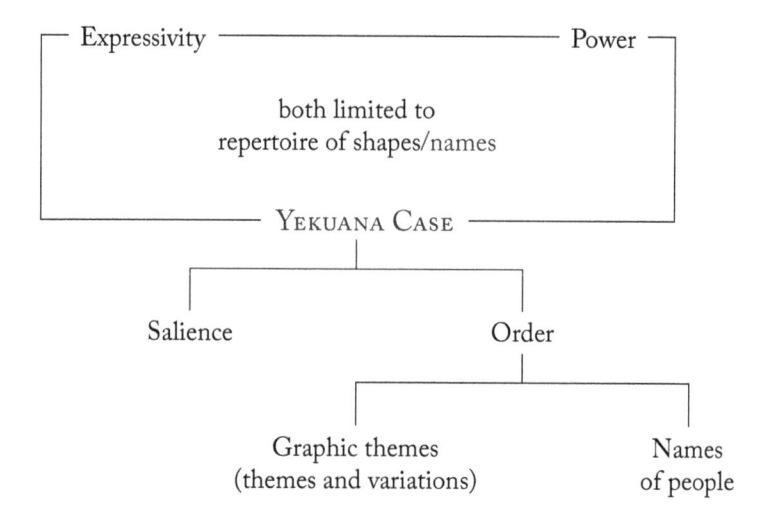

```
┌─ Expressivity ──────────────── Power ─┐
│                                        │
│           both limited to              │
│       repertoire of shapes/names       │
│                                        │
└──────────── Yekuana Case ──────────────┘
                    │
          ┌─────────┴─────────┐
       Salience             Order
                              │
                    ┌─────────┴─────────┐
              Graphic themes          Names
           (themes and variations)   of people
```

Figure 19. Ordering and salience in Yekuana pictography.

The model I am proposing is squarely focused on mental operations and the relationship between iconography and language. There is thus no point in trying to compare different arts of memory in terms of their appearance or the tools, materials, and techniques used to create their graphic systems. The only relevant dimension is the relationship between salience and ordering, encoding and retrieval, on the one hand, and power and expressivity, on the other.

One final point worth noting concerns the evolution of the arts of memory. The negative vision of pictographic traditions shared by many historians of writing is based on the idea that pictograms are fundamentally sterile—unable to develop because they are little more than abortive, individual attempts to transmit information. For them, writing did not develop out of pictography, but bypassed it completely, following a quite different track: the representation of the sounds of a language. Much research suggests, however, that American pictograms developed in coherent and autonomous ways for several centuries. In the development and evolution of the arts of memory in the *longue durée*, it is clear that they were always modular and multilinear; that is, the development or extension of one aspect of the arts of memory did not imply the parallel development of another. One local tradition might reach a high degree of complexity in the organization and ordering of memorizable knowledge without developing a refined iconography. Elsewhere, we might find an extremely codified and visually sophisticated iconography with a relatively limited logical power. This is only a question of degree, since all Amerindian pictographic traditions place more emphasis on salience than on power. As we know, pictography systems represent highly specific, identifiable knowledge. If we briefly turn our attention to the art of the Northwest Coast of North America, we will find an example of how this relationship between salience and ordering may develop.

EPONYMOUS ANIMALS: NORTHWEST COAST VISUAL CULTURE

The combined efforts of Franz Boas and Claude Lévi-Strauss turned the Northwest Coast into one of the *loci classici* of anthropological research. This Amerindian "ecumene" (Lévi-Strauss [1979] 1982), which brought several distinct cultures together in one homogenous ensemble, has been studied for its mythology, social structure, spectacular rituals of exchange, and cyclical vision of time, with a radical separation between summer and winter, each characterized by a distinct conception of social existence and relationship to nature. I doubt any reminder is needed about the value of the artistic traditions of these cultures. Northwest Coast works of art were eulogized by the Surrealists and are featured in major museums in many countries. Art historians and anthropologists have studied them at length, focusing on their different styles, mythical references, artists, and aesthetics foundations. Studies of their mnemonic role have been less common. And yet, a coastal totem pole is not merely an instantiation of a particular aesthetic idea; it was also created to preserve the memory of a name or a series of names. Marius Barbeau's (1950) formidable study of totem poles, as well as numerous other works (Inverarity 1950; Smyly and Smyly 1975; Garfield and Wingert 1967), are unanimous in affirming that, whether a pole is linked to the memory of a person, house, clan, or moiety, its function is the same: to give visual form to a specific series of names of mythical characters (crow, whale, eagle, bear, and so on) that, as a totality, designates a particular social group.

A good example is the Haida totem pole from the village of Skedans (Figure 20).

The totem pole is a sort of pictographic column, a vertical series of images of crests or "heraldic emblems," most commonly in the form of animals. Figure 20 shows a totem pole for Black-Whale House, which bears a complex name that is read from bottom to top as "Black Whale—Crow—Rainbow—Eagle." The sequence of crests not only visually represents the name of the particular social group but also proclaims its ownership or other forms of control of certain lands, hunting and fishing territories, or ritual privileges. Furthermore, the images always correspond to highly detailed narrative cycles describing the group's history, from its origin myths to more recent legends. A totem pole may contain the crest of clan chief who was especially fortunate or respected; Barbeau (1950, 2:831ff.) even describes a strange one portraying a group of eighteenth-century Russian orthodox missionaries.

The Northwest Coast totem pole is thus a multimnemonic object. It may simply depict the image or symbol of a person buried at the funerary site where it stands, or it may proclaim rights, delimit lands, describe collective origins, or evoke key events past and present. In each case, a range of functions is realized via representations, in the form of crests, of a series of names. Representing names as forms is common in Amerindian pictographic traditions, as we saw in the Kuna and Yekuana examples. Here again, the representation makes use of a sequential ordering and visual salience, but the ways in which salience is produced in totem poles are vastly more complex. By virtue of its specific shape, the totem pole offers an original visual solution to the problem of salience. It has often been noted that Northwest Coast iconography is based on the creation of what could be called an "alphabet of forms," in which each visual theme is meaningful and corresponds to a particular lexeme. This can give rise to a series

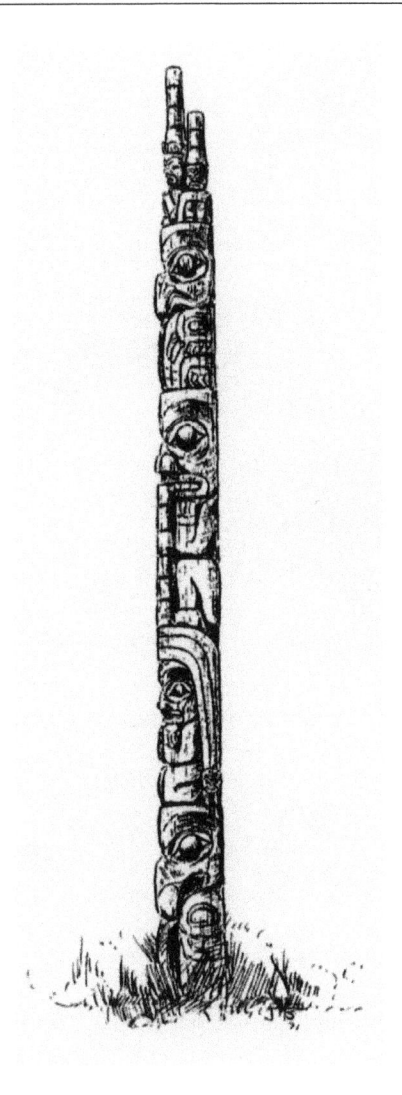

Figure 20. Haida totem pole from the village of Skedans (from Smyly and Smyly 1975).

of forms whereby the figure of an animal or human is broken down into its constituent parts: wing, fin, eye, paw, and tail (Figure 21).

An eponymous animal may thus be metonymically represented by one or more of its parts. A good example of this graphic convention is the Haida representation of the sea monster Sisiutl, whose reptilian body gives way to images of its three heads (Figure 22).

Figure 21. Some examples of the Northwest Coast "form alphabet" (from Holm 1965).

Figure 22. Representation of the sea monster Sisiutl on a Kwakwaka'wakw drum, made by Willie Seaweed, Royal British Columbia Museum, Victoria.

As Bill Holm (1965) has shown, the process by which entities and their traits (wholes and parts) are abstractly recomposed may lead to "representative" or "distributed" forms of the iconic traits used to depict various mythical creatures (Figure 23). In fact, whether the representations are "realistic" or "abstract" is less relevant in this tradition than the organization of space into a plane with a right–left opposition across a central axis. Iconic traits (or the forms of the

Figure 23. Representative space and distributive space (from Holm 1965).

visual alphabet) are then arranged in accordance with this predetermined spatial structure. This description conforms to the concepts of the "form-line" (proposed and illustrated by Holm in his work) and split representation typical of Northwest Coast imagery (Holm 1983; Holm and Reid 1975; see also Vastokas 1978, 243–59).

It is worth stressing that this aesthetic form is dynamic. Far from reducing the themes it represents to fragmentary or static representations, Northwest Coast iconography is a superb instrument for representing metamorphoses. The different iconic traits that signal the simultaneously fragmentary and emblematic presence of an animal can easily be combined, giving rise to a transformative process that constantly alters its outward appearance. This can be observed in the numerous depictions of mythical figures transforming themselves into another being, be it some fantastic sea monster, a ritual dancer, or even a shaman possessed by animal spirits. Elsewhere, I have explored the visual and mnemonic characteristics of these representations of metamorphosis as chimeras (Severi 1991), so I will not repeat it here. Suffice it to say that the anthropomorphism typical of Northwest Coast art probably owes its remarkable evocative power to the formal aspect of the sequences of transformations it depicts.

In coastal masks, paintings, and sculptures, mythical creatures (woodpecker, eagle, crow, etc.) area always represented as a specific combination of humans and animals. It follows that the types of metamorphoses described by this iconographic tradition are not composed of binary terms (animal 1 / animal 2) but always contain *three elements*: animal (in human form 1) / animal (in human form 2). Accordingly, the transformation of one animal into another always runs parallel to a latent anthropomorphism, which simultaneously orients its representational space and endows it with a graphic means of indicating salience. The human element, like a kind of musical ostinato repeating the same notes to accompany the changing melody, is always present in the background—at once revealed and dissimulated in the shift from one animal to another. This is a striking, purely visual way of signaling the logical unity of the transformative process.

The specificity of the Northwest Coast approach stands out even more clearly if it is compared to the Hopi solution to the same conundrum of how to represent complexity. Hopi ceramics make use of simple, emblematic forms that also refer to name-lexemes (cloud, lightning, serpent, and so forth), which are combined to represent, for instance, a mythical bird (Figure 24).

Figure 24. A Hopi chimera in a polychrome ceramic pot (© President and Fellows of Harvard College, Peabody Museum of Archaeology and Ethnology.)

Here too, the image's salience is reinforced, allowing it to bring together different meanings while simultaneously abetting the mental reconstruction of beings that are present only in a fragmentary form. This visual process could perhaps be compared to a puzzle or a mosaic composed of different elements, which only produce an image once they have been assembled. In the Hopi case, however, there is no latent anthropomorphism: the process is not driven by stressing the human element in the linear sequence of visual themes that are transformed into one another. Instead, it relies on the appeal to one naturally salient form (here, the bird), which then functions as an ordering principle to which heterogeneous visual themes can be attached. This process establishes what we might call a complex salience, quite different from the technique in Northwest Coast art.

To summarize, I have touched upon three graphic means of creating chimeras and thus of reinforcing the salience of an image representing a name. These complex images can either be depicted in an oriented, representative, or distributive space, or they can occupy a condensed space, which can be linear (as with the latent anthropomorphism of totem poles) or inclusive (as with Hopi ceramics, which incorporate heterogeneous elementary forms into one paradigmatic form). In Northwest Coast art, yet another form of salience can be identified. Specific substances (shells, pelts, or human hair) are incorporated into representations to reinforce the visual impact of masks and totem poles. In this way, the purely visual salience produced by the appeal to a fixed repertoire of forms is buttressed by an indexical form of salience.

In the Northwest Coast traditions, the complex trajectories of iconographic salience are paralleled by a type of logical power that is strictly limited to the transmission of names. This necessarily implies a sequential ordering of this knowledge, notably, the organized series of images in a totem pole. But this order does not constitute a principle likely to engender other forms of knowledge. It simply records the different circumstances that marked a particular social group (individual, clan, or moiety) over a given stretch of historical or mythical time. In short, although the invention of images in this tradition gave rise to an especially complex form of visual salience, the memory produced was never transformed into an organizational principle that could be applied to other domains of social life. Unlike traditions elsewhere, this was a limited, passive system for organizing the knowledge to be committed to memory. According to the analytical method outlined above, Northwest Coast iconography can be described as a system that has evolved toward remarkable degree of visual complexity, based on a progressive development of salience that is only minimally related to the establishment of order (Figure 25).

Taken as a whole, these apparently unrelated examples suggest that the development of Amerindian arts of memory is indeed modular and multilinear. It has unfolded along two principle lines: the use of taxonomic thought and the creation of a visual form of salience. Each of these levels has its own mnemonic function and endows the mnemonic tradition with a particular form of expressivity and logical power. The universe of the arts of memory is thus constituted by a defined group of mental operations.

PICTOGRAMS AND ANDEAN *KHIPUS*

What, though, of Andean *khipus*? Is there a place within this comparative schema for a technique so often compared to writing and so often described as something more than "mere arts of memory" (Urton 1998)? Can we apply the three types of relationships discussed above (mnemonic, iconographic, and

THE UNIVERSE OF THE ARTS OF MEMORY 91

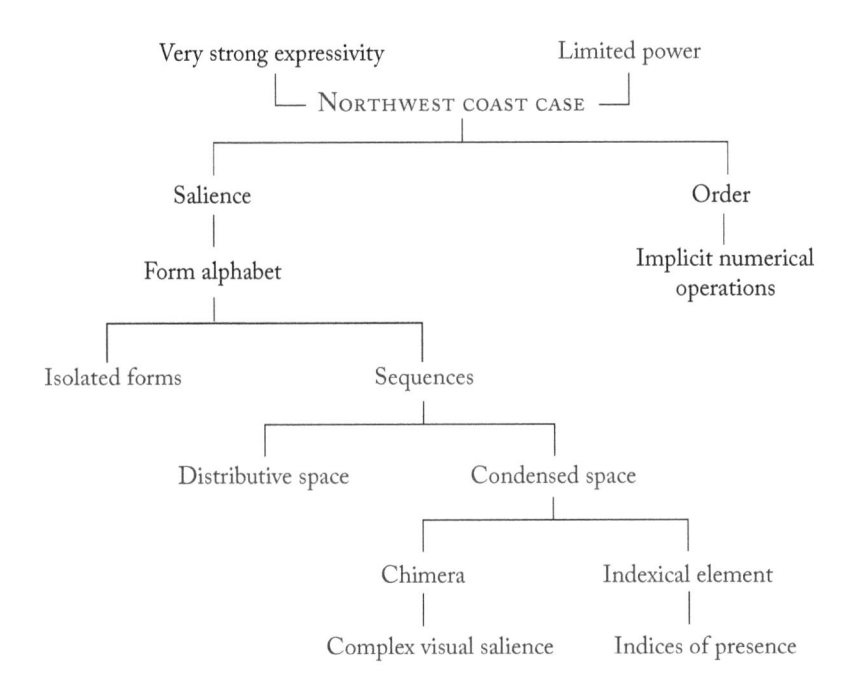

```
       Very strong expressivity              Limited power
                   └─ NORTHWEST COAST CASE ─┘
                                │
           ┌────────────────────┴─────────────────────┐
        Salience                                    Order
           │                                          │
      Form alphabet                          Implicit numerical
           │                                    operations
   ┌───────┴────────┐
Isolated forms   Sequences
                    │
            ┌───────┴────────┐
      Distributive space  Condensed space
                                │
                        ┌───────┴────────┐
                     Chimera         Indexical element
                        │                   │
              Complex visual salience   Indices of presence
```

Figure 25. Development of salience in Northwest Coast iconography.

logical) to the Incan *khipu*, a visual representation that some say was limited to numerical calculation? I would answer in the affirmative to both questions.

Let us start by outlining the logical development of the complex process of ordering that characterized this system. The technique that was historically used in *khipus* was based on a small number of organizational principles applicable to a wide range of different domains. This coherent development of the *khipus'* taxonomic principle led to the creation of a system endowed with a high degree of logical power. Visual salience, however, was limited to marking a point (the knot) in a linear sequence (the cord), albeit with a certain scope for variation. In this context, the ordering of knowledge to be represented most likely evolved toward a system that distinguished between an idea of pure quantity (based on a decimal system and applicable to a wide range of categories: people, objects, units of time or space, etc.) and the equally numerical concept of the ordinal series. The latter category was then divided into a numerical series and a linguistic one. The linguistic series was further divided into toponyms and anthroponyms, while the numerical series made it possible to represent a series of series and to organize them along decimal lines (Figure 26).

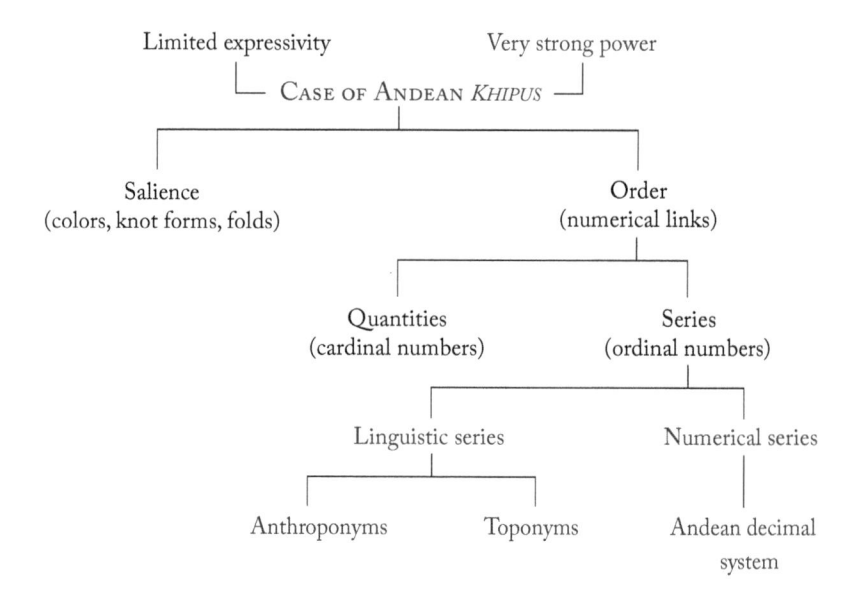

```
                  Limited expressivity        Very strong power
                         └─ CASE OF ANDEAN KHIPUS ─┘
                                    │
          ┌─────────────────────────┴─────────────────────────┐
       Salience                                            Order
  (colors, knot forms, folds)                         (numerical links)
                                                             │
                                          ┌──────────────────┴──────────────────┐
                                      Quantities                             Series
                                  (cardinal numbers)                   (ordinal numbers)
                                                                             │
                                                            ┌────────────────┴────────────────┐
                                                     Linguistic series                 Numerical series
                                                    ┌────────┴────────┐                      │
                                              Anthroponyms        Toponyms             Andean decimal
                                                                                            system
```

Figure 26. Development of order in Andean *khipus*.

Seen from this perspective, the *khipus* can be described as an art of memory possessed of a rudimentary form of visual salience and a highly complex ordering of representable knowledge. In other words, the Andean system (considered in terms of mnemonic, iconographic, and logical relations) appears to have followed the opposite path as that taken on the Northwest Coast and, indeed, in Amerindian pictographic systems more generally. My analysis focuses exclusively on those groups of relations that rely on a certain number of logical elements and mental operations. What matters is the logical universe implied by the system, not its visual manifestations. As mentioned earlier, pictographic traditions may contain implicit numerical operations, notably ordinal ones (a series or a series of series). Andean memorization techniques started with a standard task (for instance, by transcribing a series of proper names) and then distinguished between numbers and names, and between cardinals and ordinals. This allowed a further distinction to be made between qualitative categories (meant to be named) and a series of numbers produced by using a decimal base. In an essay on the "social life of numbers," Gary Urton and Primitivo Nina Llanos (1997, 173–208) convincingly demonstrate that the Andean decimal system was the result of the interaction between two organizing principles related to Andean mathematical thought: on the one hand, an organizational system based on the principle of counting from one to five, modeled on the five fingers of the hand; on the other, the systematic union of a series of opposing terms (or moieties) that underpinned Andean dualism and gave rise to what they call an "arithmetic of rectification." This does not imply that *khipus* are radically different from pictograms: the act of enumeration is often a constitutive mental operation in the latter memorization techniques as well. Without the creation of a relatively rigorous linear series, where each element has a set place within an ordinal series, Amerindian pictography would be quite impossible (whether it concerned shamanic chants, calendars, or pictorial autobiographies). The narrative form taken by these pictographic traditions should not blind us to the fact that all pictograms rely on certain arithmetic or geometrical relationships. Examples of this range from the relations of inclusion, inversion, or a shift in scale (a type of geometric commutation) present in Yekuana weaving, to the precisely calibrated, symmetrical, and geometrically oriented spaces of Northwest Coast art. What makes *khipus* stand out is thus not the mere existence of enumeration or the mathematical expression of an equilibrium among components but, rather, the emphasis they placed on the power conferred upon mathematical calculation and its application to an increasing number of potential objects. This is testimony to the complex and elegant elaboration of mathematical thought at work in the art of memory embodied by *khipus*.

In this sense, Andean *khipus* (which are logically powerful but expressively weak) and Amerindian pictograms (which are highly expressive but capable of representing only a limited range of knowledge) constitute opposite logical poles of the vast spectrum of Amerindian arts of memory. However, we must not be tempted into constructing static sets of oppositions. A tradition largely based on the ordering of knowledge always retains some latent salience, while a tradition that stresses salience can still develop implicit numerical or geometrical operations, even quite complex ones.

Armed with these new hypotheses, let us consider the intellectual battle regarding the logical nature of Andean *khipus*. Seen from a purely numerical perspective, the *khipus* recorded at least two distinct types of knowledge: a series of numbers and a series of narratives. Roughly a third of extant *khipus* (some six hundred) display no mathematical regularity. Precisely how this numerically based system was used to memorize narratives remains unclear and has provoked much debate. If we consider the work of Polish historian Jan Szeminski and place it in the broader context of the unitary system outlined above, a solution to the problem may emerge. Szeminski recently published an analysis of a long-neglected text ("Tome II" of Fernando de Montesinos's *Ophir de España*), which reveals certain aspects of the Andean oral tradition (Szeminski 2006). His analysis identifies a series of key elements, making it possible to rethink the wider chronology of the region during the Inca and pre-Inca periods. These are crucial discoveries. His textual archaeology (amounting to a codicology) evaluates and decrypts, layer by layer, the rich ensemble of indigenous exegeses contained in Montesinos's text, leading him to reconstruct a series of "narrative facts." These shed new light on whole swathes of Andean history. Szeminski's work is of vital interest to anthropologists, since he illuminates (almost unwittingly) certain formal aspects of the *oral tradition*, the last vestiges of which are found in Montesinos's manuscript. Szeminski progressively identifies the indigenous glosses and commentary that accompanied these narrative facts, discovering in the process a *mnemonically oriented means of organizing traditional knowledge*. This process of organization, evident in the Montesinos's "list of One Hundred Kings," consisted of creating a list of the proper names of kings, each of which was progressively assigned a corresponding eponym or title. For instance, the name of the king Amawte was associated with the eponym "the scholar or wise man," and his successor was given the eponym "the great plowman" (Szeminski 2006, 312). To this list of names and eponyms was attached a further list of glosses or commentaries, brief indigenous texts that Szeminski dubs "scholarly amplifications." In short, behind Szeminski's "formalist" reading of the text lies a tradition comprised of elements organized in the typically Amerindian parallelistic fashion, whereby a series of lists of names is arranged in a specific order and serves as the backbone of an oral narrative.

If we break with the futile distinction between iconography and orality in the Andean tradition and incorporate the use of knotted cords into Szeminski's model, it can help us elucidate how these *khipus* might have encoded certain texts, which were recited according to a calendrical sequence. I suggest that we abandon the term *narrative* for these mnemonically oriented lists of names. Narrative was only one of several different means of organizing knowledge in the Andean tradition. When the narrative mode was present, it was guided by a systematic means of organizing knowledge, more reliant on the association and clustering of lists of names (serving as *aides-memoire*) than on a story-like structure. It appears that, as elsewhere in the Americas, the Andean process of mnemonic codification was based on the association of three distinct classes of elements: proper names (some of which were independently meaningful); an eponym or title (e.g., "the scholar," "the great plowman"); and a gloss or commentary. If this is true, then we can imagine a corresponding form of graphic representation (perhaps capable of developing further degrees of complexity) composed of three differently colored cords for each of the classes of elements: recording proper names, eponyms, and glosses (or even events calling them to mind: famine, revolt, invasion, etc.). Approached from this angle, Szeminski's work allows us to recreate the *form* of memorizable knowledge in the Andean system, and, in turn, to understand how sequences of knots and cords served to annotate texts.

We can thus formulate the hypothesis that the Andean arts of memory (which also made use of pictographic representations) were characterized not by the existence of two radically different systems (pictographic and numeric) but, rather, by the flexible use of one unified system that could stress either expressivity or logical power. Within this variable system, where cords were normally used to record large sets of numbers (hence its power), expressivity could be generated by linking glosses to the annotations on a limited universe of proper names. Certain latent aspects of the *khipu* system could be used to simulate the logical properties of pictographic mnemonics. Seen from this perspective, *khipu* knotted strings are the very illustration of a logical possibility ruled out by most specialists: that of a *complex* art of memory, wherein ordered sequences are linked to oral glosses or commentaries that are mentally organized along strictly defined lines and, furthermore, necessarily associated with an iconic marker. This iconic marker might take the form of an object fixed inside a fold or a knot (as in the huge *khipu* analyzed by Frank Salomon),[7] or it might be a basic geometrical form (as with the *tocapu* studied by Cummins 1994), or, again, it might simply be a distinctively colored cord.

This reconstruction (which fits with theories proposed by Urton [2003] and Martti Pärssinen and Jukka Kiviharju [2004] regarding other documents) allows us to identify a characteristic element of pictography within the *khipu* system—to wit, the fact that memorization (or better, the creation of a mnemonic relation) necessarily implies the modular organization of the knowledge it represents. The parallelism typical of both systems is a clear example of such modular organization. In this way, the underlying unity of *khipus* and Amerindian pictography becomes apparent. The *khipus* offer an original and precise means of associating their constitutive logical elements (a list of names,

---

7. I refer to the field studies and remarkable analyses of Frank Salomon (2001, 2002, 2006).

variations translated graphically, and oral commentaries) as well as the constitutive dualisms that underpin many forms of Amerindian arts of memory (order and salience, expressivity and power, encoding and evocation). Andean *khipus* thus possess all the key elements of Amerindian arts of memory.

It is naturally a task for the Andean specialists to decide how to interpret the *khipus* that have as-yet-undeciphered meanings, their accompanying texts (some of which we now have access to, thanks to the work of Pärssinen and Kiviharju [2004]), and the sundry graphic designs, pictograms, *keros,* and *tocapu* that, in all likelihood, must have been associated with them. This essay has simply endeavored to suggest a possible course between the twin rocks of "social" writing and "individual and arbitrary" mnemonic devices that have bedeviled the debate on Incan *khipus* and to open up a third way, founded on the hypothesis that they share the same internal logical structure as Amerindian pictography and, thus, rely on the same mental operations. Seen from this angle, *khipus* are neither a form of writing nor mere mnemonic devices but, by virtue of both their common traits and significant differences, a coherent variant within the wider conceptual universe of Amerindian arts of memory. This universe is structured by a particular set of mental operations, which guides a form of thought that finds its expression both in images and in the mental space it occupies. In the Americas, as elsewhere, the study of processes of memorization is, by its very nature, a study of thought in action.

PRINCIPLES OF MNEMONIC ENCODING

In the first part of this chapter, I raised three issues to interrogate: the problem of opposing written and oral traditions, an approach that smuggles in a tacit notion of mnemonic techniques based simply on individual memory; the question of comparing the *artes memorandi* in the West with the arts of memory in other cultures; and the matter of situating mnemonic arts within the Western tradition itself, dominated as it is by writing. The analyses I have proposed make it possible to now respond to the first two issues. Pictograms (and perhaps also *khipus*) are both iconographic *and* oral, and the function of images in the memorization process is clearly identifiable: the images are not mere illustrations of words. To the contrary, the image plays a central role in the construction of mnemonic relations between certain visual themes and particular words, which, in turn, play a key role in memorizing texts. From this new perspective, pictograms belong to a realm of traditional, socialized, and identified practices that are used as mental artifacts. They are thus part and parcel of a mental universe that also encompasses a range of practices that the Western world has developed and deployed in culturally distinctive ways and according to its particular history.

The study of different forms of mnemonic imagery enables us to refine the distinction introduced in Chapter Two between iconography and play, and to formulate a concept of the universe of an iconographic tradition. In the Amerindian world, depending on the geographic area where they appear, pictographic practices, like *khipus*, vary in appearance, function, and connections to oral traditions. They also entail specific ensembles of mental operations within each tradition and cultural area. Almost everywhere, pictography applies the principle of translation to variants within parallelistic texts, which implies a specific association between the memory of words and the memory of images. This technique always requires three principles for the game of iconographic memory, even if, depending on the particular mode, an equilibrium must always be established between salience and order in the way signs are used. The operations of mnemonic encoding require, first, that order be imposed on the mnemonic process and, second, that imagination be exercised to enable the recall of memories through evocation. Finally, in terms of logic, the system as a whole always implies an equilibrium between expressivity and logical power. Deploying the notion of games may thus lead to identifying a universe (in the sense of a family of mental operations) that presides over the exercise of these iconographic traditions, some of which have been identified in this chapter. This makes it possible to grasp the extent and consequences of the concept of iconographic games within an iconographic tradition considered as a whole.

The mnemonic image is not the only realm where image games can be identified beyond the Western world and its particular game of art. In some situations, the image, without playing a directly mnemonic role, appears in a different light as an incarnation of a living being. Employing the method used in this chapter, how should the universe of this type of iconography be described? What kind of game results in attributing a form of life to an artifact and establishing a link of belief between the image and the spectator? These are the questions I will approach in the next chapter by examining a classic issue in the anthropology of belief: the exercise of authority.

CHAPTER FOUR

Authorless Authority
Forms of Authority in Oral Traditions

When the Florentines conquered the city of Pisa in 1406, one of their most prized war trophies was a book: a copy of the Justinian Code drawn up in the early part of the sixth century and formerly preserved in Constantinople. Previously known as the *Littera Pisana*, it was swiftly rebaptized *Littera Florentina* and transported to Florence, where it was housed in the Palazzo dei Priori and placed in a tabernacle as if it were some sacred relic. On the rare occasions when it was displayed in public, the book was placed on a table and surrounded by candles. In a rite dating back to antiquity, the monks and magistrates responsible for the codex bowed when coming into its presence. This ritual homage, so evocatively described by Settis (1986, 411–12), sums up a number of traits that together constitute the core identity of European notions of authority. Whether it is defined as the "right to command or influence others" or as a form of "power that endows with influence and the capacity to convince" (Lalande 1926), the European idea of authority is intimately tied up with writing. As Jan Assmann (1992) has shown, the practices of authorizing and memorizing the traditions of antiquity were a result of the canonization of a corpus of texts, which were attributed with a veracity once and for all. Thus, the act of wielding authority (whether it is religious, legal, philosophical, or literary) is necessarily linked to the figure of an author. The origins of an intellectual "tradition" are always traced back to the oeuvre of an author, from whom it derives its authority, whence such formulas as the "Platonic," "Homeric," or "Marxist" traditions. The canonization of a corpus of texts produces a *principle* of recognized veracity, which finds its *source* in a real or mythical author. Whether the author occupies the role of ancestor vis-à-vis the tradition (think of Solon and Greek law) or wields a contextually specific form of authority guaranteed by that tradition, the relationship between a corpus of canonized texts understood as a principle and an author as a source of authority remains fundamentally unchanged. Following Michel Foucault ([1969] 1981), we could submit the notion of the author to critical scrutiny, reducing it to a mere organizing function and separating it off from everyday speech where, as Foucault claimed, there is no space for the figure of the author. Or, along with Florence Dupont, we could stress that the "author-function" is not always coterminous with the person who actually composed the text (Dupont in Chartier and Calame 2004, 171–89).[1] Or yet again, we could argue that the term *author* refers to a specific utterance position, to a "being of thought" (Foucault [1969] 1981) rather than to an actual individual. Whichever approach we take, the fact remains that the Western concept of authorship depends on the relationship between a textual principle and its real or mythical source. Within our tradition, it is inconceivable that an authority principle reposes on something other than a canonized text or that authority lacks a clearly identifiable source. *Nulla auctoritas sine auctore*, one might say.

What, though, of so-called societies "without writing," lacking any form of canonical texts? How is authority born of a tradition wielded in such contexts? When traditional knowledge is purely oral and the idea of the author absent, how should we conceive of the principle and the source of authority arising from tradition, not just from political power? Must societies "without writing" therefore be "acephalous," as we were wont to say in the nineteenth century? Is their traditional knowledge condemned, as Jack Goody (1968, 1987) sometimes claims, to a state of perpetual disorder and deprived of any overarching structure?

---

1. In an article warning against the dangers of appealing to Latin etymologies, Florence Dupont (2004) points out that the Latin term *auctor* ("author") was only used to describe a historian and only rarely applied to poets. And even then, the historian in question must have founded a tradition (like Tacitus, for instance). In this sense, an author was, above all, a person who established a tradition and not (as in contemporary usage) somebody who created a "literary work." Moreover, the author-function could also be decoupled from the person who actually wrote the text. In such cases (Dupont takes Virgil as an example) the true "author" was not the person who composed the text but the one who commissioned it.

It is right to be suspicious of negative definitions. Societies without writing do not constitute some homogeneous bloc in stark contrast to an equivalent bloc of literate societies. They are, instead, highly diverse, and so our analysis must work up from specific case studies. The approach I adopt here cannot, however, be defined simply in terms of its empiricism. The degree of abstraction suitable to the concepts at play is also pertinent. Although I am careful to avoid the ethnocentric extension of Western concepts to other situations, I nonetheless endeavor to identify higher-level abstractions that can help us to think through a range of authoritative traditions. Thus, I do not seek to identify "authors" and "processes of canonization" within oral traditions but, instead, focus on the unpredictable forms that the *principles* and *sources* of authority can assume in such contexts.

EVIDENTIALS, PRAGMATICS, AND ARTIFACTS

Let us begin by underscoring the fact that the act of endowing a proposition with authority by describing its source is not restricted to written traditions. Such an evaluation of a proposition's truth-value may be a simple by-product of the use of language long before a particular knowledge set is instituted as a tradition. For instance, a number of Amerindian languages use a set of lexicalized particles, called epistemic or evidential classifiers, which have the role of explicitly identifying the nature of the experience that constitutes the source of a proposition and endows it with a particular truth-value (Aikhenvald and Dixon 2003; Déléage 2005, 2009, n.d.; Landaburu and Guentchéva 2002). Thus, among the Sharanahua (Déléage 2005, 45–47), the classifier *–quia* denotes a belief derived from hearsay, whereas *–quin* denotes knowledge derived from direct experience, and *–quian* direct knowledge (derived, for instance, from dreams) that cannot be shared with one's interlocutor. The use of evidential suffixes corresponds to what Jon Landaburu (2007, 23–48) calls the "grammatical management of truth." In other words, the nature of the source of authority is fully lexicalized and constitutes an integral part of the semantic structure of these languages.

This evaluation of the cognitive value of an utterance can also be communicated pragmatically by clearly defining the status of the utterer and the social conditions of the speech act. Authority, understood as a process leading to the emergence of a belief, may be the product of certain types of utterances or speech acts based on a definition of the special nature of an utterer. This is true of many Amerindian shamanic traditions, where the authority function (which is entirely dependent on ritual activity) emerges via the definition of a complex shaman-singer identity, itself based on the production of a series of contradictory acts of ontological identification. The utterer, who may use abstruse forms of communication (secret languages, esoteric metaphor, onomatopoeia, and voiced brawl breathing), is seen as simultaneously belonging to several different ontological schemata. When he engages in ritual speech, the shaman is both human *and* animal, animal *and* plant, and so on. These special forms of utterance, unusual and often restricted to ritual contexts, nonetheless reveal an attribution of authority that is always focused on a human being. Although he is never the author of his own chants (even improvised songs are the handiwork of supernatural beings), the Amerindian shaman is still, on a more prosaic level, a human utterer. It is only his ritual function that lifts his speech out of the realm of the ordinary and endows it with a particular pragmatic status (Severi [2007] 2015, 207–44).

In this chapter, I focus on another instance of defining an authority that is authorless and independent of writing. This concerns situations in which the right to wield an authority function is not assigned to a human being (however exceptionally defined) but is *transferred to an artifact.* In such cases, the object, by virtue of its mere presence, exercises an authority function, setting in motion a process that leads to establishing a belief. In such cases, what renders the utterances of tradition into something obligatory is the product of quite a different constellation of relations from the one described above. Traditional knowledge relies on the anonymous and nonhuman nature of the authority that lies at its source. In fact, the mere act of transferring authority to an artifact is insufficient to guarantee either its independence from human actors or its anonymity.

Western tradition provides us with clear examples of situations in which authority is transferred to an artifact. Classical Roman law did not distinguish between people and objects when it came to the attribution of guilt and the act of sentencing. Statues of the Emperor, for instance, by virtue of their mere presence, were able to legitimize or enforce contracts (Bettini 1992, 162). Several examples were recorded of statues being prosecuted, as when the Romans indicted a statue of the Greek general Philopemon, whose defense was entrusted to Polybus (De Angelis 2007, 37–56). In Byzantium, the word *legimus*, used to sign official documents, indicated the emperor's direct intervention in a world where scarcely anybody still spoke Latin (Settis 1986, 411). This almost incomprehensible word served as an index of the emperor's presence and authority. Closer to home, as Leah Dickerman (2001) has shown, the portrait of Lenin was used in the Soviet Union as an icon and sometimes even an index of his authority.

In all these cases, however, the authority thus indexed has already been defined. The foundational schema upon which the authority rests, which I have identified in the relationship between a text understood as a principle and the figure of the author as a source of authority, continues to function. The legitimizing principle remains fixed to a corpus of texts rather than being transferred to an object. Although the source of authority is indexed or replaced by an artifact, it is not identified with it. What interests us here, by contrast, are situations in which authority is uncoupled from any human source or avatar. Unlike the Roman and Byzantine examples mentioned above, such situations are not simply a reflection of, a response to, or the ghost of some prior coupling of a person and an authority. When celebrating a ritual or uttering a mythical chant, objects themselves can be made to bear full responsibility for the wielding of authority. In such cases, the object is *anonymous* and its identity is opaque, mysterious, or indecipherable insofar as it is not a reflection of any human identity, neither that of any participant in the ritual nor that of its actual "author" (that is, maker). In other words, the artifact has no external referent: it contains its own principle of legitimacy. As mentioned above, the source of a tradition's authority can be expressed pragmatically by endowing the utterer with a particular status. As regards the ritual use of artifacts, this status amounts to the attribution of an extremely minimal (indeed, almost null) definition of identity to the objects in question. Accordingly, the object is associated with a form of intentionality seen as *independent* of any human will and, in certain cases, as uncontrollable.

THE FANG *MVET*: SINGER, SONG, AND HARP

One fine example of this is the oral tradition of the Fang of Cameroon, analyzed by Pascal Boyer (1988). This tradition comprises a vast repertoire of songs that recount, somewhat like a saga, the shifting relations of conflict and alliance that prevailed between three tribes of giants when the world was still young. The poets tell of the adventures of the scions of Yo (ancestors of the Fang and of all humans), the people of Oku (mythical but mortal beings from far-off lands), and the Engong (a race of immortals). The two mythical tribes who do not possess the secret of immortality wage terrible wars against the others, generally allying themselves with their ancestors and ghosts. These songs, called *mvet*, are sung by poet-musicians who also play a harp-like instrument (see Figure 27).[2]

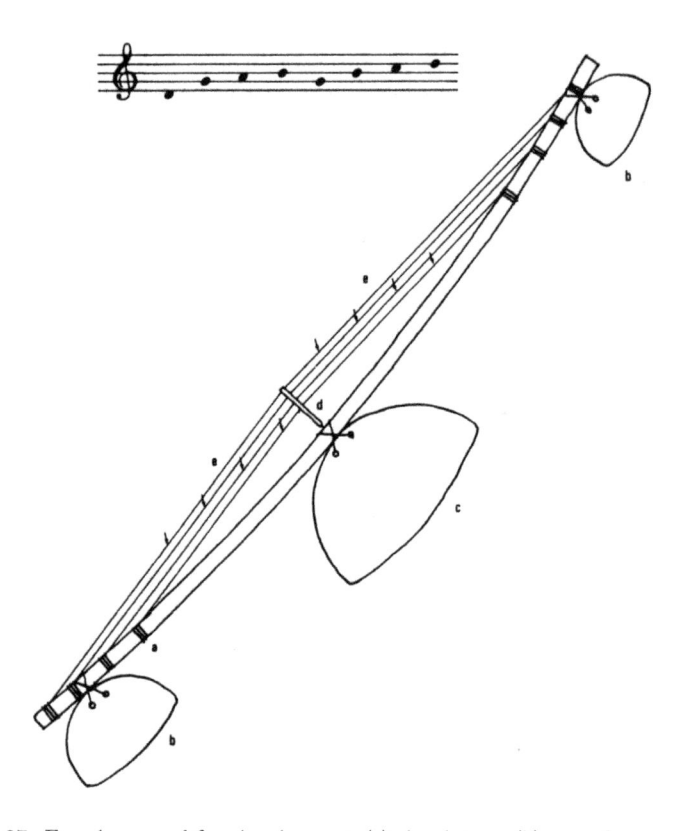

Figure 27. Fang harp used for play the mvet: (a) chord rings; (b) secondary resonators; (c) main resonator; (d) bridge; (e) strings. Image from Boyer (1988). Reproduced with the permission of Société d'ethnologie, Paris.

---

2. The *mvet* is actually a stick-zither made from a branch of raffia palm, with strings made from its bark. Four thin slivers of bark are attached to the branch at different points and placed under tension using a small stick planted halfway along its length. This stick is notched at four separate points, then each string is fitted into a notch. The strings are divided in two, giving each *mvet* eight strings in total (Nguema 1972, 10).

This song cycle boasts a richness of both style and theme that makes it one of the jewels of traditional African literature. Some of its chants are highly elaborate. We only need to look at the four-hundred-page transcription of the saga sung by Zwè Nguema (1972) in the 1960s. This is not the place to detail the wealth of this tradition, with its grand themes, genres, and schools. Instead, I want to concentrate on only one key aspect: the way in which this traditional knowledge is transmitted or handed down and, more particularly, on the relationship that is established between singer, song, and instrument in the act of utterance.

At first glance, the manner of learning these epic songs seems to follow a fairly standard pattern. Each singer is situated in a chain of transmission composed of named links going back from master to master until they reach a named but less clearly identifiable mythical character supposed to have invented the tradition. The "real" learning of the song cannot, however, be reduced to a mere process of musical or literary internalization and reproduction of past models. To learn a *mvet*, a student must acquire an individual "voice" by establishing a specific relationship with a supernatural being. Boyer's research found that, to become a *mvet* singer, the student must identify with, or, rather, *acquire*, a particular identity derived from an indeterminate or paradoxical principle, of which no one knows its true nature. In Fang terms, one must "possess" an *evur* or a *byang*. These ambiguous concepts refer to supernatural substances supposed to lodge in the "pit of the stomach" of an initiated singer. The term *evur*, normally used to refer to a "magical force" related to the ability to bewitch, here describes a principle of knowledge. To play a *mvet*, the singer needs *evur*. But this in itself is not enough: he must also have "received *byang*" by undergoing a specific type of initiation (Boyer 1988, 63). The *mvet* itself, as a "sung epic," is understood in terms of these substances, which represent in mysterious but physical form the song's veracity, efficacy, and faithfulness to a tradition.

A *mvet* is thus, by definition, "bewitching" and "a product of secret initiation." But the relationship between knowledge of a song and the initiation process does not stop there. Boyer's interlocutors repeatedly stressed that, to sing well, the singer must "really have eaten the *mvet*." This alimentary metaphor condenses a whole network of relationships that the poet-musician must establish with spirits whose voices find expression in the *mvet*. What is striking in the transcript of Nguema's *mvet* are the "interludes" where, little by little, the singer sketches out the history of his initiation. He begins by stating that "the *mvet* loved him [the singer] like a woman" and "in the end, the *mvet* loved him the ways girls love boys" (Nguema 1972, 77). The poet then repeatedly asserts that this contact with the words of the ancestors will "make him sick" and even die: "The village singer is killed by the melodies of *mvet*" (1972, 55), he sings. "I am dying for the harp. Why? I, Zwè Nguema, am dying by *mvet*" (1972, 77). Ethnographers have explained this as an allusion to the risks of initiation (Boyer 1988; Nguema 1972, 230); the dangers of revealing initiatory secrets are indeed mentioned several times in the transcription ("I run the danger of revealing the relic of *mvet*" [Nguema 1972, 231]). According to several native exegetes, this rather poorly guarded secret may involve the symbolic sacrifice of a close relative of the singer, such as his wife or brother (1972, 233ff.). Whether or not this is true, it is clear that this "death by *mvet*" transforms the singer's identity. In the interludes accompanying Nguema's account, the "dead" poet is first transformed into a series of songbirds. Later, this contact with the *mvet* saps the poet's identity, transforming him into nothing more than an instrument for the spirits' voices. The acquisition by initiation of the *mvet*'s veracity and efficacy of utterance coincides with the annihilation of the singer's human identity. Various statements by singers (appearing in Nguema's transcription and in Boyer's ethnography) support this interpretation. Singers declare that they are "merely a bar of a xylophone" or "nothing more than the string of a harp." After the initiation, the singer and his instrument, his speech, and his voice, as well as the song itself have become one composite being composed of artifact, utterance, and utterer. The three are collectively known as "*mvet*." Once these different identities have been merged into one, the initiate is defined by his dependence on a force that remains fundamentally alien to him. As one *mvet* singer expressed it to Boyer, "When I sing the *mvet*, what I say is a dream, I cannot recall it"; in the words of another, "it is the *mvet* speaking; these things are not in my heart" (Boyer 1988, 27). The veracity and the efficacy of the *mvet* are not expressed through the person of the singer or his knowledge of the song's words (which constantly change) but, rather, by the nature of the artifact he wields: his harp. It is only by analyzing the artifact that we can understand the relationship between the authority that founds the tradition (represented by the hidden voice of the spirits) and its interpreter.

When the latter defines himself as an instrument's "bar" or "key," he refers not only to the structure of the instrument but also to a specific instrumental technique. Singers often describe one particular stage in the learning process as crucial, which is worth examining in detail. First, the young Fang musician must slowly and painstakingly learn several melodic lines by heart. Once a certain degree of difficulty is reached (for instance, in simultaneously playing two lines with different rhythmic structures, one binary, the other ternary), the apprentice must make use of a different form of knowledge acquisition, which cognitive psychologists call "chunking." The young musician will have a curious experience: rather than gradually learning the lines, he struggles at length and seemingly fruitlessly to acquire them until, one day, the ability to do so appears to materialize out of nowhere. He just "knows" how to play them. Indeed, he will find that he is almost incapable of playing the two lines separately. His pride at mastering the difficult sequence is tempered by the awareness that some aspect of the music's organization escapes him. For Fang musicians, it is precisely this type of experience that brings out the "hidden voices" of the spirits. Let us examine more closely this musical form of the *mvet* spirit "presence." The following are two transcriptions of a musical extract transcribed and analyzed by Boyer (see Figure 28).

Figure 28. Two rhythmic and melodic sequences in *mvet* music from Boyer (1988, 121). Reproduced with the permission of Société d'ethnologie, Paris.

Each line is assigned to one of the player's hands: the left hand plays triplets, while the right plays a highly regular duplet. When the two hands play together, the two different rhythms intersect with one another, producing a surprising melodic fragment. If we play the two lines on a piano, it becomes clear after a few repetitions (that is, once a distinction between the acoustic shape and the background is established) that what we actually hear in the foreground is a succession of fragments made up of a repeating demitone (here, B C B C B C, etc.). The result is an extremely simple melody that emerges out of the combination of the different rhythms. These two rhythms create what is called a "resultant rhythm." This is analogous to what is produced when two tambourines play slightly different sequences. In such cases, *another* musical cell is produced—"one which is clearly recognizable, but which is played by no musician, since it is the result of the combination itself" (Boyer 1988, 121). Of the sequence played on the Fang harp, Boyer says,

> a similar effect is created. The instrumentalists' hands appear to be operating independently of one another, but the combination of the two produces a resultant melody that the instrumentalist has not played and which it seems that he cannot play, except by repeating the whole sequence. (Boyer 1988, 121)

Although this melody is, properly speaking, the outcome of an interaction between two separate melodic lines, it seems to have its own independent, autonomous existence.

Theorists of Western music call this phenomenon (which has a rhythmic and a melodic aspect) a "resultant melody." Its technical aspects do not concern us here. Suffice it to note that this *mvet* fragment embodies the vital shift from a sound intentionally produced by an instrumentalist's playing of the strings and the emergence of a "voice" that is not entirely his own. The *hidden voice* that comes of this is made up of traits belonging to prior melodic lines; these lines occupy the musician's attention both during the learning process and later, when he plays them. Through a reversal of figure and ground—which we see in numerous other contexts discussed in this book (see also the examples analyzed by Wagner 1986, 2012)—the third voice underscores a convergence between the two lines that otherwise tends to remain latent or implicit. In other words, this musical cell is not the intentional result of the playing of the melodies but, rather, seems to emerge from the instrument itself. The artifact thereby acquires its own voice—one independent of the poet. For Fang musicians, it is this voice that expresses the source of the tradition and, thus, the authority on which it is founded. Although the Fang interpret this spirit voice as the sound image of the spirits' presence, they are aware that it is the product of a particular technique;

the musicians interviewed by Boyer were in no doubt about this. Nonetheless, this voice—the voice of the tradition that it authorizes—is seen as both hidden and anonymous. The identity of "those who sing," which is independent of the player, remains somehow ungraspable and vaguely menacing. It is this paradoxical definition of identity—at once "evident," in the sense of being a bearer of "truth," and conceptually undecidable—that transforms the artifact into a source of authority.

At this juncture, it is perhaps helpful to explain the nature of this authority-wielding process in an "oral" tradition by means of an analogy. Elsewhere (in Chapter Eight and in Severi [2007] 2015), I analyze the role played by particular sculptural or pictorial visual representations—which I call "chimera objects"—in the transmission of traditional knowledge. These objects are typically composed of fragments drawn from representations of different beings. Their double or multiple reference to representations of different beings in a single image produces a form of presence that is not physically inscribed on the surface of an object or in its sculpted form but, rather, one that emerges out of their conjunction. We see this quite clearly in the following Haida mask (Figure 29).

Figure 29. A Haida mask, American Museum of Natural History, New York.

This image is reduced to a handful of traits, thereby simplifying its structure and causing the observer to perceive a representation that mobilizes both the figure of a crow and a human face. This type of chimera is a set of visual indices wherein what the viewer is given to see necessarily calls to mind an implicit presence, something invisible that is produced entirely from indices present in mental space. A cognitive principle underlies the structure of these chimeric images: the condensation of the image into a handful of essential traits relies on viewers' projective interpretation of the final form, filling in the gaps. This principle, which confers a particular salience on the image, can play a crucial role in social practices linked to memorization and the evocation of traditional knowledge. As we saw in the preceding chapter (Chapter Three), the visual salience of these images becomes a mnemonic salience, having the capacity to embody and preserve meaning. This process can be described as the intensification of the cognitive efficacy of an image that, via an act of visual inference, sets its missing parts to work. Such a process is widespread, so it would be easy to mention other examples of this kind of representation.[3]

If we return to the Fang harp, we could interpret this instrument, with its independent voice that endows it with a life of its own, as an *acoustic chimera*. Its voice is composed entirely of implicit elements of the "real" sound, and its existence depends on an act of mental reconstruction, expressed by a reorientation of aural perception. Here, as with visual chimeras, an indirect form of presence is produced, emerging from the playing of *other* melodic lines. This model of a living artifact allows us to look behind the object and glimpse the shape of an authorless voice. It can be considered an extension of the model of chimeric representation, since it produces an analogous form of salience but, this time, in the aural domain.

The notion of an acoustic chimera can be pushed further; it may guide us toward understanding other forms of exercising authority that have hitherto been opaque. In his analysis of the *mvet* tradition, Boyer tends to stress its paradoxical

---

3. If we restrict ourselves to West Africa, it is worth mentioning Frederick Lamp's (1996) analyses of ritual masks among the Baga Mandori of Guinea and, in particular, of the Tongkomba-Bana dyad. The Tongkomba incorporates elements of both land and sea, while the Bana has "a long, horizontal headdress composed of the jaw of a crocodile, the face of a human being (with Baga scarification marks and a woman's elaborately braided coiffure), the horns of an antelope, the body of a serpent, and the tail of a chameleon" (Lamp 1996, 144ff.). These characters are developed in what can only be described as a chimeric dance, when the dancer must imitate each of these animals in turn (1996, 148).

aspects, its lack of rational determination, and even its use of "empty concepts" (Boyer 1993, 121). For him, "these sagas are typically made up of confused and contradictory statements that yield no clear propositions" (1988, 17). If it is possible to speak of Fang harps as authorizing a tradition, it is because "particular objects or, rather, the specific uses to which they are put, display qualities that catch the attention in such a way that the imagination can unfold itself through a process of indefinite repetition" (1988, 40).

I would argue, instead, that we should focus our attention on the forms of the enunciation of truth with which this tradition confronts us. To this end, we must understand not merely their content but also some more abstract and perhaps generalizable traits. In the Fang case, we can identify three formal traits:

1. A series of identifications that leads to the creation of a composite being, the *mvet*, which comprises a chant, an instrument, and a singer
2. A weak definition of the identity of the source of traditional truth (a voice without a discernible author, in the sense that it is associated with an identity that is almost null)
3. The transfer of the effect of authority onto an artifact, to which a principle of autonomy is attributed by imputing subjectivity to it.

We can use this initial model to explore further examples of attributing ritual artifacts with the capacity for a type of action, rather than speech, that authorizes a tradition. In a more complex context of exercising authority over tradition, we can explore an analogous definition of the ritual identity of an artifact, especially regarding the element of apparent autonomy.

RETHINKING THE WEST AFRICAN NAIL FIGURE

In *Art and Agency* (1998), Alfred Gell made the point that the artifacts in our museums we label "primitive art" are not merely instances of a universal instinct underlying artistic creativity. Besides being the products of the particular aesthetic of the societies in which they were conceived, many of these objects were also originally treated as living beings, notably within sequences of ritual actions. Through the process that Gell calls an "abduction of subjectivity," these artifacts are endowed with their own agency. As such, they are able to become the means of expressing specific networks ("skeins") of relationships among members of society. Whether it is a question of performing a sacrifice, marking out a symbolic space, or correctly accomplishing a rite of passage, "living" artifacts play a crucial role. In such contexts, the authority wielded by an artifact in a "textless and authorless" tradition, such as that of the Fang, can only be understood as a specific expression of autonomous agency. To better understand how this attribution of the capacity for action to an artifact operates, let us reexamine one of Gell's examples of ritual agency: the use of *nkisi* nail figures (Figure 30).

Nkisi (or *nkisi nkondi*) is a term used for nail figures (sometimes called "nail fetishes") that were used throughout a wide swath of West Africa, comparable in scope to the *mvet* zone. The ethnographic record suggests that these nail figures were mainly used in legal contexts, either as a record or a guarantor of a pact or promise. The *nkisi* would punish transgressors and could also be used to wreak vengeance. Gell draws his material from the ethnography of Richard Dennet ([1906] 1968), who described the fabrication and ritual usage of *nkisi* by the Zinganga people in the Congo in the following terms:

> A palaver is held and it is decided whose *kulu* (soul) it is that is to enter into the muamba tree and to preside over the fetish to be made. A boy of great spirit or else, above all, a great and daring hunter, is chosen. Then they go into the bush and call his name. The *Nganga* [priest] cuts down the tree, and blood is said to gush forth. A fowl is killed and its blood mingled with the blood they say comes from the tree. The named one then dies, certainly within ten days. His life has been sacrificed for what the Zinganga consider the welfare of the people. They say that the named one never fails to die. . . . People pass before these fetishes (*Zinkici Mbowu*) calling on them to kill them if they do, or have done, such and such a thing. Others go to them and insist upon their killing so and so, who has done, or is about to do them some fearful injury. And as they swear and make their demand, a nail is driven into the fetish, and the palaver is settled so far as they are concerned. The *kulu* of the man whose life was sacrificed upon the cutting of the tree sees to the rest. (Dennet [1906] 1968, 93, in Gell 1998, 61)

Drawing up a table of the implicit relations (either active or passive) that the use of the *nkisi* implies (see Figure 31), Gell (adapted from 1998, 28) makes use of two main notions: the active role of the "index"—that is, "the material thing which motivates the abduction"—and the passive role of the "recipient." In this analysis, the legal, vengeful *nkisi* of the Zinganga is caught up in a chain of relations linking indices to recipients; this chain describes the object's "cumulative agency." The

Figure 30. A Congolese nail figure (*nkisi*), from Gell (1998). Reproduced with the permission of the Musée du Quai Branly and the Réunion des Musées Nationaux, Paris.

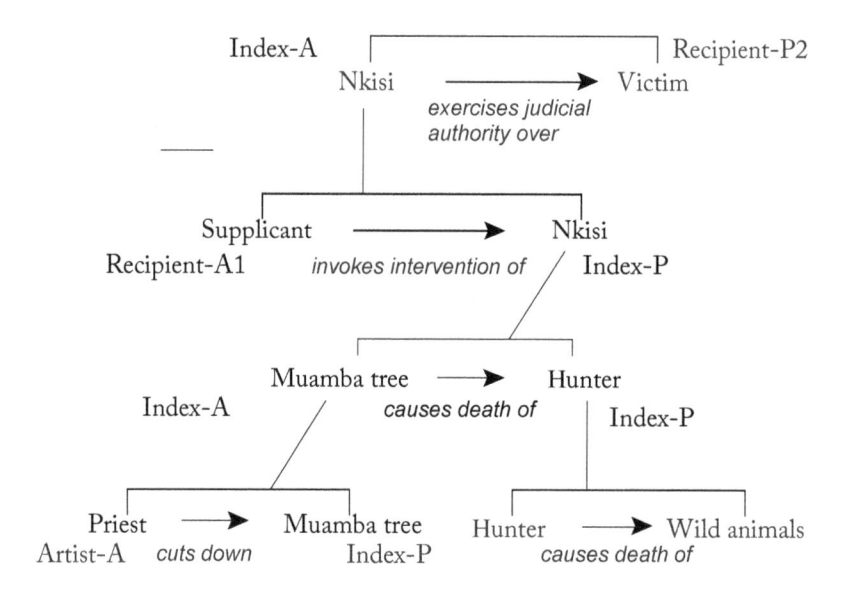

Figure 31. The skein of spatiotemporal relations mobilized by the use of the *nkisi* (adapted from Gell 1998).

authority wielded by the nail figure (as an active index) over its victim (the passive recipient) emerges out of the chain of actions comprising the supplicant's invocation of the figure, the death of the hunter caused by the muamba tree, and, finally, the priest's carving of the figure out of wood from the tree.

Gell's schema clearly shows how an object can imply a group of relations. In his own words, "An instructed person, approaching such a fetish, does not see a mere thing, a form to which he may or may not respond aesthetically. Instead, what is seen is the visible knot, which ties together an invisible skein of relations, fanning out in social space and time" (1998, 62). The idea, however, that networks of relations can be read in the use of an object leaves one central point unclarified. The nail figure is not merely the end point of a chain of actions; I would argue it should be conceived as a full agent in its own right. The goal of ritual action is to transform the status of the artifact, moving it from a position of passivity to one of activity. As Gell rightly observes, "it has the capacity to act (as a fetish) *because it has been acted upon*" (1998, 62; emphasis in original). When a nail is driven into the figure, it is cast in the role of symbolic victim and reacts against such harm. The force generated by this reaction transforms the figure from an object of a violent act into a subject of another one. Driving in the nail also transfers the priest's symbolic aggression against the muamba tree to the figure. In this one act, the object is transformed from victim into avenger at the same time as it is partially identified with the supplicant, who undergoes a parallel transformation from victim into avenger of a wrong. In this sense, we can also say that the figure acts as a substitute of the avenger; several examples of *nkisi* even show a small mirror attached to the statue (Bonhomme 2007). However, the object's behavior remains unpredictable: its intentionality always retains a certain ideal independence from that of the supplicant. Although it is hard to imagine a situation in which the action of the nail figure might run directly counter to the intention of avenging the supplicant or obtaining justice, the latter nonetheless never exercises direct control over the object. It follows that what we need to explain is not so much the series of events leading up to the object's transformation but, rather, the independence or autonomy it seems to acquire in the ritual process.

Let us go back to Dennet's narrative and try to understand the kind of dynamic transformations it involves. We are told that once a collective decision has been made, a priest is instructed to fell a tree. He strikes it and addresses it by using the name of the young hunter who is destined to die, at which point it begins to bleed like a human body. The wood of the tree is then used to make the figure. The blood of the wood is coupled with the blood of a sacrificial chicken. In this sequence, we see the young hunter's *kulu* (his ability to kill) transformed from a passive role (as an element associated with the dead hunter) into an active one (as a source of the figure's power). The ritual action revolves around the transformation of a tree trunk that represents the young hunter as the victim of a violent act into a figure that represents him as the vengeful and thus active party. But how does this transformation occur? Gell writes that the tree "brings about metonymically the hunter's death" (1998, 61). It is worth remembering, however, that, in Dennet's description, the tree is not presented as an active party or as an index. Rather, it is the priest who sets the process in motion by striking the muamba tree. It is also clear that the tree, being called the name of the young hunter, is ritually compared with a human body by virtue of its bleeding.

Let us not forget that the context in which these actions are performed is a *ritual*. The actions are situated in a symbolic space where the identities of the agents and recipients are supposed to change or, in any case, to effect transformations. However, Gell's analysis is limited to the agent/recipient pair, which obscures the dynamic nature of the ritual action and the resultant metamorphoses. He is forcing the data here, no doubt misled by a certain love of symmetry. The origin of his error, however, lies more in the very nature of the analytical vocabulary he adopts ("indices" and "recipients"). Indeed, if the young hunter dies "certainly within ten days" (1998, 61) after the priest fells the tree, it is surely because his *kulu* (soul) has become identified with that of the tree. His identity has been *progressively redefined* in the course of the ritual; this transformation is revealed as soon as the blood flows from the tree. The identification between the hunter and the tree is the crucial issue at stake in the ritual. Throughout the ritual, this identification is intensified and reinforced. The process takes place in three stages. In the first one, as we saw, a young hunter is chosen and his name is pronounced to extract, liberate, and manipulate his *kulu*. The priest cuts down a tree, which then "bleeds like a human," establishing the first identification. In the second phase, a chicken is sacrificed and, like the tree and the human, its blood pours forth. The second equivalence is brought about when the priest mixes the blood of the chicken and the tree, thereby identifying the one with the other. In the third and final phase, when the hunter dies, his symbolic identification with the tree in symbolic terms is complete: the blood the priest spills is that of the hunter.

Here, the ritual action produces changes that affect each element of the chain of identifications. The identification between the hunter and the muamba wood destined to become a nail figure is produced by two explicit acts of connotation: bleeding and naming. These pave the way for another crucial (albeit indirect) identification, which both links the figure to the hunter through a transfer of *kulu* and transforms the wood from a passive thing into an active agent. Thus, the *nkisi* is born as a ritual subject that *partakes of the nature of both tree and hunter*; its identity combines passive elements (felled tree and sacrificial chicken) and active ones (the hunter's *kulu*). The supplicant, seeking a means to get revenge, identifies himself (perhaps by using the mirror) with this ambiguous or hybrid artifact-subject, which is simultaneously passive and active. We must conclude that the *nkisi* has a hybrid nature, not a single-faceted one.

If we go beyond Dennet's ([1906] 1968) fragmentary, somewhat dated testimony and read subsequent ethnographic research, we will find confirmation of many of the conclusions of my analysis proposed above. Wyatt MacGaffey's (1986) detailed and illuminating analysis greatly broadens the scope of the *nkisi*. He first demonstrates that there is a distinction between an official public use of the fetish, close to an ancestor cult, and a private use, associated with sorcery. He also convincingly argues that the ritual use of *nkisi*—including its role in initiation (1986, 111)—is always specific, revolving around particular sets of clearly defined relations; for instance, between father and son, or mother and future child. The legal use of the *nkisi* is thus, contrary to Dennet's claims, just one example among many (MacGaffey 1986, 111–12, 140, 264). Other points raised by MacGaffey are relevant to the analysis I have been developing here. He notes that the symbolic equivalence of body and tree (which underpins my explanation of the use of *nkisi*) is so widespread in this ritual tradition as to be considered a constant, general characteristic of it (1986, 128–30). He also stresses that an *nkisi* is, first and foremost, the avatar of a dead person (1986, 137). Tombs, for instance, are invariably referred to as "the *nkisi's* house" (1986, 145), which confirms my hypothetical identification of the young hunter and felled tree. Most crucial, however, is the idea that *nkisi* is not actually a figure in the sense of a material representation of a supernatural being (as our Western gaze would lead us to assume). Rather, it is a space where several heterogeneous elements are assembled (similar to the Fang *evur* and *byang*), each of which refers back to a supernatural substance (1986, 122, 137, 139ff.). The nail figure is "the plural image" (1986, 120) of this assemblage. This explains why the prototypical *nkisi* is not a statue but, in fact, a basket or a shoulder bag (1986, 112). The statue is always conceptualized as a container of sorts. To take another example, Christian crosses in the contemporary Congo region are often considered to be *nkisi*. Of course, the content of this symbol of Jesus's martyrdom is subject to a process of radical reinterpretation in the context of traditional cults. As MacGaffey notes, Jesus is seen in the Congo more as a powerful magician than as a victim. But it is not only the content of the symbol that changes; its form is also reinterpreted. It is less a unitary symbol than the sign of transition. The horizontal line of the cross refers to the border between the visible and invisible realms, while the vertical line is a beam of power that bisects it. When the cross is understood as a *nkisi*, it is the symbol of death, since it represents "the place where paths separate." This serves to highlight a crucial point: the cross, as a *nkisi*, is not a symbol but a "statement of relationships" (1986, 119). In other contexts, the same symbol can represent the four matrilines (father, mother, mother's father, and father's father) that make up an individual's soul (1986, 123).

In other words, the *nkisi* always represents a composite being or, better yet, the sum of ritual relations established among different beings. It is in this light that we should consider its significance. MacGaffey's ethnography allows us to push still further. He claims that the vengeful *nkisi*, whose use is linked to the spilling of blood, is always made up of *antagonistic beings*: "the charm is both avenger and victim" (1986, 142). This confirms our view of the Zinganga nail figure as an entity composed of positive elements (corresponding to the aggressor's identity) and negative ones (corresponding to that of the victim).

We can only conclude that, in both the example given by Dennet and those analyzed by MacGaffey, our analytical approach must account for the *composite nature* of the ritual identities attributed to the object (rather than, as Gell would have it, an alternation between active and passive positions). This analysis casts the authority wielded by the nail figure in a new light. The figure's transition from a passive role to an active one can only be effected by establishing a chain of partial identifications, which can be described in the terms shown in Figure 32.

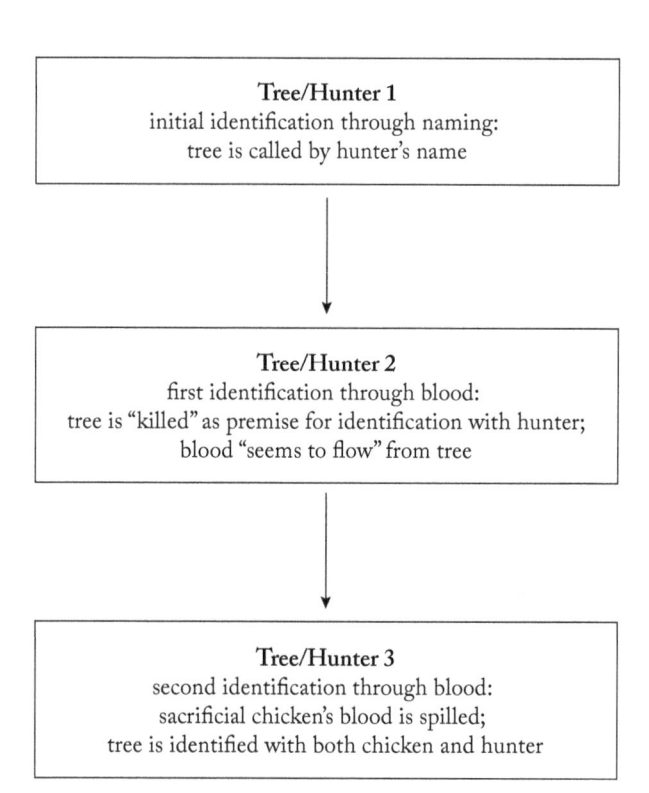

Tree/Hunter 1
initial identification through naming:
tree is called by hunter's name

↓

Tree/Hunter 2
first identification through blood:
tree is "killed" as premise for identification with hunter;
blood "seems to flow" from tree

↓

Tree/Hunter 3
second identification through blood:
sacrificial chicken's blood is spilled;
tree is identified with both chicken and hunter

Figure 32. Chain of ritual identifications attributed to the *nkisi*.

These identifications, which function as presuppositions of the actions that structure the ritual, are links in the chain of transformations that guide the symbolic transfer of the *kulu* (soul) from the body of the hunter to that of the nail figure. This analysis enables us to see the modalities of the exercise of authority attributed to the *nkisi* in a new way. These modalities involve the creation of a series of relations of identification, leading to the definition, through the artifact, of an autonomous entity, similar to what emerges, seemingly on its own, from the strings of a Fang harp. These identifications, which are serially articulated around a single connotation (of blood, a sacrificial chicken, a name, and so on) are always partial. Each participant (hunter, priest, sacrificial victim, and legal or vengeful supplicant) performs his or her part of the rite, but none of them has a direct relationship to the entire set of relations that together constitute the composite identity of the nail figure. None can be identified with the totality of the sphere of activities attributed to the ritual object. Although each contributes to the whole, the identity that inhabits this container is the *result* of the ensemble of partial identifications realized in a particular sequence of actions. We can thus say that the nail figure has a complex identity, entirely different that the everyday attribution of identity.[4] Continuing along these lines, we may now formulate responses to two main questions left unanswered by Gell in his theory of the artifact, concerning the identity of the active object and the relationships that contribute to its definition. Gell did not define the type of identity that is transferred to objects, nor did he care to specify precisely what types of relations underlie the abduction of subjectivity transferred to these objects. Without dealing with these two issues, the ritual nature of living objects like the *nkisi* is left unexplained. If this kind of object indeed plays the role of mediating social relations, it is in the context of ritual action that its agency is most often brought to fruition. In these rituals, anthropomorphism moves from a diffuse, unstable state, typical of everyday behaviors, to a stable state that can crystallize within a set of beliefs inscribed in a tradition. To understand the establishment of a stable belief, it is therefore essential to follow the production of complex or convergent identities through the establishment of ritual relations, not merely the simple transfer of an aspect of human thought to the world of artifacts.

---

4. For analyses of other instances of complex identities generated through ritual, see Houseman and Severi (1998) and Severi (2002, 2004, 2007).

THE COMPLEX ARTIFACT

Let us now return to the comparison between the Fang harp and the Zinganga nail figure. I mentioned earlier that in the *mvet* tradition, the voice of the spirits seems to emerge from the harp—a phenomenon we can conceptualize through an appeal to musical theory and the idea of a *resultant melody*. In a similar vein, the identity of the nail figure can be described as a *resultant identity* arising from the partial identifications that direct ritual action. Like the melody of the Fang harp, this identity appears to exist independently of the ritual participants. Its apparent autonomy can be explained in terms of the dynamic that animates the entire set of relations involved in its use.

In both of these cases, we see a figure (and thus a source) of ritual authority that is at once ill defined, elusive, and attributed to an artifact. This type of authority is wielded in the absence of a real person: the harp player "reduced to a string," or the dead hunter who becomes a *nkisi*. As such, its identity is negatively defined. It is at once materially produced by an intentional action (plucking the harp strings or carving the bleeding wood) and uncoupled from any direct form of intentionality.[5] Be it a harp or a nail figure, the artifact wields an authority that is both provoked and constrained, as much imagined as respected. The conclusion to be drawn is that, in traditions without written texts, authority is not wielded through reference to the figure of the author but, rather, is defined as a complex network of relations linked to ritual action. The artifact appears as the image of an ensemble of relations rather than of an individual, a mythical author, or a supernatural ghost, a consequence that depends on the production of a series of partial identifications. A tradition is thus authorized by means of an anonymous utterance. Although its agentive power and its speech emerge out of a series of clearly defined interactions, they never coincide with any direct intervention from a ritual participant. Behind the supposed presence of an utterer whose identity remains indiscernible, we can glimpse the evidential function of the object, which ties the harp as well as the nail figure to images of the truth. In other words, the space where action is attributed to the artifact (difficult to conceptualize from a Western perspective) is the space of an authorless authority.

---

5. For further discussion of this uncoupling of individual intentionality and ritual action, see Humphrey and Laidlaw (1994) and Houseman and Severi (1998).

The object can thus become a bearer of a truth. In the case of the *nkisi*, however, this can take place only through a ritual action. What happens when the agency of the object is expressed through speech? What becomes of the status of the "indiscernible subject" that appears? What are the conditions and what are the effects of its speech? What role does the image of the utterer play in such cases? An analysis of a funerary ritual in ancient Greece will allow me to formulate some answers to these questions in the next chapter.

CHAPTER FIVE

Giving Voice
When Images Speak

All speech acts imply a commingling of identity: when we make use of language, we necessarily attribute mental states to others, and we can only understand and interpret our interlocutors' utterances if we assume they are capable of doing the same. This intuitive attribution of mental capacities to others, which creates a space of shared identity, appears to be a characteristic of human beings. Although animals may give the impression of engaging in communication equivalent to our own, they are actually incapable of such behavior (Airenti 2003). In practice, however, people readily attribute this capacity to nonhumans. We have all at some point found ourselves almost involuntarily addressing animals or even inanimate objects as if they were humans. For a fleeting instant, we assume dolls, cars, or computers to be potential respondents, due to the game of interlocution triggered by our utterance. As noted in the preceding chapter (Chapter Four), this ordinary kind of experience led Alfred Gell (1998) to investigate how we attribute agency and subjectivity to objects. It is because we anthropomorphize artifacts that they can play a part in social existence. This anthropomorphism does not, however, invariably take the diffuse, everyday, and relatively superficial form discussed by Gell. In other situations, our relationship to artifacts assumes more stable forms. This is notably the case in ritual action: the progressive construction of a truth regime different than in our day-to-day existence creates a context in which our anthropomorphic thinking crystallizes and gives rise to enduring beliefs. When this happens, objects are endowed with a far more stable range of human characteristics, such as perception, thought, action, or speech. These objects cease to be merely addressed and begin to *address us* through words we lend them.

My purpose in this chapter is to explore this social context in which, as Bronislaw Malinowski put it in *Coral Gardens and Their Magic*, the meaning of a word consists "in the effect which it is believed to produce" (Malinowski [1935] 1971, 249). Under what conditions can objects speak? How are they transformed into interlocutors? Within ritual space, objects (be they statuettes, images, or fetishes) usually represent beings such as spirits, gods, or ancestors, which are all modeled on human interlocutors. These artifacts offer images of these beings; anthropologists and art historians are thus accustomed to analyzing them as iconic representations. In the context at issue now, however, such artifacts do more than merely represent spirits or supernatural beings: when they act or speak, they *replace* the entity they represent. They reinstate its presence.

The transition effected by the object from iconic representation to indexical designation involves a double shift in perspective that concerns the status of both the visual representation and the spoken word. To understand the nature of the ritual speech attributed to an image, it is necessary to ask two things: 1) How might we conceptualize iconic representation not in formal terms but, rather, through the analysis of its *context of use*? 2) Is it possible to identify the transformations (both of premises and of effects) that speech acts undergo when they are attributed to artifacts?

SPEECH AND RITUAL IMAGES

The attribution of speech to an object, even when it has no morphological impact on language, produces a fictive speaker. As such, it transforms the field of verbal interaction and the speech acts that occur within it. Thanks to the works of authors such as Dell Hymes (1981), Michael Silverstein (1976), Dennis Tedlock (1983), Keith Basso (1996), Alan Rumsey (2002, 2003), and William Hanks (2005, 2006), anthropology has firmly integrated the study of the pragmatic conditions of speech acts, through which the identities of speakers are constructed, into its conceptual toolkit. These authors have demonstrated that studying the conditions of interlocution can enrich our understanding of the meaning of traditional discourse and help us situate myths and other narrative forms in specific oral genres, and, more generally, shed new light on the uses of traditional knowledge. This pragmatic approach enables anthropologists to move beyond the mere deciphering of indigenous speech acts and endeavor, instead, to distinguish various forms of social communication and the modalities through which tradition functions. But what about the analysis of ritual speech? In this case, the links between pragmatic and anthropological approaches are problematic. Linguistic pragmatism was initially defined in strictly logical terms as the study of relations between speakers and their language (Carnap 1955; Stalnaker 1970). To yield a more complete interpretation of utterances, this entailed the analysis of the processes of metalinguistic interpretation that complement purely linguistic interpretation (Moeschler and Reboul 1998, 20–23). Since then, however, it has forked into two distinct branches: 1) the analysis of extremely simple (or fictitious) communicative acts, leading to sophisticated theoretical models (Grice 1989; Sperber and Wilson 1986); and 2) the identification of complex sociolinguistic phenomena, using contextually specific explanatory prisms (Labov 1972). To this day, practitioners tend to focus either on the wider criteria of generalized pragmatics, applicable to all communicative acts, or on the localized, specific variations that affect particular instances of linguistic performance. Numerous authors (Mey 1993; Davis 1991; Moeschler and Reboul 1998) have criticized the overly general nature of Charles Morris's initial definition of pragmatics as the study of "the science of the relation of signs to their interpreters" (Morris 1971, in Davis 1991, 3).[1] The problem doubtless lies less in the extension of field's purview and more in the sheer range of different approaches and topics to which this definition has given rise. Whether we follow Jacob Mey, who distinguishes between "micro-," "macro-," and "meta-" pragmatics, or Jacques Moeschler and Anne Reboul, who posit a linear relationship between cognitive referents and discourse analysis, the variety of topics and theories is astonishing. The unfortunate effects of this bifurcation in research strategies are clear: the degree of abstraction that Paul Grice and his followers opt for makes their models unsuitable for analyzing data from the field, while the study of specific cases raised by other authors has rarely led to wider, more generalizable conclusions from an anthropological perspective. In its relationship with social anthropology, linguistic pragmatics has seemed too abstract and based on fictitious examples, or else empirically grounded but too circumstantial and heterogeneous. This divergence is particularly striking in the study of

---

1. Here I use Steven Davis's (1991, 3) modified definition, adapted from Charles Morris's (1971, 28, 35, 43) broader comparison of pragmatics with syntax and semantics: "Syntax is the study of the syntactical relations of signs to one another.... Semantics deals with the relation of signs to designata.... And pragmatics is the science of the relation of signs to their interpreters." See also Rudolf Carnap's definition (1955).

ritual. Whereas a series of solid anthropological works (Bateson [1936] 1958; Barth 1975, 1987; Rappaport 1979, 2000; Kapferer 1977, 1979, 1983; Staal 1979, 1983, 1989; Humphrey and Laidlaw 1994; Bloch 1986, 1991) has sought to identify the constitutive traits of ritual action and to distinguish it from everyday action, linguists (even though they have produced precise descriptions of many different situations of social communication) have thus far not attempted to explore the *special pragmatics of ritual speech*. Were this to become a topic of research, their studies could converge in an approach illuminating the range of phenomena involved in this type of communication. Anthropologists, for their part, have been slow to grasp and incorporate descriptive categories from pragmatics (such as situation, setting, context, indexicality, implicature, and embeddedness) into their analyses. They have made little attempt to delve deeper into the study of the ritual use of language, limiting themselves to highlighting a few superficial aspects of ritual language (repetition, semantic poverty, use of fixed formulas, etc.) without linking them to other aspects of ritual behavior. Some of them have indeed applied John Austin's classic work on speech acts (1962) to the disparate elements of ritual speech and action (Tambiah 1985; Bloch 1974), but, as Donald Gardner (1983) points out, these approaches are either rigorous but empirically useless or else approximative and theoretically negligible.

Specialists in pragmatics agree on the existence of "social indexicality" and acknowledge that it may influence the meaning of a sentence, but they generally consider the concept to be limited to a few specific aspects of the definition of a speech context. In a text long taken as canon, Stephen Levinson (1983) recognizes relations of "totemism," "kinship," and "clan belonging" (1983, 90) among the range of "grammaticalized" social relations (i.e., those expressed in linguistic terms), but he only focuses on relationships of "rank" expressed via the use of honorifics. As Hanks has suggested (2006), this is doubtless due to the technical and conceptual difficulties of bridging the gap between the analysis of the specific context (understood as local, limited, provisional, and constructed "utterance by utterance") and a more general, stable context that is not necessarily expressed in linguistic terms. I would suggest that this may also be partly due to significant, albeit implicit, differences in how the two disciplines define their object of analysis. For linguists, pragmatics is still defined as the study of everything that is exclusively formulated through linguistic means under the conditions of a given speech context. Although they recognize the existence and the efficacy of other contextual indicators that are not expressed in linguistic terms, they almost invariably treat them as either residual or as having little influence. This linguistic definition of the field of analysis, which only takes into account the "grammaticalized" elements (Levinson 1983, 89), ignores a whole range of other phenomena that anthropologists consider integral aspects of social indexicality. Most significantly, such approaches do not provide us with the tools we need to understand the logic underpinning verbal communication in ritual contexts.

To illustrate this point, let us consider a particular verbal act that occurs during the *Naven* ritual, a Papua New Guinean Iatmul transvestite rite (Houseman and Severi 1998). During the ritual, which celebrates a youth's first "cultural act," men dress as women and women as men. They take each other's place and flaunt themselves in the public plaza where the ritual takes place. In this entirely fictitious context, Ego's maternal uncle addresses his sister's son by exclaiming, "You, my husband!"

This ritual utterance is often understood as one of a series of "recurrent behaviors" (Bateson [1936] 1958) that frames the ritual. A few details of these ritual acts will suffice: the youth's mother strips herself naked, while his mother's brother dresses in a grotesque imitation of women's clothing. He then sets out, sometimes helped by his wife, to look for his sister's son in order to give him food in exchange for precious shells. Meanwhile, the youth's father's sister, who is the female equivalent of the mother's brother, wears splendid male garb and beats the youth, her brother's son (Figure 33).

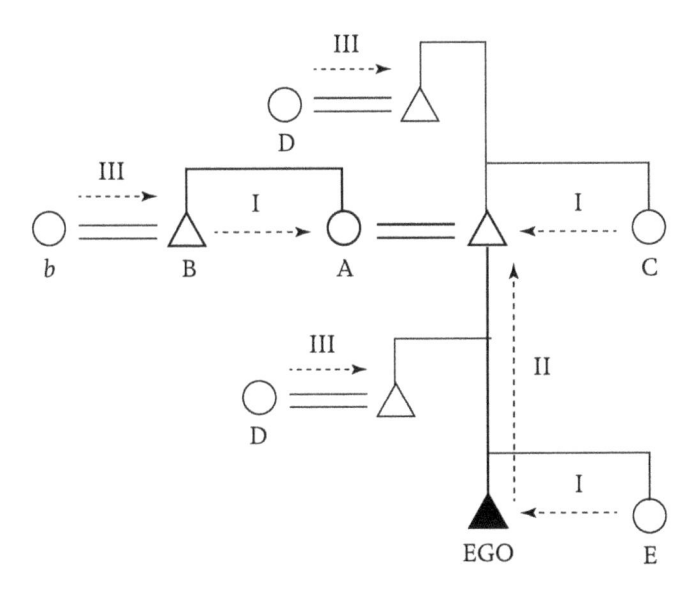

Figure 33. Relationships and behavior in the *Naven* ritual.

This sequence of actions is characterized by the fact that all the protagonists (except for Ego's mother) switch places in their everyday kin identities in terms of gender and maternal or paternal links. In this particular context, everybody considers it normal to address a mother's brother as "mother," or a young woman as "husband." Once the ritual fiction is set in train, participants try to fulfill their new roles by altering their behavior. This role reversal is not in the least intended to be mere comedy. To the contrary, it reveals a whole series of deep-rooted Iatmul associations, involving three shifts of role: a brother assumes his sister's identity and vice versa, a son that of his father, and a wife that of her husband. Because the maternal uncle assumes the identity of his sister (Ego's mother), he behaves like a "male mother" by feeding Ego. Reciprocally, because the son assumes his father's identity, he becomes his maternal uncle's brother-in-law and so gives him shells, a key part of bridewealth. If, in Iatmul culture, a maternal uncle is identified with his sister, and a son with his father, then it comes as no surprise that, within the network of ritually modified relationships, the young man can become his maternal uncle's "husband." It is only when we understand this chain of identifications that the maternal uncle's utterance, "You, my husband!" makes sense. This set of modified relationships is the paralleled by the behavior of other ritual participants: as the maternal uncle assumes his sister's identity, so the paternal aunt assumes her brother's, dressing up as a man and beating Ego. Her behavior is not that of an affectionate mother, feeding her son, but an imitation of an authoritarian father. By following this game of identities, we can understand the behaviors in the *Naven* ritual, based on the fictitious, simultaneous, and complex roles assigned to actors within this modified network of kinship relations. This distribution of roles is neither improvised, random, nor discontinuous but, rather, the result of the application of a few central rules of substitution.

Michael Houseman and I have explored the *Naven* ritual in greater depth elsewhere (Houseman and Severi 1998). Here I wish to raise only two points: first, the role of nonlinguistic communication and, second, the logical status that determines the speakers' ritual identities. In the verbal exchange between mother's brother and the sister's son, an entire series of extralinguistic markers (masks, make-up, costumes, and so on) enters into play to define the meaning of the words used, the identities of the speakers, and the nature of the relationship created between them through verbal exchanges. Among the extralinguistic means of communication, actions and images play a crucial role, since it is through them that the transformation of identity underlying the participants' behavior is accomplished. It is not possible to account for the complexity of this type of communication without first articulating the precise nature of the interaction between linguistic and nonlinguistic communication. Indeed, visual indicators play no small part in ritual action: they *reveal* the speakers' complex identities, without which the ritual action—a type of exceptional game, or what Gregory Bateson ([1972] 1999, 35–40) called a "serious fiction," as distinct from ordinary life—would be incomprehensible.

Let us now turn to ways in which the identities of the two protagonists (Ego and the maternal uncle) are defined. Many pragmatists have highlighted the fact that, in ordinary speech, the identity of the speaker (and that of the hearer) is a constitutive element of social indexicality and thus helps determine the meaning of utterances. The speaker's identity is, in fact, one of the defining features of the context of speech acts, much like the use of demonstratives such as "here," "that," and "now." Levinson (1983) gives a clear definition of the role of a person's social indexicality in ordinary communication when he states that the speaker's identity must be seen as *one* of the contextual variables that affect the meaning of an utterance. To take one of his examples, the meaning of the sentence, "I am six feet tall," changes according to the sex of the speaker (1983, 58–59). He formulates a sort of minimal concept of social indexicality, which is quite common in linguistics. This approach excludes any extralinguistic definition of the speakers' identities and deals only with highly simplistic notions of sociological meanings. Once determined to be male or female, the speaker's identity remains relatively independent of the production of meaning. Such meaning may vary (for instance, expressing pride, regret, or other feelings about being six feet tall), but it never disappears. In everyday communication, the speaker's identity can only have a limited effect on the meaning of an utterance. It cannot completely subvert or destroy this meaning, nor can it influence the usual frame of verbal interaction, which remains unchanged.

Let us now return to the ritual dialogue between the mother's brother and sister's son that occurs during the *Naven*. One of the crucial characteristics of this communication lies in the manner in which a new identity for participants is created in the ritual frame through a particular form of symbolic interaction. The interaction between the mother's brother, who *acts like* a mother *and* a woman, and his sister's son, who *acts like* a son *and* a husband, generates a specific situation of communication wherein the participants' identities are constructed through a set of extraordinary meanings. In this case, the use of language implies the instantiation of a predefined, recognizable modality of interaction. The interaction between uncle and nephew sets in train a particular game—one based on displaying the form of ironic interaction that is the meaning of the Iatmul term *Naven*. During the interaction, the speakers' identities are both contradictory and plural: each speaker is the product of a complex conjunction of two contradictory identities (wife and woman for the uncle; husband and son for the nephew). The process of "ritual condensation" that alters the speakers' identities endows the communicational context with particular contours that sets it apart from everyday interactions.[2]

Everybody who takes part in the ritual knows they are speaking "in a different way" from ordinary life. Together, they create a unique "communicative game," which, on this occasion, has a form that is determined by the speakers' complex identity. Nevertheless, within this framework (in which "You, my husband!" is relevant to the ritual), this complex identity cannot vary. During the various verbal exchanges that occur throughout the ritual, the people playing the role of the transvestite uncle can change, but the character must remain the same. Its identity is fixed by the image and describes a ritual "I," which is at once temporary, complex, and inflexible. The fact that it is precisely this hybrid character (bearing a dual identification with both the youth's mother *and* his wife) who exclaims, "You, my husband!" *signals the ritual, quasi-fictional nature of the framework itself.* Within the framework of the communication taking place between the interlocutors, the speaker's identity is not one of the variables that can affect the meaning of an utterance. On the contrary, "appropriate speech" in this context involves creating complex relationships that endow the speakers with exceptional identities. The two characters must be in a particular type of relationship for the utterance (and its meaning within the context of a generalized fiction) to be possible. The situation, then, is the polar opposite of that described by Levinson. As we saw, the meaning of the statement "I am six feet tall" may change along with the identity of the speaker. Here, by contrast, the meaning of the utterance can only be grasped if we understand how the speaker is defined through a series of contradictory identifications. As in a game of chess, we must first know the rules governing the game and the uses of all the pieces in order to understand why one piece made a certain move. Likewise, in ritual communication, we must first know what the components of a speaker's complex identity

---

2. For a fuller discussion of the form of ritual communication in the *Naven*, see Houseman and Severi (1998, chap. 7).

are in order to understand the framework and thus the context of speech acts. In logical terms, the rules governing a speaker's identity cease to be *normative* (as in everyday speech) and become *constitutive* when they are applied to an entirely new game of interaction.³ In Levinson's presentation of everyday speech contexts, the speaker's identity is defined by a series of normative rules: this identity is restricted to ordinary communication and is but one of the many possible variables that affect the meaning of an utterance. The speaker's identity can vary according to factors that are independent of the speech context, even if this leads to shifts in meaning. In a ritual context characterized by constitutive rules, however, a shift in the speaker's identity affects far more than the meaning of an utterance. Since this identity is strictly dependent on the rules of communication, a transgression of these rules would abolish the very context that defines the nature of communication.

John Searle (1979) described such speech acts as "declarations." As in the ritual dialogue between maternal uncle and nephew, this kind of verbal act implies the existence of an extralinguistic dimension, "a system of constitutive rules in addition to the rules of language." In all such cases, "the mastery of linguistic competence is not in general sufficient for the performance of a declaration. In addition, there must exist an extralinguistic institution and the speaker and hearer must occupy special places within this institution" (Searle 1979, 18–19). The declaration "You, my husband!" would lose its ritual character and thus its validity if uttered by an inappropriate speaker. The transgression of a constitutive rule, as opposed to a normative one, leads not only to a change of meaning but, more critically, to the dissolution of the special "verbal game" on which the ritual communication based (1969, 1979). The speaker's complex and contradictory identity is a *constitutive element* of ritual communication, not merely one of among various elements that enable meaning to be created. As we saw above, this constitutive aspect of the definition of identity can be entirely independent

---

3. John Searle (1969) clearly explains this distinction (originally from Immanuel Kant [1781] 1999) between "constitutive" and "regulative" (normative) rules: "Constitutive rules . . . create or define new forms of behaviour. The rules of football or chess, for example, do not merely regulate playing football or chess, but as it were they create the very possibility of playing such games. . . . Regulative rules regulate a pre-existing activity, an activity whose existence is logically independent of the rules. Constitutive rules constitute (and also regulate) an activity the existence of which is logically dependent on the rule" (1969, 33–34). Note that the special use of speech governed by constitutive rules contributes to the memorability of a set of representations within a ritual tradition (see Severi 2003, [2007] 2015).

of the utterance's grammatical form. As the *Naven* example shows, the speaker's identity (and thus the identity of the subject of the declaration "You, my husband!") is constitutive of the speech context but has no impact on the linguistic form of the utterance. It follows that, in the context of this type of utterance, the image is by no means a heterogeneous or residual element in relation to the speech act. Speech and image reciprocally entail one another.

At this stage, we can sketch out a preliminary framework for the analysis of how ritual can endow objects with speech or "give them voice." Speech acts that occur in ritual contexts possess a *specific form of complexity* that is defined less by their content than by what pragmatists call *contextual phenomena*. These phenomena concern the definition of specific "conditions of utterance," including where and when the act occurs and the nature of the speaker. To be anthropologically relevant, this context must be defined not only in linguistic terms but also with regard to other forms of communication, notably visual or gestural. To bridge the two approaches of pragmatics and anthropology, a model is needed that can account for this complexity. And as we shall see, the "animate objects" that take part in ritual communication can play a crucial role. My analysis will therefore focus on the contexts of utterance in which these objects are given voice.

How, though, can we conceive of the relationship between linguistic (or as Levinson would have it, "grammaticalized") and nonlinguistic aspects of ritual communication? As we have seen, linguists tend to dismiss everything that is not "grammaticalized" as residual to the context of utterance. Anthropologists, meanwhile, rarely turn their attention to conditions of communication. To answer the question, then, we need to construct a new referential framework and illustrate it with a case study.

HERE-NOW-I: DEMONSTRATIVE IMAGES AND SPEECH ACTS

As Hanks points out (2006), definitions of the notion of context have usually been dominated by an opposition between two approaches: one marked by the focus on a specific situation in which utterances are produced, and the other that views the conditions of speech acts as little more than an empirical instantiation of grammatical rules. Both approaches, notes Hanks, highlight only certain aspects of verbal exchanges and give a distorted picture of others. He proposes instead a model of context that allows us to identify at what linguistic level meaning is determined as well as to evaluate the role played by the social field in which the utterance occurs. Hanks suggests that two distinct levels define the context of utterance: the level he calls "emergence" and the one he calls "embedding." Emergence describes "aspects of discourse that arise from production and reception as ongoing processes" during their utterance (Hanks 2006, 117). It is thus concerned with speech, or what Hanks describes as "the verbally mediated activity, interaction, copresence, temporality, in short, context as a phenomenal, social, and historical actuality" (2006, 117). The analysis of embedding, in contrast, focuses on the broader possible limits of speech, encompassing both its cultural underpinnings and the potential meaning that either inheres in or emerges out of context. In Hanks's own words, "Embedding designates the relation between contextual aspects that pertain to the framing of discourse, its centering or groundedness in broader frameworks" (2006, 117).

Hanks remarks that these two levels of analysis remain conceptually separate in pragmatic analyses. The "emergent" aspect of contextual analysis is typically reserved for the actual location and moment of utterance. The description of the wider conceptual context takes place at a different level of abstraction—one that transcends the empirical circumstances of the speech act proper. He also notes that one of the central tensions in pragmatic definitions of their object of analysis concerns precisely the nature of the relationship between emergence and embedding: "Emergence can easily be conceived at different temporal levels, as any historian knows, just as embedding applies within the most local fields of utterance production" (2006, 117).

The different levels of embeddedness are not external to the speech act. To the contrary, they constitute active forces within the utterance. The study of the process of embedding should thus be seen as part of the study of language as practice. As Hanks writes, "to study language as practice is to focus on how actual people engage in speech" (Hanks 2005, 191). We might compare this to Ludwig Wittgenstein's remarks on logical form. In his early work, Wittgenstein saw form as an explanatory category that transcends everyday language use, but, by the time he wrote *Philosophical Investigations* ([1953] 2009), he had come to understand logical form as an inherent, active element of language. Accordingly, language use, which had previously been conceived of as the periodic (and often imperfect) instantiation of a form situated at a higher logical level (typically composed of rules), became an object of study in its own right. Similarly, Hanks conceives of context as a progression that, at each higher level, increases in complexity, but he never loses sight of the "emergent" aspects of speech acts. As we shall see, this approach allows us to reconsider the interaction between linguistic and extralinguistic aspects of ritual communication.

First, though, let us consider Hank's example. For him, the first stage in defining a context involves identifying the basic interactive situation, which Erving Goffman (1963, 22; 1972) called a pure "field of copresence" between social actors. Though superficially simple, this first stage relies on a set of key criteria: a shared experience, the occupation of the same space at the same time, and a form of reciprocity through mutual perception. These are the minimal criteria necessary for interaction to occur, comprising what Hanks (2006, 118) refers to as the "prior outside" of a speech act. If we add to this a number of "socially identifiable acts, expectations, mutual understanding among parties, and a framework of relevance" (2006, 118), we can produce a fuller and more realistic description of a verbal exchange. This is what Harvey Sacks (1992, 521–22) describes as a "setting," a situation in which the "framework of relevance" of a verbal exchange is explicitly defined. In such settings, then, actors can "formulate" explicit definitions of the field of verbal interaction (Hanks gives the example of "I'm here to meet with Martin"), whereas the use of indexicals ("here," "now," "I," etc.) were previously seen as merely evoking such definitions. Hanks (2006, 117–20) then lays out a number of minimal conditions for a verbal exchange. For instance, he defines the context of such exchanges in terms of a crucial distinction, first proposed by Karl Bühler in his *Theory of Language* ([1934] 2011), between the symbolic field (*Symbolfeld*) and the demonstrative one (*Zeigfeld*). The former corresponds to the normative rules of grammar, while the latter covers all those rules that constitute or define the verbal exchange, notably the three basic indexical coordinates (referred to as "prototypical deixis"): "here," "now," and "I." The notion is primarily linguistic, since it offers a framework for the interpretation of specific elements of language called demonstratives. These indicate the context of utterance but also go beyond grammar, since "they are referring expressions whose conventional meanings belong to the linguistic code, and yet, as indexicals, their reference on any occasion of use depends strictly on the context of utterance" (Hanks 2006, 119). Since they lack descriptive content, these terms involve or require the context, although they cannot formulate it. For Hanks, this concept is vital, since it bridges the gap between the "emergent" level of pragmatic phenomena in speech acts and the level of complex "embedding" that defines the speech context as a social phenomenon. As he puts it, "Deixis is the single most obvious way in which context is embedded in the very categories of human language" (2005, 5). In this sense, the introduction of a general field that combines contextual markers ("here, now, I") into a coherent whole allows for the integration of successive levels of contextual structuration that are increasingly encompassing and complex, without losing sight of the specifics of the verbal exchange. Hanks's notion of the "social field" broadens the concept of demonstrative field (*Zeigfeld*), to which he attributes a dimension that is both linguistic and sociological, capable of constraining or modifying the contexts of utterances. In this way, speech act analysis can be extended to vastly different social contexts while remaining rooted in the examination of schematic regularities (2006, 120).

Let us now consider the question of ritual communication in relation to the notion of the *Zeigfeld* as formulated by Bühler and then used by Hanks. As mentioned above, it is composed of three key elements in the context of utterance: the "here," "now," and "I." In Bühler's view, the dual relationship between the "symbolic field" and the "field of utterance" replaces Ferdinand de Saussure's ([1916] 1998) opposition between *langue* and *parole*. He rejects the idea of a transcendent level of abstraction (Saussure's *langue*) of which the verbal exchange (*parole*) is merely an empirical instantiation. The demonstrative field, as a space that fulfills the basic requirements of a verbal act (and the relationships among them), plays as significant a role as the symbolic field in constructing language as an act (rather than as a set of normative rules). The demonstrative field also preserves a linguistic function, since it "converts the interactive setting into a field of signs" (Hanks 2006, 118).

For Bühler, however, those phenomena that affect the demonstrative field are not limited to grammatical manifestations. He does not distinguish between the linguistic production of meaning, on the one hand, and, on the other, a series of indicators considered marginal or residual (since they are nonverbal). His vision of the *Zeigfeld* is much wider, encompassing a whole series of different communicative registers, including "gestures and other perceptible aspects of the participants, such as posture, pointing, directed gaze, and the sound of the speaker's voice, all of which orient the subjective attention focus of the participants" (Hanks 2006, 118–19).

Hanks is sometimes inclined to reduce these aspects that define the participants in a verbal exchange to what Goffman and phenomenologists call the "natural attitude," when the speaker is "awake, capable of perception, present, and partaking of the same space and time as their interlocutor" (2006, 120) in a minimally defined communicational context. Bühler's notion of *Zeigfeld*, however, is much richer than this. In his efforts to account for how participants are capable of "synthesizing sensory data from vision, hearing, and touch in a system of coordinates whose *origo* is the here-now-I" (Bühler 1990, 169ff., cited in Hanks 2006, 120), Bühler devised a concept that applies equally well to verbal and nonverbal communication. If we return to our example from the *Naven* ritual, we can see that the notion of *Zeigfeld* makes it possible to factor in a wide series of nonverbal indicators. Aside from the purely linguistic force of the statement, these nonverbal indicators constitute a crucial element of the context of the ritual dialogue between the mother's brother and the sister's son. The content of the mother's brother's words is less important than the visual image and act of his cross-dressing, which "evoke" the context and the accompanying modification of the "I." The speaker's identity must then be seen not merely as one element in a "field of demonstratives" but, in addition, as an extralinguistic element expressed through a recognizable form of interaction that is already defined as the *Naven*. It is this set of nonverbal indicators that situate the utterance in the three dimensions of here-now-I that constitute its context.

This formulation of the nature of the context in terms of the *Zeigfeld* enables us to insert a visual criterion for defining identity into an indexical taxonomy: *the ritual identity established by the image* indicates a shift in the definition of the speaking subject, which is one of the three basic dimensions of Bühler's "demonstrative context." We can describe the nonverbal means of ritually defining the maternal uncle's identity (the act of *showing himself to be different*) not as mere "decoration" but as factors that affect what it means to be "I" in the verbal act. In the ritual, neither the maternal uncle nor the uterine nephew is the same "I" as in everyday speech contexts. Bühler's innovation was to consider the two contextual fields of utterance as copresent. This allows us to see the maternal uncle's iconic act of defining himself by "showing himself to be different" as more than simply a "residual" or "heterogeneous" element of the speech act. If we place *Zeigfeld* and *Symbolfeld* on the same logical footing, then we can see this nonverbal definition of the participants' identities as constitutive of the context and meaning of the utterance. Neither visual nor verbal communication takes center stage; rather, they operate together as part of a coherent whole.

Working out from this initial example, we can imagine a series of different cases of ritual communication characterized by comparable or different shifts in what we understand by "I" (and by other elements of the *Zeigfeld*) and how different elements interrelate. This would provide us with a logically sound taxonomy—one based on a relational model composed of a finite number of terms and relations as phenomena that affect the context of ritual utterances both grammatically and demonstratively (in the broad sense that includes acts of iconic display) and thus determine the ritual communication. We might compare this reciprocal, contradictory, and gendered definition of the identities in *Naven* to other forms of complex identity definition, such as in shamanic or initiation rituals.[4] This would begin to introduce a degree of order into the heretofore heterogeneous, fragmented field of phenomena subjected to pragmatic analysis. Doing so would make it possible to analyze such phenomena in terms of the shifts in the demonstrative (and nonverbal) field of the ritual communication and the resultant construction of complex actors.

Let us pause to consider the relations between linguistic and nonlinguistic communication that the *Zeigfeld* enables us to conceptualize. As we saw, too often image and speech have been viewed as separate, even though both are present in ritual action: aesthetic approaches neglect the way in which images are actually used in rituals, while linguistic approaches treat iconography as a "residual" element in the context of utterance. However, when painted or sculpted images are endowed with speech, they involve both iconography and language. They have two modes of existence: one via the iconic invocation of a particular being onto the ritual stage, and the other by virtue of the voice they are given and the type of presence this confers on them. Ever since Charles Peirce (1955), philosophers and semioticians have been inclined to contrast icon and index as two different kinds of signs with distinct modes of producing meaning. Icons work because of an analogy of form between sign and signified, whereas indices are inherent to the object they designate. However, as the art historian Ernst Gombrich demonstrated in his well-known *Meditations on a Hobby Horse* (1971), which explores how children play with a simple broomstick, iconicity and indexicality are, in fact, inseparable in an image. "All art is 'image-making' and all image-making is rooted in the creation of substitutes" he argues (Gombrich 1971, 9). "The greater the wish to ride, the fewer may be the features that will do for a horse" (1971, 8). In other words, the more the function of substitution is relevant, the less the form matters. Furthermore, the transformation the object undergoes (from a mere instantiation of a preexisting form to the production of a presence) is not isolated or random. Once inserted into a particular relation context such as a game, it becomes the visible term of a sequence of thoughts that largely escapes any analysis of its form. In this way, the broomstick sets in train a series of inferences: if the broomstick is a horse,

---

4. On this point, see Houseman and Severi (1998, 265–78).

then the child is a knight and his young playmate a princess. Within the space created by the game, their house becomes a palace. It follows that all form, by virtue of the relational space it evokes, implies a form of presence. These two dimensions of iconic representation and indexical referencing, which semioticians keep separate, almost always coexist in ritual images.

This kind of transformation is a widespread phenomenon. Consider, for example, a mask from the Northwest Coast Amerindians. Even if such a mask is created according to the rigorous rules of traditional iconography, its creator may choose to attach human hair and animal fur to it. These seemingly heterogeneous elements endow it with a type of "agency" that can be directly deployed in a ritual scene. The literature devoted to such images rarely addresses the articulation between aesthetic form and such means that create the impression of "presence." While linguists focus primarily on "grammaticalized" aspects of verbal exchanges, art historians prefer to address the images' aesthetic qualities. Nevertheless, within the space of ritual, these objects do indeed act and are sometimes given voice. For anthropologists, it is crucial to address these issues.

At the outset of this chapter, I remarked that the analysis of speech lent to images posed two types of question. The first set of interrogations concerned the relationship between an image and a speech act. On this question, we can now conclude that, within the *Zeigfeld*, speech and image can be integrated into a single context. In this context, the role of visual communication is one of the elements that define the demonstrative field constituted by the elementary series here-now-I. Let us now turn our attention to addressing the second set of questions regarding the contexts in which such artifacts are used. How should we define the image's modes of presence without reducing them to a residual aspect of iconicity? What relationships are created between the ritual action, which produces complex identities, and the impact of the image's presence? As we shall see, these questions are central to understanding the role played by artifacts in ritual and the nature of the speech with which they are endowed.

KOLOSSOI AND *KOUROI*; OR, THE PRAGMATICS OF IMAGES

In his groundbreaking work on "The psychological category of the double" in ancient Greece, Jean-Pierre Vernant ([1965] 2006) describes a series of funerary rites characterized by a highly singular means of representing the deceased:

> In a cenotaph dating from the thirteenth century BCE were found, instead of skeletons, two blocks of stone, lying on the ground, one larger than the other, both roughly hewn into quadrangular slabs tapering toward the top to indicate the necks and heads of human figures. One was a man, the other a woman. Buried in a tomb alongside the objects belonging the dead person, the *kolossos* functioned as a substitute for the absent corpse. (Vernant [1965] 2006, 320)[5]

The *kolossos*, which is little more than a hunk of stone vaguely carved into human likeness, is a particularly clear example of the ritual presence of an image. In fact, as Vernant stresses, the stone does not "represent" the deceased; rather, it lies in the tomb in the place of the deceased:

> When a *kolossos* is used in a tomb as a substitute for the corpse, it is not meant to reproduce the features of the dead man or to create the illusion of his physical presence. What it embodies in permanent form in stone is not the image of the dead man, but his life in the beyond, the life that is opposed to that of living men as the world of night is opposed to the world of light; the *kolossos* is not an image; it is a "double," as the dead man is a double of his living self. ([1965] 2006, 320)

Elsewhere, Vernant said that the "reality of the *kolossos* seems to exclude any similarity effect or imitative project. In order to evoke the deceased, the stone must establish a distance from the living person" (1990, 33). This ritual substitute for the deceased, however, was not always entombed. It could instead be raised above the tomb in a remote and distant site devoted to the gods of Hades. In this space outside the city, "rites for the evocation of the dead were celebrated. The prescribed libations and the blood of a black ram were poured over the stela; then those present called the dead man's name three times, gazing at the stone where it was believed he would reappear" ([1965] 2006, 320).

If this stone, which kept the deceased confined in the tomb, were erected at a certain place and became part of a ritual, it allowed the living to contact the deceased. Through the *kolossos*, this "gazeless hunk of stone" (as Vernant describes it), the deceased could be brought back to the light of day and his

---

5. For a critical reexamination of this text, see Carastro (2012, 77–105).

presence made manifest. But this "presence" was also an absence: "by making himself visible in the stone, the dead man also reveals himself as being not of this world" ([1965] 2006, 320). What appeared when the deceased was invoked was not the person himself but, rather, his *psuchê*—a "soul" (sometimes represented in animal form) that abandoned his body to haunt the netherworld and that had to be fixed and mastered. This soul, which "is a wisp of smoke that vanishes beneath the ground with a little cry, like a bat" (Vernant [1965] 2006, 326), was fixed to the stone during the rite. In fact, the representation of this presence/absence was one of the fundamental raisons d'être for the ritual. *Kolossoi* were also used to create or renew relations of hospitality with absent members of the city, particularly those who had moved to colonies. Hospitable relations with such people could, as in Selinunte, be maintained by offering food to the *kolossoi* that stood in their stead. In Thera, the oath guaranteeing reciprocal obligations between residents of the metropolis and African colonists, revealed a different sequence involving figurines. To maintain ritual relations with the absent colonists, "*kolossoi* are made, this time of wax; they are thrown into a fire while the following formula is pronounced: 'let whoever breaks this oath be turned into liquid and disappear, himself, his descendants, and all his goods'" (Vernant [1965] 2006, 322).

Through these two rituals, linked to death or absence, the erect stone revealed its nature and function. In both cases, it became a site of transit, a space of ritual contact between the living and the dead (or absent). Depending on the situation, this transit could flow in both directions. In funerary rites, for instance, the dead were brought back to the world of the living in stony form. In the ritual accompanied the oath marking the reciprocal obligations of colonists, the living projected themselves into the world of the dead through the waxen figures that take their place. "Through the *kolossoi* who represent them in the form of doubles," Vernant notes, "those swearing the oath cast themselves into the fire" ([1965] 2006, 322).

The *kolossoi*, then, produced a form of presence (or rather, a paradoxical representation of absence/presence) by enacting a ritual sequence (libation, sacrifice of a black ram's blood to the stone, ritual hospitality offered to the figurines) that mobilized several essential elements: a "minimal image"; a speech act that was not written down but associated with the image through the action of calling out the deceased's name three times; and the act of "gazing fixedly" the "speechless and gazeless" stone, which stood before the celebrant of the ritual. This ritual sequence served a dual purpose: it allowed a ritual identification between, on the one hand, the *kolossos* and a man who took an oath (and pledged his very life if he broke it), and, on the other, between the stone and the deceased through funerary rites when the stone was addressed as an instantiation of the dead man's presence. In the latter case, the *kolossos* became a "religious sign": the *sêma* (or *mnêma*) of the deceased to whom the mourner directed both gaze and speech. This ancient ritual sequence persisted for many centuries. In a series of texts discussing the panoply of visual representations in Hellenic culture, Vernant ([1965] 2006, 1979, 1990) demonstrated the existence of a core continuity between *kolossoi* and the emergence, from the sixth century BCE onward, of *korai* and *kouroi* statues in ancient Greece.

Despite changes in the style, the idea of a funerary statue as a *sêma* or "psychological category of the double," acting as an "intermediary term" and ambiguous "site of transit" between the world of the living and that of the dead, spans the archaic era. One crucial aspect, however, went through a radical change. In the social world of the first city-states, dominated by a warrior elite, the funerary *sêma*, while conserving certain core traits of the *kolossos*, not only acquired a new iconic dimension but was also endowed with a ritual voice (Figure 34).

As Burkhard Fehr (1996) has shown, these iconographic representations of young people embodied a wide series of values held by the aristocratic society of ancient Greece. The young women (*korai*) were portrayed in expensive clothes, showcasing their skill in weaving and their noble origins, while the young men (*kouroi*) were represented as exemplars of equality and physical excellence. Fehr notes that the *kouroi* often have the same height and follow an identical iconographic model. These conventional iconographic traits are accompanied by certain characteristic details. The posture and attitude of the *korai* and *kouroi* discreetly denote a courtesy expected of young aristocrats, epitomized by what Fehr calls their "allocutionary smile": the statue seems to greet spectators with a smile and to address them easily. From the sixth century BCE onward, the statues begin to be accompanied by inscriptions, usually placed on the plinth that served as the statue's base (Boardman 1991). In some cases, the statue and inscription are clearly linked, either by simply stating the name of the young person portrayed ("I am Diosermes, son of Antenor" [Boardman 1991, fig. 174]) or by directly addressing the observer and thereby rendering the meaning of the allocutionary smile more explicit: "Look at me!" (Boardman 1991, figs. 174, 244). This genre of interlocution is one example of how ritual artifacts can be endowed with a voice, which could be elaborated in various ways in the array of *korai* and *kouroi*. Let us focus on one particular case, that of Phrasikleia, a young

Figure 34. Two examples of Greek funerary statues: left, a female *kore*, Acropolis Museum, Athens (© Tarker/Bridgeman Images); right, a male *kouros*, National Archaeological Museum, Athens (© De Agostini Picture Library/G. Nimatallah/ Bridgeman Images).

kore with a typical smile, wearing an expensive dress and jewelry, and, with a prominent gesture, holding a lotus bud in front of her chest. The statue, which still shows traces of the original painting, probably dates from around 540 BCE and bears the following inscription:

> I, Phrasikleia's *sêma*, shall always be called girl [*koúrê*], having received this name from the gods instead of marriage. (Svenbro [1988] 1993, 17)

Jesper Svenbro ([1988] 1993, 8–25) has devoted a magisterial analysis to this statue, from which I will extract only a few essential points concerning the subtle play between what is seen and what is read, which, for the Greeks, meant reading aloud as speech (Svenbro [1988] 1993, 18). The tradition of ancient funerary statues testifies to the persistence of naming the deceased during the funerary rituals (although not in the form of the ancient *epiklēsis*, calling out the name of the *kolossos* three times). This particular speech act still ensures the longevity of the memory of the deceased. Svenbro translates *Phrasikleia* as "she who draws attention (*phrasi-*) to fame (*-kleia*)" ([1988] 1993, 14). The young woman thus declares herself to be the preserver of the good name (*kléos*) of the noble family of Alcmeonides to which she belongs. But she is, above all, "one who displays" their *kléos*. If the name that the living are called upon to utter is, in a sense, an act of self-definition, Phrasikleia's noble identity is likewise indicated by her gesture of showing the lotus flower before her. As Svenbro notes, the flower is a complex symbol with several layers of meaning. It indicates the hearth fire, which dies down at night but comes back to life in the morning, "unquenchable" like an "unwilting" flower ([1988] 1993, 23). Moreover, the lotus flower as hearth fire, as the heart of the household, is also the symbol of its *kléos*, its renown, which sounds down the generations. Thus, Phrasikleia's gesture is a visual translation of her name: "Holding a flower in her hand, a flower unceasingly reborn, the flower of fire, the young girl enacts her *kléos* with a silent gesture. In fact, the gesture of her hand mimes her own name, Phrasikleia" (Svenbro [1988] 1993, 23).

The statue's action, just like her name, expresses the notion, "I am thus, this is my nature, this my mission: I preserve the renown of my family." From the outset, an identification emerges between the deceased and the statue that stands in her place, since they have the same function: they are both *mnêma*, memory devices. The statue's smile does not just convey a particular meaning (a simple inscription would have sufficed for that); it attracts the gaze of observers and invites them, with all the courtesy of the archaic ethos, to pronounce her name. It is only when the inscription is read aloud (the Greek verb is *ek-eipein*, "to speak aloud") that the *kléos* associated with her name will be preserved in time (Svenbro [1988] 1993, 61). The statue is in a "state of waiting": only those who have seen her gesture and been convinced by her discreet smile will give life to her desire that her name be ritually pronounced. This act of reading aloud (which echoes the threefold repetition of a deceased's name) accomplishes two typical ritual actions. On the one hand, it uses specific modalities to produce what I am calling a "complex identity," discussed in the analysis of the West African nail figure (see Chapter Four). When we focus on the relation between inscription and statue, it is clear that the word "I," which opens the text, condenses at least two possible Egos: Phrasikleia the young noblewoman, and Phrasikleia the statue. In the inscription ("I, Phrasikleia's *sêma*, shall always be called girl"), the "I" designates both the young woman and the statue, this "peculiar and ambiguous presence that is also the sign of an absence" (Vernant [1965] 2006, 323), whose function is to preserve the memory of her *kléos*. Indeed, the relationship between what is seen and what is read constructs here a complex series of embeddings that plays on the double meaning of Phrasikleia and the statue that presents her as an unmarried woman (*kore*). It incorporates a long list of characteristics referring to Phrasikleia as the visual *sêma* and to Phrasikleia as the deceased whose name preserves her memory. The interplay between the two terms *sêma* and *kore* reverberates with multiple meanings. Who is actually speaking here? Who utters the words inscribed on the plinth below the statue? The speaker's identity appears to be defined by a sort of double negation: it is clearly not the *sêma* who received the name *kore* from the gods in lieu of marriage. Nor can the maiden Phrasikleia somehow refer to herself as a *sêma*. And yet the inscription begins with an act of self-defining: "I, *sêma* of . . . ." This "I," as Svenbro makes clear, refers to *both* of the Phrasikleias: "I, *sêma* of" and "I, the young girl" are two implicit utterances that coincide in the semantic field, allowing us to understand the inscription. As Vernant (who translates the inscription slightly differently) notes, "The second name, *kore*, is that of the funerary statue who speaks in the first person, in the name and in the place of Phrasikleia, of whom it is the *sêma* and whom it has substituted, as a funerary representation, by assuming the form of a *kore*" (Vernant 1990, 81). Svenbro uses the linguistic term "grammatical singularity" to describe the inscription, but it is clear that the utterance can only be understood in terms of its relation to the accompanying image. As we saw with the Northwest Coast mask, an image can reference both iconically and indexically. By linking physical traits, such as hair or fur, to a conventional iconic schema, the mask assumes a direct presence on the ritual stage. In the case of Phrasikleia, the presence of the image as a person is produced by triggering an exceptional convergence between the visual field and the written word to be read aloud. What we have is an interplay between two modes of generating meaning: the iconic and the indexical. The result is a complex person who unifies icon and index. Svenbro interprets this in purely linguistic terms as a phenomenon pertaining to the anthropology of reading. But this "reading" is a ritual act; we need to recognize that it goes beyond the bounds of everyday communication and creates (as in all ritual) a powerful verbal game that can only be understood within the ritual framework. The articulation between image and speech is crucial to this game. Through her gesture, Phrasikleia shows us what she says and, through her epigram, she says what she shows. *Symbolfeld* and *Zeigfeld* precisely coincide, all the while remaining symmetrical to one another.

Like many ritual beings, Phrasikleia's identity is complex: her words evoke a plural speaker who is both human (the young woman) and nonhuman (the statue). But how is this reflexive representation made of words and images transformed into presence? By the voice conferred upon it by the ritual. Phrasikleia can reach beyond the iconic, conventional dimension of the *kore* and assume a direct ritual presence only because of the speech and voice with which she is endowed. This speech and this voice are those of the ritual mourner: the reader of the inscription. Thus, it becomes clear that the production of this series of cumulative identities implies the existence of a relationship to the reader—a living person who is called upon to utter Phrasikleia's name.

Writing the deceased's name in a text linked to an image is not in itself enough to preserve it. For its ritual presence to be realized, the name must be read or, more precisely, read aloud. Like the mourner in the *kolossos* ritual, the reader who commemorates the young woman must utter the name, "Phrasikleia," in order to realize her desire to be "she who preserves" the fame of her family, the Alcmaeonids. This adds a further element to those found in the *kolossos* ritual: the reading of the stela not only calls out to the deceased, but also gives her voice and so accomplishes the action required by her sense of family duty, which is inscribed in her name. It is her task to spread the *kléos* of the Alcmaeonids through multiplying the uttering of her name. Just like her (and in her place), the reader transforms her gesture ("look at what I am: a flower, symbol of the hearth fire, heart of the family") into sound.

Let us now return to the *kouroi* as a whole and see if we can deploy the analytical instruments developed through our analysis of Phrasikleia. The morphology of this type of funerary representation is well known. The *kouros*, as a valiant young nobleman, expresses "in the form of his body, the beauty and the youth that death has fixed upon him for all eternity by cutting him down in the flower of youth" (Vernant 1990, 57). The set of iconic traits that comprise the young noble's *eumorphia* do not represent an abstract or ahistorical ideal of male beauty. They belong to a world of warfare. The beauty of the *kouros* embodies what Vernant calls the radiance of "definitive youth" (independent of the deceased's actual age), a state of splendor and prestige conferred by a "good death" on the battlefield. Such "youth" belongs primarily to the gods, who are forever young. But it is also defined in opposition to the obsessive idea in Homeric society of the profaned corpse of the warrior fallen in battle and subjected to a range of posthumous atrocities. Vernant explored these cruel practices, committed with the intention of robbing the warrior of his posthumous memory. After battle, bleeding corpses were sometimes smeared with dirt and disfigured to strip them of their individual identity, clarity of features, and radiance. Corpses might also be dismembered: "chopped into bits and fed to the dogs, birds, and fish" (1989, 74).

Funerary rites thus aimed, above all, to preserve the form of the body. The statue offers a model of the body intact, inviolate: the stylistic criteria sculptors applied in representations of *kouroi* (harmony of dimension, elegance of gesture and smile, neatness of hair) mirror the funerary treatment of the warrior's corpse to preserve it from profanation. The body was washed, perfumed, and embalmed before being cremated. The warrior's hair was carefully combed, and sometimes his comrades-in-arms "cut off their own locks before committing their friend to the flames. They strew the body with their hair as if dressing it for its final journey in their youthful and virile vitality" (Vernant 1989, 66). The funerary statue is the culmination of the ritual. Its beauty is that of the corpse. But we also know that the statue is no mere representation of the deceased: it stands in his stead and, just like the "naked stone" of the *kolossos*, it offers "a handle on the deceased, a ritual means of acting upon him" (1990, 74). So how is this *eumorphia* (the definition of the *kouros* as iconic representation of the deceased) transformed into ritual presence? How does it relate to the ceremonial action? The *mnêma* is, from the very beginning, the result of carrying out a ritual. In the Homeric era, "the 'share of honor' (*géras*) due to the dead consisted of cremating the body, gathering up the bleached bones, separating them from the ashes and covering the ossuary urn with earth so as to raise a mound, at the summit of which was place a *sêma*" (1990, 54). But the *sêma* was also a means of keeping the dead person's memory alive through the ritual uttering of his name. From the very beginning, the *kolossos* was always associated with *epiklêsis*: the "repeated calling out of the name" of the deceased. People contact the dead by speaking to their statues. However, the representation of the dead is also, at a crucial moment of the ritual, entrusted to the living mourners:

> During the lamentations, at the moment when the deceased's parents bring him briefly closer to the living by letting the last flickers of life (i.e., fire) play upon his body, they simultaneously bring themselves closer to him by acting out their own entry into the shapeless world of death. They simulate the profanation of

their own bodies, by begriming and tearing out their hair, rolling in the dust, and smearing their faces with ashes. (Vernant 1989, 72)

Even before the image of the deceased was fixed into stone (as the *kouros* or, in earlier times, as the *kolossos*), the ritual required the mourners themselves to enact this image. In other words, prior to erecting the statue, the parents literally "mimed" the dead person in the precise sense of the verb *mimesthai*, "to simulate the presence of an absent figure" (1990, 65). The mourner had to present himself as a victim of the same fate that befell the deceased. Indeed, the experience of intense grief (*pothos*), involves *preserving the deceased's presence within oneself* so as not to forget him (1990, 43). As Vernant explains,

> Like all rites of passage, funerals contain a liminal period, when the deceased is no longer alive, but his visible presence in his corpse stymies his entry into the shades. . . . It is at this moment that *pothos*[6] is given ritual form: the refusal of food, water, sleep, separation from the living, the besmirching of the face, begriming with ash and dust. These practices are linked to the act of remembrance, bringing the living closer to the dead relative by placing them both in an intermediary state. (1990, 48)

The *sêma* (as a *kolossos* or a *kouros*) is the visible sign of this injunction to remember, which implies staying close to the deceased, almost identifying with him or her. This profoundly ritual aspect of the "plastic symbol" (Vernant) among the Greeks is strikingly illustrated in the *Iliad*. When Patroclus, who drove Achilles's horses, was killed, the animals froze in a posture of ritual mourning. In their despair, "they stopped short and took root, as a funeral stela erected over a tomb remains forever immobile, preserving the memory of the deceased." Similarly, "the figure on the stela or the funerary *kouros* stands upon the tomb in the place of what the deceased was, was worth, or accomplished when alive" (Vernant 1990, 44). Vernant cites the example of the stela of Ampharetus (late fifth century BCE), which bears the following inscription: "Here I hold the beloved child of my daughter, whom I held in my lap when we were both alive and saw the light of the sun: and now, in death, I hold the child still" (1990, 80).

Here we see the same interplay and partial superposition of the *sêma* and the deceased that we witnessed with Phrasikleia. The *sêma* speaks through the

---

6. Vernant (1990) translates *pothos* as the deceased's "bereft desire."

inscription that appears upon its plinth and in the place of the person whose memory it evokes. The deceased is thus present upon the ritual stage, since we can hear his or her voice; the statue's ritual presence is signaled by its being endowed with speech. When inscriptions replaced the purely oral *epiklêsis* that had been addressed to the *kolossos*, the conditions were set for the emergence of a complex speaker. Like the *kolossos*, which was little more than a standing stone, the image of the smiling young noblewoman (or, more precisely, the relationship between a plastic symbol and an inscription that endows it with speech) creates a point of transit between the world of the living and that of the dead. This point of transit (or of ritual contact) appears as two parallel processes of identification that unite the statue with the deceased *and* with the mourner. When brought face to face with a reader or ritual mourner who gives it a voice, the *kouros* is transformed, like the *kore* Phrasikleia, into a plural speaker. It "is" the young warrior whose *eumorphia* it displays, but as soon as the reader utters the words of the inscription aloud (for instance, "I am Glaukos" [Boardman 1991]), then it establishes an interplay between speech and image that alters its nature. Through a partial identification between the statue and the reader, the latter gives his voice to the former, allowing it to speak (Svenbro [1988] 1993, 61). The act of reading aloud is far more than a mere uttering of a written inscription; it is the performance of a ritual act of remembrance based on a dual modality of presence that is at once visual and aural. Where a stela declares "Remember me: I am Dionysius," it is the statue who represents the deceased's visual presence, but it is the reader's voice that gives the statue an aural presence by giving it voice. As Svenbro remarks, "If the reader proclaims aloud 'I am the *mnêma* of Glaukos,' his lips serve an inflexible ego that is not his own" ([1988] 1993, 36). During the reading of the inscription, "It is not the stela that speaks; the reader lends it his voice by reading the inscription" ([1988] 1993, 51). Once transformed into a speaking object, the statue assumes its full ritual function. The principal raison d'être of a *kouros* is the visual representation, in the form of a *sêma*, of the deceased. When the statue says (via the reading of its inscription) "I," it is the deceased who speaks. Thus, an initial identification is made between the statue and the deceased (whether buried or cremated). Through the words uttered by the statue, as well as by its courteous attitude and its smile, the statue calls out to its interlocutors, drawing in their gaze and asking them to utter its name so that it may be granted a posthumous existence. The statue pleads for the intervention of a voice—one that can utter the word "I" in its stead. The visual *eumorphia* of the *kouros* reflects the initial, explicit identification between the deceased and his *mnêma*, while the vocal register produces an implicit, but always latent, identification between the deceased and the mourner who commemorates him. Above and beyond the meaning of the words inscribed on the plinth, it is the sharing of a voice in the ritual space that enables the contact between the two parties. Voice and image tread two separate paths, but, through the two processes of identification, the statue ceases merely to represent the values of ancient Greek society and becomes the site of a ritual relationship between deceased and mourner. This contradictory relationship links the smiling, courteous image of a dead nobleman (whose *eumorphia* is, however, that of a fallen warrior, his wounds made whole and his body anointed with oil and honey) and a mourner who stands in for, and lends his voice to, the deceased. For the duration of the utterance, the two unite to become a plural speaker. The *kouros*, like the *kolossos* from which it was derived, is double: it offers an image and a presence to the deceased and, via the ritual identification, allows a mourner to commune with him. It allows the bereaved, in the depths of mourning, to come so close to the deceased that, for a fleeting moment, he can take his place. In the state of profound grief experienced in the ritual as *pothos*, the speaker enables the deceased to prolong his existence. By pronouncing the deceased's words aloud ("I am Glaukos," "I am still the warrior you knew"), then, ever so briefly, in the time it takes to perform the ritual, the mourner becomes his sonorous image.

CONCLUSION

Let us now return to our opening questions: How do images speak? What types of speakers do they become when they appear in a sequence of ritual actions? These are questions that art historians and linguists, for all their valuable insights, have largely failed to tackle. The former do not realize that images may have a presence that escapes any analysis of their form, while the latter limit themselves to purely linguistic modes of communication. What the analysis of Greek funerary rites presented here has shown is that the complexity of the speech with which images are endowed resides precisely in their *simultaneous* mobilization of verbal and visual forms of communication.

The speech act attributed to the statue both implies and produces a series of complex relations that constitutes its presence. The act of giving it voice clears a path for a series of ritual identifications, which are both simultaneous and multiple and which link mourner and deceased through two distinct types of contact: via the image and via the spoken word. The funerary statue, which fixes the deceased's ritual identity in the form of an image is, then, not a mere representation of a social ideal: present on the ritual stage, it is the center of an ensemble of ritual relations. The analysis of the *kouros* as an iconic transformation of a latent presence (historically emerging out of the figure of the funerary *kolossos*) has shown how a plural "I" takes shape: the attribution of subjectivity to the statue isolates different aspects of synesthetic perception (sight, hearing, speech) and organizes them into a series of distinct dimensions of presence. This allows two simultaneous sets of identifications, one visual, the other aural, to converge on one object according to the different registers of perception they mobilize. Thus, the statue is "given voice," becoming a complex being who bears an image of the deceased and invites speech through its smile and courteous demeanor, then incarnating the speaker through the voice it is briefly given. The "I" embodied by the statue is plural in its complexity, fixed in a single image, and, as Svenbro suggests, inflexible. We can conclude that, in this form of ritual iconography, visual and verbal characteristics reciprocally entail one another: the identity of the image is indissociable from the voice it is given.

Contrary to Gell's (1998) suggestion that the artifact progressively "replaces" a particular person through speech, we can see that it acquires presence in this ritual context by taking on certain traits of the participants' identity in the ritual. Its identity emerges out of the relations it produces. I suggest that this approach to objects endowed with speech, which relies on a distinction between normative and constitutive forms of constructing identity and on the concept of a "demonstrative field" that includes images, constitutes a new point of departure for the analysis of ritual action as well as for the dialogue between linguistic pragmatics and anthropology. Following this path, perhaps we will one day be able to not only decipher the language of objects but even to understand how and when they can speak.

In the two preceding chapters, I have presented two cases of artifacts with agency that take on life in a ritual context. The African *nkisi* and the Greek *korai* and *kouroi* have thus revealed their full complexity. I will now embark on another experiment. Instead of analyzing the *terms* of the operations of substitution and identification between persons and artifacts in a single relational context, I will consider the nature of this context and its possible variations. The context is liable to vary, either by replacing someone with a real person (who is treated exactly like an object-person) rather than by an inanimate artifact, or by conceiving of these operations of identification and substitution in a context *other* than a ritual one, without thereby returning to the provisional, instable agency Gell suggested. The case I will explore in the next chapter is the Greek funerary game, through a reading of the *Iliad*. This will allow me to introduce a new concept—the *quasi-ritual context*—and to propose a more general vision of situations in which the agency of object-persons is likely to appear.

CHAPTER SIX

Becoming Patroclus
Funerary Rituals and Games in the Iliad

> *The living are generated from the dead, just as much as the dead from the living.*
>
> —Plato, *Phaedo*

What is a ritual? At several points in the preceding chapters, I have articulated the theory of ritual action that serves as the foundation of my analyses of various cases. In *Naven or the Other Self* (Houseman and Severi 1998), Michael Houseman and I argued that a rite is determined more by its form than by its meaning or function. By "form," we meant a particular relational configuration that confers a distinctive ontological dimension on ritual interaction, which, in terms of both figure and ground, occupies a position that is distinct from ordinary social life. This dimension, which we viewed, in Gregory Bateson's terms ([1972] 1999, 35–40), as a "serious fiction," implies more than the traditional anthropological principle that the world evoked within a ritual must be interpreted according to a symbolic register.[1] It implies further, we argued, that the

---

1. An example of this can be found in E. E. Evans-Pritchard's analysis of the logic of Nuer sacrifice (1956), which Claude Lévi-Strauss traces as a series of qualitative analogies in which "a cucumber is worth an egg as a sacrificial victim, an egg a fish, a fish a hen, a hen a goat, a goat an ox" (Lévi-Strauss 1966, 224).

subjects as well as the objects of ritual action are defined by the particular nature of identity, which consists of traits that are both plural and contradictory.

We then attempted to generalize this model beyond the single example of *Naven*, which we had chosen because of its fundamental and paradigmatic characteristics, in order to overcome the limits of our approach imposed by the specific traits of that empirical case. Since the *Naven* ritual consists of a complex interaction based largely on binary pairs, Houseman went on to apply our method to cases of ritual action in which the form of interaction mobilizes sets of three terms (Houseman 2012). For my part, I proposed to extend the relational approach to situations in which language (which played a minor role in *Naven*) is the primary vehicle for the ritual action to unfold (Severi 2002, [2007] 2015). In the preceding chapters, I have proposed an interpretation of rituals in which, through an abduction of subjectivity, an inanimate *artifact* takes the place of a human subject in the action. I now want to take a further step and go beyond ritual contexts to demonstrate how the relational approach can shed light on situations where interactions are inscribed in other kinds of contexts. These may be interactions that, like certain forms of games, do not fulfill the essential conditions that define a ritual situation, or they may be ones that are not situated in a single rite but, rather, in cycles of action that mobilize various rituals.

My first exploration will extend the approach sketched in the preceding chapter (Chapter Five) concerning the ritual relationship between the dead and the living in ancient Greece. As a point of departure, I will describe the funerary games in the *Iliad* organized to honor the memory of Patroclus, and then analyze them in relation to the funeral rites and the context of the battles.

In the *Iliad*, Book 23, Homer describes the ritual orchestrated by Achilles in honor of his companion. The events that preceded this celebration are well known: in reaction to Achilles's refusal to continue fighting in the war to conquer Troy, Patroclus takes his companion's weapons and armor and goes to the battlefield in his place. During combat, he is killed by Hector, due to the secret intervention of Apollo. Furious, Achilles goes to the battlefield to avenge Patroclus and kills Hector. Nonetheless, this act of revenge does not exhaust his rage or calm his grief. Three episodes in the *Iliad* describe Achilles's intense suffering. The first one, in verse 18, involves the hero's violent reaction to the news that his friend has died:

> A dark cloud of grief fell upon Achilles as he listened. He filled both hands with dust from off the ground, and poured it over his head, disfiguring his comely face,

and letting the refuse settle over his shirt so fair and new. He flung himself down all huge and hugely at full length, and tore his hair with his hands. (*Iliad* 18: 22–27)

The second episode, one of the most famous in the epic, takes place in the middle of the night. After a meal shared with the other Myrmidon warriors, Achilles falls asleep, when the image of Patroclus appears before him.

Here a very deep slumber took hold upon him and eased the burden of his sorrows.... Presently the sad spirit of Patroclus drew near him, like what he had been in stature, voice, and the light of his beaming eyes, clad, too, as he had been clad in life. The spirit hovered over his head and said, "You sleep, Achilles, and have forgotten me; you loved me living, but now that I am dead you think for me no further. Bury me with all speed that I may pass the gates of Hades." (*Iliad* 23: 62–71)

Achilles tries to embrace him, yearning to weep with him: "Draw closer to me, let us once more throw our arms around one another, and find sad comfort in the sharing of our sorrows" (*Iliad* 23: 97–98). Right away, he realizes that only a "soul" or "shadow" remains of Patroclus, while the "spirit" (*phrénés*) has disappeared: "He opened his arms towards him as he spoke and would have clasped him in them, but there was nothing, and the spirit vanished as a vapour, gibbering and whining into the earth" (*Iliad* 23: 99–101).

In reality, Achilles's pain can be assuaged only if his mourning takes on a public form. After wiping away his tears, he turns to his duty to hold a solemn celebration, which mobilizes both ritual action and funerary games. The long ritual is a striking episode in the *Iliad*, remarkable for the excessive fury that characterizes Achilles's acts and for the constant reference to sacrifice, which, in ancient Greece, was reserved in principle for the gods. Achilles organizes a veritable holocaust of victims sacrificed in memory of Patroclus. To the "resistless and devouring might of the fire," he offers sheep, dogs, horses, jars filled with honey and oil, as well as "twelve brave sons of noble Trojans," whom Achilles slays with his sword (*Iliad* 23: 173–76). This is a unique case of human sacrifice in the Homeric epic. Once the ritual is complete, Achilles calls his warriors, invites them to sit in a circle, and challenges them to participate in a series of games.

What do the Homeric warriors compete for in the games? Achilles announces a prize for the fastest chariot racer (*Iliad* 23: 173–76). But a single competition is not enough. In honor of the deceased, Achilles announces a series of tests (races, boxing, wrestling, javelin throwing, archery, armed combat, and so on) to determine which warrior will be declared the best. Although one of Achilles's epithets is "the best of the Achaeans," he does not take part in the games, since he assumes the essential role of overseeing them. During the funeral ritual, he was both the organizer and a mourner. During the funerary games, he becomes the judge who declares which warrior has won each competition. In the Homeric era in Greece (which specialists concur in placing around the eighth century BCE), as in many other cultures, the competitive games concluded the ritual activities but were not part of the funeral itself. What, then, do the games bring to the ritual celebration? Why does the transition from one context to another, from mourning to competition, seem not only natural but necessary? What image of the deceased is expressed during the games, and how does this ludic image differ from the one presented in the funeral ritual? These are the questions I will attempt to answer by applying the relational model of ritual action.

Anthropologists have long debated the best way to interpret the relationship found in many societies between rites and games (see, e.g., Valeri 1981) and, notably, between funerary rituals and competitive games. No clear position has emerged from these discussions. Claude Lévi-Strauss's view, laid out in a few pages in *The Savage Mind*, stands out for its clarity and intuitive power (Lévi-Strauss [1962] 1966, 31–33). He questions the relationship between ludic and ritual action when analyzing the funerary practices of the Meskwaki, an Algonquin group of the Great Lakes, called the Fox by French colonists who had long waged war against them. Like the Homeric Achaeans, the Fox practiced both rituals and games to honor their warriors killed in battle. When a warrior died, tradition required that the deceased be immediately replaced by a living being. This obligation took on a double form. The first was ritualistic, individual, and ephemeral: one of the deceased's comrades-in-arms performed a dance that gave visual form to the circumstances of his death. Lévi-Strauss's source (Michelson 1925, cited in Lévi-Strauss [1962] 1966, 31) describes how one of the warriors, named Hirondelle-à-Tête-Blanche, took off on a mad race on horseback, throwing himself like his comrade had fallen and "dying" in the same way. It was a sort of funerary pantomime from which, of course, he emerged alive. In this case, the relationship between the living and the dead was individual and direct: the warrior's death was both represented and denied by the presence of a living replacement who was ritually identified with him.[2] But

---

2. The Fox rite shows certain parallels to the Apache Ghost Dance, a messianic ritual in which dancers would perform on the grave of a deceased warrior to make him immediately come back to life (see Severi [2007] 2015, 262–89).

the effect of this kind of pantomime could only be temporary, since the Fox did not believe that it prevented the soul of the vanished warrior from returning to the living.

To ensure his permanent disappearance, they performed a second, more stable form of replacing the deceased by adopting a true living person in place of the dead one. This was possible only through funerary games based on competition. The warriors were divided up into two groups of competitors: those who, for this occasion, represented the living and those who incarnated the dead. The outcome of the competition was, however, fixed: the "dead" (that is, the social group to which the deceased belonged and was thus obliged to ritually adopt a replacement) would always win over the "living," who had to reward the victors with a new warrior. In comparison to the warrior's dance, the collective game did not establish a direct relationship of identity between a living warrior and a deceased one. Rather, through competitive play, it represented the survivors' relationship to the dead by inventing another relationship, which could be called a fictive opposition between two groups of the living. To honor their dead, the group of Fox warriors was thus divided in two.

Lévi-Strauss proposes to contrast this ludic action with the prior ritual one. According to him, the ritual served to establish a social bond, while the game (notably, a competitive one) had the function of temporarily interrupting this bond by creating a dimension in which the social norm was suspended. He concludes that ludic action was based on the recognition of a dimension that was distinct from everyday life. It was a socially approved fiction in which the "separation of the antagonists," so often seen in competitive games, is the simplest example. He states, "Games thus appear to have a disjunctive effect: they end in the establishment of a difference between individual players or teams where originally there was no indication of inequality. And at the end of the game they are distinguished into winners and losers" (Lévi-Strauss [1962] 1966, 32).

I will return later to Lévi-Strauss's theoretical intuition concerning the nature of ludic action and its consequences. For the moment, note that if we adopt this perspective for the Homeric example, we cannot grasp the analogies and differences between the ritual and the game unless we clarify exactly what relationships are established in the fictive dimension of the game between Achilles, the competitors, and the image of the deceased Patroclus. During the games, within the "exceptional dimension" that functions as an implicit premise of the ludic action, something like "a real presence of the deceased" emerges (Rohde [1894] 2000, 17; Agamben 2001). As Erwin Rohde, Giorgio Agamben, and others have pointed out, the Homeric games embody a distinctive characteristic:

the ludic action is deliberately inscribed within the funerary ritual. This means that the participants do not merely compete *among themselves*; they also compete *with* Patroclus. The manner in which the warriors' competition encompasses the deceased remains to be elucidated. Although Agamben (2001) may have extended this idea too quickly to contemporary practices (such as playing cards with the dead), it is undoubtedly crucial for understanding this type of game. But how should we conceptualize the presence of the dead hero alongside the competitors? How should we evaluate the modalities and consequences of Patroclus's presence when we compare ludic and ritual action? Why and to what end do the warriors mobilized by Achilles take part in the funerary games?

All commentators on the *Iliad* have recognized that the Achaean warriors did not compete simply to win the prizes promised by Achilles to the victors (Homer lists "cauldrons, tripods, horses and mules, noble oxen, women with fair girdles, and swart iron" [*Iliad* 23: 259–60]); they competed above all to honor Patroclus. If this is what actually constitutes the collective aim of the game offered to the deceased hero, then what is the relationship among Patroclus, the competitors, and the winner of the ultimate prize who stands out from the group and receives "honor" as the best (*aristos*) of the warriors? How do these ludic relations fit into the core of a ritual that seems to follow its own logic, guided by a specific type of bond between the mourners and the deceased?

To answer these questions, we must grasp the relations mobilized by the Homeric funerary ritual in all their complexity. First, let us consider an initial difficulty. As I argued in Chapter Five, the Greek funerary ritual (especially that organized around the attribution of a speech to a *kouros* or *kôre* statue) unfolds entirely through the elaboration of an image and a verbal act that are situated within a ritual action conducted by a living participant in the present. The types of evidence gathered by Jesper Svenbro ([1988] 1993) and Jean-Pierre Vernant (1989, 1990) from written or archaeological sources make it possible to reconstitute such an act. However, the case of the *Iliad* seems quite different. The description of the ritual performed by Achilles is situated in a mythic era, for which the only evidence is the oral tradition. Achilles and Patroclus are only characters in a story. Up to now, I have been extending the study of relations of identification from ritual action performed by real people to the universe of artifacts in order to understand certain acts and words that humans attribute to them. But how should this method be applied to a narrative, shifting from a real mourner (or one who is supposedly real) to the protagonist of an epic tale? The difficulty concerns not only the shift to a narrative of an act performed in certain circumstances and under certain conditions; it also presents some difficulties in methodology. In the example of Phrasikleia discussed in Chapter Five, the vector of identification results from a redundancy organized around the word "I," which, within the verbal act, signifies *both* the mourner and the deceased. What linguistic method would enable us to trace a process of analogous identification in a poetic narrative? What kind of action or circumstance in a poet's work would authorize us to reconstruct the complex "I" of an identity constituted by contradictory traits, similar to that attributed above to the mourner in the funerary ritual?

To answer this question, the work of Gregory Nagy ([1979] 1999) on the Homeric oral tradition is useful. In recalling Milman Parry's findings and Albert Lord's comparative approach (Parry 1987; Lord 2010; see also Page 1959), Nagy reminds us that, in this form of poetry, which was governed by extreme technical rigor, individual deviation from a tradition was never allowed. In Homer, the contents of each specific action (an act of war, an encounter, a journey, a banquet) are narrowly constrained by a formula that is nearly fixed (Nagy [1979] 1999, 3). The specific form of the diction in the texts follows tradition and is always linked to a theme. The astonishing formal exactitude of the *Iliad* and the *Odyssey*, calling to mind the governing principle of verbal economy that runs throughout the epics, is proof, Nagy argues, that this poetry is not the work of an individual poet. Rather, the Greek epics are the result of a collective, anonymous, and gradual process. Its final phase took place between the fifth century BCE and the sixth century CE, at which point we still find Homeric traditions, notably on vase paintings, that do not appear in the versions of the epics with which we are familiar (Parry 1987; Lord 2010; Page 1959). This process of progressive refinement occurred through innumerable selections, rehearsals, and adjustments, transforming the vast range of local traditions sung by different skilled epic poets (*aoidoi*) into the great heritage of Panhellenic collective oral traditions that are conventionally grouped under the name of Homer. The dominant themes, artistry, unity, and verbal technique of these poems "must be assigned not simply to one poet but also to countless generations of previous poets steeped in the same traditions" (Nagy [1979] 1999, 3).

The universe of Homeric poetry coincides with that of the traditions of ancient Greece; its language and its themes are consistent with such traditions. The simplest example of the exact relationship between form and content that results from this process is the use of epithets. For example, when the Homeric poet mentions a Greek fleet, he often resorts to a formula evoking the lightness, speed, shape, or color of the ships. Achilles is repeatedly called "godlike," "son of Peleus," or "swift footed"; Zeus is "the son of Cronus" or "wide seeing." Oak trees are "ample spreading" and the sea is said to be "roaring" or, more rarely, "the color of wine." Nagy identifies two movements governing the use of these verbal definitions in the Homeric oral tradition. In the first, a process of dissemination occurs, which leads to the proliferation of certain terms, such as "divine."[3] In the second, the repertoire of epithets available to a poet appears to go through a process of selection, which limits the use of certain precise formulas to well-defined characters.

Nagy ([1979] 1999, 4) adopts Parry's (1987) distinction between fixed, generic epithets and particularized, distinctive ones. The Homeric epics make rigorous use of the latter. For example, the formula "equal to Ares," which describes a warrior as being similar to the god of war, is reserved in the *Iliad* to two characters: Achilles and his Trojan adversary, Hector (Nagy [1979] 1999, 33). A rigorous logic thus operates in the use of these verbal formulas. However, Nagy shows that the Homeric tradition does not only affect the formulas and epithets; it also selects and carefully defines the words themselves and, above all, the proper names of the characters. As a particular verbal form inscribed in speech, the Homeric proper name acquires a meaning with a direct connection to the content. To grasp the identity of a character in the epic, it is necessary to translate the proper name and associate it with the series of epithets attributed to it by tradition. For instance, Nagy ([1979] 1999, 69–78) translates the word *Achilles* as "he who has the host of fighting men (*lâos*) grieving (*akhos*)"—a definition that contains a sort of prefiguration of his destiny and the role he plays in the plot. Similarly, *Patroclus* means "he who bears the glory (*kléos*) of the ancestors" (*patroon*).

The traits of a particular character in the epic come to be defined by tradition through a process that is most likely linked to a mnemonic technique. A set of generic epithets is used ("godlike," "swift footed," "lion-hearted," and so on), which gradually become individualized in the character of Achilles through the use of a restricted group of specific epithets until the meaning of his proper name indicates, by allusion, his particular story.

This approach has the merit of illuminating both the contents of the epic and its formal aspects and, indeed, certain techniques used in ancient Greek oral

---

3. Parry (1987) shows that the use of the epithet was so widespread in the Homeric era that the adjective "divine," for instance, could be applied not only to gods, warriors, and heroes but even to animals.

traditions. In considering once again the analyses of *artes memorandi* presented in Chapter Three, the links from proper names to generic and distinctive epithets can be conceptualized as a means for focusing memory. If the name of a character has a meaning, it can be thought of as a mnemonic device. If distinctive epithets are added to a proper name as a narrative unfolds, the ways they are used makes it possible to recall the episodes to which they refer. Some features of ancient mnemonic techniques, which we know only through their results, thus appear in a new light by analyzing the relationship between proper names and epithets (and perhaps also between epithets and episodes).

This approach—which could be compared with Erich Auerbach's commentary on the Homeric style ([1946] 2003, 3–23, 26–30)—certainly merits a separate study. For present purposes, the most relevant point is that the oral tradition of the Homeric epic is a collective and anonymous phenomenon, perfectly comparable to the universe of ritual I have addressed elsewhere. The poet's language in the epic always coincides with that of tradition, and each character is defined by a series of verbal formulas, which enables the poet to gradually and accurately memorize their identities, functions, and sometimes, through the interpretation of proper names, the destiny that awaits them.

But more is involved than this. Homeric epithets not only allow an oral poet to call to mind certain characters, for instance, through a function ("herald with the resonant voice") or lineage ("Antilochus, son of Nestor"); as soon as the poet focuses on a distinctive epithet, this mode of definition through a "verbal formula" may become more complex and assume a new function. The examples Nagy has focused on the most concern the two protagonists, Achilles and Patroclus, in the ritual and funerary games that I examine next.

Let us thus return to the episode where Patroclus goes to war (*Iliad* 11: 604). He dons Achilles's armor and takes his weapons, then leaves the tent to join the battlefield, where he will be killed. Nagy ([1979] 1999, 33) points out that this is the first and only time in the poem that he is described as "the equal of Ares," the god of war: "He [Patroclus] came out, equal to Ares, and that was the beginning of his doom" (*Iliad* 11: 604, as translated in Nagy [1979] 1999, 33). By adding this description to Patroclus's proper name and other epithets, the poet here uses an epithet in principle reserved for Achilles, at least in the Achaeans's camp. Patroclus thus indirectly incarnates the figure of Achilles through the name he bears. The use of the distinctive epithet in this case no longer conveys a generic definition of a character for the purposes of memorization. Rather, it serves to provisionally transfer a verbal formula usually identifying someone else to another protagonist, much like the image of Patroclus taking up Achilles's weapons. At the same time, the transfer serves as a memory aid for an oral poet by prefiguring subsequent episodes as the plot develops.

This is undoubtedly an example of prolepsis, a verbal technique through which the memory of a character encompasses his or her future, which, in this case, is the destiny that Patroclus will meet in the epic. However, the exchange of the epithet also serves as a clue to the identification between Patroclus and Achilles, a relation that will gradually intensify as the narrative moves forward. It is thus the first time that one of them appears in the guise of the other. This example provides an initial key for exploring how the epic narrative uses its particular means to accomplish what the ritual achieves through action: an identification, partial and linked to specific circumstances, between two characters.

Let us now consider how this relationship, which the use of the epithet represents as a form of narrative prefiguration, develops in the ritual action.

THE IMAGE THROUGH THE TEXT: IDENTIFICATION, HIERARCHY, AND PREFIGURATION

The ritual begins with weeping. The need to "give due honor" to Patroclus spreads among the Myrmidons as a moral imperative. Patroclus must be given his *géras*, his share of the spoils of war. Only in this way will he be able to take refuge in Hades and no longer torment the living, as he promised Achilles. Surrounded by his warriors, Achilles "laid his blood-stained hands," which had killed Hector, on Patroclus's body. A cycle of actions is set in motion, which seems to follow two parallel trajectories: the honor rendered to his friend for his "beautiful death" (Vernant 1991, 50–74) coincides with the outrage committed against the corpse of Hector. This may explain the excess that characterizes the ritual, which all commentators on these episodes have noted. The extreme cruelty shown toward Hector's body corresponds, through a sort of hyperbole, to the extreme honor (expressed through a hypertrophic *géras*) that Achilles wishes to render in memory of Patroclus. Before performing the ritual in memory of Patroclus, Achilles takes Hector's body, "laying it at full length in the dust" (*Iliad* 23: 24), and proceeds to mutilate and humiliate it. He ties the body to his chariot and drags it along the ground before abandoning it, defiled, for dogs and birds to devour. By contrast, the body of Patroclus is consecrated through fire and the blood of sacrificial victims. "Many a goodly ox, with many a sheep and bleating goat did they butcher and cut up; many a tusked boar moreover, fat and well-fed, did they singe and set to roast in the flames of Vulcan; and rivulets of blood flowed all round the place where the body was lying" (*Iliad* 23: 30–34). Then follow the scenes in which Achilles succumbs to the grieving desire (*pothos*) to come into contact with the deceased and, almost, to die like him. Patroclus answers him with a prediction and a request. He reveals that Achilles, at the moment of his own death, will suffer the same fate ("you too Achilles, peer of gods, are doomed to die beneath the wall of the noble Trojans") (*Iliad* 23: 80–82). We know that, just as Patroclus was killed by Apollo, so, too, will Achilles. Patroclus then asks that his bones and those of Achilles be placed in the same urn. This image of the conjunction of the bodies and destinies of the deceased and the ritual mourner is matched by the gesture of the group of warriors who, later on, will cut their hair and cover Patroclus's body with it. This gesture introduces Patroclus into what could be called the common body of the warriors, signifying that, even after his death, he is still one of them. Later, Achilles performs this same gesture and places a lock of his own hair "in the hands of his dear comrade" (*Iliad* 23: 152–53; see also Vernant 1989, 66).

Next comes the scene of the sacrifice through fire (*Iliad* 22: 164ff). Achilles smears the fat of the sacrificial victims over Patroclus's body. He adds jars of honey and the oil of numerous victims: horses, dogs, sheep, and a dozen young Trojans. After several attempts to kindle the pyre, which is having trouble catching fire, Achilles prays to the winds to stir the flames, which then flare up. In the morning, he pours wine for Patroclus one last time and then begins sorting through the bones, separating those of the sacrificed animals from those of his friend's body. The burial site is marked out and the bones are gathered in a golden urn, protected by animal fat and "covered with a soft fabric" (*Iliad* 22: 255–56). The indications of a conjunction between the images of Achilles and Patroclus are so numerous in these ritual scenes that it would be difficult to deny that, even more than a public expression of *pothos*, the Homeric form of the funerary ritual is based on an identification between the mourner and the deceased. Indeed, when Homer defines Patroclus, leaving the tent he shares with Achilles to go to battle, as being "equal to Ares," he is *prefiguring* a cycle of actions that, over the course of the narrative, gradually intensify the identification between the two protagonists. During the battle, Patroclus, who had taken up his friend's weapons, already embodied the image of Achilles in the eyes of all the other warriors. But the words Patroclus speaks and the ritual actions that are organized around his death go even further.

He tells his friend, "You too Achilles, peer of gods, are doomed to die beneath the wall of the noble Trojans," and asks, "let our bones lie but in a single urn" (*Iliad* 23: 81–89). All these indications converge on a term the epic constantly employs to designate the bond that unites Patroclus and Achilles: one is the *therapôn* of the other. What is the meaning of this word? Annie Schnapp-Gourbeillon recalls that, "Rivers of ink have been spilled over the friendship between Patroclus and Achilles. It seems certain that the original meaning of their heroic relationship was already lost in ancient Greece to such an extent that it was reduced to a rather banal model of male camaraderie" (Schnapp-Gourbeillon 1979, 85). Recent work by Victoria Tarenzi (2005) clarifies this point. The term, scattered throughout the Homeric epic, often takes on a simplified meaning of "companion-in-arms" or "squire." Almost all the great warriors in the *Iliad* have their *therapôn*, such as Menelaus, Agamemnon, Idomenee, Sarpedon, and Nestor. Throughout the narrative, these *therapôntes* receive guests, take care of horses, fetch wood, or, after a battle, strip the weapons from enemies killed by their master (Tarenzi 2005, 25). But the situation with Patroclus is an exception. When he is living in the same tent as Achilles, he deals with the minute details of his master's daily life, but notably, Homer does not call him a *therapôn* in this context. The descriptor does not appear until it is used to designate a ritual relationship between Achilles and Patroclus. Nagy has shown that, in this case, the term indicates a social relationship that is less vague than "servant" or "companion-in-arms": "This word *therapôn* is a prehistoric Greek borrowing from the Anatolian languages (most likely sometime in the second millennium B.C.), where it had meant 'ritual substitute'" (Nagy [1979] 1999, 33; see also Van Brock 1959; Lowenstam 1981; Chantraine 1980).

In the literature devoted to Mesopotamian civilization (see, e.g., Bottéro 1987), we find a description of the use of the term *tarpalli*, from which *therapôn* was derived. In Sumer, this term designated the person or animal chosen to be a substitute for the king if an omen indicated he was going to die or was about to suffer a fatal destiny (Bottéro 1987, 180–84). Jean Bottéro gives the example of a ritual performed to prevent the death of an ill king. The sovereign was supposed to lie down in his bed with a small goat. The next morning, a grave was dug, and the king and the goat would climb down into it. An executioner then went through the motions of cutting their throats, but in the king's case, the execution was feigned. The body of the dead goat, called a *tarpalli*, was then treated like a human corpse: it was washed, perfumed, and dressed in the king's clothes, and a funerary rite was performed over its remains in memory of the king (Bottéro 1987, 145–65).

The *therapôn* is thus, in its religious sense, the ritual substitute for someone: he is the one who can take his place during a ritual and share his destiny. In the language proposed by Nagy, the logical conclusion is that Patroclus, "glory of the ancestors," is the ritual substitute for Achilles, "he whose host of fighting men (*lâos*) are grieving (*akhos*)" (Nagy [1979] 1999, 78). However, this etymology—the soundness of which only specialists in the subject can judge—does not suffice for an analysis centered on ritual action, such as the one attempted here. How can this general concept of "ceremonial identification" be associated with the sequence of actions that punctuate the ritual performed by Achilles? The Homeric form of this ritual, which all commentators emphasize has a singular character, perhaps even aberrant, undoubtedly refers to an identification between the two *therapôn*. But this relationship is established in quite different ways than elsewhere. By examining their characteristics, I intend to refine my analysis and anticipate an unexpected relation between ritual and funerary games.

At first, the *Iliad* presents Patroclus as the minor, subordinate double of Achilles. Patroclus lives in the latter's tent, and it is only when he is in the presence of his protector that he is described as a warrior (Nagy [1979] 1999, 33). From a purely formal point of view, the relationship between Patroclus and Achilles is thus not merely one of simple equivalence. It concerns, rather, a double relationship on two levels: one implies an identity in the character of the two warriors (who have been companions-in-arms since their youth, when Patroclus, who had killed a fellow student, was taken into Peleus's home); the other, by contrast, posits a hierarchical difference between them, with one being conceived as superior to the other. To borrow the language of Louis Dumont (1970), we could say that this relationship of identity encompasses a relationship of difference, almost a domination of one over the other, which sometimes appears clearly in the text. However, the development of the narrative and the description of the ritual gradually modify this aspect of the link between the two warriors. As soon as he leaves the tent to go into battle, Patroclus evolves to become the *equal* of Achilles. This transformation, which goes through several stages, becomes especially evident when Antiochus, by orders of Menelaus, recounts how Patroclus died:

Antilochus, come here and listen to sad news, which I would indeed were untrue. You must see with your own eyes that heaven is heaping calamity upon the Danaans, and giving victory to the Trojans. "The best [*aristos*] of the Achaeans has been killed, Patroklos, that is; and a great loss has been inflicted on the Danaans" (*Iliad* 17: 685–90, as translated in Nagy [1979] 1999, 33).

Here, we may recognize another example of the technique of exchange epithets, which Nagy has brought to light in the above passage: "the best of the Achaeans as been killed." When we hear this epithet, we modern readers (like Homer's public) assume it refers to Achilles, since "best of the Achaeans" has been a distinctive epithet usually reserved for him. It is through this new exchange that the text suggests that the death of Patroclus *prefigures* that of Achilles, just as the epithet the "equal to Ares" is applied to Patroclus as a way of prefiguring the warrior's valor, which he will prove on the battlefield. Indeed, Achilles will be killed later by Apollo, the same god who had killed Patroclus. As Schnapp-Gourbeillon remarks,

Patroclus and Achilles are, at this point, two figures rigorously indissociable figures, who represent the various manifestations of the hero's *hybris*. Patroclus dies because of the same god who will cause Achilles to die . . . a god, and not a man, will put an end to his existence. (Schnapp-Gourbeillon 1979, 85)

It should be remembered that Patroclus, despite appearances, was not actually killed by Hector. As Patroclus himself declares, Hector deserves little credit for the deed: his role in killing Patroclus came after Euphorbia and, even more decisively, after "the son of Latona," Apollo. "The death of Achilles is thus visible like a watermark in the narration of the death of Patroclus and the obsequies performed in his honor" (Schnapp-Gourbeillon 1979, 86).

This intensifying process of identification of Patroclus with Achilles reaches its peak with the announcement of the former's death when, as Nagy ([1979] 1999, 113) points out, Thetis and her sisters sing a solemn funeral lamentation *for the death of Achilles*. The text presents the latter as nevertheless alive and ready for vengeance. It is as if he were already dead and his body were prepared for the ritual *prothesis* (public display). Thetis calls her sisters to listen to her woes:

Ah me, the wretch! Ah me, the mother—so sad it is—of the very best. / I gave birth to a faultless and strong son, / the very best of heroes. And he shot up like a seedling. / I nurtured him like a shoot in the choicest spot of the orchard, / only to send him off on curved ships to fight at Troy. And I will never be welcoming him back home as returning warrior, back to the House of Peleus. (*Iliad* 18: 54–60, as translated in Nagy [1979] 1999, 182).

Thus, upon the death of Patroclus, the lamentation given is over the disappearance of Achilles. One of them replaces the other entirely this time. This is the full meaning of the term *therapôn* if it is understood, as Nagy proposes, as a "ritual substitute." Nonetheless, it is essential to recognize that Achilles and Patroclus are linked through a relationship that is considerably more complex than the one I have elsewhere designated as a "ritual identification." Composed partly of absolute equality (as when Achilles is seized by the desire to be dead, just like his friend), partly of domination (when Achilles protects his friend with no weapons), and partly of prefiguration (when Patroclus, through his death, prefigures that of Achilles), the link that makes one the *therapôn* of the other is rooted in certain aspects on the axis of symmetry and, through others, on that of complementarity. The actions taken by Patroclus transform him from a condition of being a minor double of his companion to the status of a hero in his own right, equivalent to that of Achilles. This is how he was able to become, like the latter, "equal to Ares." When he dies on the battlefield, he is thenceforth recognized, as is Achilles, as the "best of the Achaeans."

Later, ritual action will again modify the terms of their relationship. At that point, Patroclus is celebrated by Achilles and the Myrmidons as a warrior who has attained a "beautiful death," that state of "definitive youth" that makes him an almost divine hero (Vernant 1991, 50–74). Another reason must be considered for the exceptional nature of this ritual, which, furthermore, enjoins us not to treat it as a general model. Patroclus is the recipient of a solemn celebration when Achilles bows down before him, paying homage to his glorious death. During the rite, which contains a reference to the identification between the two, the hierarchical aspect of their relationship is inverted. It is now Achilles who pays tribute to his friend, the hero. During the ritual action, we can even perceive a sense of competition between the deceased and the mourner. Performing this ritual means at one and the same time identifying with and recognizing the superiority of he who, having been the first to die in battle, is the first to attain the rank of a hero, which makes him almost worthy of a cult (Nagy [1979] 1999, 9). This is the reason why Patroclus, killed in battle as the "best of the Achaeans," is celebrated not only as a victim of Apollo but also as the victor of another ordeal, one that conveys the rank of hero on a person. In his memory, the Greeks not only owe him the *kléos* and *géras*, but also a sentiment closer to a *timê*, a religious reverence that, in ancient Greece, was almost exclusively reserved for the gods but that heroes could also arouse. Later, it will be the turn of his *therapôn*, he who, for the moment, plays the role of the mourner. An altar will also be dedicated to Patroclus on Hellespont, taking the form of a fire that will never be extinguished.

In the universe of the rite as in that of the game, however, it is clear that one of them takes the place of the other. It is Achilles who proclaims and organizes the games in honor of Patroclus, and it is he who prepares and distributes the prizes to the winners. The death of his *therapôn* is a presage of his own death, just as the honor of the former is also his own. This singular relationship, which seems to combine substitutions and competition, makes it possible to enter the dimension of the funerary games, in which the two ritual *therapôntes* merge into the same double figure and where one may always take the place of the other as "another self" (Schnapp-Gourbeillon 1979, 86). The tradition of the Panhellenic games will make this ambiguous figure into a paradigmatic image of the hero. The games in honor of Patroclus become, indeed, the mythic precursor of the Olympic games in antiquity. These games are offered to Patroclus and intended to honor his memory. On Olympus, before beginning the games, a funerary ritual had to be performed. But there, the ritual was celebrated in honor of Achilles, not of Patroclus.

To summarize so far, the ritual described by Homer is marked by a series of anomalies tied to the exacerbation of the contrast between the two notable deaths—Hector is delivered to the dogs and birds, while Patroclus is honored as a hero. However, this ritual seems to be part of the same relational horizon as that of the funerary cults, distant in time and attested by sources of different kinds, which I have analyzed in Chapter Five. The ritual identification between the mourner and the deceased, which is brought about through a specific relationship linking two *therapôntes*, is much different, from a formal point of view, from the chains of partial identification that I was able to highlight earlier. This link, which is gradually accentuated as the narration moves forward, implies two opposite sides of the relationship, equality and hierarchy, in which one is subsumed by the other. While gradually intensifying the identification between them, to the point of confusing the two bodies after death, the ritual action inverts the terms of the hierarchy by making the one who was protected into the protector, and the unarmed companion into a hero, whose death is celebrated as a victory. Playing with a series of exchanges of distinctive epithets, the Homeric tradition accomplishes this complex identification through a cyclical sequence of episodes, which makes one of the terms of the relation a prefiguration of the destiny of the other. The various episodes examined above can be imagined as a *cycle of successive identities* in which Achilles and Patroclus together designate the complex presence of a deceased warrior in the midst of the living. It is this form of presence—an intermediate structure between the living and the dead—that the funerary games will develop.

FUNERARY GAMES AS QUASI-RITUALS

Let us review the episode of the funerary games in the *Iliad*. Achilles organizes a series of competitions—chariot races around the grave, javelin throwing, boxing, wrestling, armed combat, discus throwing, archery—and promises prizes of great value for the winners. In the role of judge, Achilles again shows himself to be closely linked to Patroclus. The symmetrical schema that had governed the relationship between the two men does not change during the games: that which "honors" the memory of the warrior killed in combat confirms the prestige of the one who commemorates his death. But the games also invent a form of specific interaction, absent in the ritual, that concerns the relationship established by the group of Myrmidons with the dead through the identification of a winner. Recall that Lévi-Strauss, in his study of the funerary beliefs of Fox warriors, suggested that the games contained a disjunctive function ([1962] 1966, 31–33). The ethnography he used to advance his reflection (unfortunately too fragmentary to enable a true analysis) provided him with an example of two distinct ways of effecting a ludic disjunction. The first was based on an individual relationship between the deceased and the living person who pretended to replace him, demonstrating that he could remain alive in the same circumstances that had provoked the death of his companion-in-arms. The second occurred through the staging of a game in which two groups of warriors competed: the group that, during the game, represented the living, and the other that stood for the dead. Unlike the single warrior's pantomime, this collective game did not posit a direct relationship of identity with death. Rather, it represented a link between the living and the dead through the invention of a bond between two opposing groups of the living. The creation of this new relationship highlights the theoretical possibility, within the confines of the game, of *extending the social space from the individual to the collective*. It does so by making it conceivable to move from the space mobilized by the preceding ritual, embracing a relationship between a living person and a deceased one, to a relationship that is "played" between the living and thereby reiterates their relationship to the dead—all of which is expressed on the collective level.

What aspects of this theoretical possibility might apply to the funerary games described in the *Iliad*? Here, a ritual relationship of mourning, which mobilizes a dual bond between the deceased and the celebrant, is likewise extended to a collective activity that evokes the relationship to the world of the dead. In contrast to the ritual action, which associates the group of warriors as a single collective body that includes Patroclus, the action in the games assumes a disjunctive function. The challenge in the ludic medium is to establish who is the "best of the Achaeans" in which one winner will emerge. However, as Rohde ([1894] 2000) long ago remarked, the competitors do not only play among themselves: they also play *with Patroclus*. How does this conjunction between play and rite operate in connection to the world of the dead?

In ancient Greece, all relations with the dead were based on an implicit premise: the dead oppose the living and demand the "share in the spoils" (*géras*) that belongs to them. The living, who are in debt to the dead, are obliged to offer ritual acts to them. The funerary games described by Homer do not alter this overall structure, but they construct a parallel field of relations where those who oppose the world of the dead are not a unified "world of the living" but, rather, several groups of players engaged in a reciprocal competition. During the temporal framework of these games (which is unthinkable without the ritual action), each player's action is situated within two parallel spaces: one in which the living play against other living people, and another materialized by the ritual, which stays in the background and opposes the dead to the living.

This process of duplicating the context—one being ritual, the other ludic—has a double consequence. On the one hand, it preserves the autonomy of the ludic action vis-à-vis the ritual action. The universe of the games follows its own rules, which must not be confused with the constitutive rules of the rite. The aim of the games is to identify who will win a prize. Nothing is offered to Patroclus—except the game itself. On the other hand, the constant reference in each of the actions involving ludic action to two distinct relational spaces (that of the ritual, opposing the living to the dead, and that of the games, which opposes the living among themselves) confers a double relational value on the behavior of the players.

The warrior who wins the competition in, for example, boxing or horse racing, is awarded valuable objects chosen by Achilles. The victor's public image is thus defined, in the first place, by the complementary relations established by the game between the group of players and the victor (who, for once, is not Achilles). Moreover, his image is equally defined in relation to the world of the dead. As the victor of the game, he is proclaimed the "best of the Achaeans." He thus becomes, for a time, the living image of Patroclus, who had assumed this epithet. It is through this parallel relational value that Patroclus enters the game: through play, the victor serves as a figure in the world of the living who now embodies the hero who has passed to the world of the dead.

By mobilizing two groups of parallel relationships—ludic and ritual—that simultaneously involve the games practiced among the living and the ritual commemorating the deceased, the competition among the living creates a mimetic relation with the deceased. Through the competition, a transformation takes place that makes the man who wins the game the equal of Patroclus for a defined period of time. This identificatory function is not limited to the moment when the victor temporarily assumes the title and epithet, like the deceased hero, of the best of the Achaeans; it is also confirmed several times through the nature of certain prizes given by Achilles to the victors. Among these prizes are objects of value, such as horses and sometimes women, but other prizes are "memory-objects" of Patroclus, linked to his life and his person. In this sense, they can be considered his *semata* (plural of *sema*, sign, symbol, tomb). Notable among them is the *krater* (wine vessel) that belonged to Patroclus while he was alive; articles he stripped from enemies he had killed, such as Sarpedon's spear, helmet, and shield; and the sword Achilles captured from Asteropaeus to avenge Patroclus's death. Those who win in the games will hold these objects in their hands; their triumph will redound to the honor of Patroclus. In this way, the competition creates mimesis on yet another level. Thus, the warriors are competing in the games for a specific aim: *to become Patroclus*. Just as a devotee of Apollo may offer him a *kolossos* in the shape of a triumphant god, so, too, Achilles honors Patroclus by presenting him repeatedly with the image of a victorious warrior.

It is now possible to specify the type of articulation that takes place between the ritual action and the games in the epic. After the ritual has created a domain that encompasses a particular bond between Achilles and the deceased Patroclus, the ludic activities expand this domain by extending it from Achilles to the rest of the warriors as a group. At the same time, these activities exclude all ambiguity from the relational universe of this domain. Within the ritual, Patroclus iss treated as both a victim and a victor; within the funerary games, he takes on only a positive image. The ritual action, enacted within a dual relationship between *therapôntes*, preserves the full intensity of the presence, both close and ambivalent, of the image of the deceased. The game then introduces some distance and constructs a representation in which Patroclus becomes, through the games in which the winners are not predetermined, the hero of all the warriors.

This analysis of the way in which the ritual and the games are articulated enables us to comprehend two different forms of relational complexity. The ludic action, linked to a univocal identity of the deceased it is intended to honor, seems to ignore the essence of the prior ritual action, which had condensed the contradictory traits of the identity of the mourners. The latter identity is epitomized by the bond between ritual *therapôntes* that is enacted in the Homeric form of the funerary rite. The representation of the traditional figure of the hero that the ritual generates is double and contradictory on both the axis of hierarchy and that of competition. More specifically, the ritual draws a complex image of the hero through two operations: prefiguration, whereby the hierarchical relations between the living and the dead are inverted; and identification, whereby an image is contructed out of traits that belong (or will belong) to the victor and the victim. By contrast, the game captures but one single image: that of the victor, an image that is emphasized by being generated repeatedly through the outcome of each successive competition.

Both unstable and collectively aroused, the ludic form of the identification with the deceased is constructed in parallel with its ritual form without being confused with it. This articulation between the funeral and the games designates a complex form of action with a double context, one ritual, the other ludic. This example from the *Iliad* may help us in the future to elaborate this model through other exercises in comparative anthropology.

It would be illusory, however, to categorically oppose rituals to games in some kind of typology, based on this reading of the *Iliad*, by claiming, for instance, that all games everywhere have a "simpler" structure than that of the ritual action. To demonstrate this, it suffices to note that the word *game* does not designate a class of comparable phenomena but, instead, an open and perhaps unlimited series of family resemblances (see Wittgenstein [1942] 1965, 48).

This analysis leads us away from such typologies (even if it proves useful for other ethnographic studies) in two new directions. First, it takes us toward the empirical territory of what might be called quasi-ritual interactions: situations that, without corresponding to the definition given above to ritual action, can nevertheless be studied by using this method I have been constructing, based on the identification of relationships brought about through action.[4] The Homeric funerary games are a good example of forms of interaction that can be linked to a ritual without being confused with it.

REFLECTIONS ON FUNERAL RITUALS AMONG THE WARI'

Let us now turn toward some theoretical reflections on how these analyses of ritual may be generalized. In a study of Wari' funerary cannibalism, Aparecida Vilaça (2014) deals ethnographically with two of the issues I discussed above: the condensation of contradictory identities and the degree of complexity that characterizes the ritual action in comparison to other types of interactions.

Vilaça describes Wari' cannibalism as a two-stage ritual. It is preceded by a long vigil held over the body by the kin of the deceased, who maintain physical contact with the body during their grieving but abstain from using the deceased's name, using only indirect means of reference. They then call on nonkin of the deceased to cut up, cook, and consume the body. This first stage of the ritual, when the mourning is so intense that some kin may attempt suicide to join the spirit of the deceased in the afterlife, is marked by an absolute prohibition on the kin to take part in the meal. Everything is done in their place by designated nonkin. During the second stage, which marks the end of the mourning, a hunting party is organized to go after peccaries, followed by a collective meal shared by both kin and nonkin of the deceased. During the meal, the animal they eat is explicitly called a "corpse." Vilaça points out that, for the Wari', the person is normally defined in double terms, simultaneously as "human" (*wari*) and "animal" (*karawa*).

Through the funerary cannibalism, she argues, the deceased is reduced to a single identity, that of an animal prey. The deceased's body is viewed only as a peccary, called a "corpse," and is collectively consumed at the end of the ritual cycle. Vilaça maintains that the ritual action (in this case, the funerary cannibalism) is responsible for reducing the complexity of the definition of the person. This contrasts with the interpretation that Houseman and I advanced in our book on the *Naven* ritual, through which the definition of the person is made

---

4. For an initial development of the concept based on this definition, see the texts compiled by Berthomé, Bonhomme, and Delaplace (2012).

more complex in comparison to ordinary life.[5] In the Wari' case as Vilaça presents it, there seems to be a paradox: on the one hand, the ritual does not promote any condensation of contradictory identities, while, on the other, "ordinary life" involves a more complex definition of the person through contradictory identities (human vs. animal).

It may be true that, in certain funerary rituals, something like the process of reducing the complexity of social bonds takes place, especially when the person is already defined by the condensation of opposite identities, such as Vilaça argues is the case among the Wari'. To assess this claim, however, would require a detailed review of certain ethnographic aspects of this ritual, which I have only touched on lightly so far. It would be particularly revealing to take a closer look at the special and indirect names reserved for the deceased, which, as I argued earlier, sometimes prefigure the ritual relationship that will be established between the deceased and the living. Furthermore, it would be valuable to consider evidence for the marked difference in the rite between the bodies of the living and of the dead. Vilaça argues that in the former, two definitions, human/animal, coexist, while in the latter, only one of the terms of the pair is incarnated (for nonkin during the first stage of the rite, and for everybody during the second), specifically, as an "animal prey," conveyed by the ritual identification between the deceased and a peccary. People ask nonkin during the rite to consume the body of their close kinsperson, as if it were an animal prey—even though for them it retains all the characteristics of a person ("We remember them too strongly," said one of them). When they make this request, it seems to evoke precisely a link between humans and animals through "condensation" and, within human society, between "people who have the same flesh" (that is, for the Wari', close kin) and "people who have different flesh" (nonkin).

Let us therefore look more closely at the pair *wari* (human) and *karawa* (animal), which defines human beings for the Wari', according to Vilaça, and the transformations that the ritual action makes them undergo. As a *wari* (human), a nonkinsperson consumes the flesh of a human who is ritually assimilated to the body of an animal, doing so "in the place of" (and at the request of) a kinsperson. At the same time, nonkin, as *karawa*, behave as predators. The ritual identity of the latter is thus the result of a complex series of identifications

---

5. See Houseman and Severi (1998). What follows here, however, reflects my point of view only, for which I assume full responsibility.

constituted by contradictory traits: they are both animal and human, nonkin and kin (since, although nonkin, they take the place of kin at their request). The kin who make the request are "made of the same flesh" and thus identified with the deceased but also, indirectly, with the nonkin who consume the deceased's flesh in their place. In short, if the ritual does involve some kind of decomplexification, it occurs only with regard to the body of the deceased kinsperson (or the deceased's inverse figure, the peccary called a "corpse"), but not the other participants in the ritual action.

But let us reflect further on the ritual presence of the deceased. A brief analysis of the Wari' *chicha* "drinking parties," mentioned in Vilaça's article, reveals that the binary opposition, *wari* versus *karawa*, is actually a triad, since the ritual relationship between humans and animals almost always implies the presence of the dead in the course of the ritual action. The ethnographic description informs us that during these festivals, when the hosts play the role of humans and the guests must appear in the form of animals, the guests are often also considered to be "the dead." They symbolically become the dead in at least three ways: when they lose consciousness due to the copious amounts of beer they are forced to swallow (an unconscious state that the Wari' assimilate to death); when, in the course of one of the most important Wari' rituals, the *tamara*, the dead assume the form of peccaries and come to the world of their living kin; or when the guests, in the form of animals, are ritually "killed like peccaries" by their hosts. As Vilaça notes, during these events, the Wari' take the same verbal precautions toward the guests-cum-dead that they take toward the deceased person whose body they will consume during the funerary rite. For the guests as well, the passage from a person to an anonymous body precedes the passage from a human body to an animal prey. Thus, for both the dead and the guests, a transformation of a relationship takes place.

Other forms of identification between animals and the dead are added, since the Wari' believe that animals, in turn, can manifest themselves as strangers, affines, enemies, or even sorcerers, following a progressive scale of forms of alterity that are increasingly complex, a typical Amazonian phenomenon. In short, undertaking a relational analysis of the cycle of festivals that precedes the funerary rite reveals a chain of transformations, a sort of ritual life cycle, in which condensed identities take turns appearing, so to speak, during the *chicha* drinking festivals. This movement may form the backdrop that progressively prepares the identities of the participants in the funerary ritual, who, over time, take turns being hosts or guests.

Thus, if we apply an ethnological framework for analyzing the ritual, the identities of kin and nonkin alike appear to be "complex" almost from the start or, at least, to be apprehended in a context that evokes complexity. In this regard, to speak of an identity belonging to "ordinary life" that will be ritually "decomplexified" after death entails merely a sort of optical illusion. From a wider perspective, a universe of ritualized transformations is gradually constructed through the complex identities created in the relational field of the *chicha* festivals, thus generating the cycle that the funerary ritual must conclude through a process of decomplexification. What would not be visible from the perspective of the analysis of a single ritual therefore appears clearly if we choose to go beyond and study the *cycles of ceremonial actions*, in which each ritual in the series constitutes the relevant context for understanding the others.

In the eyes of the Wari', this incessant cycle of transformations does not stop at death. The indigenous interpretation of suicide and the myth mentioned by Vilaça show that, for the Wari', "to die" is only a way for the living to reach a place where, reduced to an animal state, the dead perceive each other as exact analogues of humans. This is consistent with the perspectivist formula articulated by Tania Stolze Lima (1996) and Eduardo Viveiros de Castro (2004, 2005). The animal-dead thus rediscover, post mortem, their place among humanity. Even in the case of Wari' funerary cannibalism, it is crucial to fully consider the role of the dead in the ritual scene in order to perceive, yet again, that ritual condensation takes place and generates the type of identity based on articulated opposites.

I do not want to reduce this ritual to the perspective of *Naven*, however, much less to mask the specificities of the Wari' ethnography. Rather than reduce all rituals to a single schema, I wish simply to illustrate how the relational approach to rituals I have proposed opens up new perspectives, precisely because it allows us to interpret rituals as fields of complex relationships that are configured in different ways in each ethnographic case. The study of *Naven* made it possible to describe how certain social bonds are constructed; other rites may reveal how it is possible to modify or dissolve such bonds. From this perspective, it is possible to read the Wari' case as a variant of the relational schema I have proposed, in which the relative decomplexification of the person appears against a background characterized by a sort of "diffuse condensation," carefully prepared during the funerary rite. On the one hand, this condensation is evoked by the actions that precede the consumption of the animal prey identified with the human corpse, and, on the other, by the series of rituals that forms the backdrop upon which each rite is inscribed. This is thus a case of a figure (perhaps typical of certain funerary rituals) in which, for a time, the specific action of the rite takes place through means other than those used in the case of *Naven*. Through this analysis, what at first appeared to be a confusing paradox turns out to be coherent when viewed as a reversal of figure and ground. From a methodological perspective, this offers both a confirmation and a potential elaboration of the relational theory of ritual and, consequently, of the type of generalization it enables. It provides a confirmation in that the association between ritual action and other systems of relations appear to be comparable to that established between figure and ground in experiments in Gestalt psychology. It also represents an elaboration in that, given the above interpretation of the Wari' case, it becomes possible to move beyond the analysis of various manifestations of a single rite, as in *Naven*, to the analysis of *relations among rites* and to the study of ensembles of groups of ritual relations.

This approach also means, conversely, that we cannot follow Vilaça when she claims that, in our book on *Naven* (Houseman and Severi 1998), we based the notion of condensation on an "individualized" notion of the person. To support such an assertion, she cites a passage where we wrote, with regard to the ritual cross-dressing in *Naven*, that "the emergence of such higher-order relational totalities [in the rite] derives from the condensation of nominally incompatible relationships . . . themselves grounded in a recognition of a number of irreducible differences between men and women" (Houseman and Severi 1998, 217). In fact, links of condensation can only be established between terms marked by similarities as well as by differences, whether implicit or explicit. However, there is no logical connection between the recognition that the bodies of men and of women are marked by sexual dimorphism and the definition of the social person, in ritual or in ordinary life, in symbolically univocal terms. As we showed in our book, it is possible to recognize and describe the processes of setting up constellations of attributes that generate complex identities without denying the existence of such dimorphism. Marilyn Strathern, who argues that men see in the physiology of the female body the truth of what myths claim about their own original femininity, is likewise far from denying this (1989, 99–103).

But let us go even further. According to Strathern, the Melanesian person can be defined as a "dividual" insofar as it is composed of aspects that are *entirely defined by the relationships* in which they are involved. From this perspective, the social relationship is no longer thought of as the "result" of a biological or psychological identity that is progressively socialized, somewhat like Margaret

Mead (but not Gregory Bateson) believed, but as the very expression of this identity, which is unstable since it depends on variable interactions. Such is the case of gender in the exchange system of ceremonial gifts in the New Guinea Highlands, where the defining features of the person can mobilize changing and "complex sexes" independently of any prior biological or psychological definition. If we adopt this definition and return to *Naven*, we can easily point out that all these relational positions—the complex identities—that we described in *Naven* are dividual. The ritual identities are plural (arranged as doubles, pairs, or other formulations) precisely because they are composed of dividuals. This means that they emerge within sets of constitutive interactions (mobilizing contradictory relations) in which people, far from possessing their own identity, "are construed as depending on others for knowledge about their internal selves. They are not in this sense the authors of it" (Strathern 1989, 119). Only the conflict between these fields of contradictory relations defines the complex and indirect identity of those who participate in a *Naven*. Although Houseman and I utilized the fact of sexual dimorphism, we made no reference whatsoever to an individual conception of the person.

Far from being derived from a conception of the person, what distinguishes our book on the *Naven* ritual from Strathern's *Gender of the Gift* (1989) is the epistemological and formal nature of our approach. If the two approaches are different, it is simply because they do not choose the same point of observation on the phenomenon. In our *Naven* study, we consider relationships through the relational fields that intersect with increasing complexity during already complex interactions, at the same time as we focus exclusively on the nature of a single ritual in its various manifestations. Strathern's objective is much broader (1989, 132): to describe various systems of relationships, both ritual and nonritual, that characterize social life in terms of gift exchange throughout Melanesia by considering these relationships one by one, case by case, and system by system. The relationships she envisions always mobilize two terms (or two times two terms), which she analyzes to progressively construct a general picture of unusual complexity. Conversely, in our book, Houseman and I consider, detail after detail, the internal dynamic of a single rite, taking as our point of departure a bundle of relationships and then trying to identify certain components within it. Later, I will return to these questions, which do not concern the relation between "rite" and "daily life" but, rather, the type of complexity that this kind of analysis of "relations among relations" can attain and under what conditions.

For the moment, let me emphasize the implications of the step I have taken above: the interpretation of the apparent paradox posed by Wari' cannibalism is conceivable only if we shift from a perspective focused on the various manifestations of one ritual to the analysis of the *metaritual context*. From this level, it is essential to move to the study of the relations among relations that can be established within the cycles, where each ritual constitutes a logical condition for the interpretation of another. Parallel to the study of quasi-ritual interactions, which I have interpreted through the example of the funerary games in the *Iliad*, the analysis of metaritual situations opens up another path to the generalization of the relational approach Houseman and I initiated twenty years ago in our work on the *Naven* ritual.

THE UNIVERSE OF OBJECT-PERSONS

Let us take what we have learned from ritual and games in ancient Greece and the Wari' and return to the broader questions about artifacts that become object-persons. What are the most general features of the universe of object-persons? What game of interaction does this universe rely on? As soon as an artifact comes alive, it does not reflect a single identity, as we have seen. Through refraction, it captures a plurality of partial identities. The persistence of the bond of belief that unites it with a person can be explained by the complexity of the relationship the object mobilizes within the ritual action. As they become more complex, the bond of belief that characterizes these situations becomes more stable. Starting with the opposition, described by Alfred Gell (1998, 67–72), between the ritual use of an artifact, on the one hand, and, on the other, the daily exercise of anthropomorphism (which seems to be more unstable and more diffuse), I perceive three features that determine the universe within which the artifact may act as a living being.

The first is that the attribution of subjectivity is only one of the aspects of a relationship that is created between an object and a subject (or subjects) in the ritual action. To fully grasp what occurs in this context, it is not enough to simply describe the transformation of the artifact; the transformation of the subject (or subjects) that enter into relation with it must also be described. When the *nkisi* comes to life, the recipient acquires the ability to kill a young hunter incarnated by the artifact. When the mourner in the Greek funerary ritual speaks, he takes on a part of the identity of the deceased. Between the artifact and the subject of the ritual action, there is thus a reciprocal definition.

But even more is involved. The two other features that characterize the object-person concern the status of the mental space in which the artifact comes alive. In Chapter Nine, I will analyze the example proposed by Ernst Gombrich in his *Meditations on a Hobby Horse* (1971) and suggest that playing with the wooden horse creates belief through the gradual exclusion of doubt. Each stage in establishing the belief that defines a child's play with a broomstick horse depends on an ostensibly counterfactual premise about the artifact: from the moment a child decides to play, the broomstick "is" a horse. If this is true—if doubt is excluded—then a boy who rides it "is" a knight, a prince, or other character.

In each stage of the interaction that includes the artifact, the truth status of the action, far from being established by "magic," is the focus of constant renegotiation between those who play. In the next stage of the make-believe, might the little boy turn out to be a Moorish knight? Might the little girl who plays with him take on the role of an Asian princess or, perhaps, that of long-haired Melisande? During the play, each of the children must acknowledge that the role assumed by the other is legitimate. Moreover, all it takes is for one of their parents to show up for this world of play to suddenly evaporate. In this dynamic, two features are at work that also pertained to the rituals previously analyzed, those in Africa and ancient Greece. On the one hand, the living object plays a crucial role in the transformation of what Karl Bühler ([1934] 2011, 117) called the "here-now-I" of the enunciation. On the other, this redefinition completely saturates the inferential space of the action.[6] Outside of this space, the real boy and the prince, or the real girl and the princess (or, analogously, the mourner and the deceased) cannot coexist at the same time and under the same conditions.

When these complex links between person and artifact are created, the object and the living being acquire the same ontological status. A relation of figure and background is thus established between the universe of the living object and any other form of experience. This is the game of the ritual artifact; this is the form of the link to belief that it makes possible.

Having discussed the relationship that links Achilles to Patroclus, brought about through substitution and partial identification as well as through domination and competition during the funerary games, I wish to emphasize that

---

6. This inferential space is akin to what Aby Warburg ([1932] 1999) calls the *Denkraum* (literally, "the space for thought").

the ritual context is not the only place where the agency of a substitute may be expressed. There are other situations involving games in which various kinds of substitution are posited between humans and objects, or between humans and humans. I have proposed describing such situations as quasi-rituals, which, although lacking the usual conditions for a rite to take place, can still be described through the relational theory I have formulated for interpreting ritual action. In this regard, funerary games—which cannot be conceived of without ritual—represent an exemplary case.

It follows from these analyses that the agency of the artifact (or the substitution of one person by another) depends on the relational context within which it operates. I would therefore like to propose an outline of a taxonomy of agency, which could include the following:

1. The exercise of everyday (nonritual) agency, as conceived by Gell (1998), involving a provisional and revocable relationship that has a single term, in which an artifact is linked to a person
2. A ritual relation involving a crystallized, stable relationship among two or more terms, in which an artifact may be linked to several people
3. A quasi-ritual situation, also involving a crystallized, stable relationship but, here, having a single term, one between the substitute and the substituted.

I am obviously not talking about a taxonomy based on fixed categories. This could not be otherwise, given the very fact that, so far, we have considered only one example of quasi-ritual situations. I am proposing these distinctions for purely heuristic reasons: they make it possible to explore new terrain and move forward before attempting to draw general conclusions.

With this same experimental spirit, I wish to venture one step further and consider art as a site for the exercise of the agency of artifacts, among other things. I will propose that we adopt the hypothesis that Western art—or, rather, the domain of relationships through the gaze that this art implies—is also a quasi-ritual situation, one in which a dialogue is initiated between persons and artifacts. In short, I suggest we invert the perspective of the primitivists: instead of seeing works of art everywhere outside the West, I will consider, as a hypothesis, certain Western works of art as object-persons.

CHAPTER SEVEN

The Anthropology of Abstract Art

> *The work of art is in itself an act of knowledge and judgment. We must thus transfer the concept of aesthetic knowledge from theory to the work.*
> —Carl Einstein, "Totalitat"

I have argued so far that an object that comes alive through a ritual act does not function like a mirror image but, rather, generates a more complex form of identity comparable to that of a crystal. The mental game that consists of transforming an artifact into a person follows several stages and occurs through a set of interrelated conceptual operations: the progressive transformation of the status of the object; the saturation of the surrounding space with thought; the reciprocal definition of the object and the subject; and the identification, always fragmentary and partial, of different subjectivities with distinct aspects of the artifact. As I discussed in earlier chapters, these constitute the universe of the game of attributing subjectivity to the inanimate object.

Is this complex game present in Western art? Artists, theorists, and historians from antiquity up to the present have constantly talked about the "life," "movement," "charm," and related influences exercised by works of art. Ernst Kitzinger (1976, 107) argues that running through the entire history of Western art is "the tendency to break down the barrier between image and prototype."

Does this mean we should assimilate all works of art to a ritual object? Can we say that these attributions of life forms function in the same way in the Western artistic tradition as in, say, the complex games of identities that occur in ritual manipulations of an African nail figure? Or according to the same logic that drove a mourner to speak to a funerary statue in ancient Greece? I believe not. My objective here, to the contrary, is to specify some of the forms that the game of attributing life to artifacts has assumed in Western art. It is thus a sort of experiment with the theme of agency explored in the prior three chapters, pushing further to see how much it may reveal in this domain. I will investigate two forms of space in particular: chimeric space (where I consider the comparison of Western and non-Western art) and perspectival space (which I associate with a form of magic—the semblance of life attributed to a work of art). Before doing so, I will clarify my analytical criteria in this chapter, based on a review of Claude Lévi-Strauss's statements about art, and then consider the status of abstract act, which is crucial from a theoretical point of view, since it raises the question of whether a general anthropological theory of artistic expression is possible.

CLAUDE LÉVI-STRAUSS AND THE ANTHROPOLOGY OF ART

In Lévi-Strauss's work, there is no "anthropology of art" in the current sense given to this phrase. For him, the study of images, which should start from the artworks themselves rather than from aesthetic theories, does not constitute a subdiscipline of social anthropology. Rather, it involves analytical work that bears directly on the objective of anthropology. His studies include texts on Asian and Oceanic arts, analyses of paintings by Jean Clouet and Nicolas Poussin, and remarks on Jean-Baptiste Greuze, Paul Delvaux, Edouard Manet, and the Surrealists, Cubists, and Impressionists. He makes so many references to the visual arts that it has become customary to distinguish, on the one hand, the ethnologist who examines the arts of the Amerindians of Brazil or the Northwest Coast using a relatively technical language and, on the other, the passionate connoisseur who comments more briefly on the works of this or that Western artist. Such a view, however, overlooks the fact that, as early as *The Savage Mind* ([1962] 1966), Lévi-Strauss recognized art as one of the major themes amenable to anthropological reflection, just like myth, play, or ritual. The richness of the artistic themes evoked in his works testifies not only to his erudition but also to the striving toward universality that has always animated his thinking. I will first explore what is involved in his efforts to define "the universal type of the work of art" (Lévi-Strauss [1962] 1966, 23) and, from this, develop certain themes relevant to my subsequent analyses.

By the late 1950s, Lévi-Strauss distinguished his approach as a theoretician of art from those taken by his contemporaries, for instance, that of André Breton. In 1957, Breton published a long essay entitled "L'Art magique," largely devoted to non-Western arts. In contrast to scientific knowledge, which "always claims to extend its domination over all human invention" (Breton [1957] 2008, 62), the founder of surrealism opposed a universal "lyrical consciousness" that allowed a direct understanding of all art. According to him, art—whether primitive or modern, naïve or exotic, created no matter where or when—responds to an instinct "linked to the perennial nature of certain major human aspirations" ([1957] 2008, 53). Without being directly identified with art, magic nevertheless responds "to the same aspirations as the practice of art" ([1957] 2008, 53). Everywhere, "the work obeys its own laws; whether or not it decides to adapt itself to magical purposes, we must remember that its very origin is in magic; even if it seeks to be purely realistic, it still owes most of its resources to magic" ([1957] 2008, 73). In opposition to what he called a "civilization of professors" who, to explain the life of a tree, "do not feel entirely comfortable until the sap has been removed," he asserted that we must recognize that "all art is magic, at least in its genesis" ([1957] 2008, 73).

When speaking of magic, Breton was referring above all to "hermetic disciplines in the Western tradition," which, he argued at length, influenced European art ([1957] 2008, 64). According to him, it would be impossible to understand Victor Hugo, Charles Baudelaire, or Stéphane Mallarmé without referring to Éliphas Lévi and the esoteric tradition he represents. It would be wrong, he noted, to think that magical esotericism is a phenomenon peculiar to the West. The tradition of hermetic magic has simply translated a type of conception found all over the world into terms with which we are familiar. He said that Lévi's "unique dogma" was based on the notion that, "Since the visible is always the manifestation of the invisible . . . the truth is found in perceptible and visible things in exact proportion to the things that are imperceptible to our senses and invisible to our eyes" (Breton [1957] 2008, 64).

Breton further claimed that neither the development of civilization nor the progress of technology has ever been able to eradicate from the human soul "the hope of solving the enigma of the world and of diverting the forces that govern it to their advantage" ([1957] 2008, 83). The instinct that leads to the magical manipulation of the world remains alive everywhere. "Savage peoples have lost the magic charge that justifies their existence far less than we have," so this is why "the precariousness of their resources today contrasts with the luxuriance of their art" ([1957] 2008, 83).

In an appendix to the introduction in "L'Art magique" ([1957] 2008, 109–64), Breton published a survey consisting of a list of questions he had sent, in his own words, "to some of the best qualified minds" of the time. Some of the questions explicitly supported the theses that Breton defended in the introduction: Can we say that "civilization has dispelled the fiction of magic only to exalt, in art, the magic of fiction"? Does magic respond to an "inalienable need of the spirit"? Other questions related more specifically to the relationship between modern art and magical thinking: he asked if, from its "long time parked in the garage of imitation," could today's art emerge differently if magic were rehabilitated? Could works or artists active in modern art (such as Henri Rousseau, Giorgio de Chirico, Wassily Kandinsky, Marc Chagall, or Marcel Duchamp) be described as "magical"? Or would it be necessary to go beyond the realm of art and identify a magical role linked, for instance, to memory, played by certain objects in everyday life?

The respondents chosen by Breton—ethnologists, philosophers, art historians, artists, and writers—gave widely differing answers to these questions. Some of them, such as Martin Heidegger, cast doubt on the conceptual criteria that led Breton to oppose "magical art" and "religious art," or "classical" and "baroque" art. According to Heidegger, this confuses the "categories naming historical periods of art with categories of a theoretical or metaphysical order" that would better describe their nature (Breton [1957] 2008, 116). Others, such as Jean Paulhan, criticized the facile notion of magic used in the questionnaire: "I scarcely see any way to usefully compare two things as dissimilar as magic that is personally experienced and magic that is attributed, on extraordinarily thin grounds, to this or that time, in this or that culture" ([1957] 2008, 118).

Nevertheless, many authors agreed on one point: that a "magical art" indeed exists, crossing historical eras and world cultures. The works illustrating Breton's book—paintings by Hieronymus Bosch, François Nomé, Paolo Uccello, and Francisco de Goya; African and Oceanian masks; works by Giorgio de Chirico, Wassily Kandinsky, Salvador Dali, and Max Ernst—presented striking testimony to such "magical" art, as the author had hoped.

Among the responses to this questionnaire, one of them stands out clearly—that of Lévi-Strauss. The anthropologist, who had long studied Amerindian arts, responded to Breton's questions with a series of reflections concerning the mode of conducting the investigation as well as the very existence of a "magical art." What art did he mean, what kind of magic, and, above all, what society?

> Through history and depending on the societies, art and magic have undoubtedly accompanied each other at certain moments, separated at others, and, at yet others, crossed paths. But, to understand the relation between them, it is necessary to define the situation in terms of each society under consideration. . . . It is not at all because your survey takes magic seriously that it bothers me but, rather, because it poses the terms of art and magic in such a vague sense that it makes it impossible to conduct a serious reflection on the subject. . . . Instead of circumscribing the terms and starting from a possible definition, for example, that of magic as a set of operations and beliefs that lend the same value to certain human acts as natural causes . . . you give the weakest semantic value to the terms of art and magic; that is, you place them on a level when their meaning dissolves. (Lévi-Strauss, in Breton [1957] 2008, 123)

This declaration served as a landmark that, for many years to come in Paris, defined the relations between social anthropology and the world of art. At the time, it represented an act by the emerging field of ethnology of taking a stance in opposition to the primitivist aesthetic. The literary and artistic avant-garde, impassioned with the arts considered "primitive," cultivated a great mistrust of any anthropological approach to art. According to the primitivist aesthetic, which postulated the universality of the language of art, any object whatsoever could be understood independently of the meanings it embodied in the society where it was created. In response to Lévi-Strauss's remarks, Breton denounced "the intolerance and arrogance of today's militant ethnology, which believes it must defend what it considers to be its exclusive property" (Breton [1957] 2008, 121). He was far from being the only one to hold this idea. In the nineteenth century, Western ethnocentrism had cast serious doubt on the notion of the universality of art. During the avant-garde era, however, "primitivism" allowed for the existence of a universal art, but it refused to develop any analysis of it. In both cases, an anthropology of art had no place.

The passion, almost amounting to anger, that resonated in Lévi-Strauss's answer to Breton, who, for his part, deplored the stunning "bad mood" of the ethnologist ([1957] 2008, 120), was not linked simply to the circumstances of a personal disagreement. It recalls other critiques from the same period that this pioneering anthropologist formulated against those who, like Roger Caillois, preferred style to analysis in studies of social facts. But it also reveals certain roots of Lévi-Strauss's larger project, in which reflections on art were always an essential issue. In *Tristes Tropiques*, for example, the study of Caduveo designs gives him an opportunity to define a distinctive concept of style that extends to the analysis of forms. Thus, the entire set of customs of a people "is always marked by a style," and, indeed, such a style makes it possible to recognize that their customs form a system:

> I am of the opinion that the number of such systems is not unlimited and that—in their games, dreams, or wild imaginings—human societies, like individuals, never create absolutely, but merely choose certain combinations from an ideal repertoire that it should be possible to define. (Lévi-Strauss [1955] 2012, 178)

By making an inventory not only of all customs observed by ethnologists but, in addition,

> all those imagined in myths or suggested in children's games or adult games, or in the dreams of healthy or sick individuals, or in psycho-pathological behavior, one could arrive at a sort of table, like that of the chemical elements, in which all actual or hypothetical customs would be grouped in families, so that one could see at a glance which customs a particular society had in fact adopted. (Lévi-Strauss [1955] 2012, 178)

He thus takes on the issue of the universality of art as a site for exploring formal thought. If structural analysis is properly conducted, the study of a Native American mask should reveal abstract elements that can be applied to other artistic expressions, including the works of Western artists, whether they be a portrait by Clouet, a historical painting by Greuze, a canvas by Poussin, or a work by a contemporary artist. Lévi-Strauss admits that all art is linked to the aesthetic emotion. He likewise concedes that this experience may be universal. But the experience of art remains mysterious, in his view: What lies behind the effectiveness of a particular work? Why does the perception of certain works stir feelings of admiration and pleasure? His point of departure for this reflection is Clouet's painting of Elizabeth of Austria (Figure 35):

Let us now look at this portrait of a woman by Clouet and consider the reason for the very profound aesthetic emotion which is, apparently inexplicably, aroused by the highly realistic, thread by thread, reproduction of a lace collar. (Lévi-Strauss [1962] 1966, 22)

Figure 35. François Clouet, *Portrait of Elizabeth of Austria* (1571), Louvre Museum, Paris.

Note that, as an anthropologist, Lévi-Strauss never refers to the painter's personality. His argument relies on neither the artist's own poetics nor an analysis of the pictorial style. It focuses instead on a neglected aspect of representation in images: their *reduction in scale*. The lace collar that Clouet painted is "like Japanese gardens, miniature vehicles, and ships in bottles, what in the 'bricoleur's' language are called 'small-scale models' or 'miniatures'" ([1962] 1966, 23). This painting lets us see, in an extraordinarily faithful manner, a reduced model of the world. Lévi-Strauss asks,

> Now, the question arises whether the small-scale model or miniature, which is also the "masterpiece" of the journeyman, may not in fact be the universal type of the work of art. All miniatures seem to have intrinsic aesthetic quality—and from what should they draw this constant virtue if not from the dimensions themselves?—and conversely the vast majority of works of art are small-scale. (Lévi-Strauss [1962] 1966, 23)

To understand a real object in its totality, Lévi-Strauss notes that we tend to start with its parts. The resistance we encounter in it is overcome by dividing it into sections. The reduction in scale in images reverses this situation: in the portrait of Elizabeth, we apprehend the totality before grasping the parts. In a single glance, we dominate the whole of a representation before comprehending the elements that make it up:

> Being smaller, the object as a whole seems less formidable. By being quantitatively diminished, it seems to us qualitatively simplified. More exactly, this quantitative transposition extends and diversifies our power over a homologue of the thing, and by means of it the latter can be grasped, assessed, and apprehended at a glance. (Lévi-Strauss [1962] 1966, 23)

This reduced model of the world presents another characteristic: it is explicitly *constructed*. It is made by human hands. For Lévi-Strauss ([1962] 1966, 24), "They are therefore not just projections or passive homologues of the object: they constitute a real experiment with it." This double approach—the reduction in scale and the way of apprehending a work that leads to the experience of a certain mastery over the constructed object—makes it possible to account for the power of plastic representations and, indeed, for our latent temptation to assign subjectivity to it. It is because of this process that "A child's doll is no longer an enemy, a rival or even an interlocutor. In it and through it a person is made into a subject" ([1962] 1966, 23).

This insight gives us a better understanding of what the "magic" of a work of art might consist of. It involves a specific process of *interpreting the image* that makes it possible to constitute subjectivity. This process may involve the observer, who, in the face of the representation, "in a confused way . . . feels himself to be their creator with more right than the creator himself," and who thus constructs himself as a person ([1962] 1966, 24). Alternatively, it may involve the representation itself, which appears to be a potentially active agent endowed with its own subjectivity. Whether it is a statue, drawing, or painting, a work of art may thus acquire a *personality* close to that of a human being. This leads to the conclusion that the idea of a "life" associated with an image is not a mere exotic belief confined to faraway countries or "primitive peoples": it is, to the contrary, one of the universal roots of the aesthetic experience.

The theorist of "L'Art magique" (who himself was hesitant and tormented enough to ask for the help of a coauthor) hypothesized the existence of a universal lyric consciousness, which supposedly enabled a viewer to have an immediate intuitive contact with any art object. By contrast, the author of *The Savage Mind* proposed a parallel interpretation of the constitutive coordinates of the image and of the mental operations implied by such coordinates. Instead of the primitivist connoisseur's notion of an immediate gaze, with its appeal to a lyricism stripped of analysis, Lévi-Strauss proposes to reconstruct the mental operation implied by each invention of an image. Rather than searching, as did Carl Einstein, Georges Braque, Pablo Picasso, and Juan Gris, for the "masterpieces of Cubist art by African visual artists" (Einstein [1915] 1986, 347), Lévi-Strauss attempts to show that what is true of an African idol or a Polynesian club can also illuminate European art in unexpected ways. At the time, his approach made it possible to invert the usual perspective, with well-known repercussions to this day.

Some might object that this explanatory model, which claims to be universal, is still based on the imitation of nature. It cannot apply to an art that, for most of the twentieth century, aimed at abstraction. Lévi-Strauss expressed harsh opinions against "non-representational painting," which he criticized as "academic" and as being dedicated to "realistic imitations of non-existent models" (Lévi-Strauss [1962] 1966, 29–30). This is probably more a way of covering up the problem rather than solving it, especially since many non-Western iconographic traditions are based on principles other than the imitation of nature. The problem of "abstract" representation is neither peculiar to modern art nor confined to the Western tradition.

PRINCIPLES OF ANALYSIS: AN EXAMPLE FROM KANDINSKY

Let us stay within the realm of Western art and attempt to move further along this path. What is the best way to imagine the "magic" of a work of abstract art? In what way does it enable subjectivity to be constituted? What universe does the "small-scale model" represent? To deal with these questions, let us first turn to the painting by Wassily Kandinsky entitled *Picture with an Archer* (Figure 36).

This work marked an essential stage in the emergence of abstract art. In the 1910s, the object of pictorial representation underwent a radical transformation through the work of Kandinsky and some of his fellow artists in the Blaue Reiter movement. For them, the reference for the painter was no longer the external world cleverly reconstituted in miniature. Adolf von Hildebrand had already

Figure 36. Wassily Kandinsky, *Picture with an Archer* (1909), Museum of Modern Art, New York.

articulated the principle of this change in the object of representation, a change that was to gradually assume a crucial role in the arts of modernity. In *The Problem of Form in the Fine Arts* ([1893] 1907), he contended that all perception of space and movement presupposes an experience of form. As I discussed in Chapter Two, this thesis constituted an indispensable premise for all modern primitivists after Einstein. Given this experience, the subject of the work plays a minor role—a thesis that has influenced the interpretation of artworks to this day. For example, a still life by Jean-Siméon Chardin, representing some banal objects arranged in a corner of his atelier, could evolve into an intensely tragic image, especially during the last period of the artist's life. The subject portrayed in the image may thus be almost irrelevant to the aesthetic experience. Rather, what assumes priority is the space (the experience of the light, the relation between surface and volume, the implicit movement animating objects or, by contrast, freezing them with a strange immobility) in determining the nature of the representation. Kandinsky and his companions thus proposed a dramatic change in the interpretation of the aesthetic experience. The logic of this position can be summarized as follows: if what counts in a work of art is not the subject portrayed but the experience of the form it implies, why not imagine an art that takes this experience itself as the subject of representation? Kandinsky held that, in "spiritual" art (his synonym for "abstract"), the world is no longer the subject of representation. What the artist should aim for, by abandoning appearances, is the *mental act* presupposed by the perception of the world. If the work, "like a Japanese garden," in the words of Lévi-Strauss, reconstitutes a miniature of the world, then for abstract art it is a model of this interior space, which it attempts to reconstitute through its own means (line, surface, color, and light). In strictly visual terms, how does this passage toward an "art without image" operate in Kandinsky's work?

A close observation of *Picture with Archer* reveals that Kandinsky has brought about an inversion of the traditional function of color (which became even more apparent in his later *Abstract Improvisations* series). In Clouet's *Portrait of Elizabeth of Austria*, which followed one of the traditional aesthetic models, color still animates a space in the representation that is essentially defined by the drawing. Even if here, Lévi-Strauss asserts,

> the depiction of a lace collar in miniature demands an intimate knowledge of its morphology and technique of manufacture . . . it is not just a diagram or blueprint. It manages to synthesize these intrinsic properties with properties which depend on a spatial and temporal context. (Lévi-Strauss [1962] 1966, 25)

At the heart of this synthesis is the drawing of the object, which shows, at one and the same time, "the lace collar exactly as it is" and the lace collar with "its appearance [that] is affected by the particular perspective" (Lévi-Strauss [1962] 1966, 25). In *Picture with Archer*, however, this essential function of the drawing is called into question. The rhythms governing the perception of the landscape, expressed here in essentially chromatic terms, so fully invest the subject of the representation (the rider, his bow, his horse, his decorated mount) that the traditional balance between figure and ground in the image is reversed. It is the ground, the visual experience of a surface punctuated by light, that takes precedence over the figure and the subject portrayed.

In Kandinsky's theoretical reflection, the concept of form has a double meaning. Insofar as the form is contrasted with color, it is a specific visual means of representation (see Kandinsky 1994, 501–4, 534–700). The line demarcates, emphasizes, and distinguishes. In this respect, the concept of form implies "delimitation" as a mental operation. It is the demarcation of a contour that assumes a role as the motor of perceiving space and as the dynamic equilibrium between figure and ground. But insofar as "form" is contrasted with content, Kandinsky uses it to designate the entire aesthetic experience of space and movement. In this regard, he shares the language and ideas of Hildebrand. In fact, *Picture with Archer* simultaneously mobilizes both possible senses of the notion of form. Almost nothing distinguishes the two planes, one with the archer on horseback and the other with the landscape surrounding them. Here, a sort of *implicit hypothesis of indistinction between the landscape and the subject* characterizes the nature of the space. Light and color dominate. The rider carrying a bow has become so difficult to perceive that it is almost as if the title alone signals his presence. On the other hand, the chromatic background, which dominates the perception of the work, fully assumes *the role of form* inasmuch as it constitutes the true support of the aesthetic experience of the space. This painting, which seems at first glance to be almost without an object, is actually generated by the inversion of its constitutive coordinates. It is the color, not the design as the "demarcation of a contour," that plays the central role of revealing the form in the sense of space, movement, and light. *Picture with Archer* is an "abstract" work not because it refers to a "nonexistent reality" but, rather, because the subject represented is evoked as a mere episode, a "content" without direct relevance to the perception of the work. Indeed, where we see nothing but an absence, a lack of reference to nature, we discover a reflection on the gaze. Kandinsky develops this process for generating space, at once inseparable from color and containing conventional forms, even further according to the same logic in his series, *Abstract Improvisations*.

Breton was certainly aware of the importance of Kandinsky's work. In "L'Art magique," he even recognized that "it is under the double invocation of Chirico and the master of *Abstract Improvisations* that almost all the paintings that count in the twentieth century have developed" (Breton [1957] 2008, 120). The founder of surrealism, who, when he exhibited at the Salon des Surindépendants in 1933, had sent an "invitation of honor" to the master of abstraction to join the movement, noted,

Kandinsky's art, produced from this dark Siberia of hyperborean demonology, Chinese ideograms, and the rudiments of the art of the steppes . . . has brought aesthetic activity around full circle with his sumptuous, barbaric chords. (Breton [1957] 2008, 120)

More than the artist's style or personality, the true revolution here involves, on the one hand, the contrast between two technical notions of pictorial art (drawing and color) and, on the other, the very status of the subject of representation, which has shifted from a reduced model of the world to the experience of form as a datum in itself to be represented. Linked more closely to the interaction of constitutive elements in the work than to a paraphrase of the language of esotericism, this level of analysis has a bearing on the definition of the *universe of discourse* relevant to iconic representation. In his book *Look, Listen, Read*, Lévi-Strauss ([1993] 1997) remarks that, from an anthropological point of view, the difference between Western art and the arts called "primitive" does not primarily concern the evolution of techniques, the difference in styles, or even the lives of the artists. On the contrary, the most crucial distinction concerns the nature of the *model* represented through the work—a theme that, as we have seen, played a crucial role (although in his own terms) in Kandinsky's reflections. Lévi-Strauss states,

> Art can be considered as "primitive" in one of two senses. First, in the sense that the artist does not have sufficient grasp of the technical means or know-how necessary to realize his or her objective (that is, the imitation of a model), and as such can only signify it; an example would be what we call "Naïve" art. In the second sense, the model the artist would depict, being supernatural, necessarily escapes any naturalistic means of representation: again, the artist can only signify, but as a result of the object's excess, and not the subject's shortcomings. The art of preliterate peoples, in all its different forms, illustrates the latter case. (Lévi-Strauss [1993] 1997, 162)

I will return to this point later and develop it further. For now, it is worth noting that, in a memorable passage in *The Way of the Masks*, Lévi-Strauss ([1979] 1982) remarks that the study of objects can be conducted according to a point of view that, rather than focusing on their uniqueness, explores how they are classified by the cultures that produced them and what relations can be discovered among them. In this perspective, the object under analysis is constituted not only by what is materially realized in it but also by what could have been realized and what was excluded from the universe of possible works:

> It would be misleading to imagine, therefore, as so many ethnologists and art historians still do today, that a mask and, more generally, a sculpture or a painting may be interpreted each for itself, according to what it represents or to the aesthetic or ritual use for which it is destined. We have seen that, on the contrary, a mask does not exist in isolation; it supposes other real or potential masks always by its side. . . . A mask is not primarily what it represents but what it transforms, that is to say, what it chooses *not* to represent. (Lévi-Strauss [1979] 1982, 144)

This intuition, which may seem surprising, simply develops the analytical perspective used by Franz Boas and, before him, the entire tradition of the biology of images from Augustus Pitt Rivers to Hjalmer Stolpe. It also follows up on certain reflections in *The Savage Mind*. There, Lévi-Strauss had stated that, in response to the problem that a work poses to an artist,

> there are several solutions to the same problem. The choice of one solution involves a modification of the result to which another solution would have led, and the observer is in effect presented with the general picture of these permutations at the same time as the particular solution offered. He is thereby transformed into an active participant without even being aware of it. Merely by contemplating it he is, as it were, put in possession of other possible forms of the same work. . . . And these forms are so many further perspectives opening out on to the work which has been realized. In other words, the intrinsic value of a small-scale model is that it compensates for the renunciation of sensible dimensions by the acquisition of intelligible dimensions. (Lévi-Strauss [1962] 1966, 24)

For Lévi-Strauss, these intelligible dimensions, which constitute the latent aspects of the works, open up an enormous range of "mythic beliefs, ritual practices, and plastic works [that] remain mutually congruent when they imitate one another, and even, perhaps above all, when they seem to be contradictory" (Lévi-Strauss [1979] 1982, 148). The "story" of these cultural expressions and their "logical operations," which unfolded over an "immense territory . . . on a time scale of millennia" in the Northwest Coast, is the focus of *The Way of the Masks* ([1979] 1982, 147–48).

This perspective makes it possible to take a fresh analytical approach to the Western artistic tradition. Lévi-Strauss's recently published "Notes sur l'*Olympia* de Manet" formulates the outlines of such an approach. Instead of "seeking to place a work in the historical lineage of another one," it involves "comparing parallel attempts to give plastic expression to logical problems" and to put them in an orderly series (2008, 1671). Let us experiment with this new organizing principle by applying it to the certain themes in abstract art.

VISUAL STRATEGIES IN ABSTRACT ART

Using this approach, we can explore some of the aesthetic problems that abstract artists posed for themselves and the visual strategies they devised to address them. If we look again at *Picture with Archer*, we can see that Kandinsky faced two particular problems. On the one hand was the problem of inventing a space where color could play the role of form; on the other was that of establishing a new balance, almost an identification, between figure and ground. These problems dealt with a certain relation between space and color, for which Kandinsky's work offered an original solution. This raises further questions: In what series, based more on the comparison of plastic solutions than on chronology, should this work be placed? How should this work be understood not only in terms of what it represents but, furthermore, what it transforms? How may we discover specifically how Kandinsky, like a Northwest Coast mask maker, "is answering other past or present, actual or potential, creators" ([1979] 1982, 148)?

It may help to turn to another artist who had earlier wrestled with related challenges. In 1843, at the Royal Academy in London, William Turner exhibited two landscapes directly inspired by Goethe's *Theory of Colours* ([1810] 2006), where the problem of the relation between space and light is posed. Each painting has a double title: one describes the "subject" through which the viewer may interpret the image, while the other has a commentary on the relationship between light and color portrayed in it. These two works are entitled *Shade and Darkness (The Evening of the Deluge)* (Figure 37) and *Light and Colour (Goethe's Theory): The Morning after the Deluge* (Figure 38).

The reference to Goethe's work is direct and intentional. Turner is referring specifically to the text in which Goethe opposes warm colors (yellow, orange, and red, which he marks with a plus sign) to cold ones (blue, blue-green, and purple, marked with a minus sign). In the case of warm colors, Goethe argues, "the feelings they excite are quick, lively, aspiring," while cold ones produce "a restless, susceptible, anxious impression" (Goethe [1810] 2006, 168, 170; see

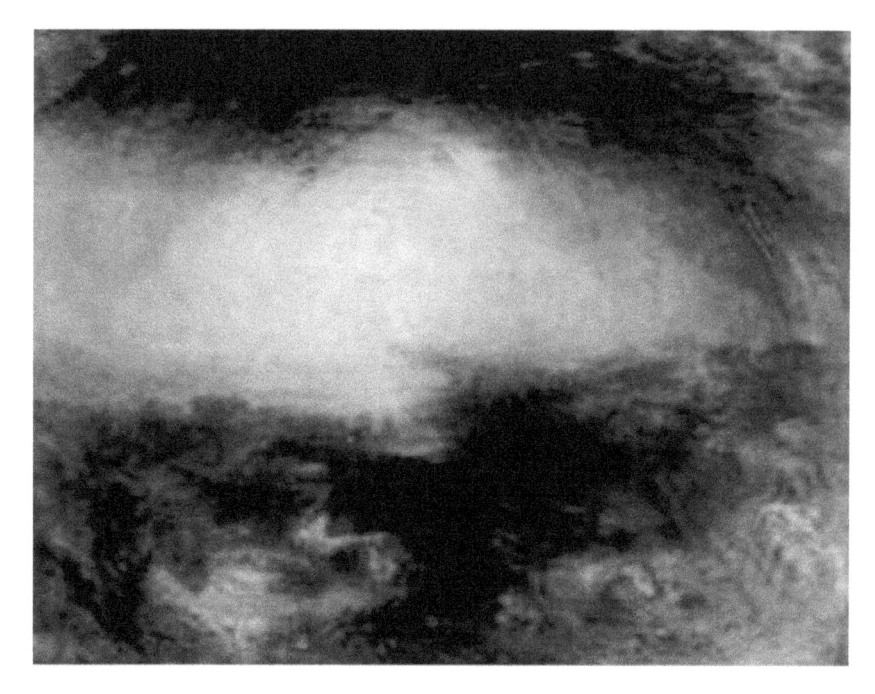

Figure 37. William Turner, *Shade and Darkness (The Evening of the Deluge)* (1843), Tate Britain, London.

also Gowing 1966, 51). He amplifies this initial opposition with a list of other contrasts that are physical, chemical, or psychological in nature (Goethe [1810] 2006, 151):

Plus	Minus
Yellow	Blue
Action	Negation
Light	Shadow
Brightness	Darkness
Force	Weakness
Warmth	Coldness
Proximity	Distance
Repulsion	Attraction
Affinity with acids	Affinity with alkalis

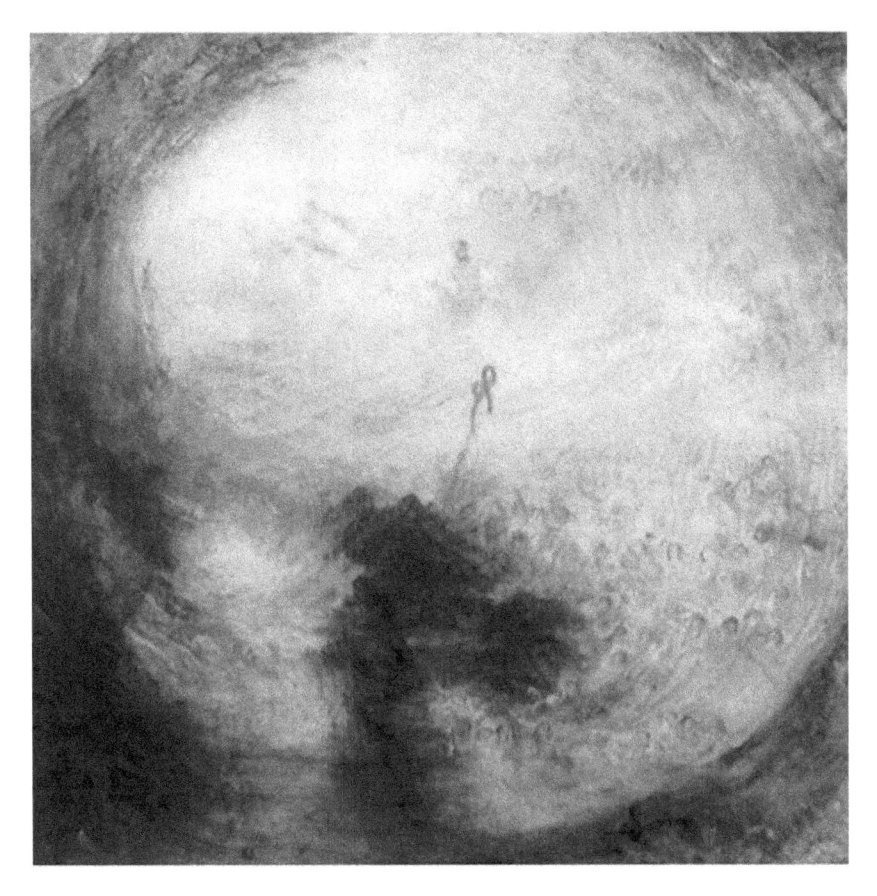

Figure 38. William Turner, *Light and Colour (Goethe's Theory): The Morning after the Deluge* (1843), Tate Britain, London.

Of these oppositions, Turner clearly privileges those that can be translated into spatial terms in his two flood paintings. In these compositions, in which graphic indications are reduced to a minimum—not even the horizon is indicated—the darkness of the cold colors express distance from the view, while the vividness of the warm colors express proximity. The effect exercised by the blues, greens, and blacks, which lead the viewer's gaze toward the background of the flood scene, contrasts with the vividness (arising from the brightness, warmth, and proximity) that emanates from the most luminous parts of the painting. Turner thus follows Goethe's theory, but he uses it to formulate a specific problem that occupied his entire life: how to understand and thus reproduce the conditions "in which reflected light became an image" (Gowing 1966, 21–23). For him, it is a matter of imagining a spherical space where indications shown on a flat surface become indications of depth using almost exclusively color. Turner's method, at once original and Goethean, consists in playing with the reciprocal influence of primary colors so that the desired shade is produced not in the painting but, rather, directly *in the eye of the viewer*. Instead of mixing colors to obtain shades, he applies "fine dots of primary colours" (Finley 1967, 366–67) on the paper or canvas, leaving it to the viewer's gaze to perform the synthesis. The artist's actions are no longer responsible for producing all the colors. It is the viewer's gaze that, by engaging with "polarization"—the phenomenon Goethe defined as the reciprocal influence of colors in a situation of simultaneous contrast—generates, at least in part, the secondary colors.

The discovery of this method, which fascinated and scandalized his contemporaries, made Turner a precursor recognized as much by Georges Seurat and the divisionists as by the American abstract painters of the 1950s (Motherwell 1999, 253, 268). Note that this approach concerns not only the chromatic effects: light also orients all the space in the landscape. Regarding the two paintings inspired by Goethe, both of which are organized in an almost spherical space, Lawrence Gowing remarks that "the whole focus of the circular images is seen to be shifting and condensing," indeed, far from the center of the canvas (Gowing 1966, 48). A comparison with other circular compositions will clarify this essential point. Consider, for instance, two works by Gottfried Wals, a German painter who worked in Rome at the beginning of the seventeenth century and who specialized in this type of composition (Figures 39 and 40).

In these landscapes, Wals presents a composition that, from the point of view of the conception of space, is not far from the project Turner pursued. The structure of space—furnished with Roman ruins in one case, stripped down in the other—makes explicit its reference to a sphere. The contrast between shadow and light in these works, where the use of color is closely monitored, is wedded to an unusually strict linear organization. For there to be depth, it is necessary for the vanishing point, around which the perspective is organized, to *enter into tension* with the center of the canvas. The vanishing point must neither coincide with the center nor be placed too far from it, since, in both cases, the effect of depth would be lost. Through this gap between the actual center of the canvas and the vanishing point of the composition, the circular organization of the composition allows the gaze to plunge into the image, intensifying the impression of depth. In this type of composition, the two factors work together so that the viewer may gain access to the space and be projected toward the horizon. In

Figure 39. Gottfried Wals, *A Roman Landscape with Figures* (c. 1616), Metropolitan Museum of Art, New York.

Wals, as in Turner, this technical feat is certainly not devoid of meaning. Most likely, it implies a meditation on the painting itself, on its character as something both illusory and faithful. In a spirit close to the Baroque, what is at play in the relation between the technical perfection of the representation and its provisional character—especially in *A Country Road by a House*, which appears to have no theme at all—is the vanity of appearances and the anxiety that can weigh them down. The more perfect the technique, the more the fictitious (and hence fragile) character of the representation becomes palpable.

By contrast, Turner works emphatically in the opposite direction. Whereas Wals, who rigorously calculated the gap between the vanishing point and the center of the circle, seeks the illusion of depth, Turner intends to represent, especially in *Light and Colour*, a vividness, a sudden irruption of light that projects outward in a curved, almost convex space. Whereas Wals establishes a relationship between a plunging view and a perception of depth by using graphic means, Turner constructs his composition strictly through the contrast of colors: warm and cold, glowing and dark, near and far. Through the juxtaposition of negative and positive colors, Turner thus seeks not only depth but,

Figure 40. Gottfried Wals, *A Country Road by a House* (1620), Fitzwilliam Museum, Cambridge.

moreover, a sort of *imminence* of space, an intensification of vision that almost causes vertigo.

As a "possible solution" to a visual problem, Kandinsky's *Picture with Archer* comfortably fits into a series that starts with Turner's two paintings. Apart from any chronology, this series would ideally be composed of solutions offered to the problem of constructing space through the use of color, on the one hand, and, on the other, the idea of a direct representation of visual experience as the subject of the work (as affirmed in the titles of Turner's canvases). This series, oriented by the logical dimensions of visual problems, could be enriched with other works and other artists. But let us return to Kandinsky. If we grant that his canvas can be included in a series that, independently of influences that one artist may exercise over another, has affinities with some of Turner's research, what may have developed from it?

Earlier, I argued that *Picture with Archer* works with two visual problems, one concerning the relation between the object and the space where it is situated, the other involving the construction of the experience of form through color. In Paris and elsewhere in Europe in the 1910s, two artists discovered other solutions to these problems. In 1913, Piet Mondrian began to shift the subject of his paintings—a representation of nature through trees portrayed in a Cubist manner and landscapes that become increasingly sparse—toward the *relations* that exist between real objects or elements in a landscape. For him, as for Kandinsky, this is a way of representing a thought process without going through a description of nature. In a 1919 article, he explains this shift clearly. He says that, in his earlier work,

> I expressed myself through nature. But if you observe the sequence of my work carefully, you will see that it progressively abandoned the naturalistic appearance of things and increasingly emphasizes the plastic expression of relationships. (Mondrian [1919] 1971, 118)

The series entitled *Pier and Ocean*, of which Figure 41 is an example, develops a method that consists of filling pictorial space with indications of relations (horizontal and vertical) that seek, through the absence of the real terms of these relations, to portray an infinite space.

Here, Mondrian finds an original solution to the problem of the relation between figure and ground, as posed by Kandinsky. The latter had played with color to trigger the experience of space and movement, which he used to invert the link between subject (the archer) and landscape. While this relation is indicated in an implicit way by Kandinsky, it becomes explicit and starkly visible in Mondrian. It forms the object of a plastic solution by becoming the subject of the representation itself.

Echoing the concerns of Goethe, Turner, and Kandinsky, Robert Delaunay, who belonged to the Parisian group of Cubists, began searching in the 1910s for an original solution to the problem of creating an illusory space through what might be called the *mental synthesis* of color. This space is specifically a spherical space, something to which Turner was also sensitive. Free from all figuration,

Figure 41. Piet Mondrian, *Pier and Ocean* (1915), Kröller-Müller Museum, Otterlo.

even conventional types, the subject of Delaunay's *Simultaneous Disk* (1913) is the encounter of colors within the gaze itself. As Albert Gleizes recognized almost immediately, "The Delaunay of the *Disks* only paints with color. He claimed that, instead of destroying, color constructed, *edifying the form*" (cited in Seuphor [1949] 1971, 28; emphasis added).

During this period (probably the happiest of his work as a painter), Delaunay not only seeks (like Turner did with regard to Goethe) to illustrate the theory of colors and dispersion of light articulated by Jean-Eugène Chevreul ([1939] 1969) in his concept of "simultaneous contrasts"; he aims, above all, to create a visual transcription of the very idea of simultaneity. Let us examine closely what is at play in his *Simultaneous Disk* (Figure 42).

The pronounced distinction between warm and cold colors, which are distributed into quarters in the work as a whole, are suddenly transformed in the central disk into a confrontation between two almost monochromatic, intensely contrasting semicircles of red and blue. The difference between the four axes that cross the entire disk horizontally and vertically, elsewhere emphasized by

Figure 42. Robert Delaunay, *Simultaneous Disk* (1913), private collection.

colors, thus seem to disappear at this spot. As a result, in the central circle, the clear distinction between the red and blue makes it difficult to perceive the drastically fainter difference between the two reds and two blues, each pair barely distinct, that form two equivalent sections of the pair of semicircles. Here, the "simultaneous contrast" implies its contrary: the visual succession of warm and cold colors, with the consonances, dissonances, and rhythms they create, have the effect of generating a central image that *unfolds in the moment*: the two reds and two blues become not only simultaneous but also almost identical. The work of the gaze is thus revealed to itself in Delaunay's disk, just as it was in Turner's final landscapes. The color is located as much in the disk as in the eye of the viewer. Here, Delaunay joins Goethe, who maintained that the world, by itself, does not have any colors at all. Only the gaze and the work of the spirit it reflects can *attribute color* to it.

Through the works of Turner, Kandinsky, Mondrian, and Delaunay, it is possible to outline a series organized around the problem of the relation between space and color, and between figure and ground. Delaunay radicalizes the process of making the forms conventionalized, which Kandinsky had attempted, leading the experience of form toward one that is noniconic. Mondrian, for his part, progressively abolishes color in order to retain only spatial relations. None of these artists "walks alone along the path of creativity" (Lévi-Strauss [1979] 1982, 148); rather, each chooses one of the aspects of the problem posed by Turner in all of these experiments with light and space.

Based on the analysis I have laid out above concerning abstract space and the mental synthesis of color that it presupposes, I would like to identify three anthropological principles of intelligibility in images: the study of the mental operations implied by iconic representation (and the process of constituting subjectivity that such operations imply); the definition of the universe of discourse that is specific to it; and the construction of an iconographic series that presents, according to Lévi-Strauss's formula, many of the visual solutions to given logical problems.

These three principles represent only the starting point for an interpretive project that I will pursue through new ethnographic data in the next two chapters. For the moment, my conclusion is that these three principles can legitimately be applied to Western art, even when the imitation of nature, so dear to Lévi-Strauss, seems to disappear. Let me now show how these principles can be applied and developed through the study of an entirely different type of space.

CHAPTER EIGHT

Chimeric Space
Perception and Projection

> *I saw an entire landscape refracted through the eye of a heron as it plunged into the water: the thousand circles that bound each life, the blue of a whispering sky swallowed up by the lake, and their emergence in another place. This is what images are: emergence in another place.*
>
> —Franz Marc, *Aphorisms*

In the Pitt Rivers Museum in Oxford, a remarkable Siberian ivory buckle is on display (Figure 43). It features the same form interpreted in two distinct ways: once as the outline of a wolf's head and once as the entire body of what is probably a sea lion. This object is more than a mere representation of two different animals by the same visual means; it is a testament to an active gaze. By placing a curved line in two different contexts, the image is transformed from a representation of an animal through imitation into a complex and composite interpretation of a form. As a material trace, the representation highlights a series of mental operations (or, simpler yet, thoughts) linked to this curve and, in both cases, helps project an invisible or potential aspect of the image.

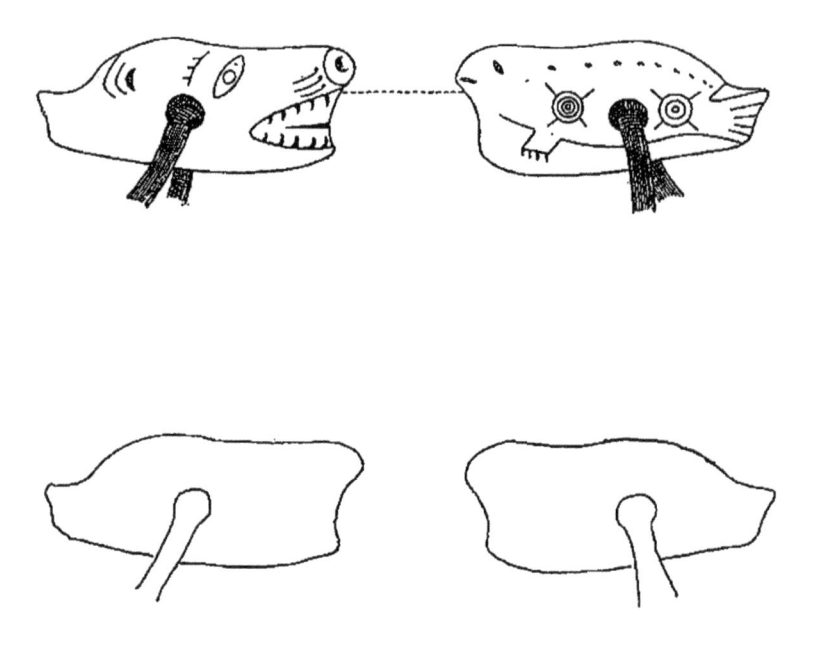

Figure 43. Siberian ivory buckle with the double image of a wolf's head/sea lion. Pitt Rivers Museum, Oxford.

I have suggested elsewhere (Severi 2003, [2007] 2015) that such representations are best understood as what I call "chimeras." Their key characteristic is the condensation of the image into a few core traits that, by causing the observer to project, produce one or more possible interpretations of the resulting form. The observable image is assumed to be part of a different form that has an implicit presence. In this type of gaze, the invisible both takes precedence over the visible and appears to frame it. I argued that this structure uses "indices" to endow the image with a particular salience, thereby enabling it to play a key role in social practices linked to memorization and the creation of traditional knowledge usually described as oral. The visual salience of these images, which is linked to their capacity to produce inference, can be transformed into a mnemonic form of salience that embodies and preserves meaning.

This initial definition of the concept, which I proposed to explain a series of empirical cases through an anthropological theory of memory, provoked much debate and opened up new avenues of research. In light of such discussions, it is worth formulating a number of new questions, starting with morphological ones relevant to ethnographic interpretation. How can the heuristic potential of the chimera concept be extended to new field sites? Can we formulate a general model of representation as "chimerical" in the same way we speak of "realistic," "abstract," or "symbolic" representations? How do chimerical representations vary across space and time? Is chimerical representation, as initially defined, restricted to non-Western art forms? And if so, how should this chimerical property of Amerindian, Oceanian, and African arts be distinguished from images in the Western tradition that have been called fantastical, double, ambiguous, or even simply "potential" (Gamboni 2004)?

Other questions touch on the purely logical properties of the concept. If, as I claimed, the essence of the chimera concept resides not in the specific morphology of the image itself but, rather, in the type of mental operations required to create and perceive such images (such as selecting visual traits, projecting, inferring, arranging sequences, and so on), then what actually distinguishes chimerical representations from other forms? What is their characteristic mode of thought, and how does this differ from others?

Finally, questions of aesthetics also emerge. From an aesthetic point of view, one of the effects of chimerical representation is to intensify an image by mobilizing its invisible aspects. On a fundamental level, however, this scarcely differs from nonchimerical art, which also requires the viewer to engage with aspects that are not materially represented in the work. Indeed, this point is invariably stressed in modern aesthetic treatises. As far back as Denis Diderot's "Notes on Painting" ([1765] 1995), we find an idea of a "machine" that, through careful attention to space and proportion, forces the invisible part of a work of art upon the viewer's consciousness:

> Try, my friends, to imagine that the entire figure is transparent, and that your eyes look out from its center. From there you'll observe the complete exterior disposition of the machine; you'll see how some parts are extended while others are contracted, how the former stretch out while the latter expand; and, consistently preoccupied by the overall effect, by the whole, you'll succeed in showing in that part of the object presented in your drawing everything that would correspond with it but that's not visible, and though displaying only one of its views to me you'll oblige my imagination to envision the opposite view as well; and it's then that I'll write that you're a surprising draftsman. (Diderot [1765] 1995, 195)

What, then, marks the form of aesthetic apprehension proper to chimerical representations? And if all art implies a process of reflection, is it possible to imagine an image that is *not* chimeric? Georges Canguilhem stated that

> to work on a concept is to vary its extension and comprehension, to generalize it through the incorporation of exceptional traits, to export it beyond its region of origin, to take it as a model or inversely, to search for a model for it—in short, to progressively confer upon it, through regulated transformations, the function of a form (Canguilhem 1963, 452).

In this chapter, I will address these questions and elaborate the concept of chimeric representation. This will enable me to refine my analytical tools (and perhaps to clear up a few misunderstandings) and to shed further light on the style of thought expressed through this particular type of iconographic tradition. I purposely avoid an approach based on a typology of representations, opting instead to identify the logic of relations embodied in images created in a specific tradition. To illustrate this shift in perspective, I draw on the analysis of iconographic examples to propose a sharper definition of the chimera and to suggest potential avenues of research based on the three perspectives outlined above: morphological, logical, and aesthetic. I then demonstrate how this new approach can be fruitfully applied to a particular ethnographic case study, the iconography of the Wayana people of northern Amazonia, and compare it to the basketry of a related people, the Yekuana.

THE VISIBLE AND INVISIBLE IN WORKS OF ART

Let me start with the aesthetic questions raised by the debate surrounding the idea of chimeric representation, specifically the issue of whether the relationship between a chimeric representation and the mental processes entailed in perceiving it are truly different from that characteristic of other works of art.

Johann Joachim Winckelmann ([1755] 1985, 72–73) once wrote, "The artist must offer more to the spirit than he does to the gaze. . . . Painting distinguishes itself by the capacity to represent invisible things, past or future." This aphorism epitomized one of the cornerstones of modern aesthetic thought—the idea that, rather than relying on passive or mechanical perception, a work of art always provokes an "active gaze" by the observer. Winckelmann, like Diderot, suggested that an aesthetic experience emerges out of the interplay between what is actually visible on a painted canvas and the process of exploration or interpretation through which the observer assumes a role parallel to that of the artist. From this point of view, an artwork exceeds and even opposes the simple concept of "image." Subjects construct themselves as observers who draw on what they see to produce an aesthetic experience that, although partially the product of the artist's imagination, only reaches fruition in the observer's own gaze. As I pointed out in, this theory has been expressed in various ways by writers from Goethe to Claude Lévi-Strauss. Goethe argued that the color is not a product of the external world in itself but, rather, of the "dormant light [that] resides in the eye," which, through the action of sight, produces the "chromatic harmony" of color (Goethe 2006, xxvi–xxvii). Lévi-Strauss spoke of the observer who, "in a confused way, feels himself to be more . . . creator than the creator himself" ([1962] 1966, 24). In the interval, an entire aesthetic tradition developed the theory that a work of art is the product of a dialogue conducted through the active gaze, above and beyond passive perception.

Michael Baxandall expresses such notions in *Painting and Experience in Fifteenth-Century Italy* (1988) in a manner that serves as a useful introduction to the ensuing analysis. When discussing the relationship between visual experience and cultural knowledge, he proposes a sort of visual experiment with a fairly simple shape (see Figure 44). What does this image represent? We can, for instance, make out a "round thing with a pair of elongated L-shaped projections on each side." Or, geometrically speaking, we can see a "circular form superimposed on a broken rectangular form" (Baxandall 1988, 29). The observer's perception of the image depends not only on the mechanical processes that regulate visual perception but, more broadly, on the interpretive skills nurtured by a particular culture, "the categories, the model patterns, and the habits of inference and analogy," or what he calls its "cognitive style" (1988, 29–30). The further knowledge that the image comes from a description of the Holy Land published in Milan in 1481 and that it bears the caption, "This is the shape of the Holy Sepulcher of our Lord Jesus Christ," adds two additional elements to our perception of the image. Baxandall notes that, as a strategy of interpretation, observers can start by consulting their experience of certain representational conventions. They may realize, for instance, that the image belongs to a particular historical convention of the ground plan, in which the lines representing the exterior walls of a building are drawn as if seen vertically from above. Next, observers who are familiar with fifteenth-century Italian architecture will understand that the circle represents a round building, perhaps with a cupola, while the rectangular wings are halls and the square inside the circle indicates the tomb itself (1988, 30–31). Thus, three cultural variables affect observers' interpretation of these otherwise meaningless shapes: "a stock of patterns, categories and methods of inference; training in a range of representational conventions; and experience, drawn from the environment, in what are plausible ways of visualizing what we have incomplete information about" (1988, 32).

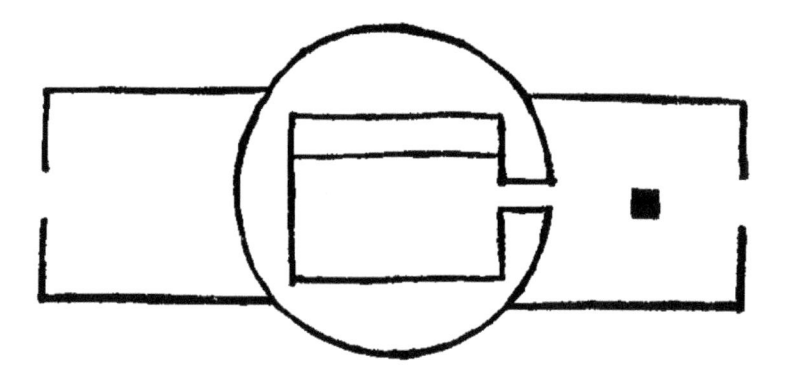

Figure 44. Plan of the Church of the Holy Sepulcher, Jerusalem (from Santo Brasco 1481, 58 v°).

It follows that, in all acts of looking, the physiological process of perception and the projection of culturally acquired knowledge are necessarily intertwined. These mental processes are inseparable from the gaze. This does not, however, imply that the relationship between perception and projection, defining how an image is construed in a given culture, is itself invariable. The visual conventions mentioned by Baxandall do not constitute some cultural grammar with fixed, enumerable rules. Instead, they are unstable, contextually variable, linked to hypothesis and inference, and continually being renewed and reinterpreted. The relationship between passive perception and the interpretative gaze varies not only from individual to individual but also according to the type of dialogue that a given visual convention (or entire iconographic tradition) proposes to the observer's gaze.

To grasp what distinguishes chimeric representation from other sorts, we must explore the modalities of the specific relationship it implies between perception and projection, and then map out the coordinates of chimeric space.

Since the notion of the chimera is unfamiliar, however, the best way to proceed may be to start with a contrasting visual convention, one that is more familiar to us, that of standard Western perspective.

PERCEPTION AND PROJECTION IN THE GAZE

The most basic relationship between perception and projection is that of *embedding*, whereby one operation is included in the conceptual framework of another. In such instances, projection takes place in an almost fixed visual framework, such as Western perspective. Here, projection (prior even to the process of semantic interpretation) entails the ability to translate static lines laid out on a surface into markers of depth endowed with implicit movement. This way of grasping an image, which strikes those of us in the West as quite natural, is far from universal. It has been analyzed in depth as a cultural device of visual interpretation, notably by Pavel Florensky ([1920] 2002), as discussed in Chapter Two. However, the process of inferring depth from two-dimensional images (to which, thanks to the convention of perspective, we have grown accustomed) is most clearly described from a formal point of view by an author I have cited several times in other chapters, Adolf von Hildebrand, notably in *The Problem of Form in the Fine Arts* ([1893] 1994) as well as other writings ([1881] 1969). For Hildebrand, works of art provoke particular mental operations not because they are based on direct observation of the real but, rather, because they emerge out of a complex process of recollection of the real image:

> To see and to represent an object are two entirely different processes. To prove this, look intently at an object and then turn your back. What remains in your mind is very different than the first impression you had of it: one part of the image has disappeared while the other traits persist. The first act is a **perception**; the second, a **representation**. The act that presides over the representation thus belongs to memory, not to perception. (Hildebrand [1881] 1969, 274; emphasis in original)

It is thus visual memory that is, properly speaking, the object of an artist's action. The artist's work involves a constant calculation of appearances. But this attentiveness to the real does not imply the attempt to imitate nature. Instead, it aims to identify an organizing principle of perception, expressed in the presence of a *form*. For Hildebrand, form is neither a property of the exterior world nor a subjective aspect of experience proper to artistic activity. Instead, it describes the "the unconscious perception of space that constantly orients our gaze" ([1881] 1969, 275). This "feeling" (which today we would more likely call an unconscious reflex) both orients our movement and location of our body in space. It follows that any image that implies depth and movement (as in the visual convention of perspective) aims not to imitate appearances but to represent space through the work of the active gaze. Hildebrand concludes that the artist's work occurs "where the representations of space are unconsciously produced" ([1881] 1969, 281). The process of discovering this mental substrate is as much a matter of exploring the labor of the looking as of provoking an unconscious feeling for space.

Here is not the place to delve in depth into Hildebrand's concept of form. Suffice it to underline one essential point: his definition of the concept provides us with a basic abstract model of embedding, which is characteristic of the visual convention of perspective. In this convention, so dominant in the West, observers can grasp the form represented and thus correctly interpret the perspective only if they know how to perceive the depth and movement suggested by the two-dimensional image.

Hildebrand, father of formalism and more a theorist of aesthetic space than a historian of art, offers us a highly idealized interpretation of the relationship between perception and projection that operates in perspective. However, the history of perspectival practices cannot be reduced to geometric rules. Once Alberti had established the ground rules of perspective, these practices gradually gave rise to a shared conceptual space, with its particular enduring traits, peculiar problems, dilemmas, rediscoveries, and resonances, all of which have gone through a complex evolution evident only through the *longue durée*. Svetlana Alpers (2005) builds on the earlier work of Baxandall and John Shearman when she compares this space to a scientific laboratory where the artist, the model, and the patron all play essential roles. This space was a sort of theater of the gaze where, from the Quattrocento to the Impressionists, all the individual elements were at some point altered: the ideology of the patron, the techniques of representation, the means of addressing the observer (Fried 1990), the poses struck by models, and so on. Within this universe, various modalities of relationships between projection and perception are possible. At the risk of oversimplification, we might say that the most straightforward means of activating projection to allow the observer to interpret a two-dimensional image has, since the Renaissance, been to endow it with symbolic value. Both Baxandall (1988) and Salvatore Settis (2005) have shown that religious iconography from the Italian Renaissance was rigorously codified according to detailed instructions given by the Catholic Church in order to guide and engage the imagination of the faithful. One clear instance of this is the representation of Christ, whereas Baxandall showed, the artist's imagination had anything but free rein. On the contrary, the portrayal of Christ was expected to conform to the description given by Lentulus, a fictitious governor of Judea described in a popular Renaissance translation of a Greek forgery (1988, 165). Lentulus, who supposedly met Christ, described him thus:

> A man of average or moderate height, and very distinguished. . . . His hair is the color of a ripe hazel-nut. It falls straight almost to the level of his ears; from there down it curls thickly and is rather more luxuriant, and this hangs down to his shoulders. . . . His forehead is wide, smooth and serene, and his face is without wrinkles or any marks. It is graced by a slightly reddish tinge, a faint color. His nose and mouth are faultless. His beard is thick and like a young man's first beard. . . . His eyes are brilliant, mobile, clear, splendid. (Zardino de Oracion 1494, quoted in Baxandall 1988, 57)

Few period depictions of Christ contradict this description. Nonetheless, within this iconographic framework, it was quite acceptable for the conceptual aspect of a representation to contradict its plausibility. Take the example of representations of Christ as a young man: in his *Crowning of the Virgin*, painted near Avignon in 1454, Enguerrand Quarton depicts the Father and the Son with the exact same face to show that the two are in fact one entity (Figure 45) (Baschet 2008, 170–72).

In similar fashion, Bramantino, around the same period, painted a *Virgin with Child* (Figure 46), depicting Mary with a facial morphology so close to that of a young man that the painting was long considered enigmatic. William Suida demonstrated that this was the result, on the one hand, of the benefactor's wish to remind the viewer of Christ's *divine* nature (which can contradict appearances and emerge even in the face of His own mother) and, on the other, of an appeal to a rare but canonical definition of the Mary as "Virgin Mother,

Figure 45. Enguerrand Quarton, *Coronation of the Virgin* (1454), Musée Pierre-de-Luxembourg, Villeneuve-lès-Avignon.

Figure 46. Bartolomeo Suardi, *Virgin with Child* (c. 1515–1520), Ambrosian Library, Milan.

Figure 47. Hieronymus Bosch, *The Martyrdom of St. Liberata* (c. 1500–1504), Doges Palace, Venice.

daughter of her son" (e.g., when Dante, in Canto XXXIII of the *Paradiso*, calls her *vergine madre, figlia del tuo figlio*) (Suida 1953, 98–100).

The same "impossible likeness" can also be found in the work of Hieronymus Bosch, as when he painted Saint Liberata, a bearded woman martyred on the cross, with the face of Christ (Figure 47). Later, an anonymous eighteenth-century German artist drew on this long tradition when he represented all three members of the Trinity with the same young man's face (Figure 48).

Visual references in Renaissance paintings to Greek, Roman, and Egyptian antiquity also involved a highly influential iconography, which has been amply studied by the Warburg school. Without dwelling on this subject, let me simply note that these basic iconographic allusions constituted a relatively stable repertoire that, in different contexts, could be quoted, modified, contradicted, or renewed. One example is Albrecht Dürer's sixteenth-century "hieroglyphs"

Figure 48. Anonymous German painter, *The Trinity* (eighteenth century), Carolino Museum, Salzburg.

adorning the Emperor Maximilian's Triumphal Arch (Figure 49), which completely reinvents an entire neo-Egyptian iconographic tradition on both a symbolic and stylistic level.

The use of symbolic images in Renaissance paintings, as Aby Warburg notes (2010), seemed to follow one of two paths: either they referred back to antiquity

Figure 49. Albrecht Dürer, hieroglyphs for the *Triumphal Arch of Emperor Maximilian* (c. 1515), woodcut print (from Dürer 1970).

(the Italian tradition), or they situated classical or Biblical scenes in the contemporary period in which the artist and patron lived (the French tradition). Juan de Flandres's *Salome* (Figure 50) is a striking example of this innovative means of introducing symbolic variety. The painting, inspired by the Biblical descriptions of Salome's sensual beauty and sublime cruelty in asking for the head of John the Baptist, shows the young princess accompanied by one of her ladies-in-waiting. Both are dressed with signal elegance, and Salome appears perfectly indifferent to the decapitated head offered by the troubled guard. In the background, two peacocks can be seen perched on the castle walls, as elegant, indifferent, and cruel as the two women in the soft afternoon light. This initial parallel is intensified by a further visual parallel: the guard and the severed head of John the Baptist are almost identical. What we see is an incarnation of controlled, apparently emotionless cruelty contrasting with an intense suffering. There is perhaps no better example of the French tradition: the text and its symbolism are present in the service of the image, with no explicit reference to the Gospel.

Figure 50. Juan de Flandres, *Salome* (c. 1496), Museum of Art and History, Geneva.

SYMBOLISM AND TRANSITIONAL SPACE

Inspired by antiquity, religious tradition, and courtly life, the symbolism of Renaissance paintings emerges out of a cross-projection of different forms of knowledge, which come together in one interpretative field. But this projection (a gaze that draws on various fields of knowledge to interpret a work of art) is not necessarily limited to the semantic domain; it can also affect representation itself. The formal frame of perspective (and the relationship between perception and projection it implies) ceases to be a mechanical reflex and becomes a consciously reflexive act. Perspective, as a visual convention, relies on the shared assumption that there exists a continuity between space as depicted and real space (including the part of real space we might term *liminal*, which marks the boundary with the space depicted without being part of it [Shearman 1992, 59]). This assumption now ceases to be implicit and becomes a *subject* of representation.

In the Renaissance, the viewer's interpretation was no longer a matter of reading a painting's symbolic meaning, as in the Middle Ages, but of interpreting the action it represents. Gestures, demeanors, and gazes are depicted that presuppose the existence of a sort of double space, one that is partly fictive, partly real, in which the observer's attention is captured. This is what Shearman, following Aloïs Riegl ([1902] 2009), calls the "transitive" nature of perspective—its formal capacity to interpolate the viewer into the image. Perspective implies not only the use of a vanishing point around which depth perception can be organized but, more precisely, of *two* points of view: one within the image itself and another projected outside the painting, which is the implicit location of the observer (Shearman 1992, 36).

When the process of projection takes the representational frame as its object, then the image included in the fictive space it reveals contains certain elements of the real space in which it is situated. As such, it represents the conditions of its own perception. This iconographic *mise en abyme* brings out what we might call the pragmatic aspects of the gaze.[1] This type of composition, which includes in the scene presented the very conditions of visual perception, marks a new

---

1. The level of analysis described by Karl Bühler ([1934] 2011) as the "here-now-I" aspect of utterances is thus also applicable to visual representations, which in turn allows us to rethink Alfred Gell's (1998) conception of the agency of images (see Chapter Four).

relationship between the exercise of perception and that of projection. Within perspectival representations, their relationship is articulated through embeddedness. Nonetheless, in this kind of relationship, the conventional aspect of vision, which frames the act of interpretation, is never represented as such. When observers engage in projection, they translate two-dimensional signs into implicit depth and movement, but they cease to be aware of the frame's formal properties that guide their perception. Their "sense of form" is very similar to Hildebrand's definition, since it works as "an unconscious reflex that unconsciously orients the position of the body and the gaze" (Hildebrand [1881] 1969, 269). This type of embeddedness is almost spontaneously triggered as soon as the observer's gaze interprets a symbolic representation, for which the perception of depth (as well as implicit movement) provides the formal context. However, when the strategy of representation becomes "transitive" (due to a reflexive awareness of the frame), the image *reveals a shift* between what is shown and what the observer infers through the act of projection. The perceptual frame and the symbolically interpreted iconographic theme are no longer bound to one another in perception. For instance, in the mysterious cloud that Andrea Mantegna paints in the shape of a knight in his *Saint Sebastian* of Vienna (Figure 51), we get a glimpse of the unconscious conventions that tacitly structure visual perception (Damisch 1972; Gamboni 2009). Here, the process of projection is made visible. Although the perceptual frame usually veils these conventions, in this case we see traces of them in the image. The embeddedness of perception and projection within perspective, which normally remains at the level of an unconscious sense of space (as Hildebrand pointed out), here shows its limits and reveals its fictitious nature.

Highlighting the liminal character of this double space first appears in the early Renaissance period, circa 1530. Shearman (1992, 59) has pointed out that, when Andrea del Sarto painted his *Madonna of the Harpies* (Figure 52), he inserted "clouds of incense" into the composition, which could only come from the altar that would originally have stood beneath the painting. This was quickly noticed and praised by Giorgio Vasari, who mentions the "haze of transparent clouds" above the architecture emerging from behind the figures (Vasari [1556] 2008, 140), which imbues the painting with a strange atmosphere (Shearman 1992, 59). It also, however, indirectly suggests the liminal space that signals the dividing line between that which the painting offers up to the eye and the space within which the painting itself is situated. The smoke unmasks the painting's fictional status and the carefully calculated illusion it generates. An alternative

Figure 51. Andrea Mantegna, *Saint Sebastian* (c. 1459), and detail of clouds from upper left corner, Kunsthistorisches Museum, Vienna.

version of this same game, but with a profane, elegant, and vertiginous twist, can be seen in Paolo Veronese's frescoes in the Villa Maser near Venice (Figure 53).

Juan de Flandres, in turn, offers us a dramatic and spectacular version of this. Toward the end of his life, when he was living in Spain, he produced a series of paintings from 1505 to 1506 that depicted Saint Michael wearing a vast black breastplate and crushing a monstrous beast beneath his feet (an example is shown in Figure 54). In the breastplate's reflective surface, the artist has depicted apocalyptic visions of corpse-strewn battlefields and burned cities that look as if they occupy the space where the viewer stands. As in his *Salome*, symbolism is present, but the conditions of its interpretation have changed. It is no longer a question of deciphering the hidden meaning of a symbol but of

Figure 52. Andrea del Sarto, *Madonna of the Harpies* (1517), Uffizi Gallery, Florence.

creating a new relationship between the fictional space of the image and that of the viewer. The painterly device of Saint Michael's reflective armor transforms the viewer from a mere reader of symbols into an active participant in the scene represented. The city in flames and the scenes of violence seem to lie behind his own shoulders, thanks to the illusion created by the mirrored image that reflects a second background located outside the painting.

The sorts of aesthetic operations discussed so far (such as the symbolic interpretations, the emergence of a transitional space, and the exploration of gazes

Figure 53. Paolo Veronese, fresco detail (1560–61), Villa Barbaro, Maser (Treviso).

through which perception and projection intermingle) are not restricted to the Renaissance, Mannerism, and the Baroque. Indeed, we see a similar exploration of the observer's double presence in Barnett Newman's mid–twentieth-century

Figure 54. Juan de Flandres, *Saint Michael Altarpiece* (c. 1506), Diocesan Museum, Salamanca.

series of abstract paintings entitled *Onements* (Figure 55). The precise dimensions of the canvas and the intensity of the light allow Newman to place the viewer both in front of *and* within the infinite and aniconic space that it represents. From Juan de Flandres to Andrea del Sarto, from Bramantino to Mantegna, and from Dürer to Newman, it is clear that shifts between the iconographic theme and the frame, and between perception and projection are an integral part of the Western tradition.

Figure 55. Barnett Newman, *Onement VI* (1953), private collection (© The Barnett Newman Foundation / Adagp, Paris).

CHIMERAS AND AMBIGUOUS IMAGES

An exhibition held in 2008 at the Grand Palais in Paris, entitled *Une Image Peut en Cacher une Autre* ("Behind One Image Another May Lie"), went beyond simply the Western tradition, presenting hundreds of "double images" from around the world. The curators, Jean Hubert Martin and Dario Gamboni, set out to show that the ways of reflexively playing with the tension between symbolism and frame transcend any particular epoch or culture. So far, I have examined how this game operates in the tradition of perspectival representation (which, from Piranesi to Goya and from Manet to Newman and Jasper Johns, is one of the axes of Western modernity). It is clear, however, that all iconographic traditions are, each in its own way, *transitive*, where transitivity refers to the implicit form of illusion (an invitation to the gaze) that it entails.[2] Thus, to understand the concept of the chimera, we must focus on the various *forms of relationship* between perception and projection that this kind of representation entails. This will help us identify the modes of relationship between the reflexive awareness of the frame and liminal space, on the one hand, and perception and projection, on the other, that are mobilized in chimeric representation.

Before we do so, however, let us deal with a point of some confusion: the difference between visual ambiguity and chimeric representation. Art historians writing about primitivist art have often used the notion of the "double image" or "potential image," along with the more general issue of visual shifts between perception and projection, to explain *all* forms of visual ambiguity in primitivist and non-Western arts alike. So, for instance, a nude by Edgar Degas that can also be seen as a landscape (Figure 56) might be compared to a Baga *A-tshol* mask that simultaneously represents several different beings (Figure 57), on the grounds that they are both "double images."

By the same logic, the Baga mask might be compared to an illustration in a seventeenth-century Mughal manuscript, which features composite, fairy-tale animals that contain within them various other animals (Figure 58), simply because both portray plural beings. From here, the comparisons might move on to Guiseppe Arcimboldo and thence to Salvador Dali or Jasper Johns. In all these examples, the same concept of a "double meaning" is at play, inviting the viewer to decipher an implicit image in addition to the immediately apparent one.

Although the search for such parallels may make for an amusing pastime, its premises are flawed. It ignores the specific, contextualized meanings of the

---

2. The techniques analyzed by Gell (1996, 1998) that, in certain non-Western arts, tend to entrap the eye in a labyrinthine representation can certainly be interpreted as cases of transitivity. Another example is Chinese funerary art, notably the Tang dynasty funerary monuments dating between 618–713, in which, as Jonathan Hay (2010) has recently shown, the representation of the tomb is portrayed from the point of view of the deceased person's spirit (see Chapter One).

Figure 56. Edgar Degas, *Steep Coast* (1892), private collection.

images in favor of considering only their strategies of visual invention. This drastically reduces them to a lowest common denominator imposed from the outside and superficially lumps them all together. As I will show, not all double or composite images are necessarily chimeric.

Let us now turn to a different sort of example, one that could properly be described as chimeric. The Getty Museum houses a remarkable helmet, dating from 350–300 BCE, labeled as the "Helmet of Philip V of Macedonia" (Figure 59). On the peak of the helmet is a composite image of a mythical creature, a sort of winged, beaked horse. This detail has led specialists to interpret the helmet as a ritual object, probably linked to Philip's cult of Perseus. However, the artifact is relevant to our discussion for yet another reason, one that will enable us to refine our terminology and analytical tools for understanding the morphology of chimeric representation and its underlying iconic logic. Along the portion of the helmet that covers the brow and surrounds the face, the creator of this remarkable object has engraved, with consummate artistry, a pair of

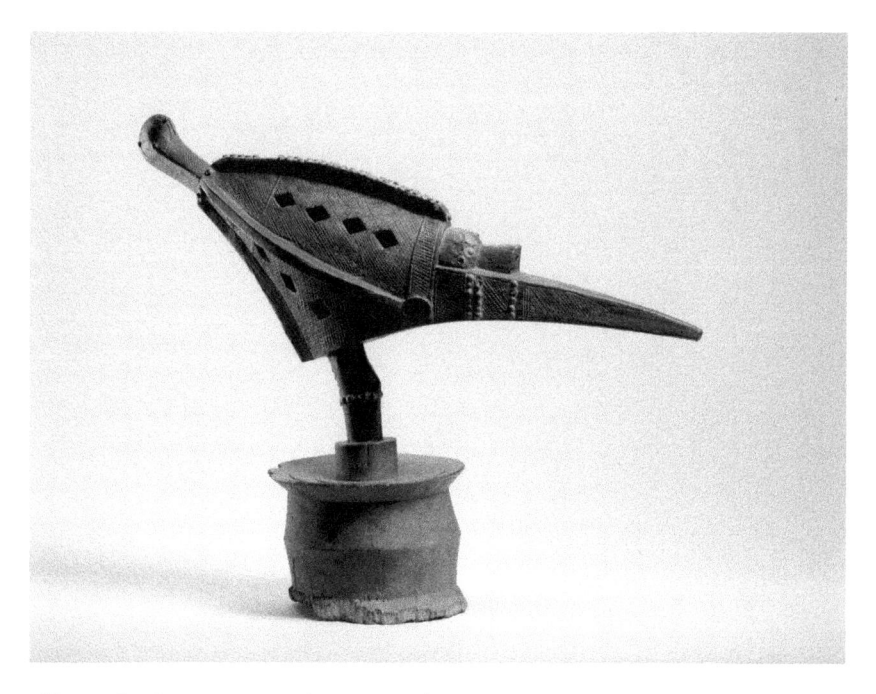

Figure 57. Baga *A-tshol* anthrozoomorphic mask, contemporary era, Guinea, Musée du Quai Branly, Paris.

eyebrows and the hair surrounding the face. This engraved hair is gracefully arranged above the forehead and continues down to the sideburns and joins the beard. The engraving along the edge of the helmet, which Riegl and Shearman call "liminal," represents the boundary between the artifact and the wearer whose presence is implied. Viewers realize that the engraving depicts the hair of the young warrior who wore the helmet. These details transform the empty space it surrounds into something perceptible and apt to trigger projection. As viewers' eyes follow the hairline engraved on the helmet from the brow down to the beard, what suddenly appears in the empty space is not the image of its wearer but, rather, an *index of his implied presence*. Thus, when helmet and warrior simultaneously appear before the viewers' gaze, it is not a "double image" that manifests itself; instead, one could say that, by making visible the relationship of a visual fragment to the empty space it entails, the sculptor has produced a plural being that works as both a visual representation and an index of presence.

This example is radically different from the forms of double or composite representation discussed above in two significant ways. First, chimeric

Figure 58. Mughal School, *The Shah Bahram-Gour Fairy Harpist on a Composite Camel* (seventeenth century), Museum of Islamic Art, Berlin.

Figure 59. Ritual helmet, called the "Helmet of Philip V of Macedonia," Getty Museum, Malibu.

representations such as King Philip's helmet never involve any *duplication* of the image. Even in the case of artifacts with elaborate details like this one, a plural representation is made up of an image for observers to see and another for them to think about. The sudden vision of the implicit, though invisible, head of the young warrior is not the result of a marginal slippage in a model of spatial organization (such as perspective) that would have its own independent existence. Rather, the plurality of the chimeric representation is, in all cases, the *very principle* of a particular organization of space that unites the exercise of both perception *and* projection. We are no longer faced with a fictive space determined by a set of abstract rules (such as geometric ones) that lead to some kind of transgression through the symbolism or transitivity of the image. Rather, the dividing line between the visible and the invisible is coterminous with the very definition of the space in question: there can be no liminal space, no interplay between what is seen and what is inferred, without this prior plurality of gaze. In short, chimeric representation is something quite different from a double image.

Let us return to the Baga mask mentioned earlier (see Figure 57, above). Although the mask plays on the boundary between what can be seen (perception) and what is inferred (projection), no duplication of the image occurs. Like King Philip's helmet (which also deploys this active principle and even multiplies it when it is viewed from different angles) and the Hopi chimera (Figure 60) I discussed in Chapter Four, the Baga mask is not a double image. The contours marking the boundary between perception and projection (such as visual fragments of birds or of the human body) do not function in the same way as icons that echo other images; instead, they serve as *indices of a presence to be deciphered*. Unlike, say, the Degas hybrid woman–landscape (Figure 56, above), chimeras do not involve any interference or echo between two iconic representations in a single visual frame. In lieu of this duplication, there is a striking interplay between an image of the totality and that of a fragment. The fragmentary image does not serve to simply reveal an implicit presence but, rather, to prefigure the possible presence of something entirely different, often even antagonistic. We do not detect the presence of two icons, either in a potential form or in a materially visible one, that evoke one another through visual ambiguity or a double meaning. What distinguishes chimeric representation is that it refers back, by dint of *fragmentary* iconicity, to a presence that is constructed through indices—a presence that only attains the status of image when the viewer's gaze mobilizes various "kinds of interpretive skills—patterns, categories, inferences, analogies—the mind brings to it," which form the "cognitive style" of a given observer in a given era (Baxandall 1988, 34, 30, 35).

This initial analysis of King Philip's helmet and of the Baga mask allows us to make two preliminary statements regarding the degree of complexity in

Figure 60. Hopi polychrome ceramic pot (see also Figure 24).

chimeric representations. The first concerns the transition from visual ambiguity arising from the shifts between perception and projection (whether implicit or explicit) in the context of a space structured by independent optical means (whether geometric or other means), on the one hand, to visual ambiguity understood as a principle of organization of space, on the other. The second statement concerns the existence of a logical relationship between an iconic representation and an index of presence. It follows that, to understand chimeric representations, it will not do to simply reduce them to instances of visual ambiguity. Instead, it is crucial to identify exactly what possibilities are encompassed in their type of complexity. Our point of departure should be a definition that takes into account both the purely optical effects of such representations and the forms of deduction they stimulate in the viewer, including the various acts of projection they trigger. I thus propose that *the term chimeric can be applied to any image that invokes a plural being by means of a single representation, which, either through purely optical means or through a set of inferences, activates its invisible parts.*

This preliminary definition further allows us to offer a response to the three questions raised by recent debates surrounding the concept of the chimera: the *morphological* question of how to define the general class of chimeric representations (and whether they are typical of non-Western arts); the *logical* question of the style of thought characteristic of this type of representation; and the *aesthetic* question of what distinguishes the process by which a viewer grasps a chimeric representation.

From a *morphological* point of view, what distinguishes this type of representation is a principle of spatial organization that triggers several different types of projection while simultaneously producing a specific "illusion" out of the shifts between the visible and implied forms.[3] Rather than a typology of iconographies (which might distinguish between "realist," "abstract," and "symbolic" images), what is relevant here is a sort of typology of spaces, understood as the gamut of possible forms of relationship between figure and ground, whether established through sight alone or through inference. It follows that representations that are fragmentary but not plural, such as Piet Mondrian's *Composition no. 1 (Lozenge with four lines)*, or ones that are plural but not fragmentary, such as Mughal illustration (Figure 58, above), should not be considered to be chimeric in the sense I am using the term here.

From a *logical* point of view, the use of the term *chimeric* is restricted to the specific type of interplay between the iconic representation (through imitation and convention) and indexical indication (through visual, tactile, or other means) of a presence whose mode of existence is primarily mental and has no material incarnation. The chimera is an image imputed by thought, but its actual realization is only perceived as an index (as in the Siberian buckle in the Pitt Rivers Museum), or as a fragment describing an image's liminal region (as in King Philip's helmet) or in terms of the ordering of a series of fragments (as in the Baga mask or Hopi chimera).

Finally, from an *aesthetic* point of view, what characterizes chimeric space is neither the stable embedding of perception and projection (in contrast to their stability in perspectival space) nor a shifting back and forth whereby perception itself becomes the object of projection but, instead, an unstable but nonfortuitous relationship of alternating complementarity between the iconographic theme and its liminal space. Within this space, a visual fragment can, of course,

---

3. Here, I am using the term "illusion" in the sense conveyed by Gombrich (1977) and Florensky ([1925] 1995).

be rendered meaningful because of the ground within which it appears, but the reverse is also possible: within this specific visual convention, figure and ground can swap roles. This is precisely what happens, in two distinct stages, with the Siberian buckle that served as the springboard for this chapter's reflections. Thus, through an active gaze that seeks out a plural being, one image (whose meaning is the result of projection) functions as a latent or realized principle of construction (or organizing framework) for the perception of the other.

Chimeric representation is characterized by both frame reflexivity and symbolic interpretation, but what appears to be the perceptual framework (even in the elementary form of a ground) can always become the principle of projective interpretation (i.e., *form* as a testimony to the work of the gaze in the Hildebrandian sense) and vice versa. The chimera is not embedded in a fixed visual frame; rather, it reflects the constant play of reciprocal presupposition between perception and projection. Since within this space, projection and perception can only function by establishing a provisional form of complementarity, figure and ground, fragment and totality, the focal and the peripheral ceaselessly trade roles.

Although the interpretation of meaning is always present, as we shall see in the following Amazonian examples, this interplay of possible complementarity between theme and frame does not principally concern the domain of symbolism. Although the fragment offered up for projective interpretation may be meaningful (representing, say, a fin, head, beak, or tail in the Northwest Coast, or a jaguar, vulture, or serpent in Amazonia), what makes possible the game of cross-referencing is this fragmentary nature—and thus its relationship to the frame. This relationship, in turn, engenders a specific form of reflexivity (quite different from the more familiar reflexivity of perspective), which makes such interplay possible. The ceaseless interplay of fragment and reflexive frame makes chimeric space iterative, recursive, and potentially infinite.

To conclude these thoughts on chimeric representation, let us return to the Haida mask, which, along with a few other examples, first inspired my research into chimeras (see Figure 29, Chapter Four). The projective interpretation of certain traits ("It's a human face!") provides the initial visual frame that indicates the presence of a human being, although the nose continues to resist easy identification. But the game can then be turned on its head, such that, if the nose is reinterpreted as a beak ("No, it's a crow!"), then the rest of the human face reconfigures itself in a sort of spontaneous anamorphosis around this beak and, instead, describes the head of a bird. Once again, the frame enables projective interpretation and vice versa. That which appeared, in the Western system, to be little more than a periodic or exceptional shifting becomes here, instead, the very organizing principle of space (what we might call *nonperspectival illusion*), no longer based on depth perception but, rather, on the awareness of the possible relations that may surge forth from an image and its background. This principle can be developed either in visual terms, from the dual opposition seen in the Haida mask to the series of fragmentary images identified in the Baga mask, or by investing in the possible relationships between image, sound, speech, and representations of movement. I must stress, however, that none of the traits identified so far is sufficient to define an ideal type of "chimeric" representation. Rather, the analysis undertaken here moves in a quite different direction; through it, I have endeavored to shed light not only on the chimera as a representation but also on the coordinates and contours of chimeric space, as well as on the underlying relational *logic* expressed by these images. Chimeras do not represent entities or beings but, rather, possible or conceptual relations between them. The idea of chimeric representation cannot be slotted into a typology of possible or actual iconographies but should be viewed instead in the context of a logic of iconic relations that play out not only in images but in the gaze-games they invoke.

WAYANA AND YEKUANA ICONOGRAPHY: CHIMERAS IN THE AMAZON

Earlier, in Chapter Three, I discussed Yekuana basket weaving, an iconographic tradition that involves chimeric images. This type of iconography, where the representations of beings are indissociable from the representations of their relations, is far from exceptional or isolated in the Amazon region. An analysis of certain features of the iconography of the linguistically-related Wayana, who live on both sides of the border of Brazil with Surinam and French Guiana, and a comparison with that of the Yekuana, will allow me to elucidate the logic of chimeric representation further. This logic is rooted in the notion of variation, which is predicated on the elaboration of a limited set of basic graphic elements that are deployed in various ways to attain greater levels of complexity.

The Wayana concept of iconographic representation (as well as certain graphic designs) is very close to that of the Yekuana. For both groups, an iconographic representation is organized around simple geometric shapes, such as triangles, squares, spirals, and intersecting or parallel lines. This type of representation is associated with the commentary and memorization of myths—although the memorization process appears to be less formalist in the Wayana tradition, which Lucia van Velthem describes as based on a general narrative schema of predation, with numerous opportunities to link mythical themes to comment on events related to daily life (Velthem 2003, 109–14). A striking feature of the Wayana is the complexity of the discourse they have developed about visual representation. For the Wayana, a geometric design is not merely the graphic sign or emblem of a mythological being, as for the Yekuana; it is also the reflection of a specific form of knowledge known as *wayaman*, which is metaphorically situated in the eyes of someone who masters the techniques of basket weaving or other skills. The *wayaman* appears as an "inverted figure" of an anthropomorphic spirit that others can see reflected in the pupils of a man or woman who makes artifacts; in fact, the *wayaman* is actually the one who is the artifact's true "author." This type of knowledge (or, to be precise, the type of gaze that reveals the "true nature" of the woven images) is above all concerned with form. This form is conceived of as a type of "thought," but also as a reflection of this "other" who lives in the weaver's eyes and "guides his hands"; it is only fully revealed when the object is created in accordance with the rules of traditional weaving. Once the form is complete, then the object will reveal its true nature and show itself to be "like a living creature." In Wayana tradition, artifacts, humans, and nonhumans may and sometimes must be adorned in the same way. Only then do they "adopt the same skin." This is a key notion, because, for the Wayana, "the skin, or rather the skin painted with a recognizable design, represents the element that makes it possible to identify the nature of a being, the means for defining its specificity" (2003, 129). Artifacts are thought of as "replicas" or "imitations" of the ancestral beings they portray because they bear the same skin; in ritual contexts, artifacts often use the images of ancestral predators, the models being the anaconda, vulture, and jaguar, and thus "replicate" or "imitate" such creatures. Due to this "identity of design," artifacts can "dance," "talk," and even "attack" like these predators. The Wayana, like the Yekuana, describe their weavings as "object-bodies," but they also claim that their creator wove the first woman into existence, so artifacts and humans are "engendered" (and given a gender) in precisely the same fashion. Not only are woven designs endowed with speech, the capacity for movement, and a sex but, furthermore, humans and animals are made from the same material as basketry because they can wear the same designs on their bodies (2003, 197, 135). As Velthem explains, the idea of "painted skin is indissociable from the idea of the copy and of reproduction, since it is by means of such skin, the Wayana claim, that all creatures are engendered. The production of an individual implies the production of a new skin—a technical gesture that depends on the observation of a prior model" (2003, 240). Seen from this perspective, the skin of a newborn child is "symbolically associated with a cloth woven of feathers," while an adult's skin is thought of as plaited designs like a decorated basket. In short, the shared identity of humans and artifacts is not, for the Wayana, based on direct resemblance but, rather, on the idea that all living creatures are defined by a specific design that is simultaneously skin, emblem, and visual name.

It would be wrong, however, to think that the appearance of a being or creature is fixed along predetermined lines. For the Wayana, everything that exists is caught up in a process of continual transformation, and, as such, it can assume the skin of one or more other beings "skin" at any moment. For instance, Velthem cites the example of dances held in men's houses. The men's house is supposed to be "inhabited by *tukuxi* fish," who, along with other animals, are painted on the central ceiling wheel of the large ceremonial house (see Figure 65, below). However, the fish are also portrayed as "long-beaked hummingbirds," so when men wearing certain masks "act like fish," they simultaneously become "long-beaked hummingbirds."

This idea of the potential and unceasing transformation of all beings is widespread throughout the Amazon. Among the Yekuana, it is expressed via the opposition between two enemy brothers, Wanadi and Odosha, who represent good and evil, respectively. The Wayana share this idea of an original duality, and they further divide the world into predators and nonpredators. Indeed, this division was one of the first tasks carried out by their mythical creator, who literally constructed the universe around the distinction between predator and nonpredator animals, vegetables, and humans. Unlike the Yekuana, however, the Wayana do not consider these creations to be individual characters with distinct personalities. Whereas the Yekuana rely on paradigmatic personalities, the Wayana think in terms of classes. Instead of contrasting a Wanadi to an Odosha, they distinguish between modes of existence that may characterize any kind of individual, whether it is an animal, vegetable, human, or artifact. This system of classification is an integral part of their traditional thought and is lexicalized in their language. Take the anaconda, one of the models of a predator. Velthem states that

> its acts of predation are so paradigmatic that not only do they evoke the wider supernatural dimension, but they can also serve to describe the acts of any other

species. This conception allows other creatures, such as caterpillars, centipedes, fish, and birds, to display predatory instincts in a supernatural setting through their association with anacondas. (Velthem 2003, 105)

When another animal acts this way, the Wayana say that the anaconda "bears the name and skin" of this particular creature. This type of categorization is not only part and parcel of their thought but is also present in their language: "This coupling of creatures is linguistically signaled by the suffix *okoin*, which means '*qua* anaconda' and is applied to the name of a particular species" (Velthem 2003, 105). Thus, for example, to the name of the toucan, *kiap*, is added the term *koimë*, yielding *kiap koimë*, "toucan-*qua*-anaconda," which is portrayed as a long-beaked serpent whose skin is covered with feathers of contrasting colors. In the same way, when an antbird is considered to be "*qua*-anaconda," it becomes a reptile that sings a birdsong. An analogous process occurs in the case of the jaguar, whose presence is signaled by the suffix *kaikuxin*, which marks the transformation of animals like the Amazon red squirrel into a "squirrel-*qua*-jaguar" (Velthem 2003, 105).

We can think of these terms as "verbal chimeras" that describe composite, changing beings that are categorized in the same class only by virtue of their suffix. The concept of a series, which is also present in Yekuana iconography, becomes considerably more complex among the Wayana. In the initiation dances analyzed by Velthem, for instance, the initiate wears a series of masks that transforms him into a composite being made up not only of different spirits (macaws, falcons, fish, sun, rainbow, and so on) but, furthermore, of different forms of these spirits as incarnations of different predators: jaguars, vultures, or anacondas (Velthem 2003, 212). This amounts to a transition from a chimera to a series of chimeric beings. In the double series of markings on the initiate's body, the concept of chimeric representation reaches unprecedented levels of complexity. The ritual becomes a site of transformation where masked youths progressively "assume the painted skin" of a series of animal, vegetable, and human spirits that are themselves subject to innumerable metamorphoses. The essential logical transition in the Wayana case involves a shift from the representation of different individuals ("personalities") to the representation of members of different classes or even (as in the ritual dance) to the representation of a series of series of chimeric beings.[4]

---

4. Velthem reports that beings considered "*qua*-anacondas" are those capable of clasping and devouring humans; those associated with caterpillars, thought of

How is this logical complexity, as well as the ontology it entails, translated into visual terms? Must we conclude that the complex Wayana system is quite different to that of the Yekuana, which seems to be restricted to the visual translation of a limited series of proper nouns? Or, to the contrary, should we conclude that the heightened degree of complexity observed in Wayana ritual action is limited to the realm of exegesis, concerning discourse but without any links to the iconography?

The representation of individual beings using simple geometric designs that we saw earlier in the Yekuana example is also present among the Wayana. Velthem (2003) references forty-seven woven designs and twenty-nine ceramic ones. However, whereas the Yekuana content themselves with simple lists of designs, the Wayana deploy a principle of categorization to produce classes of graphic designs that are divided into three distinct groups: those belonging to the anaconda body paintings; those associated with the jaguar's markings; and those evoking the skin of "anthropomorphic monsters" (a category that includes enemies, such as white people). Some of these visual motifs, while retaining their specific referent, are also used to identify groups or categories of creatures. For instance, Velthem states that "one of the paradigmatic forms of predation is the act of wounding, stabbing, or piercing." The act that summarizes such predation is "to pierce the skin with a projectile," which is characteristic not only of an arrow (an artifact) but also of several animals, including cobras, wasps, scorpions, and certain birds, notably the maguari stork (*Florida caerulae*). The Wayana consider this stork to be the prototype of piercing creatures, representing it in an iconographic motif called "maguari stork's bill" (Figure 61), which has an outline similar to the vigilant posture typical of this bird. In fact, this graphic design represents both the arrow as artifact and any predatory animal that can strike its prey like an arrow. The double arrow symbol can thus designate, in a rather indeterminate sense, "everything that pierces."

The "maguari stork's bill" provides us with one gateway past the depiction of an individual being to the representation of a category or series. The same principle can be applied to other examples. Velthem remarks that "Wayana graphic designs can be composite, simultaneously referring to several beings" (2003, 313). In such cases, the image can be broken down into several parts,

---

"*qua*-jaguars," include beings capable of "biting [humans] from within," often almost imperceptibly, during an illness (Velthem 2003, 320).

Figure 61. Duplicated image of "maguari stork's bill" design used in Wayana basketry, drawn on paper by Dola (from Velthem 2003).

each with its own distinct referent; the "crab" design, for example, also contains the design called "tapir's eye" (Figure 62). Interpretation thus relies on what Velthem calls an "internal dialogue" among forms that takes place within the graphic design itself. Thus, a creature can be represented by various designs that identify the possible transformations it can undergo; conversely, such transformations may be represented by the graphic design of a single animal that wears "on its skin" various designs representing other creatures. A vivid explanation of this concept is the paper drawing of the design called "jaguar/periwinkle," drawn by a Wayana man to explain the various creatures "contained" in the jaguar (Figure 63).

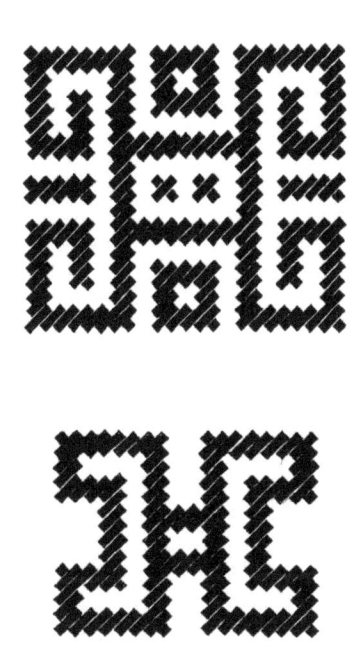

Figure 62. Complex iconography: "Crab/tapir eye" design in Wayana basketry (from Velthem 2003).

Startling echoes of these representations of a single "complex being" in the documents collected by Aristóteles Barcelos Neto among the Waura of the Xingu Basin in Central Brazil, which include representations of a supernatural anaconda composed of a string of images, each referring to a different animal (Figure 64). The Wayana system is, however, much more complex than the Yekuana. Not only do they make use of a single iconographic representation that refers to different beings, as we saw, but they also use a series of different designs to collectively designate a single being.

Thus, the ancestral predator, a being that assumes different forms through a series of metamorphoses, is represented as a collective or serial entity. The finest

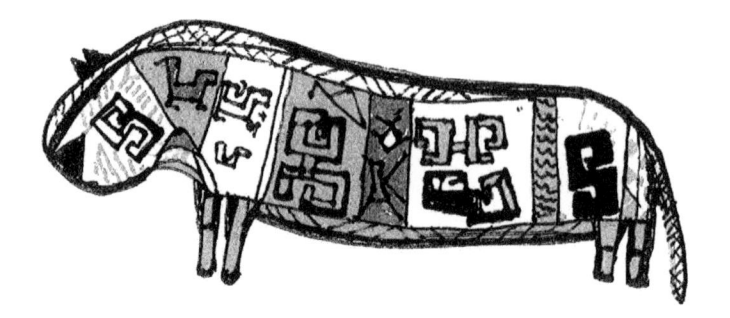

Figure 63. Drawing by Anakari depicting decorations inside a supernatural being, utilizing the "jaguar/periwinkle" design also used in Wayana basketry (from Velthem 2003).

illustration of this process is provided by the paintings that decorate the ceiling wheel of the collective ceremonial house (Figure 65). These graphic designs portray various hybrid beings (anaconda-crocodiles and fishes that "have traits belonging to mammals and birds"), which, as a set, collectively represent the "stingray-*qua*-anaconda," as shown in the *maruana* reproduced in Figure 65. This amounts to a recursive use of the selfsame classificatory principle. The Wayana chimera does more than simply bring together fragments of different creatures or various graphic designs into a single body; it also creates associations among various designs in *different* bodies. Since the designs exist independently of the surface on which they appear, they can be interconnected in a series that collectively represents a supernatural being, such as the stingray-*qua*-anaconda, which is conceptualized as a series of transformations.

Whether a graphic design represents a specific entity or a series with a different logical status, Wayana iconography is always linked to the representation of lists of proper nouns. These proper nouns do not refer to individual characters (even "disguised" or transformed ones, such as the Yekuana's Odosha and Wanadi) but to organized series of proper nouns. When these names are visually translated into graphic designs, they function as "verbal definitions" that mobilize the names of various species. When it comes to memorizing these names, the Wayana can use a process that exploits this double referential system: they can start with a single graphic design, which represents the visual name of a series of beings grouped into a single class by sharing certain taxonomic criteria; or they can trace a series of graphic designs arranged into ordered sequences,

CHIMERIC SPACE 245

Figure 64. Waura representation of anaconda (from Barcelos Neto 2002).

Figure 65. Wayana *maruana*, the painted ceiling wheel in the ceremonial house, described as a "stingray-*qua*-anaconda," Museum of Ethnography, Geneva.

which illustrate the transformations that indicate the "true nature" of a single entity.

A third possibility exists, however, based on designs in which an ancestral being is not directly represented but is indirectly identified via a relationship, expressed in purely visual terms, between two different graphic designs. One example of this is one of the representations of the red squirrel, which does not depict it literally but, instead, evokes it through its relationship to other animals. This is another means of visually translating the concept of "verbal chimera" that is so central to the Wayana aesthetic of predation, which relies on various kinds of transitions through a series. Velthem's nuanced description of two particular graphic designs illuminates the Wayana understanding of iconicity. She follows her interlocutors in distinguishing between, on the one hand, an *ukuktop*, the "perceptual image" of an animal that can be observed in the forest, including its morphology, normal behavior, food preferences, etc., and, on the other, a *mirikut*, the graphic design that represents the animal in the traditional iconography of basketry. "Although every *mirikut* is, of course, an image . . . not every image is a *mirikut*, according to the distinction explicitly formulated by the Wayana" (2003, 317). A *mirikut* enables people to interpret (or "decipher the painted skin") the "true nature" of an animal they are accustomed to seeing in everyday life. But how does this process of constant exegesis play out? Take the examples of the northern Amazon red squirrel (Figure 66) and the maguari stork (Figure 61, above), a small rodent and a bird that are familiar animals in the Wayana's environment. In traditional iconography, they are represented by two graphic designs: the double arrow we have already discussed (Figure 61, above) and a geometric figure that might almost be taken for a "realist" representation of the squirrel (Figure 66).

Figure 66. Amazon red squirrel and "squirrel" design in Wayana basketry (from Velthem 2003).

The indigenous interpretation of these images starts with an isolated design and proceeds to a group of designs. Once people admit that the design (*mirikut*) resembles the "perceptual image" (*ukuktop*) of the animal, they then shift by saying the *mirikut* differs from the *ukuktop* in that the former represents the animals' "supernatural double." The geometric design does not (just) represent the (familiar and harmless) animal but, in addition, its "monstrous, normally invisible double." Let us not forget that Wayana tradition distinguishes between different classes of designs that belong to different predators. When considered from this angle, we can appreciate that the double arrow and the red squirrel designs "both belong to" the anaconda and feature among the paintings on its underside. As such, they are associated with this predator. As members of a series, they can even form part of its representation. In this case, Velthem notes, the red squirrel design is described as the "image (*ukuktup*) and bodily painting (*mirikut*) of the anaconda" (2003, 319). Nevertheless, since the red squirrel design represents an invisible creature, it may also refer to a different predator: the jaguar. Why is this? As Velthem remarks (2003, 318), the two designs are associated because of the similarity of their body shapes, which are distinguished only by their tails: the red squirrel's tail curls outward, whereas that of the jaguar (Figure 67) curls inward.

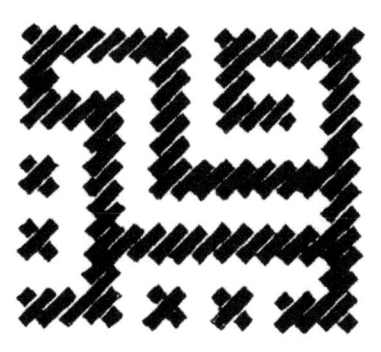

Figure 67. "Jaguar" design in Wayana basketry (from Velthem 2003).

This comparison reveals an unexpected point of connection between the two graphic designs—one that remained invisible when it was merely a question of linking the red squirrel and the maguari stork. It is not just the two graphic designs that share this point of commonality but also the two beings they represent. It follows that these two animals (when contemplated through the prism of their *mirikut*) share a "feline body," which confirms the red squirrel's jaguar-like nature or, rather, its possible existence "*qua*-jaguar." This is further evidence of the essentially serial nature of Wayana iconography: a being is not conceptualized in terms of its singularity. Its "painted skin" always defines it as a member of a class or of a sequence of possible "modes of existence."

In her discussion of these representations, Velthem justifiably describes them as "mnemonic forms." As I have argued elsewhere (in Chapter Three and in Severi 2009, [2007] 2015), mnemonic relations (unlike semiotic ones) do not involve a sign and a referent; rather, by deciphering complex images, they rely on a set of visual inferences that establish a relationship between spatial memory (in the present case, of graphic designs) and word memory. The efficacy of practices linked to memorization in iconographic traditions is not the result of efforts to imitate the referentiality used in writing; to the contrary, their efficacy is linked to the relations they establish between different levels of mnemonic elaboration. The interpretation of Wayana graphic designs relies on the same principles of order and salience that, as we saw earlier, govern Yekuana methods for memorizing proper nouns. The establishment of a particular type of order in the Wayana context affects the various iconographic series that are linked to the "series of beings" organized around the categories of predators. By making each design salient, this order makes it possible to identify each term within these series and, moreover, of each series within a broader series. In both cases, the interpretation of chimeric images presupposes the exercise of inference guided by tradition. A clear example of this is the comparison between the red squirrel and jaguar designs, which simultaneously highlights their similarity (since they share a "feline" body) and their salient differences (since their tails point in opposite directions). In other words, the Wayana graphic design (the *mirikut*) is a sort of visual name that uses iconic traits related to the natural image (the *ukuktop*) of several different creatures, which are then serialized to produce complex or composite beings. These complex entities are purely conceptual, since they would be invisible if they were not caught up in a constant process of provisional incarnations.

The way these graphic designs recurrently call attention to provisional and implicit aspects of representation (which can always break apart and multiply as a representation constantly moves toward its chimerical dimension) suggests that the underlying logic of this iconography can be explored further. One possible way to do this would be to transfer these techniques of serial referencing found in images to nonvisual forms of expression. This might lead us to investigate relations between graphic designs and "sound images," particularly among the neighboring Wayampi, where sound images (for example, in their *tule* musical compositions [Beaudet 1998]) appear to assume the role played by graphic designs among the Wayana—that is, they represent predators and their metamorphoses. Thus, we would witness a transition from the Yekuana sequences based a simple geometrical order, to Wayana serial representations, and then to the complexities of Wayampi representations that are partly visual, partly aural. We might further imagine a shift in the means of expression, as in the use that certain shamanic chants make of verbal onomatopoeia, which seems to function as a sound image of particular creatures or beings, while retaining its status as a recognizable linguistic sign.[5] In short, the domain of possible applications of this idea is vast; here, I am simply sketching out some possible avenues of exploration.

We can, however, provisionally conclude that the Yekuana and Wayana iconographic traditions discussed in this book make use of similar techniques: both in terms of the geometric representation of a series of traits (which can always be broken down into their elementary components or arranged into more complex configurations) and in terms of the variable relationship between language and iconography. In both cases, representations of the spirit world retain a hybrid semiotic character, which is "at once representative and conceptual" (Velthem 2003, 306), since their iconicity, however refined and unpredictable it may be, is always linked to a proper noun or a verbal definition (what we might call a serial name) of the entity represented. Within the latter system, which is limited to mythical narratives, we see the creation of a double relationship between iconographic representation and verbal definition. In some cases, such as with certain predators, a single graphic design is used to represent a series of creatures or the complex proper nouns of particular predators. In other cases, a series of graphic designs is used to designate a single creature, by virtue of its status as a serial name (such as the stingray-*qua*-anaconda) or as an implicit intermediary term (such as the red squirrel-*qua*-jaguar, where the identity depends on the visual similarity of the two graphic designs).

The differences between Yekuana and Wayana iconographic systems concern, first, the transition from the representation of personalized individuals to the representation of a series of constantly transforming entities and, second, the number of intermediary terms (whether linguistic or iconographic) used to refer to a specific creature. Although the ethnography might superficially suggest that we are dealing with two quite distinct systems, our analysis of the iconographic designs and corresponding mental operations reveals a deeper unity.

---

5. This project is developed in Severi (2014).

Both iconographies make use of the same logic associated with the chimeric representation of relations.

CONCLUSION

To respond to questions raised regarding the notion of chimeric representation, I have attempted in this chapter to formulate analytical tools in the domain of the anthropology of images. The preliminary analysis of a visual convention that is more familiar to most readers—the convention of perspective—allowed me to define the apprehension of an image as a variable relationship, always specific to a particular tradition, between a perceptual frame and the projection of acquired knowledge and the interpretative categories it implies. This analysis led me to focus attention on potentially universal notions, such as the interpretation of symbolism through projection, image transitivity, frame reflexivity, and the active gaze. These notions were then applied to chimeric representation, which subsequently appeared to be based, morphologically speaking, on a principle of spatial organization that produces a specific illusion out of the relationship between a visible form and a (mentally) projected form. Logically speaking, I argued that the mental operations characteristic of chimeric representation rely on a specific interplay between iconic representation and indexical indication. Finally, aesthetically speaking, I concluded that chimeric space refers to an unstable relationship of alternating complementarity between, on the one hand, an iconographic design and its liminal space and, on the other, perception and projection.

This analysis led me to the broader conclusion that chimeric representation is, above all, a *representation of relations* expressed via an image. As such, it does not belong to a typology of iconographic representations ("realist," "aniconic," "abstract," and so on) but, instead, to a logic of iconic relations. By analyzing two Amazonian traditions, the Yekuana and the Wayana, in which chimeric representation is the dominant visual convention, I have shown that identifying an implied presence through projection produces the idea of an *essence* specific to chimeric beings. Among the Yekuana, this essence is represented by key figures who are subject to continual transformation and who dominate the myth cycle. Among the Wayana, this chimeric essence develops into a plural logic that replaces the key figures with classes (and sometimes classes of classes) of hybrid entities. In both traditions, as elsewhere in Amazonia, chimeric representation is linked to an essentialist definition of a particular class of living beings. This class is based on a set of defining criteria that are entirely different from those defining species in the human, animal, or vegetable worlds. The constant interplay between fragment and frame, figure and ground, and perception and projection—a visual game that makes chimeric space iterative, recursive, and among the Wayana, potentially infinite—is perhaps characteristic not only of a particular aesthetic but, furthermore, to a *mode of supernatural existence* that is specific to Amazonia.

It follows that the study of chimeric representation may shed new light on artistic traditions as well as on the ontologies that underpin them. No doubt, this is the main challenge that a general anthropology of chimeric space in the Amazon will face in the future.

Let me now return to Western art to test yet again the analytical tools and principles I have proposed so far and see if they help uncover some hitherto unsuspected characteristics.

CHAPTER NINE

The Semblance of Life
The Epistemology of Western Perspective

> *A "living image" does not resemble its model; it aims not to resemble the appearance but the thing. To reproduce the appearance of reality is to renounce life, to confine oneself to a view of reality that sees nothing but appearance, to transform the world into a shadow.*
>
> —Robert Klein, *Form and Meaning*

In 1531, when Michelangelo completed the statue *Night* for the tomb of Lorenzo and Giuliano de' Medici, everyone agreed that it appeared to be *alive* (Shearman 1992, 105). Giovanni di Carlo Strozzi, a young poet whose family had close ties to the artist, wrote a poem saying that the statue seemed to be sleeping peacefully (Figure 68). He added that precisely *because* it was sleeping, *Night* was not inanimate and could thus wake up at any moment and reveal that it was alive:

> The Night that you see sleeping in such a
> graceful attitude, was sculpted by an Angel
> in this stone, and since she sleeps, she must have life;
> wake her, if you don't believe it, and she'll speak to you. (Saslow 1993, 419)

Figure 68. Michelangelo, detail of *Night* on tomb of Lorenzo de' Medici (1524–34), New Sacristy of the Basilica of San Lorenzo, Florence.

Since the poem ended with a challenge, Michelangelo responded with another poem in which the statue itself addresses the young poet:

> Sleep is dear to me, and being of stone is dearer,
> as long as injury and shame endure;
> not to see or hear is a great boon to me;
> therefore, do not wake me—pray, speak softly. (Saslow 1993, 419)

The statue is immobile because it is sunk in deep sleep. And it is so alive that it knows the suffering (*il danno e la vergogna*) inflicted by the Medicis on their city during that period of violent conflicts. But she refuses to see it. Michelangelo has her say that she appreciates silence and sleep; even though she is alive, she likes "being made of stone" (*l'esser di sasso*) far more than sleeping. This paradox is only an apparent one, since, in the artist's hand, the material that makes up the statue has become *living stone* (*pietra viva*): a cold stone where the soul of a living being, instead of disappearing, simply takes up a new abode ("though I've changed homes, I live on in you") (*ben ch'albergo cangi, resto in te vivo*) (Saslow 1993, 356). The theme of life attributed to works of art, which was prominent throughout the Italian Renaissance, probably appears nowhere more clearly than in the dialogue between this statue (which speaks for Michelangelo) and its young interlocutor.

This notion of a living work of art is an ancient theme (Bettini 1992, chap. 1). It was prominent in Greek and Roman writings about the arts and gave rise to reflections on perspective. Almost a century before this poem by Michelangelo, Leon Battista Alberti wrote in his treatise *On Painting* ([1435–36] 2011) that all painting using the method of perspective must exhibit *parer vivo*, the appearance or the "semblance of life" in the image (Vasari [1556] 2008). If the artist achieves this goal, the figures will show not only an accurate image of reality but also the "movements of the soul" that confirm the presence of life (Alberti [1435–36] 2011, 62).

In this chapter I will trace the epistemology of this notion. Deeply rooted in the notion of perspective, *parer vivo* is distinct from the geometric rules for composing the image, decoding depth, and interpreting movement implicit in the figures. For Alberti, as well as for Ernst Gombrich (1977) and Thomas Kuhn (1977) in our time, perspective is above all a science that applies the laws of optics and geometry to the representation of space. It thus creates what could be called a *visual truth* and belongs to the same epistemological ideal as modern science. By contrast, *parer vivo*—the principle of appearing to be alive—is a specific type of illusion. More precisely, it designates the illusion produced by perspective, the effect of reality that it can activate. It includes not only the construction of a plausible space but also the perception of life in the figures. These two features are necessarily connected, since one cannot be contemplated without the other. To outline the epistemology of this illusion, which leads to "seeing" living beings on an inanimate surface or in an immobile statue, I will first analyze the truth conditions for perspective as a scientific discipline and then describe the type of magic imbuing the image associated with it. A consideration of these two specific types of illusion and truth will make it possible to shift from the history of a practice of plastic representation, which, having been well studied in the history of art, I will not consider here, to the anthropological interpretation of a relational space where images, like the artifacts I have discussed so far, take on a kind of life and become object-persons.

First, with respect to abstract art and then to chimerical space, my analyses have made it possible to identify three anthropological principles to follow in order to comprehend how images are understood: a study of the mental operations involved in iconic representation and the processes of constituting subjectivity that these operations presume; the definition of the universe of discourse associated with them; and the implementation of iconographic series that amount to, according to Claude Lévi-Strauss's formula, visual solutions for certain logical problems.

Can this type of approach be applied to European perspective? Some twenty years ago, I noticed that a strange paradox seemed to be influencing the anthropology of art (Severi 1991, 81–85). Whereas anthropologists attempt to demonstrate the validity of their discipline for any society, whether traditional or modern, specialists in the anthropology of art continue to study almost exclusively non-Western arts or "popular," "pathological," or children's forms of Euro-American arts. Why do they never approach the "great art" of the Western world, its currents of ideas, its issues, and its great artists, while many Western art historians, from Aby Warburg to Michael Baxandall, David Freedberg, Salvatore Settis, Hans Belting, and Horst Bredekamp, have renewed their approaches by aligning themselves more closely to anthropology?

There are many reasons for this paradox. As I noted previously, some of them surely depend on a false (or timid) epistemology to which ethnologists have too frequently remained loyal. But other reasons involve the difficulty involved in the undertaking. For it must be acknowledged that, in the West, the practices, concepts, and representations developed in the field of art nearly always involve parallel developments that continually reflect other fields of knowledge. Research in both the history of art and the history of the science has come to parallel conclusions about the development of perspective. Scholars in art history, following Warburg ([1932] 1999), have shown that great Renaissance painting drew on seemingly distant fields, such as symbolism, rhetoric, and the arts of memory. Historians of science, inspired by Alexandre Koyré (1950) and others, have demonstrated that these roots also penetrated scientific traditions such as optics and ancient and Arabic geometry (Lindberg 1976; Panofsky [1927] 1991; Smith 2001; Simon 2003; Belting 2011). Before being appropriated by to art, the Latin word *perspectiva* was used for centuries in a theory of the distribution of light that continued the ancient studies of Euclid and Ptolemy. This theory was developed fully in classical Arabic culture, particularly in the works of Ibn Haytham Alhazen, before being taken up in the West by Witelo, Blaise de Parme, Toscanelli, Alberti, and Piero della Francesca (see Parronchi 1964).

Under these conditions, how are we to define the subject of an anthropological approach to perspective, when each of the areas of development and application of its key concepts (space, depth, light distribution, proportion, as well as verisimilitude, analogy, art, and artist) tends to provide only a partial view of it? Where do we locate the principle of unity around which all the practices connected to perspective can achieve coherence? A precise definition of this issue is already contained in Erwin Panofsky's writings devoted to perspective as "symbolic form." In a celebrated essay on Riegl, he wrote:

> For art criticism, it is at once a blessing and a curse that these objects (of science) necessarily put forth the pretension of being understood in some way other than from a historical viewpoint.... A method like the one that Riegl ushered in does no harm to a purely historical historiography . . . in any case no more than the consciousness theory undermines the history of philosophy. (Panofsky [1927] 1991, 197, 217)

The works of any particular artist exist within a broader context with its own distinctive type of visual thought (an exercise of thought with which images are associated). The "science of art" must not only trace the history of these forms of visual thought, but also bring to light their logical processes. In his text on perspective as symbolic form, Panofsky works on two planes. As a historian, he reconstructs the evolution of Western concepts of space and their implementation in the realm of art. As a theorist, he adopts a systematic and abstract approach. If perspective

> is not a factor of value, it is surely a factor of style. Indeed, it may even be characterized as (to extend Ernst Cassirer's felicitous term to the history of art) one of those "symbolic forms" in which "spiritual meaning is attached to the concrete, material sign and intrinsically given to this sign." This is why it is essential to ask of artistic periods and regions not only whether they have perspective, but also which perspective they have. (Panofsky [1927] 1991, 40–41)

The particular concept of perspective that developed in the Renaissance, starting with Alberti's treatise, involved the crucial notion of a "semblance of life" created by the work of art. Defining visual thought as a framework for integrating partial definitions of the concept of perspective is undoubtedly the right direction for an anthropological approach to this notion of a "semblance of life." However, Panofsky sticks to two levels of analysis—the reading of space, which he believes to be "theoretically homogenous," and the symbolic deciphering of iconography—which do not enable us to comprehend this notion. What is the most appropriate way to interpret what Alberti calls "the movements of the soul" in an image in perspective? What are the principles that make possible the dialogue—partially fictitious, partly real—between the young poet and the statue *Night*? How can we grasp the effects of substitution or the magical sense of a "presence" in the image when all we have is the rational description of the optical experience, which seems to exclude every hint of such magic? Where does that which, nowadays, is called the *life* that animates the contents of a work of art come from?

I will attempt to answer these questions in two stages. I will first reflect on perspective as a "scientific" model for experiencing reality and then study the status of the illusion it creates. To succeed in this type of analysis, the approaches used by anthropologists, art historians, and epistemologists of science need to be integrated into a common framework. In this last chapter, which is perhaps even more experimental than the preceding ones, I will thus attempt to bring them together as I take the results of my earlier analyses into new territory.

A SCIENCE OF DESCRIPTION: *IMITARE* AND *RITRARRE*

The literature on perspective is vast, so it would be impossible to provide even a brief overview of it here. Let me simply recall a few aspects of the history and definition of perspective. Panofsky's observation can serve as a point of departure: the birth of the technique of depiction involving *perspective* marked a shift from an artisanal tradition that had long been cultivated, at least in the West, by painters, architects, and sculptors, to scientific reflection. This shift took place in two steps. The first was initiated by Filippo Brunelleschi, who decided to transfer what was known during his time about the rules of visual perception to the pictorial depiction of space (Panofsky [1943] 2005, 323). The second occurred a few years later, when Leon Battista Alberti, who was a humanist and theorist as well as an architect, painter, and sculptor, published *De pictura*, the first systematic treatise devoted to perspective (Alberti [1435–36] 2011, 14, 102, 141; Parronchi 1964; Landino 1974, 117). With great precision, Alberti described the geometric rules governing the depiction of space, using a paradigm involving a cluster of straight lines emanating in 360 degrees from a central point. According to him, this deployment of radii simultaneously designated the principle of natural light distribution *and* the criterion for the pictorial depiction of space.

For Alberti, perspective was as much a science as it was an art. As a man of science, he specified its theoretical principles: *circoscrizione, composizione, e ricever di lumi* ("the drawing of profiles, the composition, and the reception of light") (Alberti [1435–36] 2011, 50, 73). As a humanist, he identified its origins among the Greeks and Romans (through Apelles, Parrhasius, Protogenes, Zeuxis, Pamphilus, and others) and defined its purpose. As a practice governed by scientific principles (*arte dotta*), Alberti said painting must create an *appearance of life* that shows "the movements of the soul."

This, then, is *parer vivo*, the principle of appearing to be alive. But which "life" did Alberti mean? As a philosophical principle, this notion was central to the Neoplatonist circle, well known to Alberti, at the court of the Medicis in Quattrocento Florence. It played a particularly significant role in the philosophy of Marsilio Ficino ([1482] 2001, [1484] 2000, [1489] 2002). Taking direct inspiration from Plotinus, Ficino asserted that matter is governed by a constant propagation of forces that make every single body a living being, whether this body has the appearance of a rock, an animal, a star, or a human being. The circulation of these energies or vital force, Leonardo da Vinci would later write, makes it possible "to perceive the breathing and the increase and decrease of the blood in the pulses . . . represented in the earth by observing the flow and ebb of the sea" (Leonardo [1883] 1970, 221). In Ficino's eyes, the symbol of the circulation of this energy is the distribution of light. According to him, the beams of light that seem to emanate from the sun and the moon, but which are actually of divine origin, propagate both the life of creatures and the love of God for the world. Conceived as an invisible principle, this love is spiritual in nature but also has a physical dimension. It is an *eros* that continually invests natural bodies, providing them with a ceaseless force of attraction. Ficino believed that the physical aspect of this universal impulse was physical beauty. In this same spirit, Leonardo subsequently wrote that if humans are constantly attracted to beauty, it is because it has an exceptional force of attraction acquired through an extraordinary intensification of light. Ficino saw in this the natural principle of love. A passionate reader of Lucretius, he even affirmed that sexual pleasure is one of the ways in which human bodies participate in the cosmic force, which possesses them beyond their will. This universal *voluptas*, having a divine origin, directs the constant creation of other human beings and, therefore, ensures the survival of the species. A synthesis of vitality, heat, and life, light is embodied in *voluptas*, the erotic energy that gives rise to corporeal shapes and drives the attraction exerted by beauty. As a translator of Plato and of the *Corpus ermeticum*, Ficino had a direct influence on a number of artists who worked in Florence during the Quattrocento (Chastel 1996). Since Alberti was one of his teachers, his exposure to the ideas behind *De pictura* is indisputable. However, Ficino's concept of life went beyond the circle of Neoplatonists in Florence. The history of science indicates that the "life" to which Alberti refers when speaking of *parer vivo* belonged to a general cosmological paradigm that dominated Renaissance thought up to at least Pierre Gassendi and René Descartes (Walker 2000; Copenhaver 1991, 2006; Yates 1964; Cassirer [1927] 2010). Characteristic of philosophers as well as astrologers and magicians, this general notion of "vital force" was formed in tandem with two great transformations of Christian doctrine that were the source of the cosmology of the European Renaissance, which was embodied in conceptions common to many authors, from Ficino to Giordano Bruno and from Pietro Pomponazzi to Tomasso Campanella, despite their differences on other points. The first transformation involved the notion of the soul: this evolved, especially among the Aristotelians of the School of Padua, from a concept as *forma assistens* (the "assisting form") to a new notion of *forma informans* (the "informing form") (Cassirer [1927] 2010, 137). If, as they said, a life animates matter (and especially the human body), this was no longer, as church doctrine formerly asserted, because they believed it contains a principle of divine origin coming from the outside. Sixteenth-century philosophers like Pomponazzi or Jacopo Zabarella now held that "the 'soul' is not added to the 'body' as an external principle of movement or animation; rather, it is the very thing that forms the body in the first place" (Cassirer [1927] 2010, 137). Indeed, the soul cannot be considered a principle independent of matter, since "The soul is the final cause that expresses the ideal 'determination' of the body" (Cassirer [1927] 2010, 127). To illustrate this concept, Zabarella drew on Plato's and Aristotle's metaphor of the human body as a ship (Sgarbi 2013): Can the "soul" of this ship be conceived of as a captain who steers it according to unfamiliar principles? Or, instead, should we imagine the soul of the ship as a principle of life conjoined to it, inherent in the very existence of the body and incarnated in this form? The answer to this choice, about which Zabarella had no doubts, was expressed clearly by Giordano Bruno: to have a soul—and thus to be alive—is, above all, to have a form. For Bruno, the principle of form is the soul of the world, the trail of the unceasing work of the "Universal Intellect," which he imagines as an "internal artifex" of nature. In the same way that our intellect produces rational categories, the soul of the world gives rise to natural species. The universe is alive precisely because it contains the principle of this thought. This objectified intellect—the source of life—is not alien to matter. On the contrary, it operates within matter:

> forming it from inside like a seed or root shooting forth and unfolding the trunk, from within the trunk thrusting out the boughs, from inside the boughs the derived branches, and unfurling buds from within these. From therein it forms, fashions and weaves, as with nerves, the leaves, flowers and fruits. (Bruno [1584] 1998, 38)

Ficino compared this "active soul inherent in the body," as a universal principle of life, to the center of a circle. As the central point equidistant from all the points that form a circle, the soul must always remain the same distance from all the forms to which it gives rise (see Cassirer [1927] 2010, 133).

The concept of the soul and its relationship to the body, which was profoundly transformed by drawing on Greek philosophy, gave rise to a new conception of the universe. In the Middle Ages, human experience was, at least in principle, considered entirely in terms of its dialogue with God. The Renaissance injected a third term into this dual relationship: the cosmos interpreted as a living being, in the image of an animal or human body. In this spirit, Leonardo wrote, for instance, that "the body of the earth is of the nature of fish, sea monsters, or whales, for it breathes water instead of air," and that "the sun never sees a single shadow" (Leonardo 2012, 248). But Tommaso Campanella probably expressed this feature of Renaissance cosmology better than anyone: "The world is a great and perfect animal, statue of God, which praises and resembles God" (Campanella 2011, 53).

As a whole, the universe was conceived as a monument—a "statue," according to Campanella—of divinity. Henceforth, humans would search for the principles of their being not in divinity but, rather, in the universe. At times, radical thinkers like Campanella and Bruno even had the temerity to invert the theological order of things and conceive of God himself as a function of this natural universe. For Bruno, "if he [God] is not Nature herself, he is certainly the nature of Nature, and is the soul of the Soul of the world, if he is not the Soul herself" (Bruno [1584] 2004, 240). Here we are approaching the limits of Renaissance naturalism. The Council of Trent decreed an end to such heresies. For having publicly upheld these ideas, Campanella was incarcerated for twenty years in Naples, and Bruno was burned at the stake in Rome.

The concept that human beings possessed autonomy, however, based on a reference to the natural world, persisted as a general feature of the humanist concept of the world. Almost a century before Bruno and Campanella, in a considerably different milieu and historical circumstances, Giovanni Pico della Mirandola ([1486] 1998) had already proposed this view. In *De hominis dignitate* ("On the Dignity of Man"), he maintained that what characterizes humans and distinguishes them from angels and animals is precisely the fact that their actions are not predetermined by God. Nowadays, this notion of freedom is seen as bearing moral and political value. But Pico della Mirandola drew quite another conclusion: because of this freedom, humans have an extraordinary ability to turn themselves into different beings. They can vegetate like plants, cry out like wild animals, dance like stars, reason like angels, or even go beyond all these creatures and meditate in the "hidden center" of their souls, where they will meet God. Humans therefore are "wonderful chameleons" that explore the universe as they explore their own nature (Wind 1968, 235).

These transformations in Christian doctrine had one result in common: the instability of beliefs. Despite the acceptance of a divine order, with its organized categories and its symbols, its angels and its constellations, the Renaissance nevertheless contained a "realm of uncertainty," a dimension of being in which "extraordinary operations" (*extra ordinem*), miracles, and magical inventions were still possible (Garin [1969] 1989, 138). Life, like beauty and eroticism, was a force that cannot be controlled. "*Vita a vi dicitur*," Campanella said: the Latin word *vita* ("life") is derived from the word *vi* ("force") (Cassirer 1998, 156). For both him and Bruno, as well as for such learned men as Agrippa von Nettenheim, Charles de Bovelles, and Faber Stapulensis, the universe was an "immense dialogue," in which apparently inanimate beings were continually engaged in an infinite series of reciprocal influences (Garin [1969] 1989, 123).

In such a cosmology, painting a "living image" was thus equivalent to inserting the work produced by an artist into this secret life that interconnected bodies in nature—something that only a few rare prodigies could occasionally make visible. The life of the figures that the artist had to make visible reflected a *voluptas* in the magical sense of the term: a force of attraction, a "movement of the soul," connecting them to other bodies through the contemplation of beauty. Even perspective, which enabled the artist to create a luminous space on a flat surface, was also considered a form of magic. In this framework, the practice of art approached the continual process of creation that gives rise to life (and thus beauty) within nature itself. For Alberti, "Nature herself shows pleasure in painting. We often see, in fact, that she makes in marbles hippo-centaurs and bearded faces of kings" (Alberti 2011, 48).

From then on, thinkers in the Renaissance could posit continuities between works of art and the wonders directly produced by nature, such as those found in the *Wunderkammern* of certain princes: polymorphous marble, corals, and nautiluses in extraordinary shapes (Schlosser [1908] 2012; Lugli 1997, 2005; Bredekamp 1996). The most cogent example of this concept is found once again in Ficino: in his *Theologia platonica*, he equated nature itself to an artist who creates living works by following "well-founded reasons" (*per certa operum rationes*) similar to those of art, while the practice of art produces inanimate works that follow "living reasons" insofar as they operate within life (*ars vivas rationes habet*). This passage deserves to be quoted in its entirety:

> If human art is nothing but an imitation of nature, and this art fashions its products by means of their definite rational principles, nature must work in the same way, but with an art that is much more enduring and full of wisdom in that it works with greater effectiveness and makes more beautiful things. But if art—which produces things that are not alive and introduces forms which are neither primary nor whole—has living rational principles, this is all the more reason to suppose that rational principles are present in nature, which does generate living things and produce forms that are living and whole. For what, after all, is human art? It is a sort of nature handling matter from the outside. And what is nature? It is art molding matter from within, as though the carpenter were in the wood. (Ficino [1482] 2001, 253)

In this analogy, which applies a logic drawn from art to the creation of matter, the operative concepts are light, warmth, force (*vis*), impetus (*ratio*), and life (*vita*). By producing their works, artists create, above all, a space penetrated by light—and light is what propagates life. Since the painted figure imitates nature by following "well-founded reasons" and by approaching an illusion of the real, it thus becomes the echo of this beauty, a synthesis of life–force–light, which constitutes the *voluptas* of nature. A number of Florentine artists, including Alberti and especially, as Eugenio Garin ([1969] 1989) notes, the young Leonardo da Vinci, were sensitive to such a vision of art.

During the Renaissance, this "cosmology" of the artistic act, considered as one instance of the set of forces that engender bodies in nature, affords us a new way of comprehending the emergence of the modern Western notion of art, which defined a new relationship between the work and the artist. In an astonishing text, Leonardo remarks that artists, independently of their will and regardless of the subject of their paintings, always tend to paint themselves. According to him, every composition of figures indirectly reflects the very appearance of its creator:

> It is a fault in the extreme of painters . . . to make most of the faces resemble their master, which is a thing I have often wondered at, for I have known some who, in all their figures seem to have portrayed themselves from the life, and in them one may recognise the attitudes and manners of their maker. If he is quick of speech and movement his figures are similar in their quickness, and if the master is devout his figures are the same with their necks bent, and if the master is a good-for-nothing his figures seem laziness itself portrayed from the life. If the master is badly proportioned, his figures are the same. And if he is mad, his narrative will show irrational figures, not attending to what they are doing, who rather look about themselves, some this way and some that, as if in a dream. And thus each peculiarity in a painting has its prototype in the painter's own peculiarity. (Leonardo 2001, 204)

It would be totally erroneous to see in these reflections, as some have suggested (Luporini 1953; Chastel and Klein 1964), an anticipation of the romantic concept of the artist or the emergence of a sort of proto-psychoanalytical unconscious. The source of such ideas lies instead in the Neoplatonist concept of the propagation of forces and shapes that govern the life of nature. Leonardo held that, just as the human *voluptas* engenders the body, light engenders natural forms; thus, as an artist, he defined himself as a "narrator of light." Furthermore, the same force that conceived the form of artists' bodies continues to operate in their activities as creators by influencing their judgment and guiding their hands. This is why artists tend to paint figures that look like themselves. Produced by the same force, they resemble one another, just as lovers' bodies resemble each another (as Ficino remarked in *De amore*) and as children resemble their parents:

> We may conclude that the very soul which rules and governs each body directs our judgment before it is our own. Therefore it has completed the whole figure of

a man in a way that it has judged looks good. . . . And in this way its height and shape are determined, and this judgment is powerful enough to move the arm of the painter and makes him repeat himself and it seems to this soul that this is the true way of representing a man and that those who do not do as it does commit an error. If it finds someone who resembles the body it has composed, it delights in it and often falls in love with it. And for this reason many fall in love with and marry women who resemble them, and often the children that are born to such people look like their parents. (Leonardo 2001, 204)

The explanation of this phenomenon is entirely dependent on Ficino's theories. Nonetheless, the Neoplatonist and Aristotelian theories associated with medicine, logic, and natural magic offer us little more than the backdrop of a general cosmology for understanding the emergence and development of the field of perspective. Artistic practices faced difficulties, found solutions, and made choices that were distinct from those encountered in philosophy. The ideal definition of the notion of "life," in particular, is far from obvious if we move from texts by theoreticians to the practices specific to painting and sculpture. From Brunelleschi onward, this ideal definition develops within a context where the act of *ritrarre* (literally "making a portrait" of appearances) is contrasted with the act of imitating. In the language of the Italian artists of the time, *ritrarre* indeed means describing what is seen as exactly as possible. However, the ideal technique of *imitare*, "imitation," of which Alberti provides the canonical version, refers to the application of the rules, independent of appearances, that the classical tradition (Vitruvius in particular) had established for achieving beauty. The founding myth of imitation was that of the Greek painter Zeuxis, who, Alberti wrote, "in making the statue of a goddess, went around choosing from several virgins, beautiful above all other women, the finest and rarest and most endowed particulars of beauty that is seen in youth, and then put them in his statue" (Alberti [c. 1436] 2013, 54; see also Lee 1974; Panofsky [1924] 1968; Cassirer [1927] 2010).

Giorgio Vasari contrasts these two processes of describing reality. In his *Lives of the Artists*, ([1556] 2008), he relates that Donatello sculpted a Christ on the cross in polychrome wood that was so lifelike and so natural that it earned the admiration of everyone in the Florentine art world (Figure 69).[1] Indeed, when

---

1. I agree with Alessandro Parronchi's hypothesis (1964, 5) that this Christ is the one in the Franciscan convent of Bosco ai Frati, of which he provides a fine analysis.

contemplating this sculpture, the viewer is struck by the "absolute realism" of this image, conveyed through the extreme tension in the agonized body, the painted traces of hair on the chest, drops of blood running down the forearms, and bruises that discolor the skin and indicate the blows received by Christ during his torture.

Figure 69. Donatello, *Del Bosco Christ* (c. 1460), Convent of Bosco ai Frati, San Piero a Sieve.

Vasari reports that Donatello's work was considered to be a masterpiece. Only Brunelleschi refused to admit his rival's victory and scoffed at his statue for being too "realistic." He derided Donatello by saying he had merely "placed a peasant on the cross, and not a body like that of Jesus Christ, which was . . . in all its parts, the most perfect human being born" (Vasari [1556] 2008, 114, 148). Donatello responded that Brunelleschi had only to "Take some wood and make one yourself" (Vasari [1556] 2008, 114). Brunelleschi then sculpted his own *Crucifix*, which is now housed in the Santa Maria Novella in Florence (Figure 70).

Figure 70. Brunelleschi, *Crucifix* (1410–15), Santa Maria Novella, Florence.

His sculpture was designed entirely in accordance with the proportions and ideal measurements of the human body advocated by Vitruvius (Parronchi 1964, 420–22) and perhaps also in accordance with the specifications in Alberti's *De statua* ([c. 1436] 2013). With this new work, which transferred to the field of sculpture the precise definition of the three dimensions used by Brunelleschi for formulating the principle of perspective in painting (Parronchi 1964, 419), the result of the bet was reversed. Everyone, including Donatello, admitted that Brunelleschi's representation of Christ was the better of the two. In accordance with his Neoplatonist sympathies, Vasari awarded the victory to Brunelleschi and thus implicitly declared the matter closed.

In painting, however, the situation was completely different. The dilemma between *imitare* and *ritrarre*—between, abstract speculation about forms and ideal proportions versus faithfulness to the visual experience and appearances—lasted for a long time in the field of two-dimensional perspective without producing any definitive solution. Some years later, far from Florence, Hans Holbein the Younger furnished a harrowing, scandalous interpretation of this opposition by choosing to radicalize not the ideal image advocated by Brunelleschi but, instead, the "naturalistic" and dramatic choice of Donatello. In 1521, he created an entombed Christ (Figure 71), where the strategy of portraying the appearances through *ritrarre* achieved a nearly hallucinatory degree of precision.

Figure 71. Hans Holbein the Younger, *The Body of the Dead Christ in the Tomb* (1521), Kunstmuseum, Basel.

Here is how Heinz Klotz describes the painting:

> The painting has the exact dimensions of the space in which a body is buried: two meters long and thirty centimeters and a half high. It is thus not much

higher than a man's chest. The grave stone comes down onto the corpse and settles very close to the lines of the body. . . . The supine body is displayed as if in a store window. The head and feet are slightly turned toward the observer . . . the mouth is open, inert, and the lips allow a glimpse of the teeth. The eye is half closed, with the pupil turned upward. The hair falls over the edge of the tomb. . . . the contrast between the noble structure of the limbs of his body and their evident distortion reveals the brutality of the treatment that Christ has had to endure. . . . the corpse shows, to a terrifying degree, the details of lifelessness. In some parts, the body has already taken on the color of a cadaver. (Klotz, in Stoïchita 1995, 425–26)

This painting was instantly seen as being exceptional. Oskar Batschmann and Pascal Griener report that it was displayed only on Good Friday and note that "only the precise nature of the wounds" made it possible to identify the body as that of Christ (Batschmann and Griener 2013, 317). Victor Stoïchita has argued that even the title, *Iesu Nazarenus rex*, was added very belatedly to the back of the board, only after fierce debate. The scandal probably arose from the fact that the inclusion of very realistic details and even the dimensions of the frame pinpoint the death of Christ to a precise instant in time and space. This image of the son of God who sacrificed himself for the salvation of humanity becomes, according to Stoïchita (1995, 427), the image "of a man condemned to death." Indeed, the martyrdom of the Savior is portrayed almost as if it were merely one death among many. Although this painting was not devoid of theological connotations, Holbein pushed the choice of portraying appearances to its extreme limit, thereby showing that, rather than confirming belief, verisimilitude in depiction can generate scandal. Within the domain of perspective, if an image intends to produce an effect of truth, it must not only follow the scientific criteria for describing reality, but it must also respect the limits of legitimate fiction. The truth of perspective assumes an exact relationship not only between realism and illusion but also, as in the case of Holbein's painting, between appearance and life.

These debates over the truth of the image raise one of the first paradoxes concerning the truth of perspective: if artists only pursue the description of appearances (*ritrarre*), they remain faithful to the visual experience, but they risk betraying their subject, as Donatello and Holbein did. Instead of the sacred image of Christ, what appears in their work is the vulgar figure of a peasant or the sacrilegious image of a condemned man's corpse. On the other hand, by following the route of imitation (*imitare*), the appearance of the living person becomes less intense and the figure approaches the perfect but lifeless model of a classical statue. The artist fashions a figure that is correct in its proportions but deprived of individuality, an image in which the "inner movement of the soul" (such as Christ's suffering) is hardly visible. In Italian art, the two principles for applying perspective emerged as a polarization (in Warburg's sense of this term)[2] between depicting an ideal image and producing a faithful description of the visual experience. These two extreme choices were sometimes seen as being mutually exclusive and, on occasion, were deliberately pursued as such, as in Brunelleschi's sculpture and Holbein's painting. More frequently, when one of these two criteria got the upper hand, the other one was still present, but it remained latent in the image as an implicit form. This was not a matter of poetic conceptions characterizing the work of one artist or another (even though that too happened) but, rather, a matter of technical choices that permeated the entire field of perspective.

This contrasting choice between reality and the idea as the subject of a work, along with the corresponding methods for constructing the image, was only the first in a series of dilemmas that characterized what might be called *field of truth* in perspective. I will explain this point later on. For the moment, I note that these two strategies of pictorial description signaled two distinct routes for spreading perspective from its sphere of origin toward other fields of knowledge. The process of directly describing appearances, which began as a technique in drawing, would go on to "guide the hand" of people (often the artists themselves) who practiced the empirical disciplines, such as anatomy, physics, meteorology, and machine construction. Imitation, which flowed directly from the theory advocated by Ficino and his circle in Florence, to wit, that ideal forms are innate, independent of appearances, and govern nature, would come to be associated with the speculative disciplines, such as geometry and rhetoric.

MODELS OF TRUTH

These debates began in the Renaissance, but they have continued in nearly identical terms up to the present time. Ernst Gombrich propounded a theory about

---

2. With Goethe ([1810] 2006), this term, subsequently adopted by Aby Warburg, indicated the reciprocal influence that two circles placed on two different backgrounds, white and black, exert on one another in both their apparent dimension and their color.

the objectivity of perspective as being based essentially on an analogy between the work of artists and scientists (Gombrich 1971, 1976, 1977, 1979). People in both of these fields observe nature and attempt to formulate a language to describe it in increasingly "objective" terms. During the Renaissance, Gombrich claims, a work of art was comparable to an "indicative proposition" about the appearance of the world, a way of indicating *how* things are (1972, 131; 1976). Perspective is *objective* because it is faithful to the visual experience and the laws of optics, and because it is independent of any other nonvisual organizational criteria, in particular, symbolic or religious ones. It is also *exclusive* because, as testimony to a type of logic that rejects any other form of representation in the past or beyond the bounds of its own civilization, it becomes the perceptible embodiment of a unique model of rationality in which the scientist and the artist come together.

This is a modern concept of perspective, which can be found in Heinrich Wölfflin (see Efal 2010) and, more recently, in Kuhn (1977), but it is debatable whether it was widespread among Renaissance theorists. It is often presented by historians of art and the sciences as being a direct consequence of Brunelleschi's brilliant intuition when he transferred the laws of optics to the realm of painting, thus providing an example of an epistemology common to modern science and art. It is true that one of the major themes of the Renaissance was an ideal analogy between the scientist and the artist. For both Alberti and Leonardo—but for different reasons—painting presented a "dignity of science."

However, virtually the only author to whom Gombrich refers is Alberti. The idea put forth in *De pictura*, which Gombrich so cherished, of defining painting in purely optical terms, far removed from erudite or symbolic references, was proposed early in Alberti's treatise ("the painter strives to imitate what is seen in light") (Alberti [1435–36] 2011, 23). The ideal of the rationality of the image embodied by the geometrical and proportional construction of space, which Gombrich also defended, was originally presented in *De pictura*: "A painting therefore will be the intersection of the visual pyramid according to a given distance after having set the center and established the lights; [an intersection] reproduced with art by means of lines and colors on the given surface" (Alberti [1435–36] 2011, 34). Even the theory, evidently so close to Gombrich's era, that attributes to art the function of making reality visible in terms discovered by artists—and which makes visible the beauty of certain landscapes solely because an artist has first revealed it to us—is found in *De pictura*: "Any beautiful thing there is in objects I claim is taken from painting," stated Alberti ([1435–36] 2011, 46).

This ideal vision, in which the scientist discovers laws that govern nature and the artist makes beauty visible, is far removed from reality. The construction of perspective as the *science of describing appearances*, as asserted in theoretical terms, appears to be far more complex and contradictory if we look at the practice of painting. I have already stated that the opposition between *ritrarre* and *imitare* over the proper construction of the figure stakes out its field of truth with an initial series of dilemmas. As soon as we approach another central theme, *historia*, that is, the relationships among figures in the composition of the subject, further alternatives to such dilemmas emerge.

POETRY WITHOUT WORDS OR BLIND PAINTING?

Let us now examine the issue of describing space. The invention of perspective obviously marked a crucial transformation in Western art. From Wölfflin to Giulio Carlo Argan, many art historians have maintained that precisely because art that uses perspective refers to Alberti's model, it is no longer based on the objects to be represented but, rather, on the more abstract notion of the unity of space:

> For the first time since classical antiquity, art presents not the image of things that have their own meaning, but it rather represents the implementation of a system of relationships where everything (object or figure) takes on significance in its relationship to the others. (Argan and Fagiolo 1989, 734)

Conceived as a technical and logical principle that precedes all representation, the first object of painting is thus space itself. This was a point Alberti made clear early on. For him, the first principle of painting is the *circoscrizione*—literally, the drawing of an outline that delimits the part of space the object occupies:

> When we watch an [object], we certainly see that there is something that occupies a place. The painter will define, then, the extent of this place and will call a similar process of tracing the edge by the appropriate term of the drawing of the profiles. (Alberti [1435–36] 2011, 49–50)

This apparently technical reasoning implies a rigorous concept of the nature of space: according to Alberti, everything that exists occupies a place. This place is the condition of its existence, and thus the painter must, above all, account for space. This concept appears to treat space and visual perception as the foundation of a painting. But in moving from the figure to the *relationships among figures*, it turns out that in reality, this is not the case. In the Albertian notion of *compositio* in a picture, "parts of the *historia* are the bodies, part of a body is a member, part of a member the surface" (Alberti [1435–36] 2011, 53). As Baxandall (1986, 130) has shown, this concept transfers to the realm of painting an organizational model borrowed from Latin rhetoric. According to the teachings of Quintillian and Cicero, the parts of a sentence must function in a precise series of articulations, which could be defined as a type of harmonic, progressive embedding of the smaller elements of discourse within broader elements (Figure 72).

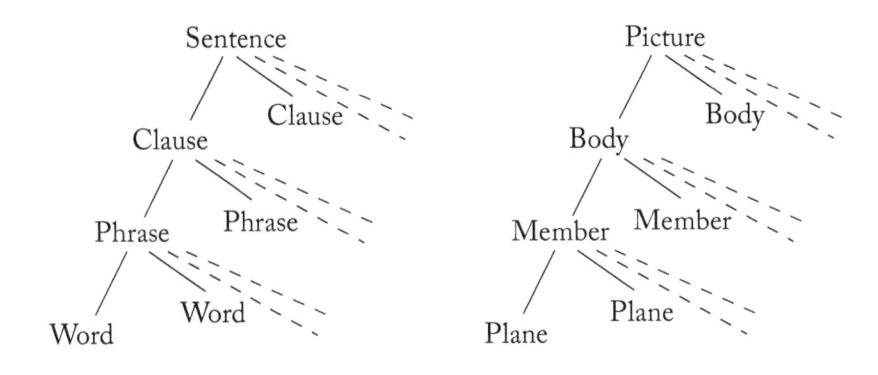

```
        Sentence                        Picture
       /    \   `-._                   /    \   `-._
      /      \      `-._              /      \      `-._
   Clause   Clause  `-._ -          Body    Body   `-._ -
   /    \                           /    \
  /      \                         /      \
Phrase  Phrase  `-._ -          Member  Member  `-._ -
 /   \                            /   \
/     \                          /     \
Word   Word  `-._ -            Plane   Plane  `-._ -
```

Figure 72. Rhetorical model of composition in painting (from Baxandall 1986, 135).

Alberti's circumscription—the outlining of the place that any figure occupies—involves a geometrically correct diagram of appearances based on perception. But the composition, which plays a crucial role in the representation of movement and action, is directly modeled on a basic principle that characterizes the grammatical structure of Latin. If the figure speaks the language of optics, the *historia* must follow the structure of the discourse, as illustrated in Figure 73.

If we examine the works of artists in the circle most closely aligned with Alberti's teachings (those in the Padua–Mantua–Ferrara axis during the mid-Quattrocento), we can see their application of these rhetorical methods for constructing a composition in painting. Baxandall cites artists such as Mantegna or Piero della

Figure 73. Giotto di Bondone, *La Navicella* (1305–13), Saint Peter's Basilica, Rome.

Francesca (Baxandall 1986, 133), but other, lesser-known paintings sometimes illustrate the point even more clearly. For instance, *Death of the Virgin* in the Pinacoteca Ambrosiana (Figure 74), sometimes attributed to a painter working at the court of Ferrara—Roberto Longhi identified the artist as Baldassarre d'Este—perfectly illustrates this conception of visual composition where every figure is defined with respect to other figures, thus reflecting the ideal form of the Latin sentence, in which every element finds its place in a preestablished hierarchy.

In this magnificent painting, the application of Alberti's method achieved an extraordinary artistic result. However, it was precisely by following this route that painting, with its prestige as *arte dotta*, could reveal its weaknesses and be reduced, in the eyes of the humanists, to an imitation of poetry. A few decades later, Leonardo vigorously challenged this concept of painting and the rhetorical model of composition. In some of his writings, he sought to define the principles that characterize painting and issued a veritable challenge to poets. His first example was a battle scene:

> If you, poet, were to portray a bloody battle you would write about the dark and murky air amid the smoke of fearful and deadly engines of war, mixed with all

Figure 74. Baldassarre d'Este, *Death of the Virgin* (c. 1450), Pinacoteca Ambrosiana, Milan.

the filthy dust that fouls the air, and about the fearful flight of wretches terrified by awful death. In this case, the painter will surpass you, because your pen will be worn out before you have fully described something that the painter may present to you instantaneously using his science. And your tongue will be impeded by thirst and your body by sleep and hunger, before you could show in words what the painter may display in an instant. In such a picture nothing is lacking except the souls of depicted beings. And in each body the integration of its parts in demonstrated from a single viewpoint. It would be a long and tedious thing in poetry to portray all the movements of the participants in such a war, with all the components and members of their bodies and their accoutrements. The painter can accomplish this . . . with great immediacy and truth, and such a display lacks only the noise of the weapons, the shouts of the terrifying victors and the screams and cries of those terrified. (Leonardo 2001, 28)

After this fiery discourse, can anyone maintain that painting is nothing more than mute poetry? Leonardo retorted that, on the contrary, poetry is simply blind painting (*orbata pittura*). He added that the painter can represent an unlimited number of things that the poet can never express because of the lack of appropriate words in the language (Leonardo 2001, 20, 22). Besides, he said, there are other notable challenges posed by anatomy, meteorology, geology; indeed, who could describe in words the meanderings of the veins that intertwine in an organ, the contours of a mountain or a cloud, the ceaseless metamorphoses of a wave in the sea? Only drawing and painting have the power to achieve this with richness and precision; only the practice of *ritrarre* leads to the truth that characterizes painting.

But let there be no doubt: for Leonardo, this descriptive ability proves the *scientific nature* of painting. This scientific quality of *ritrarre* is expressed through a property that is lacking in language—the ability to capture the *simultaneity* of things and events. He says that painting "can generate a proportional harmony in the time equivalent to a single glance, just as real things do" (Leonardo 2001, 32), something that poetry is incapable of doing because it unfolds in time. In this regard, painting resembles musical harmony, which transmits several notes "to the ear in a single instant" (Leonardo 2001, 23).

Leonardo contrasted the logic of the observer's view with the word and, similarly, the *proportional harmony of a single glance* with the structure of language. On the one hand, he considered perspective to be an especially precise instrument for describing bodies; on the other, he viewed it as one of the possible registers for the free exercise of visual thought. In his later drawings, he often chose themes in which the notion of geometrical space was especially difficult to grasp—clouds, movements on the surface of water, storms at sea—such as the drawings of the *Deluge* he imagined with pencil in hand (Figures 75 and 76). The preeminence assigned to the logic of the gaze over that of language (and to *ritrarre* over *imitare* of an ideal model) had one major consequence: the priority he gave (being perhaps the first to do so) to defining the movement of the figures.

Leonardo's emphasis on movement first and foremost was a radical departure from Alberti's emphasis on an a priori circumscribed space. For the latter, space, as the basis of all representation, was grasped as something to be displayed by following a series of rules: "Therefore let our [painters] also follow this procedure in painting. At first, let them learn the edges of surfaces . . . and then the connections of the same" (Alberti [1435–36] 2011, 77). The artist still needed to *portray the space* and then insert the figures into it: "And when we wish to realize surfaces in our work, which come from very beautiful bodies, let us always determine previously the limits wherein to direct the lines according to a definite place" (Alberti [1435–36] 2011, 56).

THE SEMBLANCE OF LIFE 277

Figure 75. Leonardo da Vinci, *Deluge* (c. 1515), Royal Library, Windsor.

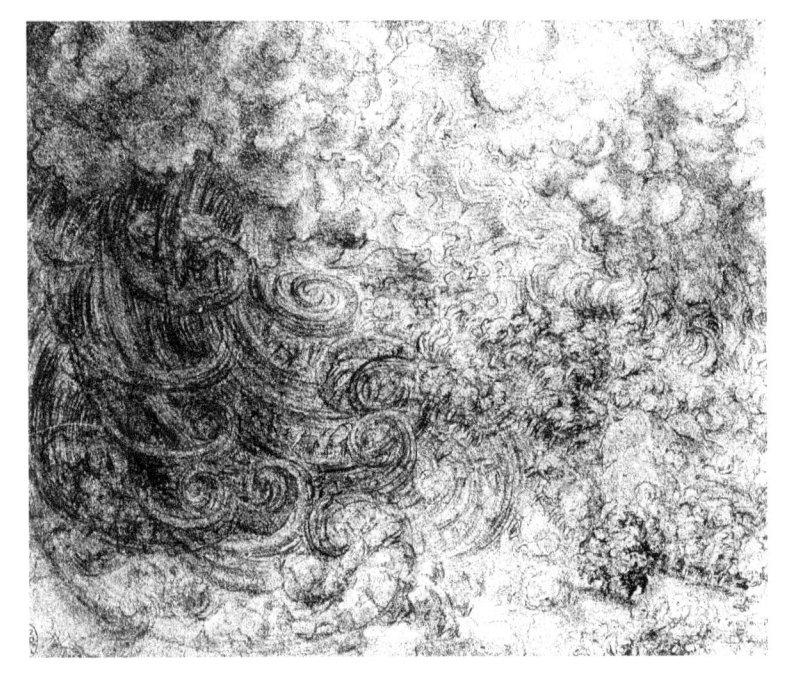

Figure 76. Leonardo da Vinci, *Deluge* (c. 1515), Royal Library, Windsor.

This abstract conception of space as a foundation for the painter's activity has enabled Panofsky to identify a pivot point between the perspective of Alberti and the history of philosophy and modern sciences. When Panofsky states that the history of perspective harks back not only to the history of the arts but also to the laws of visual thought, he is suggesting that an entirely new relationship was defined between aesthetic space and logical space. Both of these were translated by artists into the space of perception (Panofsky [1927] 1991, 67–68). For Panofsky, the true creators of the modern concept of space, defined as a homogenous, systematic, and unified extension, were the artists of the Renaissance. The perspectival method brought to the foreground a space *conceived as such* and rendered it visible. This idea was especially striking in the symbolic representation of the infinite, applied by using to the notion of a "vanishing point." This discovery, which was unique to artists, would later find a philosophical basis in the works of Bernadino Telesio and Giordano Bruno. When the latter defined spaces as *quantitas continua, physica triplici dimensione constans* ("a continuous mass existing in a threefold physical dimension"), he expressed a concept that was later evident in the ideas of Descartes and even Immanuel Kant (Panofsky [1927] 1991, 66, 139). The artist's work was not only the place for a mimesis of the shapes in nature, but also a realm in which it was possible to develop certain strategic concepts of the theory of knowledge. In this space of thought, philosophers and artists worked together. To confirm his philosophical hypothesis, Panofsky quotes a theoretician of the arts, Pomponius Gauricus, who stated in 1504 that "the place exists prior to the bodies brought to the place and must therefore be defined linearly" (Panofsky [1927] 1991, 59, 123).

This technical process, as well as the terms for thinking about space, was reversed in Leonardo's final works. Henceforth, space would be deduced on the basis of the direct visual apprehension of a figure in movement without any visible coordinates to show the way. In the text known as "Manuscript D," Leonardo wrote that the eye can never clearly perceive these "body contours" that Alberti used as the foundation of his theory of vision. In reality, Leonardo said, these contours are reduced to invisible (*insensibili*) lines: "The line forming the boundary of a surface is of invisible thickness. Therefore, O painter, do not surround your bodies with lines," he beseeched. "The line has in itself neither matter nor substance and may rather be called an imaginary idea than a real object" (Leonardo, quoted in Isaacson 2017, 269). He believed that knowledge of how the eye functions (this "minister of all functions of the mind") should be the basis of every theory and every practice in painting, effectively ruling out any priority for outlines. This new way of thinking about space did not just transform the technique of composition in painting; it overturned the logic governing the field of truth in perspective, since space was no longer defined in advance, being inferred instead. Rather than being expressed or brought to the forefront as the visual illustration of a theorem, space was deduced on the basis of what Leonardo perceptively called the *moto mentale*—the "mental motion" of the figure (Leonardo 2001, 146). The painted image was no longer the precise, almost doctrinal demonstration of an abstract element but, rather, simply the visible element of a process that perception triggered in the "seat of judgment" of the mind (2001, 37). Many examples could be cited to illustrate this strategy for constructing space. I will choose a drawing in which Leonardo represented Matilda (Figure 77), one of the most seductive women from the *Commedia* by Dante (*Purgatorio* 28: 52–70), and compare it to an engraving by Andrea Mantegna (Figure 78). In Mantegna, the outlines and the carefully calculated geometrical space occupied by the figures were defined in advance. Imitation of classical antiquity dominates in both the anatomy of the bodies and in the balance of the composition. By contrast, when Leonardo drew Matilda as a figure moving across a faintly suggested landscape, space emerged inductively as a result of choosing *ritrarre* instead of *imitare*. This enabled him to describe reality through means inherent in painting rather than through a grammatical model of composition.

Leonardo's approach was obviously at odds with Alberti's on several points. But had he also formulated his own general concept of perspective? Panofsky ([1927] 1991) and John White ([1957] 1987) presume so when they comment on the discovery of the Codex Huygens, a manuscript with drawings similar to Leonardo's style, which made it tempting to see a return to the perspective of classical antiquity. White, in particular, maintains that in another manuscript now lost but which Cellini knew about, Leonardo attempted to reformulate the entire theory of perspective by replacing Alberti's notion of rays of light as a straight line with one involving arcs of a circle (White [1957] 1987, 278). So far, it has been impossible to confirm this hypothesis from a historical viewpoint. However, let us try to compare these theories from a pure geometrical point of view.

Panofsky has established that, from the Greek vase paintings of the fifth century BCE onward, Hellenic art involved a theory of vision that was, "in its first principles, quite antithetical to linear perspective" in the modern era (Panofsky [1927] 1991, 35). More faithful to the spherical shape of the natural field of view, classical optics were not based on the hypothesis used by Alberti, who held that

Figure 77. Leonardo da Vinci, *Matilda* (c. 1515), Royal Library, Windsor.

visual perception theoretically takes place on a flat surface. Rather, classical artists used the convex surface of a section of a sphere, while classical theoreticians would constantly make "the observation that straight lines are seen as curved and curved lines as straight" (Panofsky [1927] 1991, 34). To this principle, Euclid's sixth postulate was added, according to which two parallel straight lines never

Figure 78. Andrea Mantegna, *The Flagellation of Christ* (c. 1475), Kupferstichkabinett, Berlin.

meet in infinity but always remain separated by an angle, tiny though it may be, enabling distances and relative dimensions to be calculated. From Euclid to Alhazen, the thinkers of classical antiquity and Arabic cultures made these calculations "not by the ratio of these differences, but rather by the far less discrepant ratio of the angles of vision" (Panofsky [1927] 1991, 35). Panofsky continues:

> Because it conceived of the field of vision as a sphere, antique optics maintained, always and without exception, that apparent magnitudes (that is, projections of objects onto that spherical field of vision) are determined not by the distances of the objects from the eye, but rather exclusively by the width of the angles of vision. Thus, the relationship between the magnitudes of objects is, strictly speaking, expressible only in degrees of angle or arc, and not in simple measures of length. (Panofsky [1927] 1991, 35)

This method of calculation was replaced with an entirely different one in the Renaissance, proposed by Alberti and Della Francesca. Nevertheless, despite the differences between these two visual paradigms, they were not separated logically. The classical paradigm was able to acknowledge and explain the phenomenon of marginal distortions, which Alberti's system recognized while also trying to correct or conceal them. Panofsky suggests that it is thus possible to imagine, at least from a purely mathematical viewpoint, a metasystem that includes both concepts of perspective, even if such a unity is merely theoretical or ideal rather than something that actually took place in the history of perspective. For him, Alberti's system was the only one that gave rise to a unified concept of space. What classical painting took from perspective was only an empirical and approximate principle, a schema in the shape of a "fishbone," which, without strictly following the principles of curved space established by classical optics, "approximately rendered" distances and proportions. Thus, unlike the Renaissance, the logical space of classical antiquity did not have a corresponding aesthetic equivalent.

Panofsky points out that, when the vanishing lines are extended, they "do not merge on a single point, but rather only weakly converge, and thus meet in pairs at several points along a common axis" ([1927] 1991, 38). It follows that classical art, a "purely corporeal art," failed to conform to an underlying curved space dictated by its own principles, in contrast with the surface. Hence, "its objects were not merged in painterly fashion into spatial unity, but rather were affixed to each other in a kind of tectonic or plastic cluster" ([1927] 1991, 41). Panofsky then explains:

> Yet even the Hellenistic artistic imagination remained attached to individual objects, to such an extent that space was still perceived not as something that could embrace and dissolve the opposition between bodies and nonbodies, but

only as that which remains, so to speak, between the bodies. (Panofsky [1927] 1991, 41)

Conceived instinctively by artists as an "aggregative space," classical space still did not have the status of "continuum of superior order"; rather, it was composed of *disjecta membra*. Above all, space was not represented as such. Panofsky thus concludes that, in Greek and Roman culture, space was not actually viewed as a concept ([1927] 1991, 55).

> This explains the almost paradoxical phenomenon that so long as antique art makes no effort to represent the space between bodies, its world seems more solid and harmonious than the world represented by modern art; but as soon as space is included in the representation, above all in landscape painting, that world becomes curiously unreal, and inconsistent, like a dream or a mirage. (Panofsky [1927] 1991, 42–43)

But Panofsky's comparison raises two problems: on the one hand, it seems strange that a rich and rigorous concept like the classical one never found sufficient aesthetic expression; on the other, if we turn from the Hellenistic and Roman frescoes he studied to other examples of classical painting, it is possible to identify a coherent concept of space in ancient art. Like the type of perspective used in the Renaissance, classical perspective allowed the artist to go beyond the surface and establish an illusion based on a coherent space. One example from among those Panofsky mentions illustrates this point (Figure 79).

In the foreground of this image, four dimensionally well-balanced horses appear in proper relationship to the cart and the warrior figure, even though the surface of the vase is curved. This reveals a clear perception of a dual spatial plan in the representation, involving an organization of the figures according to a type of depth and three-dimensionality that is compatible with the curved surface. If, as Panofsky argues, classical artists hewed to a "fishbone" schema, how did the artist of this vase achieve this result, so removed from any such schema? The answer lies in the strict application of a principle of geometrical coherence. This is expressed through the precise symmetry and the regular distances that determine the position and the very shape of the features that make up the cart and the bodies of the four horses. In the central pair, we can see that the horses' eyes, tails, heads, and hooves as well as the wheels of the cart are arranged in

Figure 79. *Vase with Black Figures*, second half of the sixth century BCE, Museum für Kunst und Gewerbe, Hamburg.

perfect parallelism. The two muzzles converge according to a diagram shaped like a perfectly balanced triangle. The outer pair of horses displays a carefully calculated divergence that matches the convergence of the other pair and governs both the arrangement and the dimensions of the reins and the lances. Overall, these compositional elements, without exception, converge or diverge with respect to a sequence of points that function like so many foci in a set of carefully designed sizes and relationships in space. The composition is so precise that, theoretically, we could even identify a central (but not single) point that organizes the perception of the entire composition, located halfway between the muzzles of the two horses in the foreground.

In this particular case, where is the "lack of coherence" that Panofsky sees in classical art? I would argue, to the contrary, that this image follows its own rigorous logic and geometry. Because of this rigor, we can see the internal relationships that govern its composition, including the depth, in spite of the curved surface, which otherwise would necessarily distort the viewer's visual perception of the figures. This attests to a technique created in the classical world that was able to "abolish the surface" well before the Roman-era Hellenistic style from which Panofsky draws his examples of a "fishbone" perspective. This point ought to be taken up in the future and refined further. For the time being, my hypothesis is that classical art knew of a technique that, like

Alberti's perspective, was capable of "creating the illusion," but it was conceived according to an entirely different principle, one that could be termed "radial." Such a principle was based on the proportional organization of the elements that made up the composition using "implicit foci," which were organized in pairs, as with the vase just studied: two by two, three by three, and so on. These foci indicated the intersection of axes of balance in accordance with symmetry, divergence, or other geometric criteria that governed the internal coherence of the composition.

Now let us return to the contrast that Panofsky sets up between the Renaissance and classical antiquity. It appears that this contrast is probably too rigid, and, indeed, a number of recent works have shown its limitations (see, for example, Dalai 1980). I argue that, if the contrast is restructured to include the "radial" coherence of classical space I have proposed here, we would be in a better position to grasp the theory of Leonardo's approach to space. When Alberti took the classical values expressed in arcs of a circle and reduced them to straight lines and linear measurements, he unintentionally impoverished the image portrayed in strict perspective as compared to one following the realism of perception. This is the source of the "abstract exhilaration" that characterized Alberti's works and those by painters under his influence (Chastel 1969, 91). Nonetheless, he also created a unified and homogenous concept of space, which the art of classical antiquity had never attained. By following a more realistic notion of perception, the classical artists focused their paintings on figures, thereby making space "discontinuous and unreal" (1969, 91). Leonardo advocated a theory and sometimes created a wonderful sense of space, perhaps based, as White ([1957] 1987) suggests, on a different *Nachleben* of classical antiquity, involving a return to the calculation of distances based on arcs of a circle. His space was focused on the figures and yet it was unified, as illustrated in his depiction of Matilda, where space as a totality is inferred from her implicit movement.

This comparison of Alberti and Leonardo reveals two other polarizations in the field of Renaissance perspective. The first one involves the nature of visual language and its relationship to words; the second, the relationship between figure and ground (or space), on the one hand, and, on the other, the relationship between preestablished space and inferred space. We still need to address the fourth term through which the objectivity of perspective, or its truth status, is expressed: its faithfulness to the experience of the gaze, which I have termed its "description of reality in the indicative."

THE COUNTERFACTUAL IMAGE

The use of techniques that describe appearance, even when they were associated with the rhetorical model of Latin sentence construction, by the artists who most closely followed Alberti's teachings, did not guarantee flawless loyalty to the "visual truth" of perspective. In moving from theory to practice, these techniques no longer served as a means of describing reality according to the laws of optics. On the contrary, they often became the means for imagining numerous *transgressions* of a visual experience. The perfection of appearances, a secret known by the painter, deflected such techniques away from visual objectivity (and their epistemological relationship to grammar) to continually invent transgressions of optical laws. In many cases, the image ceased to be comparable to an indicative clause as a way to refer to the optical experience and took on the logical status of a *counterfactual ostensible hypothesis*.

In Chapter Eight, we saw examples of counterintuitive representations. Enguerrand Quarton gave precisely the same face to Jesus the son and to God the father; Bramantino painted the Virgin Mary with nearly all the features of a young man to indicate that it was she who resembled her son, not vice versa. These works are surely evidence of the strategy of unreality; they were, nevertheless, directly inspired by theological doctrines. Some painters went even further. In his *Pietà*, Cosmè Tura portrayed such an implicit equivalence between Christ and the Virgin that her hand, although alive, has the same color and same stiffness as the tortured body of her son who has just died (Figure 80).

In the *Triptych* of the Frari Basilica, Giovanni Bellini achieves an analogous result through light: he projects onto the face of the Virgin and the body of the Christ child a light so white that it appears utterly "unreal" in contrast with the more "realistic" landscape surrounding them (Figure 81).

In these works, the images no longer seem to say, as Gombrich suggested of some, "this is what things in existence look like"; to the contrary, they use the conditional. In Tura's case, the appropriate paraphrase might be this: What would the Virgin look like if her suffering were so intense that her identification with her son changed her entire person, such that her hand came to resemble her son's dead hand? Bellini's triptych, with its chromatic paradox, could be translated in these terms: What if the light suddenly became exceedingly white for the sole purpose of revealing the supernatural character of the young woman and the child in her arms? And what if this made the divine presence of Christ

Figure 80. Cosmè Tura, *Pietà* (1460), Correr Museum, Venice.

become perceptible, all of a sudden, in this landscape? Henceforth, such transformations in the meaning of the image can no longer be explained merely by returning to a discourse, theological or otherwise; rather, they involve the establishment of unexpected relationships among the elements of the composition expressed in purely visual terms.

This principle of autonomy of the visual can be developed and become even more complex. In some major works, various spaces are created that contrast with natural appearances; they may be expressed in an unexpected way or may even be contradicted within a single composition. For example, when the painter's task consists of affirming a truth beyond perceptible reality—such as the notion of faith—we find no direct application, in terms of technique, of the method of perspective without some kind of artifice. Instead, various visual strategies are brought into play that intensify the artifice and even suggest a definition of space that is "impossible in nature." The strength of conviction in the image is derived precisely from such artifice, not from verisimilitude. A fine

Figure 81. Giovanni Bellini, *Triptych* (1488), Basilica Santa Maria Glorosia dei Frari, Venice.

example of this can be seen in the method of pictorial perspective used in the *Resurrection*, by Piero della Francesca (Figure 82).

Della Francesca's figure of Christ is a demonstration of scholarly, rigorous perspective; for an observer who wishes to understand not only its meaning but also its structure, it demands a particularly attentive viewing. Faithful to traditional iconography, this fresco portrays the dual victory of Christ over death and of faith over unbelief. From a visual standpoint, the composition offers nothing immediately or easily comprehensible. As Longhi as noted ([1927] 2002), the difficulty stems from the artist's application of a *hidden law*, not directly perceptible, in the organization of space.[3] Baxandall (2003) recently

---

3. Regarding this fresco, Longhi wrote: "Here once again, Piero has been called upon to portray a scene—the most triumphal scene of them all—from the Christian myth; and he has apparently fulfilled his task without diverging much from the

Figure 82. Piero della Francesca, *The Resurrection* (c. 1463), Municipal Museum, San Sepolcro.

attempted to account for this principle of organization and the virtuoso, rather unreal quality it lends to the fresco. At first glimpse, certain details seem strange. The bearded soldier, third from left, seems to be missing the lower half of his body. The point of his lance, the tree behind him, and the shape of the hill in the background refer to different spaces that are incompatible with the central perspective. The tomb is portrayed so frontally that it struggles to fit into the rest of the composition, to such an extent that Christ's foot appears to rest on a nonexistent plane. The standard he is holding reaches into a space

---

traditional staging. Nonetheless, the new wholeness of Piero's painted world and the hidden strictness of his spatial laws have necessarily led him to a triumph far different from any won, before or since, by all the more devoutly facile painters who have followed a similar scheme" (Longhi [1927] 2002, 58).

that, according to the usual rules, ought to accentuate the transition from the flat surface to the perception of depth, but it is too close to his face to allow the illusion of depth to be created. Indeed, his face owes its visual authority to a subtle tension set up between two positions that seem to be implicitly expressed in his body. Seen from the left, Christ appears to be standing in a posture that Baxandall (2003, ix) considers to be "militant" and that Longhi ([1927] 2002, 58) describes as showing "erect rigidity." Seen from the right, however, Christ looks like a majestic seated figure that harks back to the traditional iconography of the Last Judgment. These strange irregularities are significant, according to Baxandall (2003, ix), as a demonstration of the specifically visual conditions that generate the meaning of a painting through a process that occupies "the antipodes of language." As others have noted before him (e.g., Nicco Fasola, editor of Della Francesca 1942), he points out that, in this case, Piero implements not one but two patterns for organizing space. One perspective, from bottom to top, involves the group of sleeping soldiers; the other, which is more frontal and based on a higher vanishing point, independently organizes the figure of Christ. He appears to direct his gaze above and beyond the observer, thus producing the sense of authority he commands, as all commentators have noted. Through this hidden artifice, the figure of the resurrected Christ figure is thus unconsciously perceived as *independent* of the earthly space occupied by the soldiers.

The use of multiple perspectives in a composition was not unknown to the masters of perspective in the Quattrocento. In his *Death of the Virgin*, Andrea Mantegna used an analogous strategy (Figure 83). Here, the wake around the corpse of the Virgin takes place indoors, where space is meticulously indicated by the white flooring tiles. Beyond the window in the background is a landscape, perhaps riverine, using a vanishing point that is slightly to the left of the vanishing point organizing the interior space of the palace (located near the extended hand of the figure near the corpse). Because of this discrepancy between the two perspectives used—one that is barely perceptible to the eye (comparable to the use of dissonance to convey movement and intensity to a chorus of voices, as in a Monteverdi madrigal)—the solemn palace interior and the modest, empty landscape are expressed with such precision that they almost seem to be independent of one another, like two parallel, potentially antagonistic spaces in the perception of the scene.

In his *Resurrection*, Della Francesca went even further. Within the same composition are not only two parallel, slightly dissonant planes, but two *disjointed*

Figure 83. Andrea Mantegna, *Death of the Virgin* (c. 1461), Museum of the Prado, Madrid.

and partly contradictory perspectives—to the point of risking imbalance. By resorting solely to a geometrical calculation of space, the painting implies that Christ is independent from the human condition, living in a space so autonomous that he risks shattering the unity of the composition. Its strange features are thus produced by a complex visual speculation. To understand this fresco, observers must resolve the enigma presented to their eyes by these apparent inconsistencies and understand the composition as "a conversation, or a series of references among different groups of visual references" (Baxandall 2003, 139). Only after resolving these enigmas can they, in the words of Samuel Butler Coleridge ([1817] 1984, 6), *suspend their disbelief* and gain access to the structure of the image. This belief is not based on a principle of optical verisimilitude but, rather, on an interpretation of space complicated by the use of several perspectives within a single composition.

At this point, it is possible to draw an initial conclusion about the field of truth in perspective as a description of reality based on the scientific principles of optics and geometry. The contrast between Brunelleschi and Donatello illustrates the difference in approaches between imitating the principles of classical antiquity and depicting what is directly observed. As we saw in Holbein's painting, pure description does not necessarily prove the truth of the image. My reading of Della Francesca suggests that, when this truth is affirmed effectively, it is not verisimilitude that is responsible for this effectiveness but, instead, an artificial, counterintuitive organization of space.

Let there be no mistake: what Gombrich and Karl Popper called "the objectivity" of space is not absent from these works, but the nature of it changes. From a paradigm of reality, it becomes an active component of the counterfactual ostensible hypothesis that is presented to the viewer's gaze. As we shall see, the illusion of life is thereby intensified.

For now, let me summarize the conclusions of these analyses. Gombrich and Popper's scientific model defined perspective as a method for describing reality that remains faithful to the visual experience, a technique for producing an "objective" image of the world ("in the indicative," as I have termed it) that is independent of both language and all symbolism. But we have just seen that none of these characteristics is true for perspective. To the contrary, there are at least four sets of oppositions that are persistently present in perspective: between *ritrarre* and *imitare* in the construction of figures; between a rhetorical model and a purely visual model of composition; between predefined space and inferential space in the apprehension of space; and, finally, between an image "in the indicative" and a counterfactual image regarding the relationship to the reality of the image. Thus, by considering perspective from the artists' point of view, its field of truth turns out to be plural, partial, and complex.

NEW MEDITATIONS ON A HOBBY HORSE

The series of definitions of perspective that Alberti provided in his treatise designates an ideal of rationality that is far removed from painters' practices. But these questions deal with an entire field located in space and time defined by Western (and especially Italian) perspective. To grasp the true dimensions of the field of truth used in perspective, it is equally necessary to understand what contrasts with it—what Alberti (or, rather, his anonymous biographer) called the time of "gothic art" and what modern theorists of perspective reject beyond the limits of European civilization. If perspective is a "scientific" model for art, what is the opposite of art? What is not art, what is not science in the field of art and science, characterized by this ideal notion of perspective?

Implicit in most of Gombrich's writings, this contrast is presented in a short but dense text, *Meditations on a Hobby Horse* (1971). Under this harmless title, the great historian presents an ambitious theoretical position that aims to identify the bases of a "psychology of pictorial representation," the concept of evolution in the realm of art, the relationship between Western art and non-Western arts, and more generally, the logical foundations of iconic representation. Gombrich's argument is based on a clear contrast between two dimensions of a hobby horse as a symbolic object: its shape and its function.

As I stated earlier (see Chapter Five), the *function* of the hobby horse is to take the place of an absent being. In Gombrich's eyes, the common ground between the symbol and the item represented is a function independent of its appearance. The fictitious existence of the hobby horse as a toy is based on the possibility of using a broom handle as a horse (Figure 84).

When children play, they imagine a living horse by imputing its presence to the inanimate object, which thus serves as an acceptable substitute. The function restores a presence independently of the form. In this first case, Gombrich stresses the fact that the fiction is established without producing an illusion. The "horse" may be a simple stick, but it is still capable of supporting a series of functions: mobility, speed, strength, and sometimes words, thoughts, or certain emotions.

For Gombrich, as for Emmanuel Loewy (1930) and Heinrich Gomperz ([1905] 2011) before him, the substitute of a living being with an inanimate object is a response to a basic human need, which may also exist in some animals, as shown by the example of a cat that runs after a ball of yarn as if it were another animal. This involves a drive that Robert Musil (1995), in a memorable

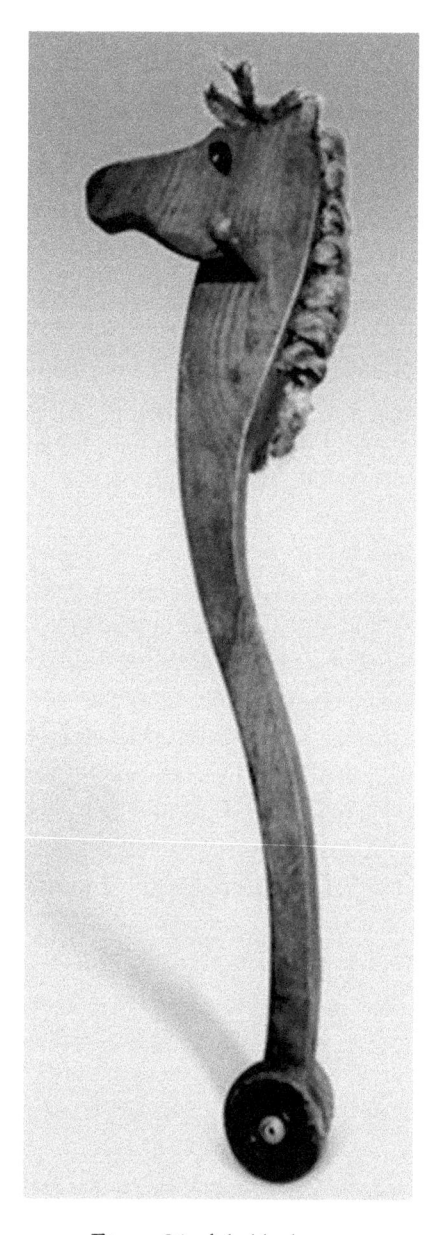

Figure 84. A hobby horse.

essay, described as *an immobile ocean bottom*. Indeed, the function of substitution *does not evolve*.

Gombrich notes that, if the shape of the object becomes too true to life, the hobby horse is *less* useful for establishing the fiction that gives it a role in play. The substituted item must remain imperfect, kept in a state of partial life. If the item becomes too realistic, it could take on life and become dangerous.

When Gombrich analyzes the visual appearance of the toy object, he further develops the terms of contrast he had suggested earlier. For him, the work of art is the foremost site for creating the illusion of reality. In *Art and Illusion* (1977), the separation of the image from its function—particularly its "magical" role in restoring something absent—is described as a condition tied to the birth of Western art, especially Greek art. Unlike the hobby horse, the work created by the Greek artist no longer reported what the subject seemed to know about what defines a real object. Rather, the work of art described a specific visual experience. The goal of a representation based on a form, systematically dissociated from any use but a visual one, is to recreate this experience using a description based on a rational method for describing space. The model for this representation is the increasingly accomplished, hence evolving, application of perspective.

This brings us to one of Gombrich's most intriguing arguments. For him, a paradoxical relationship holds between the rational method for describing space and the production of an illusion. One cannot be conceived without the application of the other, for it is precisely *because* the method for establishing the representation is rational that it can produce an illusion based on space perception. By making it possible to calculate proportions, perspective enables us not only to perceive objects or figures but also to mentally apprehend the space in which they are located. This is where "we are indeed forced to let our imagination play around with it. We endow it with 'space' around its forms" (Gombrich 1971, 17). If we can give life to the images by using our own gaze, it is because, as Gombrich writes, the space of the perspective is *saturated* with meaning. Within this space, nothing can be devoid of meaning: everything must be interpreted. Thus, even empty spaces are part of the spatial construction.

Gombrich's argument is rigorous: only an adequate and perfectible depiction can create a saturated space. This is the only type of space that can elicit the active support of our gaze. Indeed, the sequence of mental operations that produces the illusion can occur only if the representation allows us to deduce not only the exterior shape of the object represented but, in addition, its "dimensions and relative positions." In short, without geometry, there can be no illusion.

Gombrich's position can thus be summarized using a double equivalency: according to him, there is an antagonism between "formal correspondence and the replacement function of a representation" (Gombrich 1971, 16), just as a radical opposition exists among the "various rare islets"—Greek, Chinese, and Renaissance art—which are based on rational methods of describing space, versus "the ocean of ideographic traditions" that dominates the rest of the planet (Gombrich 1977, 12–15). Thus, illusion is a rare occurrence in the evolution of the human species precisely because it makes it possible, through the perfection of form, to go beyond the immobile, "preartistic," and primitive universe of function.

Two objections can be made to Gombrich's argument. On the one hand, as I have reiterated many times in these pages, illusion is far from being a phenomenon specific to Western perspective. "Primitive" or ideographic arts, which make no use of perspective, offer examples of processes that create particular types of illusion, for instance, through chimerical space. On the other hand, the production of an indexical presence of an object as, for example, a theriomorphic or anthropomorphic presence, by using it in play is not as simple a phenomenon as Gombrich implies. Far from being reduced to the simple exercise of a function, this process requires the creation of a complex logical universe. This becomes apparent if we reexamine its essential stages. First of all, the game rests on the formation of a counterfactual hypothesis: "This broom handle is a horse." Such a hypothesis involves what I have called, following Alfred Gell (1998), an attribution of subjectivity, which presumes agency, to the artifact. There are two types of attribution: an episodic attribution, which remains localized; and a systematic attribution, which produces a genuine universe of truth, conceived in close connection to the artifact's universe of agency. In this case, the ostensible hypothesis, "the broom handle is a horse," gives rise to a series of inferences that gradually transforms the identity attributed to the artifact, the identity of the participants in the game, and the identity of the place and time in which they play. This exercise in natural inference is so systematic that it produces a notably rigid context: the children at play know whether or not one of the elements of this chain of identifications is appropriate to the context of the play. In case of doubt, the explicit agreement of all participants is brought up; each time, it is necessary to decide whether one action or another is appropriate to the game. By progressively engendering belief, the game systematically excludes doubt. The crucial matter in the eyes of the children at play is not the truth status of one action or another; even if it flies in the face of any sort of verisimilitude, it can always be subjected to explicit negotiation. What is essential as elements are elaborated is sustaining the coherence of the whole.

During the play, this gradual and systematic exercise in inference produces a new definition of the artifact and a space saturated with meaning. It is like the fictitious space of depiction in perspective, which "compels us to refer every figure and every object shown to that imaginary reality which is 'meant,'" since "we cannot conceive of any spot on the panel which is not 'significant'" (Gombrich 1971, 17). Hence, if the space of the game is saturated with meaning, it also produces, just like art, its own form of illusion.

Throughout this book, I have maintained that images can mobilize two types of gaze-games. One of them, guided by a conscious and technical exercise of memory, considers the image as a text to be deciphered. The other uses the image to support the abduction of subjectivity, and, instead of deciphering meanings within the image, it generates an interpretation of pictures in terms of relations and presence. My analyses of perspective as a particular "field of truth" and of illusion have shown that the more depiction avoids symbolism, the farther it moves from the analogy with the grammar of language and the more it triggers an attribution of agency to a figure. Identifying the gradual emergence of a thought from its presence as a counterfactual image (in the conditional mode, not the indicative) makes it possible to dissolve the opposition posed by Gombrich between the rational illusion involving the technique of perspective versus the implementation of a function for restoring the presence of something absent. My examples have demonstrated, to the contrary, that within the system for representing perspective, mimesis and presence are inextricably bound to one another. The separation between form—defined as a search for an objective description of the visual experience—and function—considered as a means for magically restoring something absent—results from ethnocentric approaches in these aesthetic declensions as well as in the epistemology and history of the sciences. To understand the image portrayed through perspective and the objectivity it claims from an anthropological approach, it is not a question of contrasting these two aspects of representation but, to the contrary, of carefully assessing the relationship between them.

PERSPECTIVE AND THE ANTHROPOLOGY OF IMAGES

The outline I have presented so far of an epistemology of perspective as a model for describing and interpreting reality is, of course, incomplete and provisional. I have provided only an initial glimpse of a few polarizations that characterize the field of truth in perspective as a method for scientifically describing and interpreting reality. Many other points could be brought up, but the ones I have defined make it possible to sketch a few answers to the questions that were asked at the beginning of this study and which may be useful for defining an anthropological approach to the analysis of images. Above all, this has involved studying the mental operations involved in acts of iconic representation, the definition of their particular universe of discourse, and the implementation of iconographic series that constitute, as Lévi-Strauss puts it, visual solutions to given logical problems.

An upshot of my analyses is that the pairs of oppositions identified so far can be considered as potential answers to the problem of depicting space "as such"— a problem that surely constituted a crucial aspect of *the universe of discourse* in Italian Renaissance painting (Panofsky [1927] 1991). On the one hand, this universe of discourse had an empirical aspect, in which the city was dominant, with its contending religious and political powers, and which included images of nature. On the other hand, a theoretical aspect, both logical and aesthetic, defined perspective as a *plan for visual truth*. I have identified two alternative logical operations that iconography could mobilize within this universe: the first, in Alberti's case, was the creation of an a priori space that was expressed like a theorem; and the second, the idea of an inductive space that was deduced gradually, following an entirely different mental itinerary that started with an interpretation of a figure in motion.

But what about the fourth feature I identified? This concerns the constitution of subjectivity (or intersubjectivity) that is implied by these mental operations, this universe of discourse, and these partial responses to the problem of spatial representation. Now that we have defined the context, how should we deal with the mobilization of lifelike appearances and the interpretation of the movements of the soul that lie at their core? How should we comprehend the precise relationship between mimesis—defined as a search for an objective description of the visual experience—and the substitute of a living being as an instance of thinking about presence? In searching for answers, we discover that *parer vivo*—the theory of a lifelike appearance as peculiar to the work of art—owes nothing to geometry. Rather, it arises from *the intuition of a connection* instigated by the gaze between the subject of a representation, the person for whom it is intended, and, indirectly, its creator.

In his remarkable *Traité de l'évidence*, Fernando Gil (1993) proposes a definition of the concept of evidence that can shed light on this issue. From his text, we learn that it is necessary to distinguish two aspects of the notion of evidence. The first one, based on the equivalence between seeing and knowing (which has become traditional in our culture), applies to discourse (mathematical, for example) and refers to the "intuitive" and immediate knowledge of a phenomenon. The second is based on the idea of *active gaze*, understood as a way to establish visual contact, a relationship with another person. The intuitive connection that the semblance of life creates within perspective brings about a synthesis between these two aspects of evidence. Through spatial illusion, perspective combines a certain epistemology of the gaze—the truth of what is seen in immediate apprehension—with the notion of establishing a connection between the image and the observer, linked to concepts about the active gaze and visual contact. It is precisely because of this "realistic" development of perspective that the gazes of painted figures and of real persons share the same space. This connection, I propose, takes place in this shared space with support from the active gaze. In this space, the artist's work must not only create a good illusion in the technical sense, but it must also transform the illusion of space into evidence of a connection between the figures and viewers. In the history of Western art, perfecting the mimesis of reality through perspective as a technique for describing space, a notion to which Gombrich attributed the possibility of artistic evolution, corresponded to the emergence of complex forms of presence, something he never imagined.

FROM PRESENCE TO THE ACTIVE GAZE

In discussing chimerical space in Chapter Eight, I argued that, as a visual convention, perspective is based on an implicit hypothesis. The image posits the existence of continuity between the painted space and real space across the part of the painting that can be described as *liminal*, since it refers to the boundary that surrounds the space depicted without being part of it (Shearman 1992, 59). Within this context, the observer's interpretation moves from deciphering the symbolic meanings of the figures to interpreting the space and the action depicted. Various gestures, gazes, and postures appear in the image, which presumes the existence of a partially fictitious, partially real space in which the observer is captured. In analyzing this phenomenon, Shearman again takes up Aloïs Riegl's ([1902] 2009) classical definition and speaks of the *transitivity* of perspective, referring to its completely formal ability to indirectly create the presence of an observer committed to the image through gazing. As a visual convention, perspective involves not only a "vanishing point" that organizes depth perception in a coherent space but the existence of *two* visual foci: one located inside the painting, the other projected outside its space, thereby marking the implicit place of the observer (Shearman 1992, 36). André Chastel (1969, 147) observes that "what can be called the demonism of the gaze is analogous, from the viewpoint of [the figures'] physiognomy, to the attraction of the vanishing point, which irresistibly burrows into space through the eyes of the observer."

It is remarkable that this intuitive connection between the observer and the image can be conveyed by embedding within the iconography the very game it presupposes in visual terms. Thus, a painting may depict the act of looking at a painting. A telling example, perhaps one of the oldest, is Giotto's *Adoration of the Magi*, in which a shepherd is depicted admiring the main scene, thereby echoing the act that the observer is invited to perform (Figure 85).

This simple form, through which the transitive nature of the space is embodied in an action conferred on a figure, is undoubtedly a traditional means of intensifying the impact of the painting, as acknowledged by Alberti:

> It seems opportune then that in the *historia* there is someone who informs the spectators of the things that unfold; or invites with the hand to show; or threatens with severe face and turbid eyes not to approach there, as if he wishes that a similar story remains secret; invites you with his own gestures to laugh together or cry in company. (Alberti [1435–36] 2011, 63)

This passage has been commented on many times. Louis Marin (1975), Hubert Damisch (1993), and Daniel Arasse (2002) have emphasized that this "admonishing figure," which calls for our attention, reflects a duplication of the very notion of representation. They argue that, rather than being reduced to the naïve depiction of a visual reality, the painting displays the conditions for its own existence by demonstrating what it is—an act of depiction within an iconic discourse. Without wishing to deny this accepted thesis, I believe it overlooks

Figure 85. Giotto, *Adoration of the Magi* (1303–6) (detail), Arena Chapel, Padua.

a crucial aspect of the relationship established by the gaze. When the artist inserts an observer with an active gaze into the composition, he or she radically alters the game that the person standing in front of the picture is invited to play. Because of the liminal figure depicted, the viewer no longer wonders about the meaning of this or that part of the composition but enters mentally into the painted space. Exercising this anthropomorphic gaze gives the observer access to the dimension that Warburg (2000, 3–6) called *Denkraum*, a "space for thinking," which designates the mental act that allows the observer to move from purely executing an action to attributing this action to an image.

Considered from this viewpoint, the representation of the active gaze loaned to a "witness-figure" depicted in the painting can go beyond the merely rhetorical function of indicating the status of the sign in the pictorial discourse. It can become an essential factor in defining the pictorial space as well as displaying the agency of the figures. Federico Barocci's *Pardon of Assisi* is a good example of this dual development (Figure 86).

In this composition, greatly admired in its day, the deciphering of depth using a flat surface coincides with the interpretation of the figure in movement (Emiliani 1975, 96–99). St. Francis turns his gaze toward Christ while simultaneously kneeling and opening his arms to lead the observer into the heart of the painted space. To understand this gesture, the viewer must interpret the spatial coordinates that govern the relationships among the figures. Assigning movement to the figure gives agency to the figure in the transitional space. We move from a presence implied abstractly and implicitly, through the geometrical and projective definition of space, to the production of an alter ego (or an "I") of the observer inside the image. Clearly, the attribution of life to the painted figure of Francis rests on another implicit hypothesis, one of identification expressed in purely visual terms—and completely conditional and partial, dependent on the active gaze it engenders—between the observer and the painted image. Each one sets the other in motion. The observer moves from deciphering a symbolic image to the perception of a movement, and then from the perception of a movement of the figure to the immediate perception of an act of viewing that characterizes the observer and that is *imparted*, almost through reciprocity, to the painted image. An initial form of *connection through the gaze* is thereby established between what is actually present in the real space and what is painted in the composition.

Once this connection is established, it is possible to move from the interpretation of the movement to an attribution of complete subjectivity to the figure.

Figure 86. Federico Barocci, *The Pardon of Assisi* (c. 1575), Church of Saint Francis, Urbino.

Similarly, in Cosimo Tura's depiction of the Virgin Mary, we see her not only performing an action but also suffering over the death of her son; likewise, in Piero della Francesca's Christ, we see him not only moving but also affirming, with an imperious and distant gaze, the truth of faith. Their universe is literally brought to life by the observer's gaze through a process of saturating the inferential space. This type of space resembles not so much Gombrich's geometric dogmas but, rather, the same gradual inference that governs the creation of a universe of truth shared by the child–horseman and the child–princess in playing with the hobby horse. This is same process that takes place in the exchange of gazes between the painted figure and the observer. When gazing on Barocci's painting, the viewer accomplishes something very close to what the Greek participant in the funerary rites was doing, as we saw in Chapter Five. By speaking the name of the deceased, the mourner attributed his own voice to the *kouros* in front of him. In the same way, observers confer on the figure of St. Francis the very action that they are performing—gazing. This gaze-game, in which the transitivity of space, the interpretation of implicit movement, and the attribution of life to the image function like interdependent conditions, is one of the elements that create the appearance of life in perspective. The parallel development of the depiction *and* the connection through the gaze of the person presiding over the presence brings out the profoundly interpersonal aspect of painting in perspective. The act of viewing—or, more precisely, the act of exchanging gazes with someone—is the form of life imparted to the image and shared with the observer.

This link between the painted image and the observer, which, in the case of Barocci's painting, involves only St. Francis and the observer, can become more complex. Around 1503–1504, Giorgione painted an altar piece for the cathedral of Castelfranco Veneto, his birthplace (Figure 87).

This shows a seated Virgin with her child on her lap, dominating a landscape bathed in half-light. To her left, St. Francis shows his stigmata; to her right, Giorgione painted a man standing, clad in a suit of armor and holding a flag. Art historians have long debated his purpose: is this St. George, patron saint of painters (Longhi 1946, 24), St. Liberalis (Pignatti 1971, 49), protector of the city of Castlefranco, or St. Nicasius, to whom certain details of the armor and the flag could refer? For lack of proof, it seems that the debate will continue. But we know for sure that this painting was ordered by Tuzio Costanzo, a *condottiere* who belonged to the order of the Knights of Saint John (his family emblem appears in the center of the composition), in commemoration of

Figure 87. Giorgione, *Madonna and Child Enthroned between Saint Francis and Saint George* (c. 1502), Cathedral of Castelfranco Veneto, Castelfranco.

the death of his son Matteo on the battlefield. The figure of the young warrior in the composition in the conventional features of a saint of the church probably also refers to the recently deceased young man, although without being a portrait of him. Salvatore Settis also found indications of the presence of this young warrior in both the painting and the space surrounding it. According to his analysis (Settis 2010, 164), the painted figure in armor is only the first instance of several that represent the presence of the deceased Matteo. The gravestone sculpted in bas relief shows another image of him, while the Latin epitaph for him corresponds to the young warrior depicted in the landscape with St. Francis and the Virgin. This gravestone "responds," in the space outside the picture, to the tomb made of red porphyry that dominates Giorgione's composition. Settis argues that this series of relationships between equivalent and parallel presences, found in both the painting and the chapel where the painting is displayed, is triggered by a singular act of gazing. The Virgin looks downward (thus serving as a replication of the observer's gaze) and thus calls attention to the presence of the deceased in the porphyry tomb, the same young man who is also shown in the foreground. Matteo is shown in several forms, simultaneously as he was in life, as a fallen soldier, and the subject of mourning.

This painting is not actually a portrait of the young Matteo Costanzo killed in battle: the painter, as art historians maintain, never saw him. But his face is also not *only* that of St. Nicasius. Several features allude to him—the flag of the Knights of Jerusalem, the sarcophagus with the family's coat of arms, and the armor he wears, which is also is depicted on the tomb in the chapel. What is hidden inside the painting—his tomb, alluded to only by the red color of the porphyry—is shown in the funeral site. Conversely, what this funeral site does not suggest—his living figure—appears in the painting. To understand the unique composition of this canvas, we must take into account these multiple instances that generate a complex type of transitive connection between the painting and the space around it.

Another form of connection through the gaze is the *reciprocal* form: this is the gaze that directly meets that of the observer. The "returned gaze" that the figure offers the viewer is one of the best-known inventions of Renaissance painting. Its role becomes especially evident with the appearance (between Giorgione and Sebastiano del Piombo) of the posture described as "activity interrupted," as seen in a portrait by Lorenzo Lotto (Figure 88). Here, a young man with a small book in hand turns to the observer as if he had just paused in his reading, having noticed that someone is looking at him.

Figure 88. Lorenzo Lotto, *Portrait of a Young Man* (c. 1530), Picture Gallery of the Castello Sforzesco, Milan.

A variant on this exchange of glances is the *mirrored* gaze, suggesting an indirect or transitional presence. This kind of gaze-game often occurs in self-portraits in which the artist is both the observer and the observed. The self-portrait is still a witness-figure, an image of the gaze in action, but one that is deflected toward self-observation. Despite appearances, the self-portrait does not simply "show" the features of the artist's face. It represents his or her expression when surprised in the act of self-observance: the subject of the painting is thus the relationship to the self in all its complexity. In this case, the witness-figure no longer plays the role of adding visual commentary about a central subject depicting something else. Caught in the act of looking at himself, such a figure becomes the subject itself.

I will conclude with a few examples in which the indirect presence of the artist is suggested despite his absence from the composition. In 1523–24, Jacopo da Pontormo painted the double portrait of two friends (Figure 89).

Here, the gaze converges toward a point located outside the painted space, in front of the painting. The two friends hold a sheet of paper where a quotation from Cicero's *De amicitia* is visible. This text, which celebrates the three forms of affection (*amor*, *pietas*, and *benevolentia*) that characterize friendship, furnishes the key to the subject. These two young men were good friends of Pontormo. The two visible figures, along with the unseen artist they look at, belonged to the republican faction that opposed the power of the Medicis in Florence. In this painting, Pontormo "convened before him" his two friends (Baldinotti 2014, 132) and created a double portrait that implies a third presence, the artist's. Although invisible in the composition, Pontormo is present where the two figures

Figure 89. Jacopo da Pontormo, *Portrait of Two Friends* (1523–24) (detail), Giorgio Cini Foundation, Venice.

direct their gaze. Without painting his own image, the artist still made his presence felt, which indirectly structures the composition. We could say that he makes himself present at the very moment when he casts an actual gaze on a composition where the witness-figure has disappeared. The *semblance of life* of the two figures stems from a connection established with the unseen, indirect presence of an artist who has taken the place of the observer.

This indirect mirroring involving an artwork, an artist, and an observer can also take other forms. At the end of his life, Andrea Mantegna painted another St. Sebastian as his "spiritual testament," an image in which neither a witness-figure nor the artist appears (Figure 90). So how is it possible, in this case, to create the semblance of life and the intuitive connection that depends on it?

Let us reexamine a few key themes from his painting as we try to understand this one. As a close follower of Alberti's teaching, Mantegna always tried to imitate the art of classical antiquity as much as possible. According to Vasari, he was so adamantly opposed to the *ritrarre*, the portrayal of real things, that he even came to prefer classical statues over living beings as models for his figures. To achieve perfection of appearances, he did not hesitate to draw inspiration from inanimate objects. Vasari relates that Squarcione, who was his teacher, criticized his frescoes in the Ovetari chapel in Padua by asserting that he had "imitated ancient marbles; he claimed that one cannot learn to paint perfectly by imitating sculpture, since stone always possesses a hardness and never the tender sweetness which flesh and other natural objects that bend and move possess" (Vasari [1556] 2008, 243–44). Vasari added that Mantegna, sorely stung by Squarcione's reproaches, persisted in his belief that formal perfection was rare in reality. To achieve the ideal of beauty, it was thus necessary to employ the sublime synthesis of appearances that the great artists of classical antiquity had used. Mantegna concluded that the classical statues were "more perfect and more beautiful" than real bodies. When they were compared to the living bodies of men and women, the statues always appeared "better finished and more exact in depicting muscles, veins, nerves, and other particulars than natural figures" ([1556] 2008, 244). According to Mantegna, the statues were more effective illustrations of not only ideal beauty but also of human anatomy. Vasari believed that Squarcione had correctly identified a real flaw in the painting methods of his former pupil; a highly accomplished painter, Mantegna nevertheless remained tied to a "style which is just a little bit sharp and sometimes seems to suggest stone more than living flesh" ([1556] 2008, 244).

Today, Mantegna's work strikes us as being in search of a sometimes-paradoxical relationship between the ideal appearance of forms and the feeling of

Figure 90. Andrea Mantegna, *The Martyrdom of Saint Sebastian* (1490), Ca' d'Oro, Venice.

life. In many of his works, action, sometimes violent, is explicitly attributed to figures in marble or bronze, which are *painted as such*. On the other hand, many of his "living" figures seem to remain so faithful to the model statues that they sometimes appear to be frozen in a type of solemn rigidity. A telling example of this contrast is Mantegna's earlier *Saint Sebastian* (Figure 51, above), where he arranges statues and living bodies side by side, as if inviting us to compare them. In this picture, St. Sebastian appears as immobile and handsome as a statue. But the pieces of marble around him appear to have the muscles, veins, and ligaments appropriate to living bodies. Thus, Mantegna almost gives the impression of working experimentally. He creates a perfect (and completely theoretical) image of appearances from faithful observation of the *inanimate*. Then he transfers this model of pictorial description to the living figure, even to the point of setting up an exchange, a continual mimesis that leads from the statue to the living figure and from the figure to the statue in a sort of endless, implicit to and fro between the animate and the inanimate.

In Mantegna's later work, *The Martyrdom of Saint Sebastian* (Figure 90, above), this game is carried to extremes. Pierced by many arrows, which seem to multiply the viewpoints on his body, Sebastian casts one last glance heavenward. This extreme gesture probably represents the death throes he experienced in the last instant before death. This transitional state is emphasized by another, more discreet gesture. Sebastian advances his left foot toward the observer. His entire body reflects this movement, which is emphasized by his right foot, still raised. The viewpoint is placed so low in the composition that the figure of the saint seems to approach the observer. The position of his shoulder, like that of his elbow, indicates a slight twist. Sebastian moves his foot toward a plane that seems to be beyond the compositional space.[4] The saint is surprised in the act of crossing a threshold, a probable allusion to the passage from life to death. Less explicit is the definition of space, which is surrounded by a faux marble frame from which he seems to emerge. An observer who looks at the top of the painting—to the left, behind the coral rosary—gradually notices that this is a niche, a choice location in which statues were placed,[5] following the model of classical antiquity. Sebastian's body conforms to the skillfully calculated morphology of the classical statue, and

---

4. Joan Caldwell (1973, 373), in an interpretive essay on this painting that refers to the *Golden Legend* by Jaccobus da Varagine, sees here "a little platform."
5. This detail is confirmed by a radiographic analysis of the painting, which shows the gradual and careful elaboration of the niche (Momesso 2013, 328).

the whiteness of his skin, painted with a very thin layer of tempera, suggests the appearance of gray marble. At the same time, the expression of extreme agony on the face and the traces of blood on the skin point to a body that is still very much alive. Other, more indirect, signs of life are also present. The entire composition and the moment that it reproduces are characterized by another passage both symbolic and immaterial. The light streams in from the left while a slight breeze blowing from the right moves across the painting. Here and there it lifts the white fabric surrounding the saint's flank, and at the top, it tousles his hair. At the same time, the draperies are caught in a state of perfect immobility, with their "sharp folds as if set in ice" (Romano 1981, 10–11), and presented in such classical shapes that they, too, suggest statues. There is yet another sign of life: in the lower right, Mantegna has placed a candle on the step where Sebastian places his left foot. The candle has just gone out, for the breeze is still dissipating the smoke. Once again, this candle and this smoke bring us back to the last instant when St. Sebastian's body throbbed with life. If the theme of the painting is the appearance of life as it appears in Sebastian's death throes, Mantegna chose to depict it indirectly, in the continual passage from the animate to the inanimate. From the heroic statue of perfect appearance installed in its niche, we move on to Sebastian's body pierced with arrows and paralyzed by pain. Around the candle there is a *cartiglio* with this unobtrusive inscription: *Nihil nisi divinum stabile est, et cetera fumus* ("Nothing is stable if not divine; the rest is smoke"), which confirms that this work is a meditation on imminent death. The painting invites observers to read this phrase, carrying a message that is addressed to them and which embodies the presence of Sebastian, statue and living body, animate and inanimate. To give life to the image, Mantegna contrasts it with its opposite, the perfect appearance of the inanimate, and invites the observer to say something aloud.

Nearly all commentators establish a connection between this painting and Mantegna's imminent death. Indeed, it would be difficult to deny that, here, the words of Leonardo, according to whom "all painters paint themselves," take on a tragic dimension. The viewer senses this is a sort of indirect self-portrait of an artist who intuits the approach of death, involving the anatomical perfection of the inanimate and, conversely, the desire to seize the life belonging to the image. It is in these terms, as the intermediary figure of the witness fades away, that a type of paradoxical presence of Sebastian is produced, which is simultaneously a classical statue, an image of the saint in his death throes, and, indirectly, an implicit portrait of the suffering, aged Mantegna, who will soon die. It is through these implied connections, which make the invisible presence of the painter appear, like the unseen presence of Pontormo with his friends, that Sebastian's body takes on the appearance of life for one last moment.

THE WITNESS-FIGURE AND *CAPRICCIO*

The artists I have mentioned were bound by one rule: in no case could they go beyond the limits imposed on their subject as they engaged in activities that were often strictly tied to religious worship. It was only toward the middle of the eighteenth century that some artists, at least in Italy, claimed autonomy from their sponsors, who sometimes allowed them to invent a new iconography. In Venice, the use of the word *capriccio* (a term used as early as the Renaissance) marked the passage from mandatory reproduction of a traditional subject to the nearly free creation of a subject invented by the artist. Some, like Sebastiano Ricci, gave the *capriccio* a rather trivial meaning that harked back to depictions of landscapes with ruins. Giambattista Tiepolo, as he grew old, was the only one who embraced this theme in a series of drawings and engravings (the *Scherzi* and the *Capricci*) and gave it a new meaning (Figure 91).

The *capriccio* became a scene in which a stock set of subjects fairly similar to theatrical characters—a wise man, a young person, a warrior, a Punchinello—assemble around a statue or classical ruins and are caught in the act of contemplating it. Near them, hidden by the landscape or concealed near a bush, yet still visible, often lies a small snake, a skull, or some other reminder of death. In other compositions, Tiepolo adapted this disturbing theme in another way, for example, by drawing the tomb of Punchinello surrounded by his sad comrades or by sketching a skeleton seated next to a ruin. In one of these drawings, behind a group of characters caught in the act of gazing at a skeleton, another subtle image of death appears: a standing skeleton holding a pilgrim's staff in one hand. Death can contemplate itself ironically by miming exactly what others are doing; in a way, death is part of both the audience and the show staged by the painter. It recalls how Svetlana Alpers and Michael Baxandall (1996) describe Tiepolo's characters as a touring theatrical troupe. In this series of inventions composed toward the end of his life, Tiepolo thus established an initial definition of the genre. Drawing a *capriccio* amounted to contemplating, with irony or despair, the dread of imminent mortal danger—a *memento mori* that could reflect back on the artist himself.

Figure 91. Giambattista Tiepolo, *Scherzi e Capricci* (c. 1744), private collection, Venice.

A few years later in *The New World*, his son Giandomenico reinterpreted this new genre of visual *memento mori* with a reflective depiction of a gaze commenting on itself. Recall how Alberti gave the witness-figure the function of commenting from the sidelines on the subject of the composition. *The New World* reverses Alberti's plan: here, *every* character is a witness-figure (Figure 92). The

Figure 92. Giandomenico Tiepolo, *The New World* (1791), Ca' Rezzonico, Venice.

subject of the painting—a marionette show called *Il Mondo Novo* being performed before a small church in the background—is completely out of sight. As in the *Capricci* by Giandomenico's father, the real subject of the painting is the very act of looking—precisely what we do before the fresco. This produces a feeling of endless waiting, since we will never see what the other spectators are watching.

In this case, the connection to the viewer and the transfer of life this implies (something that was symmetrical and reciprocal in self-portraits) becomes mimetic. If the subject of the depiction is *only* the act of gazing, the space in the painting becomes the *only* space where the observer stands. The observer becomes merely one of the characters depicted in the painting, just one notch removed, so to speak, from real space. In exchange, these characters, who occupy the very same space, thus become living beings just like the observer.

When these connections—transitive, reflexive, reciprocal, and mimetic—are established between the work and its observers, the space represented in perspective, just like the broom handle of the child who wants to ride a horse, offers an opportunity for gradually saturating the relational space with life. Just like this child on a hobby horse, or like St. Francis, who opens the space of his church by spreading his arms, or the person dressed in mourning before the figure of a young man who subtly harks back to Matteo Costanzo, or the person who joins the crowd watching the *Il Mondo Novo*, the observers momentarily—almost magically—see themselves as being part of the work. This is when the painted figures take on a semblance of life before our very eyes.

By studying chimerical space, we have come to understand that the link between perception and projection sparked in perspective involves an act of embedding one operation (that of projection) within the conceptual framework supplied by the other (that of perception). Inside perspectival space, projection thus occurs in a virtually fixed visual framework where, even before deciphering the meaning of an image, the act of projecting enables the observer to translate static indications arranged on a surface into indications of depth endowed with implicit movement.

This analysis of the interpretation of perspectival space can now be linked to the definition of "semblance of life" and the concept of projection. In all the examples of complex presence I have presented, projection plays a crucial role. It is associated with the intuition of a connection between the image and the observer—an essential element of the entire system. At the very core of this operation of projection lie two very different notions of "life." The first refers to the life of a body as pure animation, what we might call an undifferentiated state of living matter, which remains connected to the unconscious interpretation of the implicit movement of a figure. Drawing on Adolf von Hildebrand's analyses, this could be termed the *experience of the form* that occurs through perspective. The second notion of the concept of life at the core of the painting indicates the living presence of an individual, or more precisely, an individual form of life. The implicit movement may render a figure virtually alive, but this is not enough. To become a person, the figure needs to do more than display a dynamic but indeterminate animation; it must become embodied in an individual presence. The active gaze that an intuitive connection to the image prompts can fully actualize or complete the figure only by conferring individuality onto it through the act of projection.

Let us revisit Michelangelo's *Night*, which opened this chapter (Figure 68, above). The statue brings to mind some of the grand themes of this great artist's work, particularly in his poetry. But where is life in this statue of a woman lying atop a tomb? In the dialogue she triggers between two humans, where she takes her place tacitly but fully. When we consider what is at play between the young Strozzi, the elder Michelangelo, and the statue, we are struck by the fact that the statue, if she speaks through the voice of a person, is not limited to taking on the role of someone else, whether mourner or decedent. As a being created by the artist but not as a substitute for him—as was the case with the mourner in the Greek funeral rite—*Night* speaks for herself. It is not Michelangelo but his creation that addresses Strozzi in response to his praise. Only in this way can the figure, like Jean de Flandres's St. Michael and Piero della Francesca's Christ, appear in the same space as the young poet and establish a relationship with him.

The figure no longer appears as a replacement for a living being but, rather, as a person as such, without mediation. The same could even be said about every painting studied in this chapter. By relying on the "demonism of the gaze" (according to Chastel) without the mediation of words, like the statue of *Night*, these works create a transitional space where a relationship *between people* becomes possible. From a theoretical viewpoint, Ernst Cassirer perfectly understood this necessary passage from the living to the individual in Renaissance thought:

> An individual soul can only be conceived of as such if it is thought of as the form of an individual body. In fact, one can say that what we call the animation of a body consists in nothing other than in this its complete individualization.

Through this, the body is distinguished from mere "matter"; through this it . . . becomes the vehicle of a definite, concrete and individual life. (Cassirer [1927] 2010, 136–137)

These remarks, which Cassirer pulled from a lecture on Renaissance psychology (which contrasts Pomponazzi's Aristotelian materialism with Ficino's Platonism), are admirably suited to painting and sculpture. In all the examples given in this chapter, I have noted that this individual life is what projection must elicit in the face of a painting or a sculpture. This form of individuality is complex, of course, since it is composed of iconographic features that are often anonymous or conventional (think of Giorgione's young warrior or Mantegna's St. Sebastian) and of features created by the unconscious experience of space (the feeling of the form according to Hildebrand's definition) felt by the observer. Ultimately, this is the source of the gaze-games, both given and reciprocated, that we as viewers attribute to the figure we behold.

It is on this unconscious foundation, where the painted figure and the observer are joined, that the most diverse chains of association can then be deployed through projection. According to the dynamic described above, the figure (whether painted or sculpted) enters the universe of visual belief. Once it becomes part of the game of exchanging gazes, the painted figure, like Gombrich's hobby horse, modifies space–time, gradually saturates the space, and uses an ostensibly counterfactual definition of the image to transform the relationship between the object and the subject of the perception. Recall that, in his essay, Gombrich remarked that a substitute image, like the broom handle, should remain incomplete to be convincing. He concluded that the elaboration of such an object added no value to it. In fact, the more rudimentary the inanimate substitute for a life function, the more effective the function of substitution. If the image of a substitute *must* remain incomplete, that in no way means that its visual aspect has no function. On the contrary, the necessary appearance of a threshold within the perceived object shows that the visual aspect is essential to its functioning in the game it takes part in. Moreover, this threshold demonstrates that this unfinished aspect is even a necessary condition for the attribution of subjectivity and for the projective operations it supports. Keeping in mind this aspect of the hobby horse, it becomes clear that *any* composition in perspective is unfinished in the same sense that the substitute for a horse is incomplete. It is unfinished because, in principle, it reflects back to a space with limits located beyond its own horizon, and because it implies (without necessarily stating) the possible and sometimes imminent inclusion in the same space of the people who are looking at it. In this case, too, the existence of a threshold of perception that coincides with the unconscious interpretation of the transitional area of the frame is essential for triggering a projection (Shearman 1992, 59).

One more point needs to be added. Even though this series of projective operations is embedded within a schema of perception involving perspectival space, it does not merely "lend" parts of the "I" to the image, as other theorists have often claimed. The psychology of form and psychoanalysis have accustomed us to reducing these processes to "the operation that consists of localizing an inner mental representation to the outside, by changing from subject to object" (Laplanche and Pontalis 1967, 342–43).

If we return to the definition of the visual process that Gotthold Lessing formulated in the *Laocoon* ([1766] 1887), we will be able to restore all of its complexity to the act of projection. Lessing showed that what we call "projection" is made up of two separate mental operations that reflect one another and give rise to visual belief. He began by establishing a necessary relationship between perception and imagination. For him,

> Since the artist can use but a single moment of ever-changing nature, and the painter must further confine his study of this one moment to a single point of view . . . evidently the most fruitful moment and the most fruitful aspect of that moment must be chosen. Now that only is fruitful which allows free play to the imagination. (Lessing [1766] 1887, 16–17)

With this initial remark, he is simply returning to a *locus classicus* of modern aesthetic thought. But this contrast is immediately followed by an enlightening intuition: for him, the use of imagination and perception is far from "free." It is precisely controlled by a constant interaction between what we commonly call "projection" and an *objectification of the projected depiction* that necessarily results from the act. Lessing argues that "The more we see the more we must be able to imagine; and the more we imagine *the more we must think we see*" (Lessing [1766] 1887, 17; emphasis added).

In the process of perception, a phase takes place involving the phantasmal projection of the features of the self onto the image, which receives them as if on a screen. At the same time, as part of the same mental operation, the self objectifies these projections and believes that they actually exist in the external, objective world. People who, through projection, perceive a figure as endowed with life do not merely complete the image; in the very movement of projecting, they "think they see" the figure, this individual life-form, as a being endowed with objective existence. This is the origin of the connection between projection and visual belief. It is not solely the exercise of thought, which I have termed "chimerical," that enriches the perception of the image; it is also the image that gives thought its status as a perceptible experience.

Through this objectification, what is generated by the gaze comes back to it as the appearance of an exterior reality. In the process, a series of projective operations takes place: an intuition of the connection, a capturing of undifferentiated life by movement, a projection of an individual form of presence. These define the conditions for the emergence of the semblance of life in the image in perspective. This is the magic of the image that the scientific theory of perspectival space produces.

In this chapter, I have presented perspective both as a particular scientific method, which applies the laws of optics and geometry to the depiction of space, and as the type of illusion that this method seeks to trigger. By analyzing the theories of Alberti and the practices of various artists, I have demonstrated that these were based not so much on the direct application of the rules of a scientific method but, rather, on the emergence of a series of polarizations: one involving the aesthetic notion of beauty as either the imitation of classical antiquity or as the description of reality; the structure of the visual composition and its relation to language; the visual interpretation of space as either explicitly predetermined by contours or as implied through the figure's movement; and the character of the image as either "realistic" or as "counterfactual." My analyses have shown that the less symbolism is involved in the depiction, the more it triggers the attribution of agency to the figures and thus conveys a notion of presence. To produce an effect of truth, a composition in perspective must not only apply scientific criteria for describing reality; it should also refer precisely to the criteria imposed on the fiction within a given tradition.

Unlike Gombrich, who contrasted the geometrical mimesis of space peculiar to art with a basic function of replacing reality with an image, peculiar to play and magic, I have shown that presence and mimesis always coexist in the realm of perspective. To understand the image in perspective, it is no longer a question of contrasting these two aspects of representation but, instead, of appreciating the precise relationship between them. Considered from this viewpoint, the *semblance of life* owes nothing to geometry; rather, it is explained by the implementation of *the intuition of a connection* brought about by the gaze, a connection between the theme of a depiction, the person for whom it is intended, and sometimes, indirectly, its creator. Beyond its subject, the work thus bears the mark of a presence shared between painted space and real space. The result is a complex network of traces that engender not only the illusion of the real but also, above all, the evidence of a connection, taking several forms, between the painted figure and the observer. Perhaps this is where we can find the heart of the *gaze-games* that led to the invention of a space of imputed relationships—a rich space where the apparent animation of the work of art, its *semblance of life*, has been preserved throughout the *longue durée* of perspective in Western art.

CHAPTER TEN

On Irrefutable Hypotheses

In the *Phaedo*, the dialogue in which Plato narrates the final hours of Socrates's life in Athens, the meeting between the teacher and his students in the afternoon before his death was dominated by neither grief nor pity. A month afterward, Phaedo, one of the students present, told some friends who had not been there that "a very strange feeling came over me, an unaccustomed mixture of pleasure and of pain together, when I thought that Socrates was presently to die" (*Phaedo* 59a). Plato was among those who were not present at Socrates's last meeting, so his account is based on Phaedo's retelling of the events.

Curiously, no trace of anguish can be found in the dialogue between Socrates and his students. The atmosphere he has created is so utterly different from sadness that Simmias, one of his most brilliant students, asks him why he seems "so ready to leave us and the gods" and to so "lightly separate [himself] from them" (*Phaedo* 63a). Socrates replies in jest, "You have a right to say that, for I think you mean that I must defend myself against this accusation, as if we were in a law court. . . . I will try to make a more convincing defence than I did before the judges" (*Phaedo* 63b). He then adds, more seriously, "I would assert as positively as anything about such matters that I am going to gods who are good masters. And therefore, so far as that is concerned, I not only do not grieve, but I have great hopes that there is something in store for the dead, and, as has been said of old, something better for the good than for the wicked" (*Phaedo* 63c). After this brief exchange, Socrates makes no further allusions to personal emotions or episodes. The argumentation follows the canonical sequence of the ancient dialectical method by analyzing the question posed, defining terms, grasping a mental image, and identifying its essence through contrasts. The reasoning remains rigorous, sometimes even difficult, up to the moment when Socrates is nearing his end. During the entire afternoon, he insists that his students demonstrate sustained attention, lucid analysis, and precise reflection, never pity. Having been well trained, they obey. Simmias and Cebes articulate some brilliant objections to the thesis Socrates formulates concerning the theoretical possibility of life after death. His students know that the jail keeper will bring him the poison at sundown.

Right from the start, Socrates throws down a challenge to his students in the form of a proposition. It is clear, he declares, that the soul can only attain truth when it is isolated in itself, separated from the body, its needs, and its senses. But this separation is itself death. The only possible conclusion is that, if the purpose of the act of thinking for the soul is to attain truth, then thinking is equivalent to the experience of death (*Phaedo* 64a–67b). This means that the activity of those who dedicate themselves to philosophy is to die or else to be dead already. We can imagine Socrates's smile at this point. But none of his students openly makes any allusion to the imminent and very real death of their elderly teacher. To the contrary, Simmias says to him in an almost lighthearted manner, "Socrates, I don't feel much like laughing just now, but you made me laugh" (*Phaedo* 64b). Socrates continues with his skillful, penetrating argument. Simmias, Cebes, and the other students make comments, add details, and raise potential objections. They deduce consequences, pose other questions, and express their disagreements. Appreciating the dialectical value of the arguments proposed, their teacher is happy about the intellectual fervor that animates this debate over the definitive or temporary nature of death in general and thus of his own death. He sometimes appears to adhere to the theses defended by Cebes or Simmias, only to turn around and energetically refute them. As usual, he exposes implicit errors and the unintended or even unacceptable consequences of what may seem at first to be trivial or irrelevant. The work of reflection should lead to a more complete comprehension of the question, just as the essence should replace an image.

This is the intellectual passion, the unceasing search for the truth, that dominates the last meeting between Socrates and his students. When any student shows personal emotions, Socrates encourages him to bring them under control. One incident that disturbs this apparent serenity so wisely constructed is when

Crito reveals his confusion, regret, perhaps even fear. He begs Socrates "to talk as little as possible" because "people get warm when they talk and heat has a bad effect on the action of the poison" (*Phaedo* 63d). Later in the afternoon, Socrates says of him, "I cannot persuade Crito, my friends, that the Socrates who is now conversing and arranging the details of his argument is really I; he thinks I am the one whom he will presently see as a corpse, and he asks how to bury me" (*Phaedo* 115c–d). In other words, Crito cannot believe that the Socrates who argues step by step, topic after topic, for the existence of a unitary soul rather than a composite one (and thus for the existence of life after death) is the same Socrates who is getting ready to die. Socrates smiles at Crito's naïveté and encourages the others to smile at him, too. In his words is a tone that seems so light and an irony so full of love that they leave an unforgettable impression on readers of the *Phaedo*. The elderly Socrates speaks in this extraordinary manner even as he prepares himself to drink the poison. A long tradition of commentary interprets this passage by emphasizing the philosopher's moral stature. Faced with Socrates's dignity, the students' doubts and fears only make their weakness more apparent. Despite their confusion, however, Socrates the philosopher and Socrates the man condemned to death are one and the same man. Affirming the unity of these two Socrates is not simply a response to a rational necessity; it is an affirmation of his greatness, his glory. Socrates's heroic behavior represents the rigorous coherence of his thought.[1] Indeed, in this exemplary episode, the soul and body of the philosopher meet the same criteria of truth. The demonstration of this unity is given in the text. If, Socrates says, the body itself can be made free from any deterioration "for an incalculable amount of time," then even more so can the soul be made free, since it contains nothing opposed to its own nature and can thus be considered indestructible (Goldschmidt 1963, 188). It is thus possible that the soul is immortal. It may not happen in everybody's case, but philosophers can sometimes attain it.

In the *Apology* (28b–d), Socrates had argued that immortality results from the exercise of a heroic virtue, a conquest comparable to that of Achilles in the *Iliad*. He specified that the virtue of the philosopher is a *ménos*, a word that indicates something more than a warrior's courage: the capacity, characteristic of the gods, to avenge an offense. But in the *Phaedo*, the question is posed in different terms: it is a matter of juxtaposing a completely theoretical idea

---

1. As Maria Michela Sassi writes, "The death of Socrates legitimates his philosophy. It functions as an image of the foundation of his thinking" (Sassi 1997, 1338).

(established "purely by means of a hypothesis" [Goldschmidt 1963, 186]) of a hypothetical experience of the soul before death with the very real experience of an imminent death. The simultaneous presence in the text of two such different points of view has a surprising effect. Instead of eliminating uncertainty, the irony with which Socrates responds to Crito gives his doubt an unexpected intensity. As Alexandre Koyré writes, all of Plato's dialogues are also "dramatic works" (Koyré [1945] 1960, 18). Certain narrative conventions play a significant role in them. Beyond Socrates's irony, which Plato highlights, it is clear that, in the *Phaedo*, there are two characters or forms of existence in Socrates. One of them persuades us with his refined, rigorous demonstration; the other moves us with his self-sacrifice. In the dialogue, we learn that the poison is slow to have the intended effect, that the jail keeper will have to return, and that Socrates, who is thoroughly engaged in his arguments, must move about so the blood will circulate and spread the poison. This juxtaposition between the philosophical argumentation and account of the Socrates's self-sacrifice, on the one hand, with the agonizing rhythm and clues that foreshadow his imminent death, on the other, sheds new light on the philosopher's main thesis: the possible existence of an immortal soul.

It is essential to be precise about his line of reasoning. Socrates never supports the existence, pure and simple, of an afterlife. On the contrary, he says that when we talk about the soul's ability to survive death, we are unavoidably speaking of a fiction. The fears and doubts this fiction inevitably arouses must be countered "with everyday incantations" (Goldschmidt 1963, 184).[2] "Perhaps there is a child within us, who has such fears," says Cebes. "Let us try to persuade him not to fear death as if it were a hobgoblin." "Ah," said Socrates, "you must sing charms to him every day until you charm away his fear" (*Phaedo* 77e). This initial definition of the netherworld as a fiction is gradually elaborated throughout the dialogue. It is worth tracing its development. Socrates had stated earlier that, although he cannot assert it definitively, he believes he will join the gods in the "other world," which gives him "great hopes that there is something in store for the dead" (*Phaedo* 63c). Later, he elaborates on this, asking,

> shall he who is really in love with wisdom and has a firm belief that he can find it nowhere else than in the other world grieve when he dies and not be glad to

---

2. The Greek word *epaidein* used in the *Phaedo* is sometimes translated as "incantations," sometimes as "charms" (*Phaedo* 77e).

go there? We cannot think that, my friend, if he is really a philosopher; for he will confidently believe that he will find pure wisdom nowhere else than in the other world. And if this is so, would it not be very foolish for such a man to fear death? (*Phaedo* 68a–b)

His student Cebes says, "There would be good reason for the blessed hope, Socrates, that what you say is true" (*Phaedo* 70a–c). The netherworld is, in other words, a useful fable. He still would like to be comforted by arguments that prove the existence afterlife, which he points out are as yet lacking. "What you say, Cebes, is true," said Socrates. "Now what shall we do? Do you wish to keep on conversing about this to see whether it is probable or not?" In the ensuing discussion, Socrates does not claim that the existence of the hereafter has the logical character of a truth. On the contrary, he is convinced that its existence cannot be proven in positive terms; it merely cannot be refuted. The existence of a netherworld, like that of the ideal city, is theoretical, "in the sense that it is comparable to the existence of geometry" (Koyré [1945] 1960, 133). This world is unreal "in the same sense that the genesis of a geometrical figure generated from its composite simple elements—lines, circles, triangles—is unreal" (Koyré [1945] 1960, 109). Socrates asserts that, if we carefully use the categories of our language, particularly by referring to the principle that "all things are generated in this way, opposites from opposites" (*Phaedo* 71a), and if we develop our argument by respecting the rules of dialectics (term, definition, image, essence), then we must, perforce, believe in the existence of an afterlife. We might say that here, for Plato as for Ludwig Wittgenstein, the truth-value of this existence therefore depends on the grammar of the language we speak; in particular, it results from an initial theoretical choice to speak of the soul as if it existed. This choice is deduced from a purely formal fact of language (Wittgenstein [1942] 1965, [1953] 2009), in this case, that it admits the opposite of the word "alive." Socrates asks Cebes, "Is there anything that is the opposite of living, as being awake is the opposite of sleeping?" "Certainly," Cebes responds. "Being dead" (*Phaedo* 71c). This is why the thesis of an afterlife, without being proven true, is *only irrefutable*. The only way we can affirm the perpetual existence of the soul is to rely on the hypothesis that something unitary and undivided must exist that contrasts with everything else that is divided, composite, and dispersed after death (*Phaedo* 78b–e; see also Goldschmidt 1963, 187). This argument does not produce a truth but, rather, dictates the conditions of a rigorous fiction.

Socrates turns to an image of Tartarus, the deepest underworld, a *terra ultra incognita* that cannot be proven to actually exist but that can be imagined well enough to draw a map of it; indeed, Socrates describes its geography in striking detail (*Phaedo* 112a–13c). This point represents a crucial passage from dialectical deduction to narration, which completely transforms the nature of the text. It is true that, in the *Phaedo*, the heroic self of the philosopher Socrates is asserted, as tradition dictates. For this reason, he has sometimes been described as a precursor of Christ, heroically consecrated to the cult of truth and ready for sacrifice. But in this same text, there is also another Socrates, another self, who is not exactly the same as the ironic and laughing philosopher. This Socrates articulates the principles of truth but admits of fiction in equal measure. Instead of excluding it from the realm of the thinkable, he takes the time to evaluate it and formulate increasingly precise versions of it by applying the same conditions as those applied to geometric entities. Victor Goldschmidt has written that, for Plato, hypotheses are like gardens: in these "gardens of writing," we can sow only through a game in order to "amass a treasure of memories" and inventions. These are gardens in which we can easily discern the path and "follow the trail" of what we seek (Goldschmidt 1963, 160).

My musings over the *Phaedo*, which I have read as both a treatise on philosophy and as a narrative, suggest that this dialogue is also "like a garden." Instead of attempting to resolve the question of the existence, real or imaginary, of a hereafter, Plato imagines a parallel world, all the while defining its logical status with great precision. His strategy is to teach his students how to accurately describe unreal phenomena—having an existence that is merely irrefutable—before examining their truth-value. From this perspective, the two Socrates—the one who remains a philosopher in front of his students and the other who may go to Tartarus because of his mad audacity and his *ménos*—are linked to each other in a relationship of figure and ground. Without contradicting each other, these two images of the philosopher's self reveal the existence of two parallel ontologies—and two registers of text—to which one or the other Socrates belongs.

A universe of inescapable fictions, of merely irrefutable hypotheses, one that engenders a dual ontological belonging—it is hard to imagine a more fitting description of the universe in which the object-persons that have populated this present book live, act, and interact with human beings. This takes us back to the story of Kafka's letters that opened Chapter One. In the game he initiated, the doll and the little girl who lost it have, in truth, exchanged their universes of belonging. The doll is present in the Berlin botanical garden as a living little girl:

she speaks, she smiles, she travels to distant lands, she gets married. Within the bounds of this game, the reciprocal is also true: the girl herself is able, thanks to the letters read to her by Kafka, to take her place in the universe of artifacts and define herself in relation to them. She can see the faraway places her doll visits, she attends her wedding and meets her doll's fiancé, and she contemplates the castle where they will live. All the conditions are brought together to define the resulting relationship as an ontology. It results from the attribution of subjectivity to an artifact and from the modification of the subject who corresponds to it, in accord with the modality of the progressive saturation of the inferential space that we have seen in so many other cases. Within the same culture, and, I believe, in every culture, several ontological levels are present, linked to the exercise of thought by an image, as perhaps we now better comprehend.

To analyze this simultaneous presence of different planes of reality in Chapter Two, I pointed out that an iconographic tradition cannot be defined solely by a specific iconography, with its *topoï*, styles, authors, and periods. Such a tradition almost always mobilizes specific instructions, ideas, values, and interactions that, by forming a system, generate the game in which playing with the images is acceptable in a given historical or cultural context. The recognition of the dual levels that constitute an iconographic tradition has broad consequences for the interpretation of cultural differences. Indeed, it is possible to distinguish variations that concern one or the other of these levels—iconography or game—and their interrelationships.

I showed that this approach has reflexive consequences, since it allows us to better understand the nature of modern primitivism. This movement, which tries to be extremely tolerant toward other iconographies, is rigid toward the game they deploy vis-à-vis the image. For the primitivists, an object must always be a work of art. As such, it must refer to an interiority, a space for exploring the psychic life of an exemplary figure of modern subjectivity—the artist. And it is through the artist that observers will gradually discover the latent aspects of their own experience of themselves. I have chosen to reverse this perspective and to consider, on the one hand, the production of images in particular circumstances to be inseparable from the exercise of thought (and thus universal), and, on the other, the game of Western art as one of many possible games that can be played with the image, rather than the only game possible.

In Chapters Three and Four, I identified at least two games linked to images, different from the modern Western game of art and the relation established between the artist and the work. One of them is the game of memory, which mobilizes the notion of iconography associated with the conscious exercise of a technique for memorization. The other is the game of attributing agency to an object, which engenders a link of belief between the image and the observer and leads to thinking of the image as a living, acting being. An exercise in methodology, devoted to different forms of mnemonic images in certain Amerindian societies, allowed me to further clarify the distinction between iconography and play. It also allowed me to formulate the concept of the universe of an iconographic tradition, defined as a specific family of mental operations that take place, in this case, on three levels: taxonomy and salience at the semiotic level; codification and evocation at the mnemonic level; and power and expressivity at the logical level.

I then posed the question of interpreting object-persons according to the same method. What is the universe of object-persons, those artifacts to which subjectivity is attributed? What is the family of mental operations that makes them exist? To formulate answers, I first made a distinction between two contexts: an everyday context in which the belief linked to the transformation of an object into a person always remains revocable; and a ritual context in which the belief attached to the agentive or subjective character of the object is more complex and persistent over time.

I argued that, as soon as an animated object acts in a ritual situation, it no longer functions like the image in a person's mirror but, rather, like a crystal. The animated object captures not only a single identity but a plurality of partial identities. Therefore, the persistence of belief over time may be explained by the relational complexity that the object mobilizes through the ritual action. The bond of belief that characterizes these situations becomes more complex, thus more stable. I tested this new interpretation in two different but comparable cases in which ritual action mobilizes artifacts. In the first case, I examined situations where the presence of an authority and a human person are not directly associated. During the celebration of a ritual or the utterance of a mythical chant, it is the object itself that bears the entire responsibility and weight of the exercise of authority. The object-person is anonymous, bearing an identity that is opaque, mysterious, or indecipherable in the sense that its identity does not reflect that of any particular human being—neither that of any participant in a ritual nor that of its material "author." The artifact is devoid of all external reference, since it bears the principle of its own legitimacy. During its ritual use, the West African *nkisi* figure has close to a minimal definition, almost nil, of identity. The object is associated with an intentionality, conceived as independent of all human will and even, sometimes, as uncontrollable.

To understand this situation ethnographically and the type of definition of ritual identity of the artifact that, in this case, engenders the link of belief (and hence the authority attributed to it), I analyzed a model of the traditional transmission of knowledge among the Fang. This model comprises three formal traits: a series of identifications that leads to the creation of a complex being, the *mvet*, consisting of a text, a musical instrument, and an enunciator; a weak definition of the identity of a source of traditional truth (a voice without a discernible author, which barely revealing an identity); and the transfer of authority to an artifact when humans attribute a principle of autonomy to it through the imputation of subjectivity. This model seems to be fitting for both the Fang harp and the ritual use of the nail figure. When a specific musical technique is used, the Fang harp acquires a type of voice that is independent of the singer-poet's intention through a process that can be understand as the elaboration of a chimeric sound. The chimeric voice is composed entirely of implicit elements of the real sound emission, which arise only through an act of mental reconstruction. The identity of the nail figure is constructed in an analogous manner. The *nkisi* never represents a single person but a multiple being or, more precisely, the set of ritual relationships that are established between different beings. This complex identity, which results from the chain of transformations orienting the ritual action, provides the artifact with its overt function and authority.

Chapter Five was devoted to the study of another ritual in which an artifact "takes the place" of a person—the ritual substitute of the dead that the Greeks called *kolossos*. The *kolossos* deploys a presence or, rather, a paradoxical representation of an absence–presence, by following an ensemble of ritual actions (a libation, an offering of a ram's dark blood on a stone, the ritual hospitality made to the figurines). This ensemble mobilizes three terms: a "minimal image"; a word, nowhere inscribed, but articulated in association with the image by calling out the deceased's name three times; and a gaze, which leads the mourner to stare attentively at the rough stone placed before him. In a series of texts devoted to representations in the Hellenic world, Jean-Pierre Vernant (1990, 1991, 164–85) established an essential continuity between the *kolossos*, which were almost nonfigurative, and the emergence, around the sixth century BCE, of the *kouroi* and *korai*, representations of deceased men and women, respectively. When the representation of the deceased takes on form in the funerary statue and an epitaph is read aloud, the statue is transformed into an artifact endowed with speech. My analysis followed these actions and words step by step. When the inscription is read aloud and the statue says "I," it is actually the deceased who speaks: this is the first identification established between the statue and the deceased (whether buried or cremated). The statue calls out through the words it utters as well as through its courteous attitude and its smile. It addresses the interlocutors, attracts their gaze, and asks them to utter its name, an act that is indispensable to the deceased's posthumous existence. In this way, the statue is asking for a voice to intervene, a voice that can say "I" in its place. If the visual form of the *kouros* or *kôre* reflects an initial, explicit identification between the deceased and his or her *mnêma*, the speech act brings about an identification between the statue and the mourner who commemorates the deceased. This is a striking example of the act of "thinking through an image," which modifies the context and the impact of the ritual act. The voice and the image do not follow the same path, but through the two series of identifications, the statue becomes the site where a ritual relationship between the mourner and the deceased is created, rather than merely serving as an example of the values of ancient Greek society. In the time it takes to repeat the name, the two of them, mourner and deceased, coincide in a single plural being. The *kouros* or *kôre* is thus double, like the *kolossos* that represented their precursors. It conveys an image and a presence to the deceased and, through the ritual identification, enables the mourner to enter into contact with the mourned. Through the utterance of the name, far from "replacing" a particular person term by term, as Alfred Gell (1998) suggested, the artifact acquires a presence by embodying several aspects of identity derived from the participants in the rite. Its identity, like that of the *nkisi*, is the result of the relationships it brings about. The object and the living being acquire the same ontological status: a relation of figure and ground is thus established between the universe of the living object and some other form of experience. Such is the game of the ritual artifact that comes alive within the framework of a ritual, and such is the nature of the link to belief that enables this to happen.

Following this analysis, I then argued in Chapter Six that ritual contexts are not the only place where a substitute may express agency. There are other situations where these games of substitution, revealed through the study of living artifacts, can be set up between humans and objects, or even between humans and humans. I explored the funerary games in the *Iliad* and other occasions elsewhere that involve substitution and identification, proposing to give them the provisional label of "quasi-rituals," since, although they may not involve the usual conditions for enacting a ritual, they nevertheless can be interpreted through the theory of relational action I have proposed.

For purely heuristic reasons, I suggested an initial taxonomy for the relations of substitution and identification that were revealed by examining the issue of agency in artifacts. The everyday, nonritual exercise of agency, as discussed by Gell, involves a provisional, revocable relation, established through a single term, in which the artifact corresponds to only one person. More complex, a ritual relation constitutes a crystalized, stable relation, established through two or more terms, in which the artifact may correspond to several people. Finally, the example of a quasi-ritual situation is an intermediary case: it involves one relation, established through a single term, between the substitute and the entity it substitutes, but, unlike everyday occasions, the quasi-ritual relation involves a crystallization that is stable over time.

In the same experimental spirit, I then took a further step in Chapter Seven and presented the hypothesis that Western art (or, more precisely, the domain of relations through the gaze that this art involves) is also a quasi-ritual situation in which a dialogue between humans and artifacts unfolds. Accordingly, I considered certain works of art as if they were complex persons—as an enactment of a sequence of relations between images. By bringing together what is held up to view in the work of art with various subjectivities, including the observer, the image thereby acquires a semblance of life.

After exploring some preliminary questions about the very possibility of an anthropology of Western art, I analyzed three types of space found in different forms of art: abstract, chimerical, and perspectival. I showed that an artistic tradition linking William Turner to Wassily Kandinsky, Robert Delaunay, and other artists constituted a decisive stage of involving the observer's gaze in the work through the mental synthesis of color. In doing so, the artist confers on the work of art itself a form of life generated through perception and visual thinking. In the examples I discussed, the work participates in this process, which, through a game of action and reaction between the image and the act of looking, creates a space through colors. A form of life is thus made possible through the interplay of the space of the work of art and the eye (and the spirit) of the observer who interprets it and makes it become real.

Next, through a reexamination of the concept of the chimera in Chapter Eight, I proposed setting up a comparative axis between perspective in Western art and different forms of representation in non-Western arts. Through the hypothesis of a specific relation of embeddedness between perception and projection, I examined the genesis of transitional spaces in which painting becomes the means of indicating the site where the presence of the observer is progressively integrated into the image. A novel form of double space is generated; within this space, the image and its observer are situated in the very same place and thus acquire an identical status. In this way, the painted figures indirectly acquire the form of life characteristic of the one who gazes upon them.

Chapter Nine explored the history of perspectival space, especially in the Italian Renaissance tradition. Using the anthropological approach to living artifacts that I developed through the course of the book, I examined the forms of existence found in the grand ideal that dominated the whole of the European Renaissance: the ideal of art as a method for representing the appearance of life. In Italy, this was theorized as the semblance of life. All the cases explored in this book revealed that the agency of the gaze, considered as a specific kind of relation to the image, is one of the sources for intensifying the image by means of mobilizing its invisible aspects. Through acts of gazing, other forms of thinking appear: one involving the game of projection and objectification; another conveying the sense that the image has some kind of link to the observer; yet another giving the impression that figures in motion in an image have seized upon an undifferentiated form of life; and, finally, the projection of these complex forms of presence through perspectival space to create the semblance of life.

In all the cases explored through these pages, the relations between these configurations of thought appear to be analogous to the relationship between figure and ground. As soon as one emerges, the other remains in a latent state, waiting but not disappearing. In the future, it will be necessary to go even deeper into these games of alternation between different planes of reality—games that constitute an essential aspect of what anthropologists usually call a "culture." For the time being, I will simply point out that they always take place in a mental space characterized by the type of thinking that Plato, notably in the *Phaedo*, described as merely irrefutable hypotheses. Such is the space of thought—that intermediary territory between truth and falsehood—where object-persons are active, speak up, or exchange gazes with humans.

Sometimes, like the lost doll in the Berlin botanical garden, these object-persons may suddenly disappear. They leave behind a sudden, intense sensation of absence within us. Perhaps now we understand that what we miss, in essence, is the *terra ultra incognita* that the absent object-person embodies: a universe of irrefutable hypotheses, which we yearn to see proven true but which will remain forever unproven, forever merely irrefutable.

References cited

Agamben, Giorgio. 2001. *Infanzia e storia: Distruzione dell'esperienza e origine della storia.* Turin: Einaudi.

Aikhenvald, Alessandra, and Robert M. Dixon, eds. 2003. *Evidentiality.* Oxford: Oxford University Press.

Airenti, Gabriella. 2003. *Intersoggettività e teoria della mente: Le origini cognitive della comunicazione.* Turin: Bollati Boringhieri.

———. 2015. "The Cognitive Bases of Anthropomorphism: From Relatedness to Empathy." *International Journal of Social Robotics* 7 (1): 117–27.

Alberti, Leon Battista. (1435–36) 2011. *Leon Battista Alberti: On Painting.* Edited and translated by Rocco Sinisgalli. Cambridge: Cambridge University Press.

———. (c. 1436) 2013. *On Sculpture, by Leon Battista Alberti.* Translated by Jason Arkles. Morrisville, NC: Lulu.

Alhazen, Ibn Haytham. (1083) 1989. *Book of Optics: The Optics of Ibn al-Haytham (1083).* Edited by Abdelhamid I. Sabra. London: Warburg Institute.

Alighieri, Dante. (1308–20) 2008. *The Divine Comedy.* Book 2, *Purgatorio.* Edited and translated by Robin Kirkpatrick. London: Penguin Classics.

Alpers, Svetlana. 2005. *Les vexations de l'art: Velasquez et les autres.* Paris: Gallimard.

Alpers, Svetlana, and Michael Baxandall. 1996. *Tiepolo and the pictorial intelligence.* New Haven, CT: Yale University Press.

Antoine, Jean-Philippe. 1993. "Mémoire, lieux et invention spatiale dans la peinture italienne des xiiie et xive siècles." *Annales ESC* 48 (6): 1447–69.

Arasse, Daniel. 2002. *Léonard de Vinci: Le rythme du monde*. Paris: Hazan.
Argan, Giulio Carlo, and Maurizio Fagiolo. 1989. "Premessa all'arte italiana." In *Storia d'Italia*, vol. 1, 729–90. Turin: Einaudi.
Ascher, Marcia, and Robert Ascher. 1981. *Code of the Quipu: A Study in Media, Mathematics and Culture*. Ann Arbor: University of Michigan Press.
Assmann, Jan. 1992. *Cultural Memory and Early Civilization: Writing, Remembrance, and Political Imagination*. Cambridge: Cambridge University Press.
Assmann, Jan, and Aleida Assmann, eds. 2003. *Hieroglyphen: Altägyptische Ursprünge abendländischer Grammatologie*. Archaologie der Litterarische Kommunikation 8. Paderborn: Fink Wilhelm Verlag.
Auerbach, Erich. (1946) 2003. *Mimesis: The Representation of Reality in Western Literature*. Translated by Willard R. Trask. Princeton, NJ: Princeton University Press.
Austin, John L. (1962) 1975. How to Do Things with Words, 2nd ed. Edited by James O. Urmson and Marina Sbisa. Oxford: Oxford University Press.
Ayer, Alfred. 1936. Language, Truth and Logic. London: Penguin Books.
Baillargeon, Renée. 1995. "Physical Reasoning in Infancy." In *The Cognitive Neurosciences*, edited by Michael S. Gazzaniga, 181–204. Cambridge, MA: MIT Press.
Baldinotti, Andrea. 2014. *Pontormo e Rosso: Divergenti vie della "maniera."* Catalogue de l'exposition. Florence: Mandragora.
Barasch, Moshe. 2003. "Renaissance Hieroglyphics." In *Hieroglyphen: Altägyptische Ursprünge abendländischer Grammatologie*, edited by Jan Assmann and Aleida Assmann, 165–91. Munich: Fink Wilhelm Verlag.
Barbeau, Marius. 1950. *Totem Poles*, 2 vols. Anthropological series 30. Ottawa: Department of Resources and Development, National Museum of Canada.
Barcelos Neto, Aristóteles. 2002. *A arte dos sonhos*. Lisbon: Musée ethnologique.
Barth, Fredrik. 1975. *Ritual and Knowledge among the Baktaman of New Guinea*. Oslo: Norwegian Universities Press.
———. 1987. *Cosmologies in the Making: A Generative Approach to Cultural Variation in Inner New Guinea*. Cambridge: Cambridge University Press.
Baschet, Jérôme. 2008. *L'Iconographie médiévale*. Paris: Gallimard.
Basso, Keith. 1996. *Wisdom Sits in Places*. Albuquerque: University of New Mexico Press.
Bateson, Gregory. (1936) 1958. *Naven: A Survey of the Problems Suggested by a Composite Picture of the Culture of a New Guinea Tribe Drawn from Three Points of View*, 2nd ed. Stanford, CA: Stanford University Press.

———. (1972) 1999. *Steps to an Ecology of Mind: Collected Essays in Anthropology, Psychiatry, Evolution, and Epistemology.* Chicago: University of Chicago Press.

Batschmann, Oskar, and Pascal Griener. 2013. *Hans Holbein.* London: Reaktion Books.

Baudelaire, Charles. (1859) 1976. "L'exposition universelle de 1855." In Œuvres complètes, vol. 2, edited by Claude Pichois, 574–97. Bibliothèque de la Pléiade 7. Paris: Gallimard.

Baxandall, Michael. 1986. *Giotto and the Orators: Humanist Observers of Painting in Italy and the Discovery of Pictorial Composition, 1350–1450.* Oxford: Oxford University Press.

———. 1988. *Painting and Experience in Fifteenth-Century Italy*, 2nd ed. Oxford: Oxford University Press.

———. 1993. "Pictorially Enforced Signification: Saint Antonius, Fra Angelico and the Annonciation." In *Hülle und Fülle, Festschrift für T. Buddensieg*, edited by Albert Beyer, 31–39. Alfter: VDG Verlag.

———. 2003. *Words for Pictures: Seven Papers on Renaissance Art and Criticism.* New Haven, CT: Yale University Press.

Beaudet, Jean-Michel. 1998. *Souffles d'Amazonie.* Paris: Société d'ethnologie.

Belting, Hans. 2011. *Florence and Baghdad: Renaissance Art and Arab Science.* Translated by Deborah Lucas Schneider. Cambridge, MA: Belknap, Harvard University Press.

Berinstein, Dorothy. 1999. "Hunts, Processions, and Telescopes: A Painting for an Imperial Hunt by Lang Shining (Giuseppe Castiglione)." "Intercultural China," special issue, *RES: Anthropology and Aesthetics* 35: 170–85.

Berlin, Isaiah. 1976. *Vico and Herder: Two Studies in the History of Ideas.* London: Chatto and Windus.

———. 1990. "Giambattista Vico and Cultural History." In *The Crooked Timber of Humanity: Chapters in the History of Ideas*, 49–69. London: John Murray.

Berthomé, François. 2009. "Démêler, raccommoder: Analyse interactionnelle de quelques dispositifs de conciliation." In *Paroles en actes*, edited by Carlo Severi and Julien Bonhomme, 139–62. Cahiers d'anthropologie sociale 5. Paris: L'Herne.

Berthomé, François, Julien Bonhomme, and Grégory Delaplace, eds. 2012. "Cultivating Uncertainty: Ethnographies of Opaque Sociality." *HAU: Journal of Ethnographic Theory* 2 (2): 129–312.

Bettini, Maurizio. 1992. *Il ritratto dell'amante.* Turin: Einaudi.

Beurdeley, Cécile, and Michel Beurdeley. 1971. *Giuseppe Castiglione, peintre jésuite à la cour de Chine*. Paris: Bibliothèque des Arts.

Blaise de Parme (Blasius of Parma). (c. 1390) 2001. *Questiones super tractatus logice magistri Petri Hispani*. Edited by Joël Biard and Graziella Federici-Vescovini. Paris: Vrin.

Bloch, Maurice. 1974. "Symbols, Song, Dance and Features of Articulation: Is Religion an Extreme Form of Traditional Authority?" *European Journal of Sociology* 15 (1): 55–81.

———. 1986. *From Blessing to Violence: History and Ideology in the Circumcision Ritual of the Merina of Madagascar*. Cambridge: Cambridge University Press.

———. 1991. *Prey into Hunter: The Politics of Religious Experience*. Lewis Henry Morgan Lectures. Cambridge: Cambridge University Press.

———. 2012. *Anthropology and the Cognitive Challenge*. Cambridge: Cambridge University Press.

Boardman, John. 1991. *Greek Sculpture: The Archaic Period*. London: Thames and Hudson.

Boas, Franz. (1927) 2010. *Primitive Art*. Mineola, NY: Dover Publications.

Boas, George, and Arthur O. Lovejoy. 1935. *A Documentary History of Primitivism and Related Ideas*. Baltimore: Johns Hopkins Press.

Bolzoni, Lina. 2001. *The Gallery of Memory: Literary and Iconographic Models in the Age of the Printing Press*. Translated by Jeremy Parzen. Toronto: University of Toronto Press.

———. 2004. *The Web of Images: Vernacular Preaching from Its Origins to St. Bernardino da Siena*. Translated by Carole Preston and Lisa Chien. Burlington, VT: Ashgate.

Bonhomme, Julien. 2007. "Réflexions multiples: Le miroir et ses usages rituels en Afrique centrale." *Images Revues* 4.

Bonita, Ruth, Robert Beaglehole, and Tord Kjellström. 2006. *Basic Epidemiology*, 2nd ed. Geneva: World Health Organization.

Bottéro, Jean. 1987. *Mésopotamie: L'écriture, la raison et les dieux*. Paris: Gallimard.

Bouchy, Anne. 2003. "Une voie de 'l'art premier' dans le Japon du XVIIe siècle: La statuaire d'Enku, pérégrin de l'Essentiel." *L'Homme* 165: 143–72.

Boyer, Pascal. 1988. *Barricades mystérieuses et pièges à penser: Introduction à l'analyse des épopées fang*. Paris: Société d'ethnologie.

———. 1992. *Tradition as Truth and Communication*. Cambridge: Cambridge University Press.

———, ed. 1993. *Cognitive Aspects of Religious Symbolism.* Cambridge: Cambridge University Press.

———. 1994. *The Naturalness of Religious Ideas.* Berkeley: University of California Press.

———. 2002. *Religion Explained: The Evolutionary Origins of Religious Thought.* New York: Basic Books.

Brasco, Santo. 1481. *Itinerario alla Santissima città di Gerusalemme.* Milan: Leonardus Pachel et Uldericus Scinzenzeler.

Bredekamp, Horst. 1996. *La nostalgie de l'antique: Statues, machines et cabinets de curiosités.* Paris: Diderot Éditeur, Arts et sciences.

Brehier, Émile. 1968. *Histoire de la philosophie.* Vol. 2, *Le xviie siècle.* Paris: Presses Universitaires de France.

Breton, André. (1957) 2008. "L'Art magique." In *Œuvres complètes*, vol. 4: *Écrits sur l'art et autres textes*, edited by Marguerite Bonnet, 49–275. Bibliothèque de la Pléiade 544. Paris: Gallimard.

Brown, Peter. 1967. *Augustine of Hippo: A Biography.* Berkeley: University of California Press.

Bruno, Giordano. (1584) 1998. *Cause, Principle and Unity, and Essays on Magic.* Edited and translated by Richard J. Blackwell and Robert de Lucca. Cambridge: Cambridge University Press.

———. (1584) 2004. *The Expulsion of the Triumphant Beast*, 2nd ed. Translated by Arthur D. Imerti. Lincoln: University of Nebraska Press, Bison Books.

Bühler, Karl. (1934) 2011. *Theory of Language: The Representational Function of Language.* Translated by Donald Fraser Goodwin in collaboration with Achim Eschbach. Amsterdam: John Benjamins.

Butler, Samuel. (1872) 2002. *Erewhon.* Mineola, NY: Dover Publications.

Caldwell, Joan. 1973. "Mantegna's St. Sebastians: Stabilitas in a Pagan World." *Journal of the Warburg and Courtauld Institutes* 50 (36): 373–77.

Campanella, Tommaso. 2011. *Selected Philosophical Poems of Tommaso Campanella: A Bilingual Edition.* Edited, translated, and annotated by Sherri Roush. Chicago: University of Chicago Press.

Candea, Matei. 2016. "De deux modalités de comparaison en anthropologie sociale." *L'Homme* 218 (2): 183–218.

Canguilhem, Georges. 1963. "Dialectique et philosophie du non chez Gaston Bachelard." *Revue Internationale de Philosophie* 17 (66): 441–52.

———. (1968) 1994. Études d'histoire et de philosophie des sciences concernant les vivants et la vie. Paris: Vrin.

Carastro, Cléo. 2012. "Fabriquer du lien en Grèce ancienne: Serments, sacrifices, ligatures." *Métis* 10: 77–105.

Carnap, Rudolf. 1955. "On Some Concepts of Pragmatics." *Philosophical Studies* 6: 89–91.

Carruthers, Mary. 1990. *The Book of Memory: A Study of Memory in Medieval Culture*. Cambridge: Cambridge University Press.

———. 1993. "The Poet as Master Builder: Composition and Locational Memory in the Middle Ages." *New Literary History* 24: 881–904.

———. 1998. *The Craft of Thought: Meditation, Rhetoric and the Making Of Images 400–1200*. Cambridge: Cambridge University Press.

———. 2002. "Avant-propos à l'édition française." In *Machina memorialis: Méditation, rhétorique et fabrication des images au Moyen Âge*, translated by Fabienne Durand-Bogaert, 7–8. Paris: Gallimard.

Cassirer, Ernst. (1906) 1950. *The Problem of Knowledge: Philosophy, Science, and History since Hegel*. Translated by William H. Woglom and Charles W. Hendel. New Haven, CT: Yale University Press.

———. (1927) 2010. *The Individual and the Cosmos in Renaissance Philosophy*. Translated by Mario Domandi. Chicago: University of Chicago Press.

———. 1998. *The Philosophy of Symbolic Forms*. Vol. 4, *The Metaphysics of Symbolic Forms*. Edited by John Michael Krois and Donald Phillip Verene, translated by John Michael Krois. New Haven, CT: Yale University Press.

Cavalcanti, Guido. 1957. "Rime VIII." In *Poeti del Duecento*, Vol. 2, edited by Gianfranco Contini, 429. Naples: Istituto della Enciclopedia Italiana Fondata da Giovanni Treccani.

Chantraine, Pierre, ed. 1980. *Dictionnaire étymologique de la langue grecque*. Vol. 4, *Histoire des mots*. Paris: Klincksieck.

Chartier, Roger, and Claude Calame. 2004. *Identités d'auteur dans l'antiquité et la tradition européenne*. Grenoble: Jérôme Millon.

Charuty, Giordana. 1997. *Folie, mariage et mort: Pratiques chrétiennes de la folie en Europe occidentale*. Paris: Le Seuil.

Chastel, André. 1969. *Le mythe de la Renaissance, 1420–1520*. Geneva: Skira.

———. 1989. *Mythe et crise de la Renaissance*. Geneva: Skira.

———. 1995. *L'Humanisme: L'Europe de la Renaissance*. Geneva: Skira.

———. 1996. *Marsile Ficin et l'art*, vol. 5. Geneva: Librairie Droz.

———. 2014. *Léonard de Vinci. La peinture: Écrits et propos sur l'art*. Paris: Hermann.

Chastel, André, and Renzo Federici. 1964. *Arte e umanesimo a Firenze al tempo di Lorenzo il Magnifico: studi sul Rinascimento e sull'umanesimo platonico.* Turin: Einaudi.
Chastel, André, and Robert Klein. 1964. *Léonard de Vinci: La peinture.* Paris: Hermann.
Chevreul, Jean-Eugène. (1839) 1969. *De la loi du contraste simultané des couleurs.* Paris: Léonce Laget.
Civrieux, Marc de. 1970. *Watunna: Mitologia Makiritare.* Caracas: Monte Avila Editores.
———. 1980. *Watunna: An Orinoco Creation Cycle.* Translated by David M. Guss. Austin: University of Texas Press.
Coleridge, Samuel Butler. (1817) 1984. *Biographia Literaria.* Vol. 2, *The Collected Works of Samuel Taylor Coleridge: Biographical Sketches of my Literary Life and Opinions.* Princeton, NJ: Princeton University Press.
Copenhaver, Brian P. 1991. "A Tale of Two Fishes: Magical Objects in Natural History from Antiquity through the Scientific Revolution." *Journal of the History of Ideas* 52–53: 373–98.
———. 2006. "Magic." In *The Cambridge History of Science*, vol. 3, 518–40. Cambridge: Cambridge University Press.
Cummins, Thomas. 1994. "Representation in the Sixteenth Century and the Colonial Image of the Inca." In *Writing without Words: Alternative Literacies in Mesoamerica and the Andes*, edited by Elizabeth Hill Boone and Walter D. Mignolo, 188–219. Durham, NC: Duke University Press.
———. 2002. "Los Quilkakamayoc y los dibujos de Guaman Poma." In *Libros y escrituras de tradicion indigena: Ensayos sobre los codices prehispánicos y coloniales de México*, edited by Carmen Arellano Hoffmann, Peer Schmidt, and Xavier Noguez, 185–217. Zinacantepec, Mexico: El Colegio Mexiquense.
Dalai, Marisa, ed. 1980. *La prospettiva rinascimentale: Codificazione e trasgressioni.* Florence: Centro Di.
Damisch, Hubert. 1972. *Théorie du nuage.* Paris: Le Seuil.
———. 1993. *L'Origine de la perspective.* Paris: Flammarion.
Dampierre, Éric de. 1992. *Harpes Zandé.* Paris: Klincksieck.
Das, Veena. 2007. *Words and Things.* Berkeley: University of California Press.
Davis, Steven, ed. 1991. *Pragmatics: A Reader.* Oxford: Oxford University Press.
De Angelis, Francesco. 2007. "Dei luoghi e della memoria: Pausania, Filopemene e la fruizione della Periegesi." In *Arte e memoria culturale nell'età della Seconda*

Sofistica, edited by Orietta Dora Cordovana and Marco Galli, 37–56. Catane: Edizioni del Prisma.

De Chirico, Giorgio. (1912) 2014. "Meditations of a Painter." *Lexander Magazine* (9 October). https://www.lexandermag.org/giorgio-de-chirico-two-essays-on-metaphysical-art-and-selected-poetry/

Déléage, Pierre. 2005. "Le chamanisme sharanahua: Apprentissage et épistémologie d'un rituel." PhD. diss., EHESS, Paris.

———. 2007. "Les khipu: Une memoire locale?" *Cahiers des Ameriques Latines* 54–55: 231–40.

———. 2009. *Le chant de l'anaconda: L'apprentissage du chamanisme chez les Sharanahua (Amazonie occidentale)*. Recherches américains 8. Nanterre: Société d'ethnologie.

———. n.d. "L'usage de l'évidentialité dans les mythes et les chants chamaniques sharanahua." Unpublished manuscript.

Della Francesca, Piero. 1942. *De prospectiva pingendi (c. 1474–1482)*. Edited by Nicco Fasola. Florence: Le Lettere.

Dennet, Richard E. (1906) 1968. *At the Back of the Black Man's Mind: Notes on the Kingly Office in West Africa*. London: MacMillan.

Derain, André. 1955. *Lettres à Vlaminck*. Paris: Flammarion.

De Sanctis, Francesco. (1870) 1965. *Storia della letteratura italiana*. Florence: Sansoni.

Descola, Philippe. (2005) 2013. *Beyond Nature and Culture*. Translated by Janet Lloyd. Chicago: University of Chicago Press.

Descola, Philippe, Gérard Lenclud, Carlo Severi, and Anne-Christine Taylor. 1988. *Les Idées de l'anthropologie*. Paris: Armand Colin.

Diamant, Dora. 1998. "Ma vie avec Franz Kafka." In *J'ai connu Kafka*, translated by François-Guillaume Lorrain, 228–29. Arles: Solin-Actes Sud.

Dickerman, Leah. 2001. "Lenin in the Age of Mechanical Reproduction." In *Disturbing Remains: Memory, History, and Crisis in the Twentieth Century*, edited by Michael S. Roth and Charles G. Salas, 77–110. Los Angeles: Getty Research Institute.

Diderot, Denis. [1765] 1995. *Diderot on Art*. Vol. 1, *"The Salon of 1765" and "Notes on painting."* Translated by John Goodman. New Haven, CT: Yale University Press.

Dietrich, Nikolaus. 2010. *Figur ohne Raum? Baume und Felsen in der attischen Vasenmalerei des 6 und 5, Jahrhunderts v. Chr.* Berlin: Walter de Gruyter.

Doll, Richard, and Bradford Hill. 1950. "Smoking and Carcinoma of the Lung: Preliminary Report." *British Medical Journal* 2: 746.

Dumont, Louis. 1970. *Homo Hierarchicus: The Caste System and its Implications*. Chicago: University of Chicago Press.

Dupont, Florence. 2004. "Comment devenir à Rome un poète bucolique? Corydon, Tityre, Virgile et Pollion." In *Identités d'auteur dans l'antiquité et la tradition européenne*, edited by Claude Calame and Roger Chartier, 171–89. Grenoble: Jérôme Million.

Duranti, Alessandro. 2015. *The Anthropology of Intentions: Language in a World of Others*. Cambridge: Cambridge University Press.

Dürer, Albrecht. 1970. *Das gesamte graphische Werk 1471 bis 1528*. Munich: Rogner & Bernhard.

Efal, Adi. 2010. "Reality as the Cause of Art: Riegl and Neo-Kantian Realism." *Journal of Art Historiography* 3: 1–22.

Einstein, Carl. 1914. "Totalitat." *Die Aktion: Wochenschrift für Politik, Literatur, Kunst* 4: 345–47.

———. (1915) 1986. "La sculpture nègre." In *Qu'est-ce que la sculpture moderne?*, edited by Margit Rowell, translated by Liliane Meffre, 344–53. Catalogue de l'exposition. Paris: Centre Georges Pompidou, Musee National d'Art Moderne.

———. (1921) 1922. *Scultura africana*, translated from the German. La civiltà artistica 8. Rome: Valori Plastici.

Emiliani, Andrea. 1975. *Federico Barocci: Catalogue de l'exposition*. Bologne: Alfa.

Evans-Pritchard. E. E. 1953. "The Sacrificial Role of Cattle among the Nuer." *Africa: Journal of the International African Institute* 23 (3): 181–98.

———. 1954. "The Meaning of Sacrifice among the Nuer." *The Journal of the Royal Anthropological Institute of Great Britain and Ireland* 84 (1–2): 21–33.

———. 1956. *Nuer Religion*. Oxford: Oxford University Press.

Ewers, John C. (1939) 1979. *Plains Indian Painting: A Description of an Aboriginal American Art*. New York: AMS Press.

Faure, Bernard. 1993. "Fair and Unfair Language-Games in Chan/Zen." In *Chan Insights and Oversights: An Epistemological Critique of the Chan Tradition*, edited by Steven T. Katz, 158–80. Princeton, NJ: Princeton University Press.

Fehr, Burkhard. 1996. "Kouroi e korai: Formule e tipi dell'arte arcaica come espressione di valori." In *I Greci: Storia cultura arte società*. Vol. 2, *Una storia greca: Formazione*, edited by Salvatore Settis, 785–846. Turin: Einaudi.

Ficino, Marsilio. (1482) 2001. *Platonic Theology*, vol. 1, bks I–IV. Translated by Michael J. B. Allen with John Warden. Cambridge, MA: Harvard University Press.

———. (1484) 2000. *Commentary on Plato's Symposium on Love*, 2nd ed. Translated by Sears Jayne. Washington, DC: Spring Publications.

———. (1489) 2002. *Three Books on Life*. Translated by Carol V. Kaske and John R. Clarke. Tempe, AZ: The Renaissance Society of America.

Finley, Gerald E. 1967. "Turner: An Early Experiment with Colour Theory." *Journal of the Warburg and Courtauld Institutes* 30: 357–66.

Flam, Jack. 1984. "Matisse and the Fauves." In *Primitivism in Twentieth-Century Art: Affinity of the Tribal and the Modern*, edited by William Rubin, 211–33. New York: Museum of Modern Art.

Florensky, Pavel. (1920) 2002. "Reverse Perspective." In *Beyond Vision: Essays on the Perception of Art*, edited by Nicoletta Misler, translated by Wendy Salmond, 201–72, 299–306. London: Reaktion Books.

———. (1925) 1995. *Lo Spazio nell'arte et il tempo*. Edited and translated by Nicoletta Misler. Milan: Adelphi.

Foucault, Michel. (1969) 1981. "What Is an Author?" In *Language, Counter-Memory, Practice: Selected Essays and Interviews*, edited by Donald F. Bouchard, translated by Donald F. Bouchard and Sherry Simon, 113–38. Ithaca, NY: Cornell University Press.

Francis, John de. 1990. *Visible Speech: The Diverse Oneness of Writing*. Honolulu: University of Hawaii Press.

Freedberg, David. 1995. *The Power of Images: Studies in the History and Theory of Response*. Chicago: University of Chicago Press.

Frege, Gottlob. (1879) 1972. "*Begriffsschrift*: Conceptual Notation." In *Conceptual Notation and Related Articles*, edited and translated by Terrell Ward Bynum, 101–204. London: Oxford University Press.

Fried, Michael. 1990. *La Place du spectateur: Esthétique et origines de l'esthétique moderne*. Paris: Gallimard.

Gamboni, Dario. 2004. *Potential Images*. London: Reaktion Books.

———. 2009. "*Nubes cum figuris*: The Interpretation of Clouds as a Modern Paradigm of Artistic Perception and Creation." In *Wind und Wetter: Die Ikonologie der Atmosphäre*, edited by Alessandro Nova and Tanya Michalsky, 259–66, 362–72. Venice: Marsilio.

Gardner, Donald S. 1983. "Performativity and Ritual: The Mianmin Case." *Man* (n.s.) 18: 346–60.

Garfield, Viola E., and Paul S. Wingert. 1967. *The Tsimshian Indians and Their Arts*. Seattle: University of Washington Press.

Garin, Eugenio. (1969) 1989. *Moyen Âge et Renaissance*. Translated by Claude Carme. Paris: Gallimard.

Gelb, Ignace. (1952) 1963. *A Study of Writing: The Foundations of Grammatology*, rev. ed. Chicago: University of Chicago Press.

Gell, Alfred. 1996. "Vogel's Net: Traps as Artworks and Artworks as Traps." *Journal of Material Culture* 1 (1): 15–38.

———. 1998. *Art and Agency: An Anthropological Theory*. Oxford: Clarendon Press.

Gil, Fernando. 1993. *Traité de l'évidence*. Grenoble: Jérôme Millon.

Gnoli, Gherardo, and Jean-Pierre Vernant, eds. 1982. *La mort, les morts dans les sociétés anciennes*. London, Paris: Cambridge University Press, Maison des Sciences de l'Homme.

Goethe, Johann Wolfgang. 1982. *Italian Journey: 1786–1788*. Translated by W. H. Auden and Elizabeth Mayer. San Francisco: North Point Press.

———. (1810) 2006. *Theory of Colours*. Translated by Charles L. Eastlake. Mineola, NY: Dover Publications.

Goffman, Erving. 1963. *Behavior in Public Places*. New York: The Free Press.

———. 1972. "The Neglected Situation." In *Language and Social Context*, edited by Pier Paolo Giglioli, 61–66. New York: Anchor Books.

Goldschmidt, Victor. 1963. *Les Dialogues de Platon: Structure et méthode dialectique*. Paris: Presses Universitaires de France.

Goldwater, Robert. (1938) 1986. *Primitivism in Modern Art*, enlarged edition. Cambridge, MA: Harvard University Press/Belknap Press.

Gombrich, Ernst H. 1971. *Meditations on a Hobby Horse and Other Essays on the Theory of Art*. London: Phaidon.

———. 1972. "The 'What' and the 'How': Perspective Representation and the Phenomenal World." In *Logic and Art: Essays in Honor of Nelson Goodman*, edited by Richard S. Rudner and Israel Scheffler, 129–49. London: Macmillan Publishers.

———. 1976. *The Heritage of Apelles: Studies in the Art of the Renaissance*. Ithaca, NY: Cornell University Press.

———. 1977. *Art and Illusion: A Study in the Psychology of Pictorial Representation*, vol. 5. London: Phaidon.

———. 1979. *The Sense of Order: A Study in the Psychology of Decorative Art*. London: Phaidon.

Gomperz, Heinrich. (1905) 2011. "On Some of the Psychological Conditions of Naturalistic Art." Translated and edited by Karl Johns. *Journal of Art Historiography* 5: 1–19.

Gonzales Holguín, Diego. (1608) 1989. *Vocabulario de la lengua general de todo el Peru llamada lengua qichua, o del inca*, 3rd ed. Lima: Universidad Nacional Mayor de San Marcos.

Goody, Jack, ed. 1968. *Literacy in Traditional Society*. Cambridge: Cambridge University Press.

———. 1987. *The Interface between the Oral and the Written*. Cambridge: Cambridge University Press.

Gowing, Lawrence. 1966. *Turner: Imagination and Reality*. New York: Museum of Modern Art.

Grice, Paul. 1989. *Studies in the Way of Words*. Cambridge, MA: Harvard University Press.

Guaman Poma de Ayala, Felipe. [1615] 1980. *El primer nueva coronica y buen gobierno*. Edited by John V. Murra and Rolena Adorno. Mexico City: Siglo Ventiuno.

Guillaume, Paul, and Thomas Munro. 1926. *Primitive Negro Sculpture*. New York: Harcourt, Brace & Co.

Guss, David M. 1989. *To Weave and Sing: Art, Symbol, and Narrative in the South American Rainforest*. Berkeley: University of California Press.

Guzzo, Augusto, and Romano Amerio, eds. 1956. *Opere di Giordano Bruno e di Tommaso Campanella*. Milan: Ricciardi.

Haddon, Alfred C. (1895) 1979. *Evolution in Art: As Illustrated by the Life-Histories of Designs*. London: Walter Scott, Charles Scribner & Sons.

———. 1910. *History of Anthropology*. New York: G. P. Putnam's Son, Knickerbocker.

Hanks, William F. 2005. "Explorations in the Deictic Field." *Current Anthropology* 46 (2): 191–220.

———. 2006. S.v. "Context, Communicative." In *Encyclopedia of Language and Linguistics*, 2nd ed. Edited by Keith Brown, 115–28. London: Elsevier.

Hanks, William F., and Carlo Severi. 2014. "Translating Worlds: The Epistemological Space of Translation." *HAU: Journal of Ethnographic Theory* 4 (2): 1–16.

Harrison, Simon. 1990. *Stealing People's Names*. Cambridge: Cambridge University Press.

Hay, Jonathan. 2010. "Seeing through Dead Eyes: How Early Tang Tombs Staged the Afterlife." *RES: Anthropology and Aesthetics* 57–58: 16–54.

Hayes, Patrick J. 1985. "Naïve Physics I: Ontology for Liquids." In *Formal Theories of the Commonsense World*, edited by Jerry R. Hobbs and Robert C. Moore, 71–107. Norwood, NJ: Ablex.

Herrmann, Wolfgang. 1978. *Gottfried Semper im Exil. Paris: London 1849–1855: zur Entstehung des "Stil" 1840–1877*. Bâle: Birkhauser.

Hildebrand, Adolf von. (1881) 1969. *Gesammelte Schriften zur Kunst*. Köln, Opladen: Westdeutscher Verlag.

———. (1893) 1994. "The Problem of Form in the Fine Arts." In *Empathy, Form and Space: Problems in German Aesthetics, 1873–1893*, edited and translated by Harry Francis Mallgrave and Eleftherios Ikonomou, 227–79. Los Angeles: Getty Center for the History of Art and the Humanities.

Hoffman, Walter J. 1891. "The Mide-Wiwin, or 'Grand Medicine Society' of the Ojibwa." *Seventh Annual Report of the Bureau of American Ethnology*, 143–300. Washington, D.C.: Government Printing Office.

———. 1897. *Graphic Art of the Eskimos Based upon the Collection in the National Museum*. Washington, D.C.: AMS Press.

———. 1898. *Comparison between Eskimo and Other Pictographs of the American Indians*. Bureau of American Ethnology Miscellaneous Papers. Washington, D.C.: Government Printing Office.

Holm, Bill. 1965. *Northwest Coast Indian Art: An Analysis of Form*. Seattle: University of Washington Press.

———. 1983. *Smoky Top: The Art and Times of Willie Seaweed*. Seattle: University of Washington Press.

Holm, Bill, and William Reid. 1975. *Form and Freedom*. Houston: Institute for the Arts, Rice University.

Homer. (1898; 800 BCE) 1999. *The Iliad*. Translated by Samuel Butler. Mineola, NY: Dover Publications.

Houseman, Michael. 2012. *Le rouge est le noir: Essais sur le rituel*. Toulouse: Pressus Universitaires du Mirail.

Houseman, Michael, and Carlo Severi. 1998. *Naven or the Other Self: A Relational Approach to Ritual Action*. Translated by Michael Fineberg. Boston: Brill.

Humphrey, Caroline, and James Laidlaw. 1994. *The Archetypal Actions of Ritual*. Oxford: Oxford University Press.

Hymes, Dell. 1981. *"In Vain I Tried to Tell You": Essays in Native American Ethnopoetics*. Philadelphia: Philadelphia University Press.

Inverarity, Robert B. 1950. *Art of the Northwest Coast Indians*. Berkeley: University of California Press.

Isaacson, Walter. 2017. *Leonardo da Vinci*. New York: Simon and Schuster.

Jakobson, Roman. 1959. "On Linguistic Aspects of Translation." In *On Translation*, edited by Reuben Arthur Brower, 232–39. Cambridge, MA: Harvard University Press.

Jinlang, Hou, and Michèle Pirazzoli-t'Serstevens. 1979. "Les chasses de l'empereur Qianlong à Mulan." *T'oung Pao* 65: 1–3, 13–49.

Jolles, André. (1930) 2017. *Simple Forms: Legend, Saga, Myth, Riddle, Saying, Case, Memorabile, Fairytale, Joke*. Translated by Peter J. Schwartz. London: Verso Books.

Kandinsky, Wassily. 1994. *Kandinsky: Complete Writings on Art*. Edited by Kenneth C. Lindsay and Peter Vergo, translated by Peter Vergo. Boston: Da Capo Press.

Kant, Emmanuel. (1781) 1999. *Critique of Pure Reason*. Translated and edited by Paul Guyer and Allen W. Wood. Cambridge: Cambridge University Press.

Kapferer, Bruce. 1977. "First Class to Maradana: Secular Drama in Sinhalese Healing Rites." In *Secular Ritual*, edited by Sally Falk Moore and Barbara Meyerhoff, 91–123. Assen: Van Gorcum.

———. 1979. "Ritual Process and the Transformation of Context." *Social Analysis* 1: 3–19.

———. 1983. *A Celebration of Demons: Exorcisms and the Aesthetics of Healing in Sri Lanka*. Bloomington: Indiana University Press.

Keane, Webb. 1997. "Religious Language." *Annual Review of Anthropology* 26 (1): 47–71.

———. 2011. "Indexing Voice: A Morality Tale." *Journal of Linguistic Anthropology* 21 (2): 166–78.

———. 2015. *Ethical Life: Its Natural and Social Histories*. Princeton, NJ: Princeton University Press.

Kitzinger, Ernst. 1976. *The Art of Byzantium and the Medieval West: Selected Studies*. Bloomington: Indiana University Press.

Klein, Robert. (1970) 1979. *Form and Meaning: Writings on the Renaissance and Modern Art*. Translated by Madeline Jay and Leon Wieseltier. New York: Viking Press.

Kleist, Heinrich von. (1810) 1972. "On the Marionette Theatre," translated by Thomas G. Neumiller. *The Drama Review: TDR* 16 (3): 22–26.

Koyré, Alexandre. 1950. "L'apport scientifique de la Renaissance." *Revue de Synthèse* 67 (1): A29–A50.

———. (1945) 1960. *Discovering Plato*, 3rd ed. Translated by Leonora Cohen Rosenfield. New York: Columbia University Press.

———. (1958) 1968. *From the Closed World to the Infinite Universe*. Reprint, Baltimore: Johns Hopkins University Press.

Kristeller, Paul O. 1979. *Renaissance Thought and its Sources*. New York: Columbia University Press.

Kubick, Gerhard. 1987. "Tusona-Luchazi Ideographs: A Graphic Tradition Practised by a People of Central Africa." *Acta Ethnologica et Linguistica, Series Africana* 18: 1–327.

Kuhn, Thomas S. 1977. *The Essential Tension: Selected Studies in Scientific Tradition and Change*. Chicago: University of Chicago Press.

Kūkai, Kōbō Daishi. 2010. *Kūkai on the Philosophy of Language*. Translated by Shingen Takagi and Thomas Eijō Dreitlein. Izutsu Library Series on Oriental Philosophy, Book 5. Tokyo: Keio University Press.

Labov, William. 1972. *Sociolinguistic Patterns*. Philadelphia: University of Pennsylvania Press.

Lalande, André. 1926. *Dictionnaire de la philosophie*. Paris: Presses Universitaires de France.

Lamp, Frederick. 1996. *Art of the Baga: A Drama of Cultural Reinvention*. New York: Museum for African Art, Prestel Publishing.

Landaburu, Jon. 2007. "La modalisation du savoir en langue andoke." In *L'Énonciation médiatisée*, edited by Jon Landaburu and Zlatka Guentchéva, 23–47. Louvain: Peeters.

Landaburu, Jon, and Zlatka Guentchéva, eds. 2002. *Modalités épistémiques*. Paris: Peeters.

Landino, Cristoforo. 1974. *Scritti critici e teorici*, vol. 1. Edited by Roberto Cardini. Rome: Bulzoni.

Laplanche, Jean, and Jean-Baptiste Pontalis. 1967. *Vocabulaire de la psychanalyse*. Paris: Presses Universitaires de France.

Lee, Rensselaer W. 1974. *Ut pictura poesis: La teoria umanistica della pittura*. Florence: Biblioteca Sansoni.

Leonardo da Vinci. (1883) 1970. *The Notebooks of Leonardo da Vinci*, vol. 2. Revised edition. Edited and translated by Jean Paul Richter. New York: Dover.

———. 2001. *Leonardo on Painting: An Anthology of Writings by Leonardo da Vinci.* Edited by Martin Kemp, translated by Martin Kemp and Margaret Walker. New Haven, CT: Yale University Press.

———. 2012. *Leonardo on Art and the Artist.* Translated by Ellen Callman. Mineola, NY: Dover Publications.

Lessing, Gotthold Ephraim. (1766) 1887. *Laocoon: An Essay upon the Limits of Painting and Poetry.* Translated by Ellen Frothingham. Boston: Roberts Brothers.

Lévi-Strauss, Claude. (1955) 2012. *Tristes Tropiques.* Translated by John and Doreen Weightman. Reprint, London: Penguin Classics.

———. (1962) 1966. *The Savage Mind.* Translated by George Weidenfeld and Nicolson, Ltd. Chicago: University of Chicago Press.

———. (1962) 1991. *Totemism.* Translated by Rodney Needham. Reprint, London: Merlin Press.

———. (1979) 1982. *The Way of the Masks.* Translated by Sylvia Modelski. Seattle: University of Washington Press.

———. (1993) 1997. *Look, Listen, Read.* Translated by Brian C. J. Singer. New York: Basic Books.

———. 2008. "Notes sur l'*Olympia* de Manet." In *Œuvres*, 1670–1672. Bibliothèque de la Pléiade. Paris: Gallimard.

Levinson, Stephen. 1983. *Pragmatics.* Cambridge: Cambridge University Press.

Lévy-Bruhl, Lucien. (1922) 1978. *Primitive Mentality.* Translated by Lilian A. Clare. New York: HarperCollins.

Lindberg, David C. 1976. *Theories of Vision from Al-Kindi to Kepler.* Chicago: University of Chicago Press.

Linhartová, Věra. 1997. "Sur un fond blanc: Écrits japonais sur la peinture du IXe au XIXe siècle." *Arts Asiatiques* 52: 167–68.

Loewy, Emmanuel. 1930. *Origins of the Visual Arts.* Vienna: Academy of Sciences.

Longhi, Roberto. 1946. *Viatico per cinque secoli di pittura veneziana.* Florence: Sansoni.

———. (1927) 2002. *Piero della Francesca.* Translated by David Tabbat. Riverdale-on-Hudson, NY: Sheep Meadow Press.

Lord, Albert. 2010. *The Singer of Tales.* Cambridge, MA: Harvard University Press.

Lowenstam, Steven. 1981. *The Death of Patroklos: A Study in Typology.* Koenigstein: Hain.

———. 1997. "Talking Vases: The Relationship between the Homeric Poems And Archaic Representations of Epic Myth." *Transactions of the American Philological Association* 127: 21–76.

Lucco, Mauro. 2014. *Mantegna*. Milan: Skira.

Lugli, Adalgisa. 1997. *Wunderkammer: Le stanze delle meraviglie*. Turin: Umberto Allemandi.

———. 2005. *Naturalia et mirabilia: Il collezionismo enciclopedico nelle Wunderkammern d'Europa*. Milan: Mazzotta.

Luporini, Cesare. 1953. *La mente di Leonardo*, vol. 2. Florence: G. Sansoni.

MacGaffey, Wyatt. 1986. *Religion and Society in Central Africa*. Chicago: University of Chicago Press.

Macke, August, and Franz Marc. 1964. *Briefwechsel*. Cologne: DuMont.

Malamoud, Charles. 2009. *Le Jumeau solaire*. Paris: Le Seuil.

Malinowski, Bronislaw. (1935) 1971. *Coral Gardens and their Magic*. London: Routledge.

Mallery, Garrick. (1893) 1972. *Picture Writings of the American Indians*, 2 vols. New York: Dover.

Mallgrave, Henry, and Efisios Ikonomou, eds. 1994. *Empathy, Form and Space: Problems in German Aesthetics 1879–1893*. Los Angeles: Getty Center for the History of Art and the Humanities.

Mangione, Corrado. 1964. *Elementi di logica matematica*. Turin: Boringhieri.

Marin, Louis. 1975. *La Critique du discours: Sur la Logique de Port-Royal et les Pensées de Pascal*. Paris: Éditions de Minuit.

Matisse, Henri. 1991. *Écrits et propos sur l'arte*. Edited by Dominique Fourcade. Paris: Hermann.

Mauelshagen, Franz. 2003. "Entzauberung vor der Entzifferung: Conrad Gessner und die zoologische Rezeption des Hieroglyphica Horapollons im 16 Jahrhundert." In *Hieroglyphen: Altägyptische Ursprünge abendländischer Grammatologie*, edited by Aleida Assmann and Jan Assmann, 221–43. Munich, Fink Wilhelm Verlag.

Merlan, Francesca, and Alan Rumsey. 2015. "Language Ecology, Language Policy and Pedagogical Practice in a Papua New Guinea Highland Community." *Language and Linguistics in Melanesia* 33 (1): 82–96.

Messina, Maria Grazia. 1993. *Le Muse d'oltremare: Esotismo e primitivismo dell'arte contemporanea*. Turin: Einaudi.

Métraux, Alfred. 1958. *Le Vaudou haïtien*. Paris: Gallimard.

Mey, Jacob. 1993. *Pragmatics: An Introduction*. Oxford: Blackwell.

Michelson, T. 1925. "Notes on Fox Mortuary Customs and Beliefs." *Fortieth Annual Report of the Bureau of American Ethnology* (1918–19). Washington, DC: Bureau of American Ethnology.

Moeschler, Jacques, and Anne Reboul. 1998. *La Pragmatique aujourd'hui*. Paris: Le Seuil.

Momesso, Sergio. 2013. "Andrea Mantegna: San Sebastiano." In *Pietro Bembo e l'invenzione del Rinascimento*, edited by Gaspar Beltramini, Davide Gasparotto, and Adolfo Tura. Venice: Marsilio.

Mondrian, Piet. (1919) 1971. "A Dialogue on Neoplasticism." In *De Stijl*, vol. 2. Edited and translated by Hans L. C. Jaffé, 117–26. London: Abrams-Thames and Hudson.

Morin, Olivier. 2011. *Comment les traditions naissent et meurent*. Paris: Odile Jacob.

Morris, Charles W. 1946. *Signs, Language and Behavior*. New York: Braziller.

———. 1971. *Writings on the General Theory of Signs*. Approaches to Semiotics 16. Boston: De Gruyter Mouton.

Mosca, Antonio. 2005. "Jean-Yves Girard, le logicien scélérat." *Critique* 701: 743–57.

Motherwell, Robert. 1999. *The Collected Writings of Robert Motherwell*. Berkeley: University of California Press.

Munn, Nancy D. 1973. *Walbiri Iconography: Graphic Representation and Cultural Symbolism in a Central Australian Society*. Ithaca, NY: Cornell University Press.

Murra, John. 1991. "'Nos hacen mucha ventaja': The Early European Perception of Andean Achievement." In *Transatlantic Encounters: European and Andean in the Sixteenth Century*, edited by Kenneth J. Andrien and Rolena Adorno, 73–89. Berkeley: University of California Press.

Musil, Robert. 1995. "Toward a New Aesthetic." In *Precision and Soul: Essays and Addresses*, rev. ed. Translated by Burton Pike and David S. Luft, 193–207. Chicago: University of Chicago Press.

Musil, Robert, and Philippe Jaccottet. 1984. *Essais, conférences, critique, aphorismes, réflexions*. Paris: Le Seuil.

Musée du Petit Palais. 1996. *La Cité interdite: Vie publique et privée des empereurs de Chine 1644–1911*. Catalogue de l'exposition du Musée du Petit Palais. Paris: Musées Nationaux.

Nagel, Alexander, and Christopher Wood. 2010. *Anachronic Renaissance*. New York: Zone Books.

Nagy, Gregory. 1990. "Sema and Noesis: The Hero's Tomb and the Reading of Symbols in Homer and Hesiod." In *Greek Mythology and Poetics*, 202–22. Ithaca, NY: Cornell University Press.

———. (1979) 1999. *The Best of the Achaeans: Concepts of the Hero in Archaic Greek Poetry*, rev. ed. Baltimore: Johns Hopkins University Press.

Newman, Barnett. 1990. "Art of the South Seas." In *Selected Writings and Interviews*, edited by John P. O'Neill, 98–102. New York: Knopf.

Nguema, Zwè. 1972. *Un mvet de Zwe Nguéma, un chant épique fang*. Edited by Herbert Pepper and Paul P. de Wolf. Paris: Armand Colin.

Nolde, Emil. 1949. *Das eigene Leben*. New York: Wolff Books.

Nooter-Roberts, Mary, and Allen Roberts. 1996. *Memory: Luba Art and the Making of History*. New York: Museum of African Art, Prestel Publishing.

Orléan, André. 2004. "What is a Collective Belief?" In *Cognitive Economics: An Interdisciplinary Approach*, edited by Paul Bourgine and Jean-Pierre Nadal, 199–212. Berlin: Springer.

Page, Denys. 1959. *History and the Homeric Iliad*. Berkeley: University of California Press.

Panofsky, Erwin. (1924) 1968. *Idea: A Concept in Art Theory*. Translated by Joseph J. S. Peake. Columbia: University of South Carolina Press.

———. (1927) 1991. *Perspective as Symbolic Form*. Translated by Christopher S. Wood. New York: Zone Books.

———. (1943) 2005. *The Life and Art of Albrecht Dürer*. Princeton, NJ: Princeton University Press.

Parronchi, Alessandro. 1964. *Studi su la "dolce" prospettiva*. Milan: A. Martello.

Parry, Milman. 1987. *The Making of the Homeric Verse: The Collected Papers of Milman Parry*. Edited by Adam Parry. Oxford: Oxford University Press.

Pärssinen, Martti, and Jukka Kiviharju. 2004. *Textos andinos*. Madrid: Universidad Complutense de Madrid.

Peirce, Charles. 1955. *Philosophical Writings*. New York: Dover.

Piaget, Jean. (1923) 2001. *The Language and Thought of the Child*. Translated by Marjorie and Ruth Gabain. London: Routledge.

———. (1926) 2007. *The Child's Conception of the World*. Translated by Joan and Andrew Tomlinson. London: Routledge.

Pico della Mirandola, Giovanni. (1486) 1998. *On the Dignity of Man*, rev. ed. Translated by Charles Glenn Wallis, Paul J. W. Miller, and Douglas Michael. Indianapolis: Hackett Publishing.

Pignatti, Terisio. 1971. *Giorgione*. London: Phaidon.

Pirazzoli-t'Serstevens, Michèle. 1996. "Giuseppe Castiglione." In *La cité interdite: Vie publique et privée des empereurs de Chine, 1644–1911*, edited by Gilles Béguin, 266–71. Paris: Musée du Petit Palais.

Pitt Rivers, A. Lane-Fox. 1906. *The Evolution of Culture, and Other Essays*. Edited by John Linton Myres. Oxford: Clarendon.

Plato. (360 BCE) 1966. *Apology* and *Phaedo*. In *Plato in Twelve Volumes*, vol. 1. Translated by Harold North Fowler. Cambridge, MA: Harvard University Press.

Quilter, Jeffrey, and Gary Urton, eds. 2002. *Narrative Threads: Accounting and Recounting in Andean Khipu*. Austin: University of Texas Press.

Rappaport, Roy A. 1971. "Ritual Sanctity and Cybernetics." *American Anthropologist* 73 (1): 59–76.

———. 1979. *Ecology, Meaning and Religion*. Berkeley: North Atlantic Books.

———. 2000. *Pigs for the Ancestors: Ritual in the Ecology of a New Guinea People*, 2nd ed. Long Grove, IL: Waveland Press.

Riegl, Aloïs. (1902) 2009. *Le portrait de groupe dans la peinture hollandaise*. Translated by Aurélie Duthoo. Paris: Hazan.

Rogers, Howard. 1988. "For the Love of God: Castiglione at the Qing Imperial Court." *Phoebus* 6 (1): 141–60.

Rohde, Erwin. (1894) 2000. *Psyche: The Cult of Souls and Belief in Immortality among the Greeks*. Translated by W. B. Hillis. Reprint, London: Routledge.

Romanini, Angiola Maria. 1980. *Arnolfo di Cambio e lo stil novo del gotico italiano*. Florence: Sansoni.

Romano, Giovanni. 1981. "Verso la maniera moderna: Da Mantegna a Raffaello." In *Storia dell'arte italiana*, edited by Federico Zeri, 3–85. Turin: Einaudi.

Rose, Berenice. 1969. *Jackson Pollock: Works on Paper*. New York: Museum of Modern Art.

Rosenberg, Harold. 1983. "Mondrian: Meaning in Abstract Art I." In *Art on the Edge: Creators and Situations*, 39–49. Chicago: University of Chicago Press.

Rossi, Paolo. (1979) 1987. *The Dark Abyss of Time: The History of the Earth and the History of Nations from Hooke to Vico*. Translated by Lydia G. Cochrane. Chicago: University of Chicago Press.

———. (1983) 2000. *Logic and the Art of Memory: The Quest for a Universal Language*. Translated by Stephen Clucas. London: Athlone Press.

———. 2001. *Logic and the Art of Memory: The Quest for a Universal Language*. Translated by Stephens Clucas. Dorset: Continuum.

Roth, Michael S., and Charles G. Salas, eds. 2001. *Disturbing Remains: Memory, History, and Crisis in the Twentieth Century*. Los Angeles: Getty Research Institute.

Rubin, William, ed. 1984. *Primitivism in Twentieth-Century Art: Affinity of the Tribal and the Modern*. New York: Musem of Modern Art.

Rumsey, Alan. 2002. "Aspects of Ku Waru Ethnosyntax and Social Life." In *Ethnosyntax: Explorations in Grammar and Culture*, edited by N. J. Enfield, 259–86. Oxford: Oxford University Press.

———. 2003. "Language, Desire, and the Ontogenesis of Intersubjectivity." *Language and Communication* 23: 169–87.

———. 2014. "Bilingual Language Learning and the Translation of Worlds in the New Guinea Highlands and Beyond." *HAU: Journal of Ethnographic Theory* 4 (2): 119–40.

———. n.d. "Language and Tacit Communication in New Guinea and Beyond." Unpublished manuscript. Canberra: Australian National University.

Russell, Bertrand, and Alfred North Whitehead. 1910. *Principia mathematica*. Vol. 1. Cambridge: Cambridge University Press.

Sacks, Harvey. 1992. *Lectures on Conversation*. Edited by Gail Jefferson. Oxford: Blackwell.

Salomon, Frank. 2001. "How an Andean 'Writing without Words' Works." *Current Anthropology* 42 (1): 1–27.

———. 2002. "Patrimonial Khipu in a Modern Peruvian Village: An Introduction to the Quipocamayos of Tupicocha, Huarochiri." In *Narrative Threads: Accounting and Recounting in Andean Khipu*, edited by Jeffrey Quilter and Gary Urton, 293–319. Austin: University of Texas Press.

———. 2006. *Los Quipocamayos: El antiguo arte del khipu en una comunidad campesina moderna*. Lima: Instituto Francés de Estudios Andinos.

Saslow, James M. 1993. *The Poetry of Michelangelo: An Annotated Translation*. Reprint, New Haven, CT: Yale University Press.

Sassi, Maria Michela. 1997. "La morte di Socrate." In *I Greci: Storia, cultura, art e società*, vol. 2. Edited by Salvatore Settis, 1323–39. Turin: Einaudi.

Saussure, Ferdinand de. (1916) 1998. *Course in General Linguistics*. Edited by Charles Bally and Albert Sechehaye, translated by Roy Harris. Reprint, Chicago: Open Court Classics.

Schlosser, Julius von. (1908) 2012. *Les Cabinets d'art et de merveilles de la Renaissance tardive*. Translated by Lucie Marignac. Paris: Macula.

Schnapp-Gourbeillon, Annie. 1979. "Les funérailles de Patrocle." In *La mort, les morts dans les sociétés anciennes*, edited by Jean-Pierre Vernant and Gherardo Gnoli, 77–88. Cambridge, Paris: Cambridge University Press, Maison des Sciences de l'Homme.

Searle, John R. 1969. *Speech Acts: An Essay in the Philosophy of Language*. Cambridge: Cambridge University Press.

———. 1979. *Expression and Meaning: Studies in the Theory of Speech Acts*. Cambridge: Cambridge University Press.

Semper, Gottfried. 1989. *The Four Elements of Architecture and Other Writings*. Cambridge: Cambridge University Press.

Seo, Audrey Yoshiko, and Stephen Addiss. 2010. *The Sound of One Hand: Paintings and Calligraphy by Zen Master Hakuin*. Boston: Shambhala Publications.

Settis, Salvatore. 1986. "Continuità, distanza, conoscenza: Tre usi dell'antico." In *Memoria dell'antico nell'arte italiana*. Vol. 3, *Dalla tradizione all'archeologia*, edited by Salvatore Settis, 373–486. Turin: Einaudi.

———, ed. 2001. *I Greci. Storia, cultura, arte, società*. 3 vols. Turin: Einaudi.

———. 2005. *Iconografia dell'arte italiana 1100–1500: Una linea*. Turin: Einaudi.

———. 2010. *Artisti e committenti fra Quattro e Cinquecento*. Turin: Einaudi.

Seuphor, Michel. (1949) 1971. *L'Art abstrait*. Vol. 1, *1910–1918: Origines et premiers maîtres*. Paris: Maeght.

Severi, Carlo. 1989. "Un primitivisme sans emprunts: Boas, Newman et l'anthropologie de l'art." *Cahiers du Musée National d'Art Moderne* 28: 55–60.

———. 1991. "Anthropologie de l'art." In *Dictionnaire de l'ethnologie et de l'anthropologie*, edited by Pierre Bonte and Michel Izard, 81–85. Paris: Presses Universitaires de France.

———. 1991. "Una stanza vuota: Antropologia della forma onirica." In *Il sogno rivela la natura delle cose*, edited by L'Associazione Museion, 226–74. Catalogo della mostra del Museo d'Arte Moderna di Bolzano. Milan: Mazzotta.

———. 1992. "Présence du primitive: Masques et chimères dans l'œuvre de Joseph Beuys." *Cahiers du Musée National d'Art Moderne* 42: 31–47.

———. 1994. "Vestiges, merveilles et chimères: Sur la collection ethnographique." *Annales du Centre d'Art Contemporain du Château de Kerguehennec* 1: 1–12.

———. 1998. "Oggetti magici e oggetti del pensiero: Primitivismi a confronto." In *Dalla meraviglia all'arte della meraviglia*, edited by Gabriella Roganti, 35–53. Modena: Galeria Civita di Modena.

———. 2002. "Memory, Reflexivity and Belief: Reflections on the Ritual Use of Language." *Social Anthropology* 10 (1): 23–40.

———. 2003. "Warburg anthropologue, ou le déchiffrement d'une utopie: De la biologie des images à l'anthropologie de la mémoire." "Image et anthropologie," special issue, *L'Homme* 165: 77–129.

———. 2004. "Capturing Imagination: A Cognitive Approach to Cultural Complexity." *Journal of the Royal Anthropological Institute* 10 (4): 815–38.

———. 2007. "Learning to Believe: A Preliminary Approach." In *Learning Religion: Anthropological Approaches*, edited by Ramon Sarró and David Berliner, 25–41. Oxford: Bergham Books.

———. (2007) 2015. *The Chimera Principle: An Anthropology of Memory and Imagination*. Translated by Janet Lloyd. Chicago: Hau Books.

———. (2008) 2012. "Primitivist Empathy. *Art in Translation* 4 (1): 99–132.

———. (2008) 2016. "Authorless Authority: A Proposal on Agency and Ritual Artefacts." *Journal of Material Culture* 21 (1): 133–50.

———. (2009) 2012. "The Arts of Memory: Comparative Perspectives on a Mental Artifact." *Hau: Journal of Ethnographic Theory* 2 (2): 451–85.

———. 2013. "Philosophies without Ontologies." *Hau: Journal of Ethnographic Theory* 3 (1): 192–96.

———. 2014. "Transmutating Beings: A Proposal for an Anthropology of Thought." *Journal of Ethnographic Theory* 4 (2): 41–71.

Sgarbi, Marco. 2013. *The Aristotelian Tradition and the Rise of British Empiricism: Logic and Epistemology in the British Isles, 1570–1689*. Dordrecht: Springer.

Shearman, John. 1992. *Only Connect . . . Art and the Spectator in the Italian Renaissance*. Princeton, NJ: Princeton University Press.

Silverman, Eric, 1993. *Tambunum: New Perspectives on Eastern Iatmul (Sepik River, Papua New Guinea) Kinship, Marriage, and Society*. Minneapolis: University of Minnesota Press.

Silverstein, Michael. 1976. "Shifters, Verbal Categories and Cultural Description." In *Meaning in Anthropology*, edited by Keith H. Basso and Henry A. Selby, 11–57. Albuquerque: School of American Research.

Simon, Gérard. 2003. *Archéologie de la vision: L'optique, le corps, la peinture*. Paris: Le Seuil.

Sperber, Dan. 1982. "Apparently Irrational Beliefs." In *Rationality and Relativism,* edited by Martin Hollis and Steven Lukes, 149–80. Cambridge, MA: MIT Press.

———. 1985. "Anthropology and Psychology: Towards an Epidemiology of Representations." *Man*, n.s., 20 (1): 73–89.
Sperber, Dan, and Deirdre Wilson. 1986. *Relevance, Communication and Cognition*. Cambridge, MA: Harvard University Press.
Smith, A. Mark. 2001. *Alhacen's Theory of Visual Perception*, vol. 1. English translation and commentary on book one of Alhacen's *De aspectibus*, the Medieval Latin version of Ibn Al-Haytham's *Kitab Al-Manazir*. Philadelphia: American Philosophical Society.
Smyly, John, and Carolyn Smyly. 1975. *Totem Poles of Skedans*. Seattle: University of Washington Press.
Sperber, Dan, and Deirdre Wilson. 1986. *Relevance*. Cambridge, MA: Harvard University Press.
———. 1995. *La contagion des idées*. Paris: Odile Jacob.
Staal, Frits. 1979. "The Meaninglessness of Ritual." *Numen* 1 (26): 2–22.
———. 1983. *Agni: The Vedic Ritual of the Fire Altar*, vols. 1–2. Berkeley: University of California Press.
———. 1989. *Rules without Meaning: Ritual, Mantras, and the Human Sciences*. New York: Peter Lang.
Stalnaker, Robert C. 1970. "Pragmatics." *Synthèse* 22: 272–89.
Stoïchita, Victor. 1995. "Ein Idiot in der Schweiz: Bildbeschreibung bei Dostojewski." In *Beschreibungskunst, Kunstbeschreibung: Ekphrasis von der Antike bis zur Gegenwart*, edited by Gottfried Boehm and Helmut Pfotenhauer, 425–45. Munich: Wilhelm Fink Verlag.
Stolze Lima, Tania. 1996. "O dois e seu múltiplo: Reflexoes sobre o perspectivismo em uma cosmologia tupi." *Mana* 2 (2): 21–47.
Strathern, Marilyn. 1989. *The Gender of the Gift: Problems with Women and Problems with Society in Melanesia*. Berkeley: University of California Press.
Suida, William. 1953. *Bramante pittore e Bramantino*. Milan: Ceschina.
Sullivan, Michael. 1973. *The Meeting of Eastern and Western Art*. London: Thames and Hudson.
Svenbro, Jesper. (1988) 1993. *Phrasikleia: An Anthropology of Reading in Ancient Greece*. Translated by Janet E. Lloyd. Ithaca, NY: Cornell University Press.
Szeminski, Jan. 2006. "Avant les Incas: La tradition orale comme source historique. Le Livre II du Ophir de España de Fernando de Montesinos." *Annales: Histoire, Sciences Sociales* 2: 299–338.
Tambiah, Stanley J. 1985. *Culture, Thought and Social Action: An Anthropological Perspective*. Cambridge, MA: Harvard University Press.

Tarenzi, Victoria. 2005. "Patroclo terapon." *Quaderni Urbinati di Cultura Classica* 80 (2): 25–38.

Tarski, Alfred. 1956. *Logic, Semantics, Metamathematics*. Oxford: Oxford University Press.

Tedlock, Dennis. 1983. *The Spoken Word and the Work of Interpretation*. Philadelphia: University of Pennsylvania Press.

Thom, René. 1980. *Modèles mathématiques de la morphogenèse*. Paris: Christian Bourgois.

Urton, Gary. 1993. "Contesting the Past in the Peruvian Andes." In *Mémoire de la Tradition*, edited by Aurore Becquelin, Antoinette Molinié and Danièle Dehouve, 107–44. Nanterre: Société d'Ethnologie.

———. 1998. "From knots to narratives: Reconstructing the art of historical record keeping in the Andes from Spanish transcriptions of Inka khipus." *Ethnohistory* 45 (3): 409–38.

———. 2003. *Signs of the Inka khipus: Binary coding in the Andean knotted-string records*. Austin: University of Texas Press.

Urton, Gary, and Primitivo Nina Llanos. 1997. *The Social Life of Numbers: A Quechua Ontology of Numbers and Philosophy of Arithmetics*. Austin: University of Texas Press.

Valeri, Valerio. 1981. S.v. "Rito." *Enciclopedia*, vol. 12, 210–43. Turin: Einaudi.

Van Brock, Nadia. 1959. "Substitution rituelle." *Revue hittite et asianique* 65: 117–46.

Vasari, Giorgio. (1556) 2008. *The Lives of the Artists*. Translated by Julia Conway Bondanella and Peter Bondanella. Reprint, Oxford: Oxford University Press.

Vastokas, Joan M. 1978. "Cognitive Aspects of Northwest Coast Art." In *Art in Society: Studies in Style, Culture and Aesthetics*, edited by Michael Greenhalgh and Vincent Megaw, 243–59. London: Duckworth.

Vega, Garcilaso de la. (1609) 1991. *Comentarios reales de los Incas*. Edited by Angel Rosenblat. Buenos Aires: Ernece Editores.

Velthem, Lucia H. van. 2003. *O belo é a fera: A estética da produçâo e da predaçâo entre os Wayana*. Lisbon: Museu Nacional de Etnologia, Assírio & Alvim.

Vernant, Jean-Pierre. (1965) 2006. "The Figuration of the Invisible and the Psychological Category of the Double: The Colossus." In *Myth and Thought among the Greeks*, translated by Janet Lloyd and Jeff Fort, 321–32. New York: Zone Books.

———. 1979. "Naissance d'images." In *Religions, histoires, raisons*, 105–37. Paris: Maspero.

———. 1989. *L'Individu, la mort, l'amour: Soi-même et l'autre en Grèce ancienne*. Paris: Gallimard.

———. 1990. *Figures, idoles, masques*. Conférences du Collège de France. Paris: Julliard.

———. 1991. *Mortals and Immortals: Collected Essays*. Edited and translated by Froma I. Zeitlin. Princeton, NJ: Princeton University Press.

Vico, Giambattista. (1744) 1984. *The New Science of Giambattista Vico*, unabridged translation of the third edition (1744). Translated by Thomas Goddard Bergin and Max Harold Fisch. Ithaca, NY: Cornell University Press.

Vilaça, Aparecida. 2014. "Le contexte relationnel du cannibalisme funéraire wari'." In *L'Image rituelle*, edited by Carlo Severi and Carlos Fausto, 38–53. Cahiers d'anthropologie sociale 10. Paris: L'Herne.

Viveiros de Castro, Eduardo. 1998. "Cosmological Deixis and Amerindian Perspectivism." *Journal of the Royal Anthropological Institute* 4 (3): 469–88.

———. 2004. "Exchanging Perspectives: The Transformation of Objects into Subjects in Amerindian Ontologies." *Common Knowledge* 10 (3): 463–64.

———. 2005. "Perspectivism and Multinaturalism in Indigenous America." In *The Land Within: Indigenous Territory and the Perception of Environment*, edited by Alexandre Surrallés and Pedro García Hierro, 36–73. Copenhagen: International Work Group for Indigenous Affairs (IWGIA).

Voltaire. (1749) 1978. *Zadig and L'Ingénu*, 2nd ed. Translated by John Butt. Penguin Classics. London: Penguin Books.

Vygotsky, Lev S. 1978. *Mind in Society: The Development of Higher Psychological Processes*. Edited by Michael Cole, Vera John-Steiner, Sylvia Scribner, and Ellen Souberman. Cambridge, MA: Harvard University Press.

Wagner, Roy. 1986. *Symbols That Stand for Themselves*. Chicago: University of Chicago Press.

———. 2012. "Figure–Ground Reversal Among the Barok." *HAU: Journal of Ethnographic Theory* 2 (1): 535–42.

Walker, Daniel P. 2000. *Spiritual and Demonic Magic: From Ficino to Campanella*. Philadelphia: Pennsylvania State University Press.

Warburg, Aby. (1932) 1999. *The Renewal of Pagan Antiquity: Contributions to the Cultural History of the European Renaissance*. Edited by Kurt W. Forster, translated by David Britt. Los Angeles: Getty Research Institute for the History of Art and the Humanities.

———. 2000. "Mnemosyne: Einleitung." In *Gesammelte Schriften (Der Bilderatlas Mnemosyne)*, vol. 2.1. Edited by Martin Warnke, 3–6. Berlin: Akademie Verlag.

———. 2010. "From the Laboratory to the Museum." In *From Yodeling to Quantum Physics*, vol. 4. Edited by Marc-Olivier Wahler and Frédéric Grossi. Bilingual edition, Paris, London: Les Presses du Réel, Art Data.

———. 2011. *Frammenti sull'espressione*. Edited by Susanne Müller, translated by Maurizio Ghelardi and Giovanna Targia. Pisa: Edizioni della Scuola Normale.

Wassmann, Jürg. 1988. *Der Gesang an das Krokodil: Die rituellen Gesange des Dorfes Kandingei an Land und Meer, Pflanzen und Tiere (Mittelsepik, Papua New Guinea)*. Basil: Ethnologisches Seminar der Universitat, Museum für Völkerkunde, Wepf & Co.

———. 1991. *The Song to the Flying Fox: The Public and Esoteric Knowledge of the Important Men of Kandingei about Totemic Songs, Names, and Knotted Cords (Middle Sepik, Papua New Guinea)*, Boroko, Papua New Guinea. Translated by Dennis Q. Stephenson. Port Moresby, PNG: National Research Institute, Cultural Studies Division.

White, John. (1957) 1987. *The Birth and Rebirth of Pictorial Space*. Cambridge, MA: Harvard University Press.

Whitehouse, Harvey. 2004. *Modes of Religiosity: A Cognitive Theory of Religious Transmission*. Walnut Creek, CA: Altamira Press.

Winckelmann, Johann Joachim. (1755) 1985. "Thoughts on the Imitation of Greek Works in Painting and Sculpture." In *German Aesthetic and Literary Criticism*, edited and translated by Hugh Barr Nisbet, 32–54. Cambridge: Cambridge University Press.

———. (1825) 1975. *Il bello nell'arte: Scritti sull'arte antica*. Edited and translated by F. Pfister. Turin: Einaudi.

Wind, Edgar. 1963. *Art and Anarchy*. London: Faber & Faber.

———. 1968. *Pagan Mysteries in the Renaissance*. London: Faber & Faber.

Wittgenstein, Ludwig. (1942) 1965. *The Blue and Brown Books: Preliminary Studies for the Philosophical Investigations*. New York: Harper & Row.

———. (1953) 2009. *Philosophical Investigations*, 4th ed. Translated by G. E. M. Anscombe, edited by Peter M. S. Hacker and Joachim Schulte. Oxford: Blackwell.

Wittkower, Rudolf. 1977. "Hieroglyphics in the Early Renaissance." In *Allegory and the Migration of Symbols*, 113–28. London: Thames and Hudson.
Worringer, Wilhelm. 1908. *Einfühlung und Abstraktion*. Munich: Piper Verlag.
Yates, Frances. 1964. *Giordano Bruno and the Hermetic Tradition*. London: Routledge and Kegan Paul.
———. 1966. *The Art of Memory*. London: Routledge and Kegan Paul.

Hau Books is committed to publishing the most distinguished texts in classic and advanced anthropological theory. The titles aim to situate ethnography as the prime heuristic of anthropology, and return it to the forefront of conceptual developments in the discipline. Hau Books is sponsored by some of the world's most distinguished anthropology departments and research institutions, and releases its titles in both print editions and open-access formats.

www.haubooks.com